The Franco-Prussian War transformed the map of Europe and ended a century of French dominance on the continent. In this first volume of his acclaimed two-part history, Quintin Barry offers a penetrating study of the opening phase of the conflict — from the diplomatic crises following 1866 to the decisive battle of Sedan and the collapse of Napoleon III's Second Empire.

Drawing extensively on German and French sources, Barry reconstructs the planning and execution of the campaign with exceptional clarity. At its centre stands Helmuth von Moltke, the architect of Prussia's victories and the first true modern professional commander. The book follows Moltke's strategic conception, the mobilisation of the German armies, and their relentless advance through the battles of Weissenburg, Wörth, Spicheren, Borny-Colombey, Mars-la-Tour, Gravelotte, and Beaumont — engagements that culminated in the encirclement and surrender of the French Army at Sedan.

Combining rigorous scholarship with accessible narrative, Barry places events within their wider political and technological context: the rise of the General Staff system, the strains of rapid mobilisation, and the interplay between Bismarck's diplomacy and Moltke's operational genius.

Supported by detailed maps, contemporary illustrations, and comprehensive orders of battle, Volume 1 of this study stands as both an authoritative reference and a compelling account of the fall of an empire and the birth of a new German nation.

Quintin Barry was a retired solicitor and employment judge who had a distinguished career in both the public and private sectors, including roles within the NHS and local radio. A lifelong history enthusiast, he was the author of numerous well-regarded books on military and naval history. His notable works include a two-volume history of the Franco-Prussian War of 1870–1871, a history of the Austro-Prussian War of 1866, and the first modern account of the Russo-Turkish War of 1877–1878. Barry was particularly known for his in-depth study of the life and career of Helmuth von Moltke. Barry's work is highly regarded by historians and enthusiasts of military and naval affairs. Sadly, Quintin passed away in early 2025.

Helmuth von Moltke (Pflugk-Harttung)

THE FRANCO-PRUSSIAN WAR 1870–71

Volume 1

The Campaign of Sedan: Helmuth von Moltke and the Overthrow of the Second Empire

Quintin Barry

Helion & Company Ltd

To Diana

Helion & Company Limited
Unit 8 Amherst Business Centre
Budbrooke Road
Warwick
CV34 5WE
England
Tel. 01926 499619
Email: info@helion.co.uk
Website: www.helion.co.uk
X (formerly Twitter): @Helionbooks
Facebook: @HelionBooks
Visit our blog at https://helionbooks.wordpress.com/

Published by Helion & Company 2007. This paperback edition 2025
Designed and typeset by Helion & Company
Cover designed by Paul Hewitt, Battlefield Design (www.battlefield-design.co.uk)

ISBN 978-1-806721-04-7

British Library Cataloguing-in-Publication Data.
A catalogue record for this book is available from the British Library.

For details of other military history titles published by Helion & Company Limited, contact the above address, or visit our website: http://www.helion.co.uk

We always welcome receiving book proposals from prospective authors.

Contents

List of Illustrations

Key to Sources

Bork *Deutschlands große Jahre 1870/71 geschildert in Liedern* (Munich, 1889)
Hohenlohe-Ingelfingen *Aus meinem Leben* (Berlin, 1897–1908)
Illustrierte Kriegs-Chronik 1870–1871 (Leipzig, 1871)
Klein *Fröschweiler Chronik* (Munich, no date)
Lindner *Der Krieg gegen Frankreich 1870–71* (Berlin, 1895)
Pflug-Harttung *Krieg und Sieg 1870–71, ein Gedenkbuch* (Berlin, 1895)
Rousset *Histoire Générale de la Guerre Franco-Allemande (1870–1871)* (Paris, no date)
Rousset *Les Combattants de 1870–71* (Paris, 1895)
Scheibert *Der Krieg 1870–71* (Berlin, 1914)

List of Maps and Plans

Acknowledgements

The writing of this book stretched over a long period of time, in the course of which I received both inspiration and practical help from many people.

I should particularly like to record my gratitude to Professor Michael Foot, who long ago encouraged me to start; to the late Colonel Philip Howes, who read the manuscript and made a number of valuable suggestions; to Lindsay Cadle and Jean Hawkes whose efforts finally put volumes 1 and 2 respectively into an acceptable state of readiness after they had bravely undertaken the painful task of deciphering my appalling handwriting; to Michael Embree and Bruce Weigle for providing the orders of battle; to Nigel Vichi for his work in preparing the maps; to Duncan Rogers of Helion & Company for all his help with the illustrations and in preparing the book for publication; and of course to my wife and family, who endured without complaint my frequent and prolonged absences of mind when I was engrossed in the events of 1870–71.

In addition, the publishers wish to acknowledge the following:

Birlinn Ltd for permission to reprint an excerpt from *A Day of Battle: Mars-la-Tour, 16 August 1870* by David Ascoli, p. 339, published Birlinn (www.birlinn.co.uk), 2001.

Cambridge University Press for permission to reprint an excerpt from "Remarks on the preconditions to waging war in Prussia-Germany, 1866–1871" by Wilhelm Deist, appearing on p. 325, *On the Road to Total War* by (eds.) Stig Förster & Jvrg Nagler, Cambridge University Press, 1997.

Harvard University Press for permission to reprint an excerpt from *Napoleon III and the German Crisis 1865–1866* by E.A. Pottinger, pp. 193–194, Cambridge, Mass.: Harvard University Press, Copyright © 1966 by the President and Fellows of Harvard College. (Harvard Historical Studies, 75)

Thomson for permission to reprint three excerpts from *The Franco-Prussian War: The German Invasion of France 1870–1871* by Michael Howard, pp. 24, 267 and 423, published London: Rupert Hart-Davis, 1961.

Introduction

In the introductory essay to his study of 'Moltke and the German Wars 1864–1871,' Professor Arden Bucholz suggested that 'Moltke is a much more remarkable individual than anyone has noticed up to now.'[1] In support of this proposition, he set his account of Moltke's achievements during the wars of German unification firmly in the context of the time, pointing out that since the outbreak of the First World War the modern mind had been so affected by the subsequent course of history that nineteenth century Germany could not fail to be considered in terms of the dreadful times of Nazi Germany and the Holocaust.

In order, therefore, properly to appraise Moltke's life and work it is necessary to consider his influence on Prussian and German history, and on the theory and practice of war, in a nineteenth century context. He was, as Professor Bucholz points out 'one of the first of a new breed: the modern, self made, technically educated, professional officer.'[2] He was very much more than this. By the force of his wide ranging intellect, as well as the stunning successes of the Prussian military machine for which he was largely responsible, he came to dominate European professional thinking in the decades that followed. He completely changed the basis upon which armed forces were trained and managed and prepared for war, and the way in which they were directed in combat. His tenure of the office of Chief of the Prussian General Staff coincided with huge advances in technology and was so influential that, when he left it, the entire military landscape had been fundamentally altered.

Thus Moltke's personal imprint on the history of his country was profound. There was another crucial factor of the time which made this possible; his remarkable career would have followed a different course had it not coincided with that of Otto von Bismarck. Had Bismarck not come to power in 1862, it is unlikely that the conduct of Prussian foreign policy would have created the conditions for the three wars of unification, which Moltke went on to fight and win. Nor is it easy to identify any other Prussian statesman who would have so managed the internal affairs of the country to overcome the political objections to William I's reform of the army, which Moltke was able to lead so successfully. On the other hand, without Moltke Bismarck might have found it difficult to bring his policy to such a swift, clear-cut and successful conclusion. There were of course a number of able Prussian soldiers any of whom would have made a perfectly competent Chief of the General Staff; but it is very doubtful that any of them could have matched Moltke's record of success or his complete mastery of his profession.

Moltke's leadership and his development of the General Staff put into Bismarck's hands a weapon upon which he could rely absolutely. And, notwithstanding the fierce disputes which particularly characterised their relationship in the later stages of the Franco-Prussian war, Bismarck did not misuse that weapon. As Professor A J P Taylor observed, 'Bismarck planned wars but they were little wars; and from the moment that he had got his war, he was thinking how he could stop it, with limited cautious aims.'[3] Bismarck's anxiety to limit the scope of the Prussian war aims lay at the heart of his struggle with Moltke and the other military leaders, who objected violently to what they believed was political interference in military matters. But it was this wise restraint on Bismarck's part that ensured that the extraordinary achievements of the Prussian army and its German allies were rewarded with secure political success.

Although Bismarck did occasionally overstep the proper boundary between statesman and soldier, it was nonetheless surprising that Moltke, who in theory perfectly accepted that political considerations must ultimately be paramount, should in practice have been so inflexible.After the King had decisively resolved the most bitter of the disputes between the two men in Bismarck's favour, Moltke, who was still uncharacteristically angry, recorded his understanding of the basis of the relationship. 'Up till now,' he wrote in a memorandum to William, 'I have considered that the Chief of the General Staff (especially in war) and the Federal Chancellor are two equally warranted and mutually independent agencies under the direct command of your Royal Majesty, which have the duty of keeping each other reciprocally informed.' As Professor Craig observed in quoting this passage, 'coming from the Chief of Staff who, until 1859, had not been permitted to report directly even to the War Minister, this was a remarkable claim.'[4] Moltke never abandoned his unyielding insistence that political considerations should not be allowed directly to shape military decisions, and this stubbornness was the one serious flaw in his intellectual make up.

Moltke was almost unique among modern military thinkers not only in being able to devise a coherent military philosophy but also in having the opportunity of putting it into practice upon the largest stage. Throughout his career he had devoted himself to a rigorously thorough study of war as it must be waged in the new industrial era. He saw clearly that the technological advances had rendered obsolete many of the basic precepts of organisation and tactics which had not previously changed much in a couple of centuries. His study was informed by a close attention to the practical experiences of other armies in handling the new conditions in which they were operating.

It was in the intellectual preparation of his senior commanders that Moltke's particular genius was especially evident. The 'Instructions for Large Unit Commanders' which he produced in 1869 has justly been described as 'one of the most influential and enduring operation instructions ever written.'[5] Basing this on his analysis of the strengths and weaknesses revealed by the Prussian Army in 1866, Moltke was assisted in its production by some of his most trusted assistants. It was to serve as the basis of German military thought for more than seventy years. In this document, Moltke distilled all the key lessons that had been learned in combat, emphasising that the whole basis of the conduct of war had been changed.

> The handling of large army units is not to be learned in peacetime. One is limited to the study of individual factors, particularly the terrain and the experiences of earlier campaigns. But the advance of technology, especially improved communications and new weapons, in short completely changed circumstances, causes the means through which victory was previously achieved – and even the rules laid down by the greatest commanders – to appear to be inapplicable in the present.[6]

Moltke was careful not to lay down a fixed set of strategical principles. Strategy was, as he said, little more than 'a system of expedients.' He asserted that

> the teachings of strategy go little beyond the first premises of sound reason; one can hardly call them a scholarly discipline. Their worth lies almost entirely in practical application. What counts is to comprehend in good time the momentarily changing situation and after that to do the simplest and most natural things with steadiness and prudence. War thus became an art that many disciplines serve. Steadiness and prudence alone do not by a wide margin make the highest commander, but where they are lacking they must be replaced by other qualities.[7]

Moltke in this way insisted on a flexible approach to questions of strategy; but in spite of this, later writers worked hard to crystallise and redefine his philosophy by comparing it with that of great commanders of the past. General Caemmerer, for instance, concluded that

> Moltke precisely and distinctly accentuated the principles which reveal his departure from traditional strategy. But as he did so in a Royal decree – Instructions for Generals – where terseness is most essential, and which, being confidential, had to be kept secret, he had of course no occasion for discussing the novelty of his doctrines somewhat in a manner unavoidable in an ordinary manual.[8]

However, at times during the war of 1870–71, Moltke did not enjoy the benefit of a complete understanding of his strategy on the part of some of his subordinates. Among the cadre of senior staff officers with whom he had worked so closely he naturally found his best support; on the other hand, some of the army commanders to whom they nominally reported did not always implement Moltke's intentions as he would have wished. The staff officers had been handpicked by Moltke; but although he took part in the selection of army commanders, that was a process which was formally within the province of the Military Cabinet. Steinmetz, whose reputation as a fighting corps commander had been made in the Austro-Prussian War, proved a disaster in command of the First Army. Prince Frederick Charles on occasion led the Second Army a good deal more cautiously than Moltke would have liked, but had the benefit of the reliable Stiehle as his Chief of Staff. The Crown Prince interfered much less in Blumenthal's handling of the Third Army; theirs was a team that had worked together very successfully in 1866. Blumenthal, notwithstanding his overweening vanity and his propensity constantly to grumble, as displayed in his ineffable diaries, was an outstanding army Chief of Staff in whom Moltke had absolute trust. The Crown Prince of Saxony had proved a capable adversary in 1866, and Moltke's high regard for him was generally justified, save occasionally during the siege of Paris. Manteuffel and Goeben were able army commanders; so was Werder, although Moltke persistently underrated him. When the pairing of the Grand Duke of Mecklenburg-Schwerin and Colonel von Krenski, his chief of staff, proved inadequate on the Loire, Moltke moved decisively to correct the situation by sending the absolutely reliable Stosch to clear up the mess. The corps commanders were for the most part experienced leaders who knew what to do and did it well. They benefited from the continuity of the higher command of the Prussian army. As Professor Bucholz noted: 'often it was the steady move up of men who experienced combat. If they survived they were promoted and saw combat again and again.'[9]

Moltke's achievement in creating a General Staff capable of the efficient management of the complex structure of a modern army has been the subject of intensive study. It has never been better summarised than by Professor Sir Michael Howard in his magisterial history of the Franco-Prussian War.

> His work consisted not in innovation but in bringing to the selection and training of staff officers the personal dedication and the mercilessly high standards of some great impresario or savant. Indeed Moltke's reflective temperament, the breadth of his interests and the fine-drawn austerity of his appearance all suggested a figure from the realms of arts or letters rather than that of the camp; and the affection and respect in which he was held by his officers was that of disciples and pupils rather than of subordinates. By temperament he was a liberal humanist, but by rigorous self discipline he made himself the most exact and exacting of specialists and he trained the General Staff in his own image.[10]

It was upon these so-called 'demigods' of the General Staff that Moltke particularly depended. Their thorough training had been validated in the wars of 1864 and 1866. Their close relationship with him gave Moltke professional support of a quality that few of the great commanders have enjoyed. But although Moltke had himself been on the staff for practically the whole of his military life, he thoroughly understood the reality of war on the ground, as well as having a clear grasp of all the organisational and logistical elements upon which success depended. He never forgot his first battlefield experience when on the losing side at Nisib in 1839; and he had, as Professor Bucholz observes, 'a fingertip feel for the combat battlefield, a sixth sense.'[11]

The military instrument which Moltke had perfected faced its supreme test in 1870–1871. Throughout the war Moltke displayed a complete and well merited confidence in the ability of the units and individuals that comprised the Prussian army to carry out the tasks confronting them, even though their adversary had hitherto been seen as the strongest military power in Europe.

Any comparison between great commanders, practising their profession in different times and different circumstances, is ultimately a futile exercise; but Moltke's record of success in the course of the wars of unification speaks for itself, and on any view entitles him to be regarded as one of the truly great commanders in military history. This account of his conduct of the Franco-Prussian war is intended to do no more than illustrate his successful application of the principles of war which he had evolved. But it is also an account of the adversaries Moltke faced, and above all of the achievements of the men under his command who fought and died in a series of dramatic campaigns which, in a few short weeks, destroyed the French Second Empire, and then, in a very different kind of war, smashed the armies of the Government of National Defence.

1

From Nikolsburg to Ems

The completeness of the Prussian success in 1866, and the speed with which it had been achieved, took all Europe by surprise. The brilliance of the victory brought Helmuth von Moltke in an instant out of the shadows to become the best known soldier in Europe. His own comments after the ending of the campaign were expressed in measured terms. He wrote to his cousin Edward Ballhorn on August 8 that 'even if I do not rate my share in the matter so highly as you do out of goodwill towards me, I have at least the comfortable consciousness of having done my duty. The grace of God was clearly with us, and we can all wish ourselves joy of the consequences, for indeed it was a matter of life and death.' He was not unmindful, however, of the extent of the achievement; 'a campaign so swiftly ended is unheard of; after exactly five weeks we are back in Berlin.'[1] He felt, though, profound distaste for the 'fulsome praise' which he received, which he said upset him for the whole day. As he saw it, he and his comrades had merely done their duty, and he reflected on the 'indiscriminate censure' and 'senseless blame' that would have been his lot if, like Benedek, he had returned home in defeat. For his luckless adversary he felt the deepest compassion. 'A vanquished commander! Oh! If outsiders could form but a faint conception of what that means! The Austrian headquarters on the night of Königgrätz – I cannot bear to think of it. A General, too, so deserving, so brave, and so cautious.'[2]

The international political consequences of the Prussian victory were of course profound. The expectation, or at least the hope, felt by many in the French government at the outset of the war that it would in some way lead to some useful benefits for France meant that Napoleon's acquiescence in Bismarck's terms for ending the war left a very bad taste in their mouths. There immediately began a struggle to develop a policy that would lead to France after all getting something out of the situation. Drouyn de L'Huys in particular clung to the belief that, in exchange for neutrality, France would be able to present a bill to Prussia in the form of a request for territorial compensations and get a favourable response. It was, after all, what Bismarck had at times led Napoleon to expect. But by the time the details of the invoice were finally settled, the terms of peace were ready for signature at Nikolsburg, and Bismarck had no difficulty in brushing aside Benedetti, the French Ambassador, when he sought to raise the subject of payment.

The feeling, as Thiers put it, that 'it is France that is beaten at Sadowa,' was a powerful one. The events of July 3 cast a long shadow, and thereafter defined the fundamental relationship between France and Germany. Emile Ollivier, who was to become French Premier in 1870, was in no doubt as to its significance, both for the government he led and for his nation.

> The first cause of the War of 1870 is to be found in the year 1866. It was in that year, to be marked forever with black, it was in that year of blindness when one

Bismarck (Pflugk-Harttung)

error was redeemed only by a more grievous error, and when the infirmities of the government were made mortal by the bitterness of the opposition; it was in that accursed year that was born the supreme peril of France and of the Empire.[3]

In the first shock of the news from Northern Bohemia there had been sharply divided views in Paris about the feasibility of armed action.

> The higher levels of the French Army expected intervention as a matter of course and were innocent of any abnormal anxiety on the subject… Canrobert, Valazé, Chasseloup-Lambert, Bourbaki, and Vimercati all awaited or actively promoted military steps. The prevailing mood in the upper echelons of the army appears to have been one of readiness and even eagerness.'[4]

Napoleon himself, however, remained firmly of the view that France was not ready to risk war. He told Cowley, the British Ambassador, that the stationing of an army of observation on the frontier, as had been urged by the Austrian Ambassador Richard Metternich, 'in the present excited state of Germany… would have no effect. On the contrary, insolent questions as to his intentions would be put to him, and war would be the consequence. But he was not prepared for war, nor could he be under two months.'[5] This was also the view of foreign observers; the astute Colonel von Löe, the Prussian Military Attaché in Paris, had been saying much the same thing before the outbreak of war, and views of this kind, strongly supported by Moltke, sustained Bismarck when he called Napoleon's bluff over the Nikolsburg terms.

Napoleon's demand for compensations, as a modern historian has pointed out, originated rather as a ministerial policy than as a popular demand. For this reason it had been pursued during the Nikolsburg negotiations too late to achieve anything; and perhaps it was always half hearted because the policy was seen as likely in any case to prove ineffective. Since it was devised as a means of removing what was supposed to be popular dissatisfaction with the whole of French policy during the recent German crisis, it is certainly true that 'French opinion as a whole was only indirectly responsible for the policy.'[6] Goltz, however, the Prussian Ambassador, held firmly to the view that the demands for compensation were indeed 'brought about by the state of public opinion in France.' He told Cowley that Eugénie had said to him 'that she looked upon the present state of things as "le commencement de la fin de la dynastie".'[7] At all events, Napoleon had to content himself with the publication in September of a diplomatic circular in which he represented the events of the last three months as a triumph of French policy, and in which he sanctimoniously disavowed any self interest in the territorial aggrandisement of France.

But the shock to the French system caused by the stunning Prussian victories was not just a matter of injured pride, although in terms of the Bonapartist dynasty it was always a matter of what was apparent rather than what was real. So profound was the feeling of dismay that gripped many that moved in court circles in France that it fuelled thereafter Napoleon's concern to achieve some success to offset the effect of the Prussian victory; as the years went by, his failure to do so created a vicious spiral which was to exercise a fatal influence on the decision making process in July 1870.

No war could ever be properly regarded as entirely inevitable, but the language of both contemporary observers and subsequent historians can make it seem so. When those whose responsibility it is to take decisions that may lead to war come to believe that sooner or later it is in any case inevitable, the most effective moral brake upon their progress down the slope is removed. It is at this stage that, necessarily, the influence of those who will have the conduct of the war itself, the military leaders, may become decisive. And if they can see that there exists the possibility that the military balance will at some time in the future begin to tip against them, that influence may be directed towards immediate action. The complexities of the mobilisation of an army in the second half of the nineteenth century exerted for this reason a strong thrust on the accelerator.

Certainly the language of those at the centre of events suggested that a Franco-Prussian conflict could not be avoided. In Paris, Colonel Claremont, the British military attaché, summed up the generally held view of most foreign observers of French military opinion when he wrote:

> That the war against Prussia is certain at some future date does not seem to be doubted for a moment by any officer in the Army. Time may modify their views, but I never saw them so excited on any subject; the most sensible, the quietest, and most reasonable amongst them say openly that it is a question of existence for the Emperor, and that the aggrandisement of Prussia renders it imperative that they should again have the Rhine as their frontier line.[8]

It was a view which Cowley repeated to Lord Stanley, albeit with a different emphasis. Although, as he remarked, he was generally 'mistrustful' of his own judgement on internal matters, he wrote: 'I hear on all sides that there is great dissatisfaction in the country, and particularly in the Army, not that people care one sixpence about an extension of the frontier, but that they cannot stomach the favour displayed by the Emperor towards Prussia. War is in general looked upon as inevitable.'[9]

Public opinion, at least as he perceived it, continued to weigh on Napoleon's mind as 1866 drew to a close. France, he told Cowley, was suffering under 'une malaise et une mécontentment' which, although not justified, he believed to be due 'entirely to the position which Prussia had taken and which has aroused or rather revived, the ancient animosity of the French towards her.' He went on to complain that intentions were attributed to him which 'together with the insinuations of the German press that France would be obliged to restore Alsace and Lorraine to Germany, were doing incredible mischief.'[10] Jingoistic press comment in these terms, on both sides of the border, kept the temperature high. In May 1868, for example, an anonymous pamphlet appeared in France publicly advocating a 'sharp, short but decisive' preventive war with the object of defeating Prussia before she reached a position of equal military strength.[11]

Almost certainly Napoleon privately recoiled from the horror and uncertainties of war with Prussia; but both he and Eugénie were prepared to stoke up the fires of French belligerence whenever they supposed it might help. During his abortive attempts to acquire Luxembourg in 1867, he told Goltz that if the Dutch King signed the proposed agreement and the Prussians refused to evacuate the Federal fortress that they still garrisoned there, he did not see how war could be avoided. A few days earlier, a more convincingly menacing tone was displayed by Eugénie, when according to Cowley she told Metternich that they 'were very much annoyed with Prussia', but that they were not grumbling, 'for a great nation should not complain until she is ready to act....military preparations were proceeding on a grand scale and she hoped that everything would be ready by the end of the year.' Metternich concluded that she felt 'that war with Prussia is inevitable, sooner or later, and that both sides are playing for position.'[12] The danger remained that utterances of this kind could be drawn from France's leaders whenever it was supposed that public opinion was or might become discontented with the regime; Napoleon was regularly speaking to Cowley of the state of opinion in France as being such that 'matters could not remain for any length of time in their present uncertain state'.

And yet Napoleon was not lacking in sources of advice that were both cooler and better informed than those available to him in the hothouse atmosphere of Paris. Stoffel, his military attaché in Berlin, sent home a stream of thoughtful and analytical reports on the state of the Prussian army and, from time to time on the general situation. When expressly asked by Napoleon to report on the prospects of war, he set out his views on August 12 1869 in unambiguous terms:

> 1. War is inevitable, and at the mercy of an accident. 2. Prussia has no intention of attacking France; she does not seek war, and will do all she can to avoid it. 3. But Prussia is far sighted enough to see that the war she does not want will assuredly break out, and she is, therefore, doing all she can to avoid being surprised

> when the fatal accident occurs. 4. France, by her carelessness and levity, and above all by her ignorance of the state of affairs, has not the same foresight as Prussia.[13]

Stoffel's opinions were entirely consistent with those of Benedetti, the French Ambassador, who also emphasised repeatedly that France need have no fear of an unprovoked assault by Prussia. Bismarck's objective, he wrote on January 5 1868, was

> not to attack us, as I have said, and as I repeat at the risk of assuming a grave responsibility, because this is my profound conviction; his end is to free the Main and to reunite South Germany to the North under the authority of the King of Prussia; and I would add that he proposes to achieve it, if necessary, by force of arms should France openly obstruct this.[14]

Although feelings on the other side of the Rhine were somewhat calmer than those in France, a sense that conflict must sooner or later arise was wide spread. Moltke was one of those who had always regarded war with France as inevitable. His own responsibility was, as he saw it, to be ready for it whenever it came. In May 1867, writing to his brother Adolf, it seemed to him unlikely to his regret that this would be in the immediate future, since

> the Luxembourg question will hardly lead to war just at present. Louis Napoleon must be aware that he is not prepared for it; but he cannot say so to his vain Frenchmen; public opinion is much excited in Paris, fomented by party spirit, and an explosion is not impossible. Nothing could be better for us than that war, which is bound to come, should be declared at once, while Austria is, in all probability, engaged in the East.[15]

In the following year, musing on Napoleon's position, he wrote to Adolf: 'I cannot believe that the domestic difficulties of France would ensure peace. On the other hand he will only play the "va banque" of war when he sees no other way of holding on. The better guarantee lies in the fact that France alone is too weak, and Austria not ready.'[16]

In Germany, as elsewhere in Europe, there was a generally held understanding that the most serious threat to the general peace was to be found in French territorial ambition. This belief, added to the traditional German fear and dislike of the French character, certainly confirmed Moltke in his view that war was bound to come. In 1860 in one of his earlier memoranda, he had noted that France 'aims at the annexation of Belgium, the Rhenish provinces, and possibly Holland. Further she would have the certainty of such territorial gains in the event of the Prussian armies being held upon the Elbe or Oder.'[17] The bruises inflicted by Königgrätz upon French national pride would certainly bring the risk of conflict closer still. In November 1866 Moltke found it necessary to strengthen the process of intelligence gathering in France, appointing the 33 year old Captain Alfred von Schlieffen to Löe's staff in Paris with the object of building up a reliable picture of French war planning.

The climate of opinion in Court circles reflected the general perception in Prussia of French attitudes. The Crown Prince, by no means a bellicose influence, observed in February 1867 to Bismarck that 'there is no denying the fact that our policy is endangered by the malevolence and ambition of France. We must face the danger boldly, but it is too great for us to provoke; I am, however, greatly reassured by the decided manner in which you expressed the desire to me on January 31 to avoid a war with France.'[18] Looking back, Bismarck himself felt that perhaps he had overrated the risk of war with France, which he never supposed he could avoid, but which he sought to delay as long as he could.

> I did not doubt the Franco-German war must take place before the construction of a United Germany could be realised. I was at that time preoccupied with the idea of delaying the outbreak of this war until our fighting strength should be increased. I considered a war with France, having regard to the success of the French in the Crimean War and in Italy, as a danger which I at that time overestimated.[19]

He repeatedly emphasised his sense that it would be folly to ignore the tides of history, as for instance when he observed to von Werthern, the Prussian minister in Munich, in February 1869 that

> German unity would be favoured by violent events I too regard as probable. But the vocation to induce a violent catastrophe is quite another matter. Arbitrary intervention in the evolution of history on purely subjective grounds has always resulted in merely knocking down unripe fruit; and that German unity is not at this moment a ripe fruit is in my opinion obvious.

And later in the same year he defined his own responsibilities in familiar terms. 'At least I am not so arrogant as to assume that the likes of us are able to make history. My task is to keep the currents of the latter and steer my ship in them as best I can. The currents themselves I cannot direct; even less am I able to create them.'[20] For the moment, Bismarck's most immediate task after the victory over Austria was to clothe the new North German Confederation with constitutional reality. He embarked on this in the autumn of 1866 and by the spring of the following year had obtained the necessary legislative sanction. He had at first contemplated allowing the post of Chancellor of the Confederation to pass into other hands, while he remained Minister President of Prussia; but he soon realised the practical advantage of combining the offices in his own person.

Against this background of profound mutual suspicion and sensitivity to imagined slights to national pride, the events of the next four years thrust Prussia and France towards confrontation. In the war scare that arose during the Luxembourg crisis, Bismarck had perhaps no very strong feelings about the subject matter of the crisis itself; if German public opinion, or more importantly, that of William, had let him, he would no doubt have acquiesced in a French acquisition that might for the moment have assuaged injured French feelings as perceived by those advising Napoleon. But he soon realised that it was not feasible, and gratefully accepted the solution the neutralisation of the fortress which, in May 1867, was the result of the London Conference. Moltke was not entirely satisfied; although the military value of the Prussian garrison of Luxembourg was very questionable, he was soon enquiring of Roon whether they would have a fresh fortress to make up for it. 'The strengthening of Saarlouis would be the most obvious choice, but not counting the fact that the terrain, especially on the right bank of the Saar, is unfavourable to a more extended fortification, we have but lately learned the difficulties any fortress in the immediate vicinity of the frontier causes us.' It would, in any case, not be finished in time to be of any help in the immediate crisis.[21] By July, Moltke had firmly concluded that any scheme for expanding Saarlouis should be ruled out, believing that railways would be more valuable than fortresses on the frontier; and in the event the project was not pursued.

One of Moltke's most important tasks was to establish and maintain close links with his opposite numbers in the South German States. Even before the Treaty of Prague was signed, Bismarck had taken a decisive step to bolster Prussia's military security when he signed secret defensive treaties with Bavaria, Württemberg and Baden. Principally directed at that time against any revanchist policy on the part of Prussia, they were nonetheless important in creating a climate of military co-operation. The publication of the treaties in 1867, at the height of the Luxembourg crisis, gave a clear warning to France which, however, her leaders chose to ignore; Napoleon was one of those who believed right up to the end that when it came to a showdown Prussia would have to fight alone.

The military leaders of South Germany were readier than their civilian colleagues to accept pragmatically the necessity for close co-operation in relation to the apparently inevitable war, although Moltke was still obliged to take account of the limitations imposed on his conversations with them by political realities. On May 13 1868, for instance, reporting to Bismarck on his conference with the Bavarians and Württembergers, he noted that 'the question is not to demand from the South German states what is militarily correct for the attainment of the war object, but to demand what they can and will perform with due regard to their own security.' An attack on France with superior forces would keep all of the French forces busy and so protect all Germany. 'But it would involve a political initiative as well as greater readiness in a military sense than South Germany had yet acquired.'[22] The notion that a Prussian offensive was necessary if the South German states were to be brought in was one which continued to inform Moltke's thinking in the months ahead. He could not, of course, predict what would be the occasion of the outbreak of war, but he was in no doubt that it would come soon.

Accordingly he worked assiduously to prepare the army of the North German Confederation for the imminent conflict. In June 1867 he accompanied the King and Bismarck to the Paris exhibition. As usual he quietly observed all that there was to see; of a parade of some 40,000 French troops in the Bois de Boulogne he noted: 'Equipment very fine: horses good,' and he took the opportunity to meet and talk to prominent French military leaders, such as Niel and Canrobert, as well as having conversations with Napoleon and the Tsar. The latter, he thought, was 'anxious for peace and a policy of restraint.' As usual, he recorded all this in letters to his wife Marie.[23]

Such leisure as Moltke had, however, now possessed a different focus. With the proceeds of a grant from the grateful Prussian Landtag, he was able to investigate the purchase of a suitable estate. In August 1867 he found what he was looking for at Creisau near Schweidnitz in Silesia. For the rest of his life Creisau was to provide him with a deep source of satisfaction and opportunity for peaceful contemplation. With Marie he spent a happy summer there in 1868; but his joy in her company in their new home was to be short lived. That autumn she contracted a fever and, after weeks of suffering, died on Christmas Eve. Moltke was devastated. To Adolf he wrote: 'I cannot desire her to awake again, she has led a life of rare happiness and escaped the sadness of her old age. Her open face and pious character made her beloved by everybody.'[24] His sister Augusta was with him. On December 26 she wrote to her daughter:

> Perhaps no man has ever mourned for his wife so deeply, dearly and entirely as Helmuth mourns for his. No one could have been more comforting, more attentive, more helpful at her bedside than he, more thoughtful or devoted....The first day he seemed only to think that she was released from her long and bitter pain. But now he feels how lonely he is, and what he has lost in her, with the whole strength of his love and reverence. Outwardly and inwardly he is transformed; the shell had burst that held back the tenderness and depth of his feelings.[25]

The potential effect on Moltke, and the consequences for his nation, was not lost on others. The Queen, in her letter of condolence, had it much in her mind, when she wrote: 'May this confidence, your consciousness of a rare fidelity to duty, the memory of a faithful friend who you mourn, and your vocation for the service of King and fatherland give you strength to endure manfully these times of sufferings.'[26] And she sent for Augusta, stressing to her the national importance of maintaining Moltke's well-being. The fear was that his withdrawn personality might leave him to retire progressively from public life and ultimately give up his post. As the Queen saw it, it would be Augusta's duty to go with her husband to live with Moltke to help him come to terms with his shattering loss; and so it was arranged.

Marie was never thereafter far from his thoughts. When at Creisau, he daily visited her grave to lay flowers upon it, and memories of her featured constantly in his letters. Outside his work Creisau was his chief concern; he ceaselessly and energetically worked to restore the manor house and improve the estate, laying out parkland and building bridges and roads. Always he displayed a characteristic attention to every detail of the work as it progressed, with careful regard for strict economy in expenditure as well as continuous concern for the welfare of the estate workers. He spent as much time there as he could, usually with members of his large and devoted family. And all the time he worked tirelessly to prepare for the war to come; but neither he nor anyone else could have guessed that the entirely unexpected issue of Spanish politics would provide the spark that ignited the conflagration.

The issue of the Hohenzollern candidature for the Spanish throne has aroused deep controversy as to the extent of Bismarck's involvement, and how far the crisis, which it provoked, was the product of careful calculation on his part. Some of the facts are even now obscure. It seems however that Bismarck was by the autumn of 1869 encouraging consideration by the Spanish government of a Hohenzollern prince as a candidate for the vacant Spanish throne. Any enquiry into the truth of the matter is not in the least helped by any consideration of Bismarck's 'Reflections and Reminiscences' in which can be found no suggestion that he might in any way have set about the promotion of the candidacy, but merely that he was politically and militarily 'indifferent to the entire question,' to the development of which before the crisis of July 2 1870 he makes no reference.[27] He suggested in his

King William of Prussia (Lindner)

memoirs that a successful candidature would have no military significance, observing that 'no Spanish government, and least of all an alien king, would possess power enough in the country to send even a regiment to the Pyrenees out of affection towards Germany.'[28] It was a view that is entirely at odds with the general tenor of the opinion he expressed in his detailed advice of March 1870, to the effect that it would be worth one to two army corps to Prussia for there to be a Hohenzollern on the Spanish throne.

As events turned out, the circumstances ultimately enabled Bismarck, by brilliant opportunism, to turn the developing situation to Prussian's advantage, thereby taking a long stride to his ultimate purpose. That, in the end, it involved the long foreseen war with France was not necessarily within his contemplation from the outset.

Throughout, however, his handling of the matter was thoroughly devious. Bismarck no doubt saw a Hohenzollern candidature for the vacant throne of Spain as having distinct advantages to Germany economically, militarily and politically, whatever he was later to claim. On March 9 1870, he set out the arguments in favour of the plan in a lengthy secret memorandum to King William in which he urged that a meeting of key figures including Roon, Moltke and the Crown Prince (who was opposed to the idea) should consider the matter. William's marginal notes on his memorandum display his great distaste for the proposal, and his absolute refusal to give orders to either Leopold or his father, Karl Anton of Hohenzollern, that Leopold must accept the throne.

The proposed meeting for which Bismarck had called took place on March 15, when the King's most trusted advisers added their own voices in support of that of Bismarck, but the King was still most unwilling to act in the matter. In order to preserve the utmost secrecy, this was not a formal ministerial discussion, but rather an exchange of views at a private dinner party. That war was considered a possible outcome may be judged from an exchange between Delbrück, the President of the Federal Chancery, and Moltke. 'But if Napoleon takes it ill, are we ready?' asked Delbrück. Moltke nodded emphatically.[29]

Left to his own judgment, however, Leopold declined the offer. Bismarck now tinkered with the possibility of putting forward Leopold's younger brother Frederick to fill the vacancy, but by the end of April, he too had indicated that he did not wish to accept the throne. Bismarck was for the moment baulked; in his extreme annoyance, he commented to Delbrück that 'the Spanish affair has taken a wretched turn. Indubitable reasons of state have been subordinated to the private inclinations of princes and to ultramontane female influences. Irritation over this has for weeks been placing a heavy burden on my nerves.'[30] By no means finally defeated in his promotion of the candidature, however, he proceeded to engage in further secret negotiations with Prim, the Spanish dictator, who may or may not have received bribes from Bismarck. After further pressure had been applied through Karl Anton, Leopold was prevailed upon to indicate, at the beginning of June 1870, that after all he would be prepared to accept. Bismarck's long and patient effort to wear down his royal master achieved its objective when, on June 21, King William 'with a heavy, very heavy heart' agreed to the acceptance of the throne by Leopold.

Having thus far achieved his object, Bismarck was at pains to exclude every possibility that he might be seen to have been the moving force in the whole affair and through Bucher, his trusted envoy, he was most careful to advise Prim how to proceed in the matter of making public Leopold's accession to the throne.

His extremely cautious approach towards the next stage of the matter was, however, rendered entirely nugatory by pure chance. The telegram from Prim's envoy, Salazar, reporting Leopold's acceptance, did not make clear the extent to which the negotiations had been finalised, and as a result Prim adjourned the Cortes, the Spanish parliament, until the autumn. The secret could not be kept for long. Soon, there was a leak; and the crisis that erupted on July 2 began with Prim's confirmation to the French Ambassador in Madrid of the true position. Seventeen days later, France was to declare war; but as a result of the intricate manoeuvres that ensued it was Bismarck who, in the end, succeeded in dominating the situation. Those seventeen days have been minutely examined by historians in seeking to establish exactly the causes of the outbreak of war, and careful attention has been paid to Bismarck's active and adroit handling of the matter which at times did not seem likely to produce the result for which he hoped.

When the diplomatic explosion began, the German posture at any rate could hardly have been more peaceful. Bismarck had, as was his wont, retired to his estate in Varzin; the King was taking the waters at Ems with Abeken, a relatively junior Foreign Office official, in attendance; Leopold was completely out of touch with events in Austria; and Karl Anton was at home at Sigmaringen. Moltke, as usual, was with his family at Creisau. Certainly no more convincingly innocent demeanour could have been presented by Prussia's rulers, which was entirely suited to the earnest surprise with which they received the outrage of the French government.

The first intimation of the French response to the situation came when Le Sourd, the French Chargé d'Affaires in Berlin, called upon von Thile, the Secretary of State, to enquire what the Prussian government knew of the matter. The response was entirely predictable. 'Nothing,' said Thile; although he was personally aware that a Hohenzollern had been considered, this was a matter for Spain, and for Prussia the affair did not exist. To von Werther, the Prussian Ambassador in Paris who was quite outside Bismarck's confidence in the development of the candidature, the French government's comments were direct and forceful. Interviewed on the eve of a long-planned visit to King William at Ems, Werther was left in no doubt of the ferocity of the French reaction to the crisis, and he promised to convey this to the King at Ems.

Bismarck's first consideration of the French démarche was that it was 'very impertinent,'[31] and he at once began to rally his diplomatic forces to resist the challenge. His most urgent task was to prevent the French getting to King William, or at any rate if they did to prevent his pacifically inclined sovereign from making concessions. Werther's proposed visit to Ems, which actually took place on July 6, was going to be dangerous in that respect if he was all too faithfully to describe to William the bellicose noises that were being made in Paris. William's response was indeed to write to Karl Anton to raise with the latter the dangers implicit to the situation.

In Paris, on the day before, an interpellation in the Corps Legislatif had been addressed to the government by a left-centre deputy named Cochery, and on July 6, Gramont, the French Foreign Minister, responded in terms which were unmistakable in their tone. Remarking that their respect for the rights of others did not oblige the French to permit a foreign power to place 'one of its Princes on the throne of Charles V', he concluded by saying that the government would 'know how to do our duty without hesitation and without weakness'[32] - a declaration that was greeted with tumultuous applause by the deputies.

The shape of the ultimate casus belli was becoming clearer; but curiously, Bismarck's immediate response from Varzin to Gramont's declaration was withheld for 24 hours. When it came, it was couched in terms that might have been expected, finding the language that Gramont had used to be 'insolent and bumptious beyond all expectation'[33] and certainly, international reaction to the speech gave Bismarck every excuse to feel aggrieved, if this were the posture he should choose to adopt. Lord Lyons, the British Ambassador in Paris, saw very clearly the diplomatic cul-de-sac which Gramont had entered, reporting to Granville on July 7 that 'the explosion of chauvinism in France is very unfortunate and very alarming. The government undoubtedly desire and hope at the present moment to carry their point without actual war; but they have burnt their ships and left themselves no possible means of escape.'[34]

On July 8, Benedetti, the French Ambassador, who had been urgently recalled from leave, set off to Ems for a royal audience with William with whom, on the following afternoon, he had a lengthy but inconclusive interview. Benedetti's account of the King's response, to the effect that he felt quite unable to give orders to Karl Anton or his son in the matter 'lessened neither our perplexities nor our apprehensions,' as Ollivier, the French Prime Minister, wrote,[35] particularly as the King had conceded to the Ambassador that Bismarck had been kept informed.[36] Benedetti's representations at this meeting had, however, not been without some immediate good effect from the French point of view. As a result of his discussion with Benedetti, William sent Werther back to Paris, a step which caused Bismarck very great alarm, if only because he feared that Werther would be much too accommodating to the French demands. In Paris, Ollivier, who was by no means himself an aggressive statesman, now began to feel that the die was cast, writing on July 10 to Gramont that 'from this moment war seems to be forced upon us: it only remains for us to make up our minds to it fearlessly and with energy.'[37] Steps were accordingly taken to prepare for war, not the least important of these being an order to the army in Africa to prepare to return home.

News of these preparations alarmed William, and demonstrated plainly to Bismarck the extent of the crisis now at hand. His response was immediate. From now on the General Staff were to be kept informed at every turn, and his own readiness to accept that war might be the outcome was manifest, even though he sought to calm William's fears while discouraging him from influencing Leopold's decision - since if the Hohenzollerns were to withdraw, at least Prussian prestige ought not to be compromised by involvement in the decision. Unknown to Bismarck, however, William had already taken the crucial situation to send an aide, Colonel von Strantz, to Sigmaringen.

Back at Ems, on July 11, William again saw Benedetti, and in his anxiety to prevent a rupture of relations, he was quite unable to avoid presenting an appearance of extreme shiftiness, most particularly with regard to Leopold's absence from any form of contact at such a critical moment. Benedetti left this meeting quite unsatisfied, and reported in detail to Gramont.[38]

Bismarck, meanwhile, was chafing to get to grips with the negotiations himself, since he feared, entirely correctly, that William would do nothing to take advantage of what he regarded as a unique opportunity. On the same day as his meeting with Benedetti, the King confirmed his agreement that Bismarck should come to Ems and on the next day, July 12, he set off from Varzin in an open carriage. Seeing an old friend standing by his doorway as he set off, he made a gesture which unmistakably indicated that he thought himself to be going off to war.[39] Moltke, too, was summoned to Berlin, but reacted rather less flamboyantly than Bismarck. Out driving with his brother Adolf and his family, he was stopped by a telegraph boy. He read the telegram and put it without comment in his pocket. Nothing could be gleaned from his demeanour except that he was even quieter than usual. When they got home, he jumped down from the carriage, saying only: 'It is a stupid thing. I have to go to Berlin tonight,' and spent most of the rest of the day in his study before setting off.[40]

Strantz, meanwhile, had endured a frustrating delay on his railway journey to Sigmaringen, which he reached on the night of July 11. There he found Karl Anton, in Leopold's continued absence, now willing to take the decision for him. In the early hours of July 12, Karl Anton decided upon a renunciation, and that morning telegrams went out from Sigmaringen announcing Leopold's withdrawal from the candidature.

Of all the recipients of that momentous news, no-one received it with greater shock than Bismarck, as on that morning he made his way into his Berlin residence. His immediate reaction was, he wrote, 'to retire from the service because after all the insolent challenges which had gone before, I perceived in this extorted submission a humiliation of Germany for which I did not desire to be responsible.'[41] On his copy of the telegram from Abeken, opposite the words 'the Prince must himself communicate directly with Madrid', he scribbled angrily 'communicate? Why? What about? And what?' Another marginal note on the same telegram commented sarcastically 'very kind!' and underlined the word 'consent' adding 'to what???'[42] These marginalia give a clear indication of the extent of his pent-up fury that day. In his own account of the matter, he records that he got the news at dinner with Moltke and Roon, although the evidence seems clearly to point to his having received it on his arrival at Berlin. Historians have questioned how seriously he intended his projected resignation, and although of course he was invariably quick in his emotional reactions, it is to be doubted at that stage that he really supposed that he must throw in the towel or that the issue between France and Germany was so easily to be resolved. At all events he at once resolved to send von Eulenburg, the Prussian Interior Minister, to Ems in his place, while he himself remained in Berlin. Eulenburg could be counted on to exert a positive influence on William in the crucial days ahead.

And indeed Bismarck now seemed in that quarter to have some very serious problems. At Ems, William received the news of the renunciation with profound relief, while in Paris the first reactions were ecstatic. Guizot said enviously that it was the greatest diplomatic victory he had ever seen, while Thiers felt that 'Sadowa was almost avenged.'[43] But some malign spirit must have hovered over the deliberations of the French government, because instead of accepting Leopold's renunciation which, as Ollivier pointed out, undoubtedly must have involved the King's participation, it was felt necessary to obtain some more formal satisfaction. The still very strong tide of public feeling in Paris was not assuaged by Karl Anton's renunciation and, borne along by this, Gramont took the fatal steps that were to carry France over the precipice. On the afternoon of July 12, he suggested to Werther, by now returned from Paris to Ems, that it would be helpful for William to write an explanatory letter to Napoleon, and Werther undertook to pass this suggestion on to the King. That evening, after a meeting between Gramont and Napoleon, Benedetti was sent two telegrams with orders to see William again to seek an assurance that he would not again sanction Leopold's candidature. The second of these, in even stronger terms, was sent at Napoleon's instance, and alarmed Ollivier. The firm tone of these instructions was, Gramont emphasised, due to the strength of public opinion. The next day at Ems, when Benedetti acted upon these orders, was to prove decisive.

While all this had been going on, the British government had been anxiously but ineffectually trying to stop the slide to war. On July 10, just prior to Karl Anton's renunciation, Lord Lyons considered war a question of hours because 'the French are getting more and more excited. They think they have got the start of Prussia this time in forwardship of preparation…If the excitement goes on, the French may choose to pick a quarrel on the form of the renunciation or some other pretext, even if the Prince retires.'[44] This objective and prescient comment in a private letter to Lord Granville, the Foreign Secretary, gives a pretty fair assessment of the real willingness of Paris to let matters come to an open breach. Lyons saw at once that the renunciation would not in itself be enough for the French government; Gladstone and Granville hastened to tell the French that if war did occur, it would be upon France that responsibility for it would fall. In truth, however, there was little that any other government could do to influence a situation that had now acquired an impetus of its own.

Werther's report to the King about Gramont's suggestion went by courier to Ems during the night of July 12, but did not actually reach there until the critical events had already taken place. In Ems, Benedetti, immediately he got his instructions by telegram, felt obliged to act on them as soon as possible, in part because the threat of Bismarck's expected arrival now hung over his hopes of extracting the desired assurances from the peaceably disposed Prussian King. William, however, had by now already been alerted to the danger and, as he took his morning stroll in the park at 9 o'clock on July 13, he was cautious in his response to Benedetti's message through an adjutant asking for an immediate audience, saying only that he would see him later. He then settled down to read the morning papers, which carried the news that the renunciation had now been made public. Accordingly, he sent over by his adjutant a copy of one of the newspapers to Benedetti, who was still in the park. The latter replied confirming that the news was known to him and, still through the adjutant, William returned his compliments and thanks.

Benedetti now pushed his luck too far. Turning his steps once more towards the path of the King, he met him near the entrance to the park. William amicably opened the conversation which Benedetti, however, turned once again towards the subject of the assurance which he had been told to get. This assurance, William insisted, he could not possibly give; Benedetti pressed the point and finally asked the King directly if he could report that the King would not permit Leopold to renew the candidature. He had gone too far. The King brought the conversation to an end by declaring, as he later wrote: 'It seems to me, Mr Ambassador, that I have so clearly and plainly expressed myself to the effect that I could never make such a declaration, that I have nothing more to add.'[45] In spite of this, it is not perhaps entirely clear that either of the protagonists were conscious of any supremely important event having taken place. Each duly reported what had occurred, Benedetti in a series of four telegrams and a despatch to Paris, and William in a note to Abeken; and that night, or possibly next day, William wrote a detailed account of the meeting.[46]

In Paris, meanwhile, on July 13, the government was still under extreme pressure. The day had begun without most of the members of the Cabinet even knowing of the demand for an assurance, a fact which greatly excited Marshal Le Boeuf, the War Minister, who claimed to have stopped his preparations as a result of the previously announced renunciation. In the Corps Législatif on the other hand, Gramont had a rough time at the hands of deputies demanding that the national dignity be avenged.

At Ems on July 13 the King saw Eulenburg at noon. At 1 p.m. Strantz arrived with the written text of Karl Anton's letter of renunciation and by 2 p.m. Abeken and Eulenburg had persuaded William, with the aid of Bismarck's advice and warnings, not to see Benedetti again but to tell him through the adjutant that he had received confirmation of the renunciation and that he regarded the matter as settled. Finally, accepting this, the King authorized Abeken to report to Bismarck - which, at 3.30 p.m., he duly did.

But even now William's pacific intentions almost got the better of Bismarck's influence when, that same afternoon, he allowed his adjutant to say to Benedetti that the ambassador could report to Paris that he, the King, approved of the renunciation. Benedetti, in the absence of the assurance for which he had asked, could only renew his request for an audience. But, by now, Werther's report of Gramont's suggestion had arrived at Ems, and Abeken and Eulenburg had no difficulty in prompting in the King the most extreme indignation at such an inconceivable request. By 5.30 p.m. the refusal of a further audience was absolute. The discussions were at an end.

Back in Berlin, Bismarck had also been having a busy day. Feelings there were running so high that, in the events which had happened, Prussia simply could not accept the humiliation which the renunciation had caused. A provocative telegram was dispatched to Werther. News came through Gortschakoff in St. Petersburg that Gramont did not regard the matter as being at an end. The British Ambassador to Berlin was told that Prussia would require assurances that there would not be a sudden French attack. Bismarck sent to the newspapers the information that Württemberg had been deeply offended by the latest French demands, even though at that time he did not really know what those demands were.

But none of these activities were to compare in importance with his dinner on the night of July 13. Moltke and Roon were again his guests. According to Bismarck, they were dejected and without appetite and during dinner a telegram was sent off to Ems urging that the King return to Berlin in view of 'the growing exasperation of public opinion over the presumptuous conduct of France'. By now, quite plainly, Bismarck was himself bent upon war even if the way things were going were by no means to his satisfaction. Suddenly, however, the means to achieve his end arrived with Abeken's telegram from Ems.

Bismarck's account of what followed has, no doubt correctly, for once been accepted as substantially accurate. With the sense for public relations that he always displayed, he perceived in the telegram a superb opportunity. Obtaining from Moltke immediate reassurance that the army was ready - that, in effect, the sooner war came the better - he sat down to produce a short summary of Abeken's telegram for publication. He read it to his guests, upon whom the effect was immediate. 'Now it has a different ring', said Moltke; 'it sounded before like a parley; now it is like a flourish in answer to a challenge'. And Bismarck took care to explain the provocative effect that the widespread publication of the amended version would cause. The two generals cheered up enormously, confident that they now had their war and confident in its outcome. Roon remarked grandly: 'Our God of old lives still and will not let us perish in disgrace', while Moltke, less characteristically for so reserved a man, said: 'If I may but live to lead our armies in such a war then the devil may come directly afterwards and fetch away this old carcass.'[47]

Bismarck's prediction of the effect upon public opinion was, of course, quite right. His editing can hardly be said to have corrupted Abeken's meaning but the emphasis was now entirely clear. The French had asked for an assurance, and had been abruptly rebuffed. No-one could suppose that such an insult could be accepted by a French public already thoroughly overstimulated into making demands that were, in the circumstances, grossly imprudent and, indeed, quite unnecessary.

That night and the next day brought fresh confirmation of the position. French military preparations were accelerating, and Gramont was openly predicting war in the absence of the assurances which Benedetti had sought. For William, who had truly done what he could to avoid war, the events of July 14 must have been a saddening experience. He cannot have been surprised to receive the urgent suggestions that he return at once to Berlin, and once he had seen the publication of the Ems telegram in the newspapers, he remarked emphatically: 'That is war'. He announced that he would indeed return next day to Berlin. That afternoon at the railway station at Ems, he met Benedetti briefly but courteously. There was no discussion between them and, two hours later, the envoy returned to Paris.

There, on the morning of July 14, Ollivier was reflecting upon the statement he was to make to the Council of Ministers recording his government's diplomatic triumph, when Gramont burst in on him. 'My dear fellow, you see before you a man who has received a knockdown blow!' In his hand he held Le Sourd's report of the Ems telegram. 'We can delude ourselves no longer,' said Ollivier. 'They propose to force us into war.'[48]

Werther had already been ordered by Bismarck to see Gramont and to take his leave of him. Presided over by the Emperor, the Council of Ministers met at 12.30 to consider the text of the Ems telegram, and were in little doubt as to its implications. That night, after heavy pressure from Gramont and Le Boeuf, the Council decided upon its response; next day, a declaration was to be made to the Chambers of the reasons why the government now regarded war as inevitable.

On the evening of July 15, William arrived in Brandenburg where he was met by Bismarck, Moltke, Roon and the Crown Prince, and as they went on towards Berlin, they discussed what must now be done. At the railway station at Berlin, Thile was waiting with news of the declaration by the French government. Although short of a declaration of war, (which was only finally delivered on July 19) it really amounted to just that, and it was taken as such by the German people as well as by their ministers. William made his way from the station to the Palace through wildly enthusiastic crowds. Moltke had no difficulty in persuading his colleagues of the need for immediate mobilisation, and that night the orders went out. For the second time in four years, Bismarck had obtained the war he needed at the time when he judged he needed it and for the second time, it would be Moltke's task now to justify the confident advice which he had given his government.

2

Strategic Planning

When it appeared possible, in the course of the negotiations which followed the battle of Königgrätz, that France might be rash enough to embark on military intervention, Bismarck asked Moltke what he would do. Moltke succinctly replied: 'I should adopt a defensive attitude towards Austria, confining myself to the line of the Elbe, and in the meantime prosecuting the war actively against France.'[1] Moltke assumed that, faced with a victorious Prussian army and the whole of the rest of the German forces, France would only risk war if a deal had been done with Austria to continue fighting. In that case, he doubted the feasibility of conducting an offensive war in the east, which he reckoned would effectively require all his forces; he proposed therefore to leave four corps, about 120,000 men, to deal with Austria, and concentrate the rest of the available forces against France. In a detailed paper, which he presented to Bismarck on August 8, he reviewed the probable situation. He ruled out the possibility that the French would violate Belgian neutrality, which would bring England into the war. He assumed that the French would advance between Luxembourg and Rastadt, and planned to await this attack behind the Rhine. Conducting a defensive war would not have been his choice; but, he wrote, this 'should not be avoided, considering the large object to be gained thereby. Even if the outcome should not be entirely successful, Germany would for all time be assembled around Prussia.' There was, he considered, no question of a voluntary cession of German territory in order to avoid war; such a policy would destroy completely Prussia's claim to the future leadership of Germany.[2] Making maximum use of the rail network, he reckoned on having assembled 150,000 Prussian troops between Mainz and Mannheim by September 9, assuming he could start the operation by August 22. Of the South German contingents, on which he believed he could count in any war against France, the Bavarian army would already be close at hand. The total North German forces would reach 240,000; after garrisoning the western fortresses he would have 200,000 available for operations in the field, with another 100,000 from South Germany.

A key part of the process of Moltke's war planning was the gathering of intelligence to enable him to assess probable French strategy. For this he depended on reports from the capable Prussian military attaché in Paris, Colonel von Löe, to whom he had sent Alfred von Schlieffen as an assistant in November 1866. Among other assignments, they went to Lyon to look at the system for transporting munitions to Metz, and to the north of France to discover the intended mobilisation plans for the artillery. The necessary information was collected without great difficulty, as was key data about the movement of the Army of Africa to France on mobilisation.[3]

In the following year, the Luxembourg crisis obliged Moltke to reconsider his plans in the light of the proposed demilitarisation of the fortress of Luxembourg. One option would be to enlarge the small fortress of Saarlouis, midway between the Grand Duchy and the Bavarian Palatinate. But this would require as an

Moltke in the saddle, by Speyer (Bork)

immediate garrison the whole of the infantry of one division, materially weakening the field army; and, since the work would take a considerable time, the unsettled political situation might mean that it was not ready in time. On the other hand, the French would probably not be ready to conduct a major war until the following year, and even after the current reorganisation of the French army the North German Confederation would probably be strong enough on its own to meet it successfully without having to count on south Germany. The French planned to increase their battalion strength from 700 men to 1000 men; however, he calculated that

> after organising a field army, a third of which in any case be composed of raw levies, France would have exhausted its reserves, and replenishment and new formations could be effected by recruitment or by volunteers, while our Prussian Landwehr forms a nucleus from which even the army of operations can be reinforced. In the French artillery the number of guns will have been increased to 1014, but not the number of trained artillery men, while Prussia can this year put 1240 guns into the field.

In these circumstances, the Saarlouis option did not appeal to him. 'I see more security for us in the hastening of extending our railroads than there would be in construction of any fortifications.' Without the completion of new main lines to the Rhine, the seven corps which the existing network could concentrate on the Rhine by the thirtieth day of mobilisation would not suffice for an invasion of France, which Moltke saw as the most effective means of defending the Rhineland province. Only about 80 miles of track would be needed, the cost of which could be treated as loans to the railway companies. 'If the state should be required to advance a few millions for hastening the completion of the projected lines, that would be entirely justified by the political situation.'[4]

The war ministry was evidently not as discouraged by Moltke's views on the utility of a new fortress at Saarlouis as he might have expected and continued to work on the scheme. Roon sent the outline proposals to Moltke, who returned them on July 6 with a crisp dismissal of the project. If he was obliged to conduct a defensive war on the Rhine, the operation to relieve Saarlouis would be difficult; if on the other hand, he was to act offensively, the fortress would be unnecessary. He did not think much of the place as a depôt to support an advance. A fortified camp, of which the new fortress would form part, had the disadvantage that if it was not occupied by an army, it would be extremely weak, and its occupants would in any case be harassed by long range artillery fire. 'So far, in the annals of war, the history of fortified camps is in most cases connected with their capitulation, and I would recommend the construction of such a camp least of all at Saarlouis, where, for instance, the range of the forts on the Felix Hill reaches to beyond French territory.' Nor would there be, he concluded, any material advantage in the series of smaller forts planned to prevent the enemy making any use of the German rail network.[5]

Later in 1867, notwithstanding the resolution of the Luxembourg crisis, it became apparent that the French were still making preparations for war, and Bismarck asked Moltke, who was away at Creisau at the time, for a written opinion on the military situation. Moltke replied in two letters of September 6 and 9. He was not surprised by the French activity, which was due to the French need to make good serious defects in their military organisation, to increase the defensive strength of the army, to speed up mobilisation, and finally in order to be able to respond to an unexpected outbreak of war. He expected the process of military reform in France to continue, even if the international situation remained stable. In reviewing the steps the French were actually taking, he did find the strengthening of the navy rather odd. 'It is a fact that the French navy is superior to ours, even if no additional steps are taken to increase it; still a report of such a contemplated increase might easily excite the mistrust of other maritime powers, though they would keep aloof in the conflict.'[6]

What was more significant, he thought, was the marked strengthening of the French army. The total of trained men had been increased by 70,000; the number of horses available suggested that the French could now mobilise as quickly as the Prussians; and the field artillery had been increased by 34 batteries. On the other hand, the re-equipment of the French infantry with the Chassepôt was going only slowly, and the planned increase in recruitment had not taken place. In a reference to recent French diplomatic activity, Moltke noted that Napoleon's efforts to build an Austrian-South German alliance had not borne fruit; without support, the French army would not be able to carry on a campaign that autumn. Looking in detail at some of the more extravagant reports of French preparations, Moltke concluded that they considerably overstated their extent and significance.

The continued refinement of Moltke's strategic plans was helped by an increasingly sophisticated scheme for the rapid movement of troops on mobilisation. Wartensleben, who headed the railways department of the General

Staff, worked continuously to accelerate the mobilisation process; he calculated that each new railway line provided the opportunity to speed up mobilisation at the rate of one corps per week. The key, as ever, was to achieve complete coordination among the fifty-three railway companies, of which only fifteen were state owned and five partly state owned. In November 1867 the time allotted for bringing the army to the point where it commenced its forward motion was thirty-two days; next year this was down to twenty-four days and by January 1870 to twenty days.[7] As this process went on the likelihood that a premature French offensive could make significant headway was greatly decreased, and Moltke could be even more confident that he would be able to complete his initial deployment without interference from the enemy.

Moltke's mind was in any case turning increasingly to the desirability of taking the war to France. His instinctive dislike of standing on the defensive was reinforced by the indications that if war came France would stand alone; and in an undated paper of 1867 he prepared march tables for the alternative possibilities of an advance against the French on the Metz-Thionville line, or on the position between Point à Mousson and Nancy. On November 16 he prepared a detailed discussion paper in preparation for a meeting with his department heads outlining the deployment possibilities and the first operations that might be undertaken. Looking ahead to the following spring, he assumed that it would be necessary to leave a part of the army to watch Denmark and Austria. These detachments would amount to one division at Dòppel against Denmark and two and a half corps around Görlitz to face Austria. This would leave ten corps; two corps, the Guard and the X Corps would remain their home garrisons, providing a central reserve of 65,000 men available for use against either France or Austria as the situation demanded.

For the operations against France he envisaged deploying 250,000 men in four armies, each two corps strong; if the central reserve was released, one corps would be added to each of the Second and Third Armies. Whether it would be necessary to stand on the defensive would depend on the speed of French mobilisation; if this was completed first, he expected an advance by the French army to take place by the twenty fifth day. There were, he suggested, a number of possible lines which that advance might take. A movement of large forces against Köln and Koblenz was not probable; more likely was an advance from Metz-Nancy towards Mainz and Mannheim. Moltke estimated that he should meet such a thrust around Homburg on the thirtieth or thirty second day; he suggested that a position should be prepared on the Upper Blies, demonstrating that he took seriously the possibility that the French would be able to get their act together and strike first. He expected that such an advance would be supported by an offensive from the direction of Strasbourg, which did not unduly trouble him; the two corps facing it would fall back, if they had to, towards Koblenz, while the French southern force would be at risk of being outflanked on its left. When and where a decisive battle would be fought would depend on the outcome of the early encounters, but might await the bringing up of the central reserve.[8]

If the Prussians completed their mobilisation first, Moltke intended to advance directly on the main French army, whatever line it was taking; to ensure that he encountered it with the maximum force he proposed a very tight concentration and an advance on a narrow front, twelve miles broad as the frontier was crossed, reducing to eight miles two days later. 'Thus we could deploy any day 250,000 men for battle, not only to the front, but also towards the flank, should the French advance to the attack from either the Nied or the Seille.' His objective was to drive the French army away from Paris, and this would determine the line of his advance; to achieve it, he was prepared to risk a threat to his communications. If in fact the French did not advance, Moltke proposed to cover Metz and advance towards Pont à Mousson.[9]

The possibility that the French might seize the initiative continued to occupy Moltke's mind, and on March 21 he drafted a paper to review the possibility that they would do so. In this case he reckoned they could have 70,000 men on the Rhine by the twentieth day of mobilisation, but whether they advanced precipitately in this way or waited until their concentration was complete, the Prussian mobilisation plans worked out in November would not be altered. If the French did advance in this way, they would undoubtedly embarrass the scattered Prussian detachments which they would encounter; Moltke accepted that he would have to abandon the left bank of the Rhine at the point of attack. Confident that he would soon roll back the French advance, he was of the opinion that the retreating Prussian forces should not destroy the railway. He had no doubt that by the twentieth day he would in any case have brought so large a force up to the right bank of the Rhine that there was no danger of 70,000 French troops being able to effect a crossing.[10]

In all the plans which Moltke had prepared since 1866, he had proceeded on the basis that the South German states could not be counted on, but in the scheme he produced in April 1868 (which he later personally endorsed as being a 'final, and governed by present conditions, sketch of a plan of operations') he assumed that their forces would be involved although operating independently. Still preparing for the possibility that he would have to fight France alone, he now proposed to hold back two corps, to operate as a reserve but also to produce a strong force to cover the North German coast, since he supposed that France would not leave its fleet unused. This left him eleven corps of 360,000 men, which was equal to the strength of the French army; a material superiority would be achieved if from 40,000 to 60,000 men joined from the South German states.[11] He still planned to operate in four armies. The First Army would assemble around Wittlich, supporting if it could its advance guard at Trier but falling back if the French launched an offensive through Luxembourg. If they did not, the First Army would link with the Second Army, which would concentrate on the line Homburg-Zweibrucken. The Third Army, moving forward from railheads in Mainz, would operate as a reserve. If the French did launch an early offensive into the Palatinate, which Moltke was now coming to view as probable, he intended that the Second and Third Armies should meet them in a defensive position in front of Mainz. The role of the Fourth Army would in any case be to cooperate with and support the South Germans. Since an invasion of France itself was the best protection for Southern Germany, the Fourth Army would, if the French did not cross the Upper Rhine, move forward in unison with the rest of the army. If the French did cross the Upper Rhine before his concentration was complete, Moltke had no doubt that they would be made to pay for it:

> the V and XI Corps would march up the Rhine on the right bank, would receive the Württembergers and Badeners in Bruchsal and Rastadt, advance on the enemy's communications and compel him to turn about. We should not be afraid of this partition of our fighting forces and we can carry out the offensive with our main force towards the west after the arrival of our second transport echelons, because the enemy has also divided his forces and abandoned all connections between them.[12]

Moltke was already at this stage pencilling the names of his army commanders. The only surprise among these was the selection of either Herwarth von Bittenfeld or the Grand Duke of Mecklenburg-Schwerin (with von Schlotheim as Chief of Staff) to command one of the armies. The final shape of his plans was now beginning to emerge. He now based these on having a total of 430,000 men, rising to 480,000 men, in his four armies. At this stage, in the absence of a firm agreement with the South Germans, he was necessarily sensitive in his assumptions as to the most effective deployment.

This uncertainty he now set about removing, meeting on May 13 with representatives from the general staffs of Bavaria and Württemberg. The discussions proved useful, and he reported on the same day to Bismarck on their outcome. Theoretically, as he pointed out, nothing was necessary save that the South Germans should mobilise promptly and place themselves at Prussia's disposal. In practice however, it was not so simple:

> The offensive and defensive alliance is always an incomplete form of mutual help, and has just so much value as each party of the alliance is able to give help. In this relation conditions of proportion are by no means equal. The North furnishes an army, the South furnishes contingents; we have a war lord, the South but a confederation Commander in Chief; the South with the best intentions can but furnish us with a coalition.[13]

Moltke drew attention to the kind of problems that had arisen in 1866, and warned that all that could be asked of the South Germans was what they could and would perform with due regard to their own security, which could be defined in discussion. He returned to what was a central tenet of his strategic planning against France: 'We believe that the lower as well as the upper Rhine is best protected by an army on the central Rhine. The South German States need a firm guarantee that we will be there in time and in great strength, in order to come to a decision as to their measures, and that guarantee I can give.'[14] This was the key to unlocking the full potential of the South Germans, and in the event Moltke was thereafter able to plan, as in 1870 he was able to operate, with the full strength of Bavaria, Württemberg and Baden at his disposal. What was vital, as he pointed out to Bismarck, was that they should mobilise in accordance with the Prussian timetable, which meant they must be ready to move on the twenty first day.

Following these talks Moltke prepared a draft plan of operations on which he proposed to base the agreements that must be worked out with each of the South German States. He divided the paper into two parts, in the first part dealing with the concentration of the army in the event of war with France alone, and in the second with the case of Austria taking part. As usual he planned active operations rather than a static defence of key points: 'the most assured protection to the strong lower, as well as the weaker upper Rhine would be given by a decisive offensive with superior fighting forces into France, and it requires but a timely concentration of the means at hand to take that offensive.'[15] Again based on operating with four armies, this plan called for the south German forces to be embodied in the Third Army, serving as the left wing and concentrating around Landau; and for the Fourth Army, concentrating in front of Mainz, to act as the reserve. He calculated now on having nearly half a million soldiers at his disposal; the general principles of his plan largely followed his previous scheme of November 1868, save for the effective incorporation of the South German forces. For the North Sea coast he set aside 40,000 men, of which 25,000 comprised two Landwehr divisions each of 10,400 men. He took seriously the initial threat posed by the powerful French navy: 'Should a French landing expedition be intended, it undoubtedly will occur in the North Sea and probably in the very first stages of hostilities. If the French fighting forces are attacked in their own country, the French will hardly undertake such an operation.'[16]

In the event of Austria taking part, Moltke recognised that he must divide his forces unequally, standing on the defensive with the weaker part and seeking a knockout blow with his main force. He was in no doubt that his first target must be France where, with superior numbers, he could hope to gain a victory in the first days of the campaign. If that gave the Austrians the chance to occupy Silesia, or even Brandenburg and Berlin, nothing decisive would have been lost, and it was entirely possible that such an advance would bring Russia into the war. It was a strategy that called for boldness. The split on which he decided would given ten corps for the advance into France, with three corps to face Austria. The role of the Bavarians would be determined by their own interests; these would be to cover the Rhine Palatinate and to take up a position in the east protecting Munich, which Moltke found perfectly agreeable, since the Austrians must detach an army of observation to watch them.[17]

Interestingly, Moltke revisited this draft scheme of operations in March 1869, to add a section based on the possibility that France would occupy Belgium. Since this would undoubtedly cause a war with England as well as Prussia, Moltke concluded that such an operation would occur as part of a deliberate intention to bring about war with Germany. It would require a French army of 120,000, committed to a campaign entirely detached from the main campaign in Alsace-Lorraine; he calculated that the maximum size of the French forces advancing on the Rhine could not exceed 200,000 men. He toyed with the idea that he might almost entirely ignore a French advance through Belgium towards Aachen, and instead himself march on Paris; he would have only 120 miles to cover before reaching his enemy's capital; the French, on the other hand, would be 320 miles from Berlin.[18] He preferred, however, the idea of an advance from the line Luxembourg-Pont à Mousson, converging in the direction of Sedan. He would have found it hard at that time to predict the circumstances which would in due course take him to this small city of no great military significance.

The possibility that Austria would take up arms in support of France was always present in Moltke's mind, and in the final draft of his mobilisation and deployment plan he reviewed its implications with care. This was during the winter of 1868/9, by which time he could rely upon having six through railway lines to the

Palatinate; if the French were to make the maximum use of their much inferior network in the frontier area, they would have to be split into two groups, around Metz and Strasbourg respectively, separated by the Vosges. Austria's potential hostility was of critical importance to the initial deployment. Moltke repeated the basic principles of previous memoranda on the subject:

> If the political situation brings about a war of France against Prussia then the attitude of Austria will be either decidedly hostile or at least very doubtful. Should we oppose one half of our army to each of these two powers, we would be superior to neither. Therefore the first thing to be considered is: against which enemy will we in the start assume the defensive with minor forces, in order to advance offensively as strong as possible against the other?[19]

Although the Rhine offered a strong defensive barrier, merely to stand on the defensive against France could cost Prussia the support of the South German states. Ultimately the position could be turned; in Bohemia, on the other hand, it might take a long time to bring the Austrians to a decisive battle. By now Moltke was firmly of the opinion that it was better by far to attack France first whatever happened. If it came to the crunch, Prussia must not hesitate to bring on the crisis.

> Neither Austria nor France is strong enough to carry on a war without allies against Northern Germany. As soon as Austria commences its mobilisation we should immediately declare war against France ... If we invade French territory, then the French sentiment will not wait for Austria. France is not only the most dangerous but the most ready enemy, and we will be certain to encounter our enemy very soon it is probable that after the first unsuccessful battle a change in the Dynasty will occur in France, and as we do not desire to take anything away from France we may soon be able to come to terms with the new Government or new Monarchy. Considering all these reasons I suggest that we designate ten army corps for an offensive against France and three army corps for a defensive against Austria. For the reinforcement of the latter and for the active defence of the coast a mobile Landwehr division should be formed, and the 17th Division should be kept back for observation against Denmark, that division to be replaced in the IX Army Corps by the Hessian Division.[20]

As he had concluded in his previous paper, against the whole strength that the Austrians would be able to develop for an advance from Bohemia to Berlin, which Moltke still thought was the line they were most likely to take, he could oppose only a total of 113,600 men. The odds were a little better than they appeared, however; it took Austria four months to get ready in 1866, and there was no reason to think that she could do much better now. And Austria would have to detach significant forces to watch both the Bavarian and Russian frontiers. All the same, the pressure to get a quick result in the west was very considerable. There,

> it is of main importance to take the field against France quickly and in superior numbers. Less complicated than for the defensive against Austria is the plan of operations for the offensive against France. It consists mainly in seeking out the enemy's main force and to attack it where found. The only difficulty lies in executing this simple plan with very large masses.[21]

The masses were very large indeed; with the South German forces, Moltke would have 360,000 men at the outset to oppose 250,000 French troops, and later 386,000 to 343,000.

In considering where the French Army would actually be found, Moltke rejected the possibility that it would attempt to turn his flank either through Belgium or Switzerland. As to the former, 'not counting political difficulties with England, the violation of Belgium's neutrality offers too little hope of success to be probable;' and he went on to note that 'France would encounter no less difficulties should it attempt to carry out operations through Switzerland and to join hands with Austria.'[22] He therefore assumed that the French would concentrate on the line Metz-Strasbourg, and that their principal objective would be to advance on the Main, with the intention of separating North from South Germany. To meet such a threat, a concentration in the Bavarian Palatinate south of the Moselle would achieve the best possible position which, assuming the French concentrated in two groups to maximise their railway system, would be on the inner line of operations between them. For Moltke, the only question was whether 'we, without running danger of being interfered with in our first concentration, can transfer the point of concentration across the Rhine into the Palatinate and to the immediate French frontier, and this question, according to my opinions should be answered affirmatively. Our mobilisation is prepared down to the very last detail.' He noted that on the twelfth day the first of his troops would detrain near the French frontier, by the fifteenth day the combat troops of two army corps would be in position, by the twentieth day he would have 300,000 men there, and by the twenty fourth day the armies would be complete with their trains. 'We have no reason at all to suppose that the concentration of the French army to a mobile footing, for which so far they have no experience, can be made quicker. Since Napoleon Bonaparte's time France has known only partial mobilisation.'[23]

For the moment he adhered to his plan for four armies, three being concentrated around Wittlich, Neunkirchen-Homburg and Landau-Rastatt respectively, with a fourth in reserve in front of Mainz. The assembly of the armies would be covered by holding Saarbrücken and Trier. Even if the French moved very quickly indeed, he thought it very unlikely that they could strike at the Second Army, which would be the furthest forward, before the nineteenth day of mobilisation, by which time he expected the Second Army to have concentrated some 104 battalions, 108 squadrons and 60 batteries around Homburg. And if by then the position of the main French Army was still unclear, it was his intention to use four cavalry divisions, supported by an infantry division, to obtain the necessary information.

All along, Moltke aimed at a swift knockout blow. Years later he summarised the reasons why this was essential: 'Calling into service all those capable of bearing arms; the strength of armies; the difficulties of sustaining them; the enormous cost of being under arms; the disruption of commerce, manufacture, and agriculture; the battle-ready organisation of the armies and the ease with which they are assembled, all press for early termination of the war.'[24]

With his final plan, which was subject to only minor modifications in the next two years (the last of which were made in July 1870), Moltke could feel that he was entirely ready for the challenge whenever it came. Now he would wait in absolute calm; whatever happened would not deflect him from carrying out plans which he knew to be correct. Some years after his death Bismarck, who was best qualified of all to express a view, said of Moltke that he was 'a rare human being, a man systematic in the discharge of his duty, with a quite special character; absolutely reliable and at the same time cold to the very heart.'[25]

3

The German Army after Königgrätz

The military machine which Moltke had worked tirelessly to perfect in the inter war years had grown substantially since the battle of Königgrätz; and he had seen to it that the essential lessons of 1866 had been learned by all branches of the army. Events were to prove that in 1870 he had in his hand a military instrument that was stronger by far than any that had ever previously taken the field in Europe. The management of such a huge force, and the need to maximise the effectiveness of the technological developments now available to it, demanded a corresponding increase in the competence and thoroughness of its leaders.

Although the industrialisation of Germany was accelerating sharply by 1870, a large part of its population still lived in small communities and drew their livelihood from an essentially agrarian economy. In Prussia in particular, however, the elementary school system had ensured that there was a rising standard of education. It was one of the factors noted by Stoffel in 1868 as accounting for the moral superiority of the Prussian Army over all other European armies. As a result of the principle of compulsory education, he wrote, 'the Prussian Nation is the most enlightened in Europe, in the sense that education is diffused among all classes of society.'[1] Its institutions were, he thought, based on two great principles, compulsory education and compulsory military service; and on these Prussia 'as upon two majestic columns, has placed itself in the first rank, among the enlightened nations of Europe.' The political and economic events of the past century had created a real sense of national identity in the German population. The military traditions of Prussia, and its recent spectacular successes in advancing the cause of German unity, had contributed to a widespread acceptance of military obligation, as did the sober, patient and obedient inclinations of the German people. All of these factors ensured that the raw material of which the Prussian Army was composed provided its leaders with a force that was unequalled in its ability to respond not only to the shock of combat, but also to the demands made by the new technology.

With the completion of the army reforms in 1867, conscripts were now required to serve for three years, followed by four years in the reserve, and five years in the Landwehr. Across the North German Confederation this provided a peace time strength of some 304,000 men; in the South German states the total of the standing army provided a further 78,000. Placed on a war footing, the total strength of the German armies increased dramatically. At the outbreak of war the overall effective strength of the army of the North German Confederation was 988,064; the South German states increased this figure by a further 200,325. As a result of the military conventions concluded with these states, the structure and organisation of the armed forces of Bavaria, Württemberg and Baden had been revised to conform to the Prussian model.

In 1870 the Prussian army originally consisted of eleven army corps, based upon the eleven provinces of Prussia; this included three new corps, the IX, X and

Prussian troops 1870, by Knötel: 1 - Dragoon, 2 - Cuirassier, 3 - Hussar, 4 - Uhlan, 5 - Pioneer, 6 - Jäger, 7 - Line Infantry, 8 - Horse Artillery (Scheibert)

XI Corps which had been formed since 1866, based upon the provinces then acquired. In addition there were the Guard Corps, which had no territorial base, being recruited from the nation as a whole, and the XII Corps, which was formed from the former Royal Saxon Army. The independent contingents of the two Mecklenburgs and Brunswick were incorporated in the three new army corps, which had been established. The contingent of the Grand Duchy of Hesse became the 25th Division. The Bavarian Army consisted of two army corps; Württemberg and Baden each provided a complete division of all arms.

The effect of the local recruitment of each army corps struck Stoffel with particular force.

> It is a very interesting thing, especially for a stranger, to observe the different Prussian army corps with reference to the physical and moral qualities which distinguish them from each other, for being recruited in different provinces, each has its own characteristic features … The various corps of the Prussian army differ so much both physically and morally, that the General Officers are compelled to alter the principles of leading, and commanding them.[2]

But what was common to all the units of the Prussian army was the high standard of training of all arms, and the constant improvement of all aspects of the army's organisation, particularly since 1866. The activity shown, Stoffel thought, was prodigious.

> They are like a swarm of bees. To understand this incessant labour, the distinctive qualities of the nation must be remembered. Its sentiment of duty, application, taste for labour, pushed to extreme limits, as it were, by the necessity recognised by everyone, of completing the military instruction of the men, in a very short period, on an average not exceeding two and a half years.[3]

The North German Confederation field army consisted of a total of 396 infantry and rifle battalions, 320 squadrons of cavalry, 214 batteries with a total of 1,284 guns, and 44 pioneer companies. Behind them stood a substantial force of garrison and depot troops. Of the field army, one infantry division (the 17th Division) and four Landwehr divisions were withheld in order to cover the possibility of a French landing in Schleswig-Holstein; all told these forces accounted for 65 battalions, 28 squadrons, 18 batteries with 108 guns and 5 pioneer companies. The field army of the three South German states added a total of 78 battalions, 62 squadrons, 50 batteries with 300 guns and 9 pioneer companies. The overall strength of the combined field armies was 519,100 with 1,584 guns.

The basic peace time organisation of an army corps consisted of two divisions, each comprising two infantry brigades and a cavalry brigade. Each infantry brigade consisted of two line regiments, each of three battalions, one of which was designated as a fusilier battalion. In each corps one infantry brigade had in addition a fusilier regiment. Fusiliers were treated as light infantry, although in practice the rapid development of the training of infantry and their use of the Dreyse breech-loading rifle had more or less removed the distinction between them. Each corps possessed in addition a jäger battalion recruited from men who were the best marksmen and those most familiar with wooded and rough terrain. The cavalry brigade consisted of from two to four cavalry regiments. To each army corps was also attached a field artillery regiment comprising three field divisions each of two heavy and two light batteries, and a horse artillery division. One field artillery division was attached to each division; the remaining field artillery division and the horse artillery comprised the corps artillery. On a war footing, the cavalry brigades were organised into independent cavalry divisions, each of two brigades, one cavalry regiment also being attached to each division. In addition either one or two pioneer companies were attached to each infantry division.

In the years since 1866 Moltke and his staff had been carefully analysing the lessons to be learned from that campaign. So indeed had everyone else; the crushing defeat of the Austrian army in so short a space of time demanded an explanation, and foreign commentators, especially for instance in England, were in the forefront of those finding the explanation in the superiority of the breech loading needle gun. More intelligent or better-informed observers knew differently. A Russian observer, Major General Dragomirov, said that 'It was not the needle gun by itself that won the victories of 1866, but the men who carried it', while Stoffel, as early as September 1866, was putting the position even more plainly. He had, he reported, interrogated a great number of junior officers and NCOs, both Prussian and Austrian, in order to get a fair view of the influence of the needle gun. 'People have assigned to the weapons of the Prussian infantry the greatest share in its victories. But it is a great error. The superiority of the weapons has been only a secondary cause.'[4] What gave the Prussian infantry such a decisive advantage was the coolness and steadiness in battle with which they used a weapon that was, of course, far superior to the muzzle loaders of the Austrians, as a result of which 'the first Prussian volley always stopped the Austrian advance, and they generally retired in disorder, when, thanks to the rapidity of loading, the independent fire completed their defeat.'[5] The quality of the Prussian infantry would be even more seriously tested in the future, since they would never again go to war with a weapon that was so overwhelmingly superior to that of the opposition. But they had already shown enough in 1866 to demonstrate that they were at least the equal of any infantry in Europe.

Before 1866 one potential disadvantage of the breech loader had been thought to be the likelihood that infantry would, because of the ease of loading, waste ammunition; but a post war enquiry found that this had not at all been the case; a total of only 200,000 rounds was fired by the Prussian infantry at Königgrätz, an average of about one per man. Not much, therefore, needed to be done about fire discipline; but the casualty rate sustained by the Austrian infantry, advancing in column in closed formations, pointed to the need to review infantry tactics, particularly against an enemy well armed with breech loaders. As a result, Prussian infantry usually (but not invariably) eschewed mass formations, preferring where possible to advance in open order. There was a continuous review of ways in which the Dreyse needle gun might be improved, and a number of suggestions made; however, as William remarked to Stoffel, 'It is no light matter to alter 1,000,000 rifles, if it is not quite clear that the proposed alterations offer a real and incontestable advantage.'[6]

What was evident to anyone who properly examined the success of the Prussian infantry was that it had a lot to do with the quality of its officers. Prince Krafft zu Hohenlohe-Ingelfingen, himself an artillerist, remarked that there were many examples that demonstrated this: 'every infantry officer who has been in action could give you plenty of them, all showing how in our army the company officer is the soul of the infantry, that he breathes his spirit into them, and with what unlimited confidence our men follow their officers.'[7] Stoffel, who regularly attended the post war annual manoeuvres of the Prussian Army, said much the same of the company commanders: 'by their general and professional knowledge, by the zeal, and the spirit of progress, which animates them, they are the soul and nerves of the Prussian Infantry, and greatly contribute to render it formidable.'[8]

There was no comparable satisfaction with the performance of the other arms in Bohemia. Moltke's 1868 review of some of the essential lessons to be learned from the campaign of 1866 spelt out some of the serious failings in co-operation that had been noted. The infantry had 'in every respect, in marching as well as fighting, performed excellently.' But unfortunately it had been supported 'inadequately by the artillery, and by the cavalry as good as not at all.'[9] Hohenlohe summed up the position from the stand point of a gunner:

> The results obtained in the campaign of 1866 told most unfavourably against the artillery [which] on almost every occasion, entered upon the scene far too late and with far too small a number of guns. In the course of all the engagements the infantry found itself exposed to the murderous fire of an artillery very superior in number to ours, and in order to reply and to defend itself and have recourse to its own fire of musketry.[10]

In fact, the suggestion that the Austrian artillery was superior was something of an over simplification. By 1866 the re-equipment of the Prussian army with steel guns was still incomplete; about one third of the Prussian guns were smooth bore. As Stoffel reported: 'All the Prussian officers of artillery have repeatedly assured me that these guns, were nothing but an encumbrance, from the first to the last day of the campaign.'[11] And, as he also pointed out, the Prussians were almost always on the offensive, which meant that the Austrian artillery had the advantage of firing from prepared positions and on occasion had the opportunity to use measured ranges. On the other hand, as Hohenlohe noted: 'Nachod and Trautenau were chance encounters, in which both adversaries had to similarly change their formations, while at Königgrätz the Second Army, for its part, was able as soon as it came on the scene to deploy a mass of artillery superior to that of the enemy.'[12]

A lot, therefore, needed to be done. Although there had been some considerable reservations among artillerists about the introduction of steel guns, especially since a number of these had exploded in action, the work of reequipping the Prussian artillery was soon completed. The bursting of a number of guns in 1866 was found to be due to faults in the breech mechanism, which were easily corrected. The superior accuracy of the steel guns over the bronze guns of their French opponents was soon to be convincingly demonstrated.

Practically, much more use was to be made in future of the artillery. Moltke required that 'the commander must rush forward and conduct reconnaissance prior to the occupation of every artillery position. In the choice of a position, concern for effectiveness always comes before cover.'[13] He also introduced a major change in Prussian artillery doctrine; in future, the loss of a battery was to be risked if this was necessary in the overall interest of the army.

> There are circumstances in which the artillery has the duty of sacrificing itself in order to gain time for the other arms and to relieve the enemy's pressure. An unshakeable endurance to the last moment can, therefore, be necessary, indeed in the highest degree favourable, even if it should ultimately lead to the loss of the guns.[14]

It was also necessary, he thought, that artillery commanders should be kept much better informed of the army's immediate objectives.

The role of the cavalry had been particularly affected by technological change. The idea that this most glamorous of arms should be held back in order to strike a sensational and decisive blow at the critical moment derived from an age in which its speed and impetus could overcome the musketry and artillery fire opposing it. By 1866 this was no longer true; infantry could now repulse cavalry attacks without the need to form square. Stoffel recorded an incident from the battle of Gitschin, in which an infantry battalion, facing ten Austrian squadrons,

> allowed the cavalry to advance within 200 paces, receiving them with a volley from the entire battalion, followed at once by independent firing. At the first volley 50 to 60 Austrian troopers fell, and the two squadrons at the head of the column turned tail. Independent firing was kept up on the next two squadrons which came within 100 paces of the battalion, and then dispersed, drawing the entire column after them in confusion.[15]

Moltke, noting the increased effectiveness of infantry fire, gave directions for the employment of cavalry which placed greater emphasis on the role of the divisional cavalry units in reconnaissance. But he still envisaged a requirement for shock action by the reserve cavalry, which must 'usually wait inactively for hours' until 'the time for its intervention has arrived. As a rule this will first be the case when the coherence of the enemy battle line loosens and when the enemy infantry is shaken by great losses.'[16] Whether in covering the retreat of an army after an unfavourable outcome, or in pursuing a defeated opponent, Moltke required that a cavalry commander 'has to hold his masses as ready as possible. They must not be engaged too early.'[17]

Like their opponents, the German commanders had gained considerable recent experience, but had perhaps learned rather more from it. Although the French could look back to the Crimean War and to the Italian War of 1859 as well as to their very different military experience in Africa and in Mexico, the campaigns of the German leaders in the Danish War of 1864 and the Austro-Prussian War of 1866 (during which a number of present day colleagues had fought on opposite sides) were perhaps more relevant to the military situation in 1870. One of the most noteworthy features of the German leadership was its age. When war broke out, the Prussian King himself was 73 and Moltke was 70; one of his army commanders at the start was Steinmetz, who was 74. On the other hand, Prince Frederick Charles was 42, and the Crown Prince was only 39. Of those who succeeded to army command during the course of the war, Crown Prince Albert of Saxony was 42, von Manteuffel was 61, and von Goeben 53. But it was the corps commanders at the outset who were noticeably older than might be expected, with an average age of 61. Only Prince August, the 57 year old commander of the Guard Corps, and the Saxon Crown Prince and Goeben, were under the age of 60; von Hartmann, the commander of the II Bavarian Corps, was 75. In spite of this, they displayed tremendous drive and energy throughout the war; a recent historian has pointed out that 'it has nowhere been remarked that, for all their years, Moltke's senior subordinates demonstrated an extraordinary resilience and physical stamina.'[18] They also displayed great personal bravery and at times an almost excessive eagerness to get into combat. The IX Corps lost two commanders in action, and there was a high casualty rate among senior officers throughout the war.

The senior appointments that were made necessarily reflected the successes of the Prussian army in 1866. Moltke's decision to appoint Steinmetz to the command of the First Army was not however made without some considerable anxiety. Born in 1796, Karl von Steinmetz served in the Wars of Liberation, being awarded the Iron Cross for bravery in 1814. Thereafter, his rise was slow; he was still only a lieutenant colonel in Berlin during the March Days, when he took part in street fighting. In the next 18 years, he rose to the rank of full General and was in command of the V Corps during the Austro-Prussian War, where his reputation was made in his series of victories at Nachod, Skalitz and Schweinschädel; here, the boldness and aggression he displayed had earned him the name of the 'Lion of Nachod', and were of course among the qualities that had led to his appointment. He was, however, strong willed to the point of eccentricity; Verdy, who headed the intelligence section of the General Staff, was among those who had serious doubts about the wisdom of the appointment.

> The nominations certainly aroused some misgivings. The universal and high appreciation of the merits of this gallant fighting general was merited in every respect. But however high his military capabilities were, his personal qualities and his independence of character were such as to make it difficult for his superiors to deal with him, and made friction probable if he, at the head of an army, was subordinate to a higher command.[19]

Alfred von Waldersee, a future Chief of the German General Staff, was blunter in his assessment of Steinmetz. 'Even in 1866 he was three quarters cracked, and now he is four years older. He will not be at fault in the matter of energy and action, but these things are no good by themselves.'[20] Moltke may have hoped that Steinmetz's Chief of Staff, Major General von Sperling, would be able to keep him in order, but in this he was disappointed. Though 'a clear headed, circumspect, and resolute officer, even his eminent military as well as personal qualities were not able to prevail with such a character as that of General von Steinmetz.'[21] Blumenthal was envious of the tasks assigned to the First Amy. 'General von Steinmetz appears to me to have the pleasantest and easiest task allotted, as long as the neutrality of Belgium and Luxembourg is respected by the French. He will, if God grants him health and life, have all the laurels.'[22]

There seems, in fact, to have been some lack of enthusiasm at the top about the appointment of Prince Frederick Charles to the command of the Second Army. At a Council of War at Potsdam on July 17, the senior appointments were considered. The Crown Prince, who was in attendance, observed:

> It was noteworthy how no-one would speak right out when the question came up as to Prince Friedrich Karl and his appointment to a high command, until His Majesty in some excitement insisted on an expression of opinion, and then how all were unanimous that the Prince should head that army (the Second Army as it is entitled) which the King would accompany and so be on the spot to exercise special control.[23]

Frederick Charles was a most cautious and thoroughly professional soldier of limited imagination; Waldersee wrote later of him that he

> was a man of only mediocre intellect – a man of slow understanding, as they say; he read with deliberation and did not like to have matters reported to him hurriedly, as he found it difficult to follow. By dint of iron diligence he sought to make good the shortcoming and he held fast by what he had once mastered; moreover he had a good memory. His whole heart was devoted to the military calling from the close of his university career.[24]

He was the son of King William's brother, Prince Charles, and was born in 1828; from the outset he was destined for a military career, in the course of which he formed a great and close friendship with Roon, then a major, upon whom he modeled himself closely. In the Danish War he had begun in command of a corps, succeeding to the overall command on Wrangel's resignation. In the campaign of 1866, his leading of the First Army had been generally competent, although frequently over cautious; there was, however, some suspicion that he was jealous of

South German troops, by Knötel. From l to r: Württemberg Reiter, Artillery, Infantry; Bavarian Infantry, Artillery, Cuirassier, Chevauleger (Pflug-Harttung)

the success of his cousin, the Crown Prince. And whatever feelings he may have ruffled, his appointment in 1870 was entirely to be expected. Like his cousin, he had the benefit of an immensely able Chief of Staff in the reliable Major General von Stiehle, of whom Waldersee noted the general regard: 'A great deal is thought of Stiehle, Prince Frederick Charles's Chief of Staff. I do not know much of him, but in any case he brings freshness and youth to his work.'[25]

The Crown Prince's appointment to the command of the Third Army was an entirely logical step. Containing as it did a large proportion of South German troops, political considerations obviously reinforced the military and dynastic reasons for his appointment. Although relatively very young, being born in 1841, he had proved a most successful commander of the Second Army in Bohemia in 1866, and was popular both with his troops and with the touchy and self-important royal personages with whom he now had to deal. He was much liked by Queen Victoria, his mother-in-law, and very much influenced by the liberal views of his wife, the Princess Royal. In 1870, as in 1866, his very able if outspoken Chief of Staff, Lieutenant General Karl von Blumenthal was to play a crucial role in the development of policy. He had been born in 1810; his father, a cavalry captain, was killed at Dennewitz in 1813. Like Moltke, he at first rose only slowly through the junior ranks of the army, and by 1848 was still only a first lieutenant. Also like Moltke, he had married an English wife. Later, however, his career picked up; after serving successfully in the Danish War, he was appointed to the command of a brigade early in 1866 and then upon the outbreak of the Austro-Prussian War was

Count von Roon, Prussian Minister of War (Scheibert)

appointed as Chief of Staff to the Crown Prince. Blumenthal was delighted with the appointment. 'The position is exactly the one I should have most desired. The youthful buoyancy of the Crown Prince's nature suits me much more than the severe earnestness of Prince Frederick Charles. Lightheartedness is the spirit in which to go to battle.'[26] Blumenthal's habit of rather over-confident self-expression had led to some potential difficulty between himself and Moltke in July 1866, when a letter to his wife fell into the hands of the Austrians and was published in the press. In his diary, he recorded what had happened.

> Certainly the letter was mine in substance but it had been mistranslated from the English in which language I had written, and, moreover, the sense had been intentionally perverted. I should not have been much disturbed about it, only, unfortunately, Moltke had been somewhat roughly handled by me in it, and he is the last of men I should wish to pain, for I honour him exceedingly. It was very mortifying to me to have made myself a laughing stock through this letter, and be represented to the world as a conceited ass.[27]

Moltke brushed the matter aside, and in spite of incidents of this kind, he recognised very clearly Blumenthal's outstanding abilities and placed a great deal of trust in him.

Crown Prince Albert of Saxony began the war in command of the XII (Saxon) Corps. He had been born in 1828; he too was from the outset committed to a military career, entering the army at the age of 15. In the fighting in Schleswig-Holstein during 1848–9, he was attached to the Prussian staff; thereafter, he was briskly advanced through the ranks to that of lieutenant general at the age of 24. At the coronation of King William I in 1861, he met for the first time Marshal MacMahon, his future adversary, at that time serving as French Ambassador in

Berlin. In 1866, he had commanded the Saxon Army in the Bohemian campaign; in the course of an almost unbroken series of defeats for the Austrian Army, the Saxon contingent nonetheless fought well under his competent leadership. In 1870, he was to rise to the command of the Army of the Meuse, at which time there was assigned to him as Chief of Staff Major General von Schlotheim, who had opposed him when serving in the same capacity in the Army of the Elbe at Königgrätz.

Edwin von Manteuffel, whose political influence had been so great, was now to have a further opportunity to demonstrate his military ability. In 1870, he began the war in command of the I Corps. In 1866, he had been in command in the Elbe Duchies as the crisis mounted, and later, during the war, succeeded Vogel von Falkenstein as commander of the Army of the Main, which he led in a successful campaign against the armies of South Germany. In 1870, after the fall of Metz, he was held in sufficient regard by Moltke to be appointed to the command of the reconstituted First Army and, later, to the Army of the South.

August von Goeben had had in many ways the most varied and interesting career of the senior German commanders. Born in 1816 in Hanover, he joined the Prussian army at the age of 17; but three years later, since there seemed little prospect of action, he resigned his commission to serve in the Carlist Wars in Spain. During the next four years, he rose to the rank of colonel there, and saw a good deal of combat, being wounded five times. Penniless, he published an account of his adventures in 1840; and in 1842, he rejoined the Prussian service. He rose rapidly, commanding a brigade in the Danish War and a division in 1866 during the campaign in Germany. In 1870, he was appointed to command the VIII Corps forming part of Steinmetz's First Army; later, he was to succeed Manteuffel in command of that army.

The brothers Gustav and Konstantin von Alvensleben, who commanded the IV and III Corps respectively, had both had long and distinguished careers although neither had risen particularly swiftly. Gustav, the elder, had been the King's Adjutant General in 1866, and in this position had been among those that had urged upon Moltke a much earlier concentration of the entire Prussian army. Konstantin had commanded a brigade in 1866, until succeeding to command of the Ist Guard Division upon the death in action of Hiller von Gärtringen at Königgrätz.

Of the Bavarian Corps commanders, Ludwig von der Tann was to play a much more prominent role in the Franco German War than his elderly colleague Jacob von Hartmann. Von der Tann was born in 1815 and joined the Bavarian Army at the age of 18. His family was close to the Bavarian royal family and he rose quickly, becoming Lieutenant General at the age of 45. In 1866, with extreme reluctance because of his bitter opposition to the war upon which his country then embarked, he took the post of Chief of Staff of the Bavarian Army. In this capacity he did his best to overcome the incompetence and irresolution of the Federal leadership; and was rewarded, after the war, by fierce attacks on his incompetence by political opponents, as a result of which he was obliged to embark on a successful libel action to protect his reputation. Hartmann had commanded an infantry division in 1866, performing competently in several of the battles fought against the Army of the Main.

The advantage that the German army might possess over its adversary was noted in one contemporary commentary. Observing that 'the German armies are in the highest state of efficiency that can be reached, by scientific preparation for war, by concentration, by compact discipline, and by forethought,' the writer went on to note that

> the army knows to whom it has to look – men like General Roon and General Moltke to plan its operations, leaders like the Crown Prince and the Prince Frederick Charles to command it in the field, inspire its troops with a confidence strengthened by past experience and habitual deference to supreme authority. In the French army, we cannot say that the present aspect of affairs is equally satisfactory. That great evolution of military reform, which the Prussians have accomplished, is in France, incomplete. The Imperial government does not possess the unequivocal or undivided confidence of any class of French citizens. The Emperor, whose will is the only tangible form of authority, does not boast of high military talents, and has been unfortunate in several of his military experiments. After him, there is in France no general of such indisputable pre-eminence and authority that he could at once give the vigour and unity of paramount command to the whole military system. The experience of the First Empire abundantly showed how dangerous it is to divide the command of the army among officers of rival pretensions, even when the supreme head of the state was a Napoleon. There is therefore at present in France nothing of that strict unity of command and complete preparation for the war, which is believed to exist beyond the Rhine. On the contrary, opinions are divided in high quarters on many essential points. And the inevitable consequence is, that where the highest authorities are not completely resolved upon a course of action, a certain tinge of irresolution penetrates to the regimental officers, and the discipline and cohesion of the whole mass is perhaps somewhat relaxed. These are not favorable conditions to take the field against a powerful and well-advised enemy.[28]

It was to prove a very accurate analysis.

4

The French Army and its Leaders

Among military leaders in France, confidence in the outcome of a war with Prussia remained high. In 1867 Marshal Randon exclaimed: 'Oh! then let us hasten to remember those military virtues of our fathers; that will be worth more than the needle gun.'[1] And a survey in 1870 of the French Army, although noting that the outcome of the Austro-Prussian war had 'awakened doubts where no doubts existed before as to the relative strength of the great continental armies', expressed confidence that nonetheless 'upon a great emergency the French nation will, as of old, put forth an amount of energy and resource capable of surmounting' the perils that it faced.[2] Emile Ollivier recorded that the Minister of War, Marshal Le Boeuf, who had been appointed in 1869 on the death of his able predecessor, Marshal Niel,had advised the Emperor that 'we are stronger than the Prussians on a peace footing and on a war footing.'[3] And Ollivier and his Cabinet had been confidently led to expect that the army was ready for immediate hostilities both by the Emperor and by the late Marshal Niel who had said that 'in a fortnight we would have an army of 415,000 men.' Other generals had said much the same.

The army in France was at the centre of Bonapartist tradition. It had played a crucial role in the coup d'etat of 1851 and, as Richard Holmes pointed out in his profound analysis of the development of the French army in the years preceding Sedan, the maintenance of Napoleon's regime was entirely dependent upon the army, and if he lost control of it, the Empire could not survive. French military tradition decreed that it should display panache and vigour in attack; and the confidence that this would bring victory perhaps contributed to the development of 'le Système D – on se débrouillera toujours', or muddling through. Certainly the emphasis on élan and ésprit militaire provided a real contrast to the sober organisational skills of the German armies. The historically high reputation of the French army had been confirmed by their victories in Italy at Magenta and Solferino. These hard fought engagements, which reflected rather more credit on the courage of the troops than on the skill of the higher leadership, followed upon a prolonged record of success in Africa and in the Crimea. These campaigns had given the French leadership considerable confidence in their ability which, unfortunately, proved not to be soundly based.

The Prussian victory at Königgrätz came as a shocking surprise to the French army, which was thereafter obliged to re-examine its view of the Prussian army and its recent development while at the same time, of course, paying heed to those technological advances that were as apparent to the French leaders as they had been to the Prussian General Staff.

In France as elsewhere the view was generally held that it was effectively the needle gun that won the war of 1866; but Niel in particular saw the urgent need for a thorough reorganisation of the French system of recruitment, and for improved administrative procedures. The paper he wrote in November 1866 contained a number of echoes of Roon's proposals to William. Randon, the incumbent

Emperor Napoleon III (Scheibert)

Minister of War, objected; but the Emperor supported Niel's case for universal short-term service, and Randon was, in due course, dismissed and replaced by Niel. The Emperor's objective was to achieve a total manpower of a million men, but this was possible only by the re-establishment of the Garde Nationale, which had been dissolved in 1851, and by their employment in much the same way as the Prussian Landwehr. Niel's most far-reaching proposals were, however, found to be unacceptable to the French Cabinet, and in the end they were heavily watered down. In the Legislature, too, they aroused vigorous opposition. Interrupting Niel's speech, Jules Favre shouted that he was turning France into a barracks; Niel replied 'as for you, take care you don't turn it into a cemetery.'

The proposals for the Garde Nationale were insufficient to turn it into an effective well-trained force, and in any case Niel's early death had deprived it of the one man who could be depended upon to pursue its development with enthusiasm. The proposed annual intake of 172,000 men into the regular army was calculated to produce, by 1875, a force capable of being mobilised that was 800,000 strong; but by July 1870, nothing like this could be attained. Le Boeuf reckoned on 497,000, of which he counted upon 300,000 being available within three weeks, and this was notwithstanding a parliamentary decision sharply to reduce the military budget.

The central direction and organisation of the French army was, in many respects, far behind that of the Prussian system. Instead of a tightly organised General Staff, the French army was run by an arrangement of 'directions', and specialist committees, which resulted both in excessive centralisation and an extremely conservative approach to military development. The peacetime army was organised solely on a regimental system which was believed to facilitate the creation of ésprit de corps. The regiments were distributed in depots with no regard to the point of origin of the soldiers concerned, the principle of territorial recruitment having been discredited. It was to these base depots that during mobilisation regiments reported to collect their equipment before being sent to join their regiment at its current location, which for about half of the regiments of the French army was elsewhere. Only then could the regiment be despatched to join the brigade, division and army corps to which it was assigned.[4] The homogeneity which this gave the army was still regarded as late as 1870 as a very positive advantage, Chesney and Reeve distinguishing between Prussia 'where local habits and institutions have great hold over the populations' and France where 'the great unity of the nation overwhelms and obliterates these distinctions.'[5] Attempts from 1859 onwards to organise the French army on a regional basis entirely failed to create an organisation in any way comparable to the regionally based German army corps. Niel had been concerned not only with the size of the army, and with its re-equipment with modern weapons; he had also addressed the question of mobilisation. In 1868, building on a paper exercise of the previous year intended to calculate the number of army corps that could be created, he had called for the establishment of permanent brigades, divisions and army corps. This was not, however, done; and in 1870 these units came into existence with none of the advantages that would have been possessed by a previously settled and self confident organisation.[6]

Within the French army, there were considerable tensions. There was a marked distinction between the treatment of the Imperial Guard and of the rest of the Metropolitan army; while the Armée d'Afrique, which had developed its own traditions and tactical doctrines, was in many ways an entirely separate organisation, effectively being an army within an army.

During the years leading up to the Franco-Prussian War, the position of the engineers and of the artillery was a privileged one, and this coincided with the decline in the reputation and morale of the cavalry. As a result of the army's re-equipment with the Chassepôt rifle, shock tactics were believed by some to be a thing of the past, although traditionalists remained determined to assert the aggressive role of the cavalry on the battlefield. The ineffectiveness of the French cavalry in its reconnaissance role in 1870 was to be demonstrated again and again, not least because of their insistence in conducting reconnaissances in strength when they could have achieved very much more with small patrols of the size so effectively employed by the Germans.[7]

The confidence of the French army was, not unreasonably, materially strengthened by a comparison of the equipment with which the two armies would fight the coming war. In the matter of equipping his infantry, Napoleon had taken one crucial step, and that was to adopt the Chassepôt breech-loading rifle. It was, in fact, considerably superior to the Dreyse needle gun in every way except calibre. This was particularly true in terms of the range over which it could be fired accurately; it was sighted to 1,320 yards compared with the 660 yards of the needle gun. In addition, the Chassepôt was a much more reliable weapon, and was capable of more rapid fire, delivering eleven rounds a minute against the seven rounds a minute of the needle-gun.[8] Unfortunately, the French infantry had received insufficient training in the use of the new rifle and, in particular, tended to waste ammunition by firing too rapidly. It gave the French, however, a formidable advantage, and over a million of these weapons had been supplied by the outbreak of war. The fears that the ease of reloading would lead to a waste of ammunition were noted and an inspection report of 1867 commented that the infantry liked the Chassepôt 'because it fires fast, that is to say often; it would be better if they liked it because it fires accurately. Men could then be more easily persuaded to fire accurately rather than often, and thus to conserve their ammunition, a thing so important in war.'[9]

Napoleon also had a secret weapon in the mitrailleuse, and this too gave the French an enormous potential advantage. This early machine gun had twenty five 13mm. rifled barrels which rotated and fired in turn, producing a maximum of 200 rounds a minute; it was sighted to 1320 yards but was effective over a range of not far short of 2,000 yards. Very little was known about it either by the Germans or, indeed by the bulk of the French army, whose leaders had not properly thought through its most effective tactical employment. Largely because of the secrecy associated with its introduction, the French infantry were not trained in its use, and in practice the weapon proved not particularly effective, partly because of its tendency to break down and partly because of the incorrect tactical use which French commanders made of it.[10]

Napoleon had always taken a close personal interest in the artillery. Here too the French had had every opportunity to take advantage of technological progress, but in the event entirely failed to do so. The Krupp works, like all arms dealers looking for customers on all sides of any potential European conflict, had in fact endeavoured to sell its steel breech loaders to the French government; but it is recorded that their brochure was filed away in the French War Office, endorsed dismissively 'Rien à faire.'[11] In spite of Imperial concern, the French artillery went into battle with significantly less effective equipment. One of the reasons for the superiority of the German artillery was their reliance on percussion fuses; the French used very defective time fuses. The rifled muzzle loaders which had served the French well in 1859, were considerably inferior to the Krupp beech loaders in both range and accuracy. The French artillery was also very much less well organised. It had undergone a series of substantial reorganisations in the previous two decades but it was suggested by General Susane, Director of Artillery in 1870, that it was worse prepared for war than it had been under the Bourbons.[12]

The French administrative system, the 'intendances', had had a poor record in the wars of the Second Empire, with an indifferent supply system and marked inefficiencies in the transport system. It has been argued persuasively that the principal failures ascribed to the system were due to causes other than its own incompetence, such as defective staff work and the extraordinary nature of some of the transport systems imposed on it, as well as a series of command decisions that were bound to overtax the supply. system of any army.[13]

But perhaps the most striking contrast between France and Germany was between the work of the staffs. Although the number of staff officers available in the French army in fact exceeded those in Germany, it was widely believed that there were insufficient. While the Germans expected, and almost always got, from their staff officers a remarkably high level of technical competence and a consistent and striking use of their own initiative, the French reduced the work of the staff to the purely clerical.

Given time, Niel's reforms might have permeated sufficiently through the army both to improve its morale and to improve the professionalism of its leaders, but by 1870 there had not been nearly enough time for the benefits of reform to be felt, and nor was the size of the army available on mobilisation anything like as great as Niel's original plans had intended.

The final total of troops available to Napoleon at the outbreak of war was 567,000, of which 230,500 were non-effective, or in garrisons or depots, or in Algeria, leaving him immediately a field army of 336,000. This was a figure very close to Moltke's peacetime calculations of the likely French strength. In addition, there were the Gardes Mobiles. The German official history is scathing about the value of these, describing them as 'in a very primitive condition, weak in organisation and of little real use ... in fact this reserve was a mere heap of armed men in uniform, only suited at best to fight behind walls.'[14]

Finally, there was the Garde Nationale, which was in a still less developed state.

Even so, the size of the French army was still sufficient to pose a serious threat to South Germany if it could be mobilised and deployed with sufficient rapidity. Le Boeuf had been working hard to improve the mobilisation plans but here again the French arrangements were, in practice, simply not good enough. For one thing, only a third of the infantry regiments were in the same garrison as their depot, so that on mobilisation, the troops reporting for duty were obliged to make two journeys. Then, too, the French railway system was not so well adapted as the German to enable rapid concentration at the key points. There were only four railway lines to the frontier, terminating at Metz, Thionville, Nancy and Strasbourg respectively. Although the railway companies themselves worked hard to cope with the demands made on them, the French staff work was far short of the meticulous preparation that was absolutely necessary and which their opponents had for years devoted to the problem. The consequence was inevitable; although it has been suggested that 'given lack of organisation and central control, it is perhaps surprising that the chaos that prevailed on French railways in late July and early August 1870 was not worse.'[15]

Nonetheless one distinguished commentator writing at the beginning of the twentieth century expressed the view that this army was the finest force that France ever put into the field,[16] an opinion which at least suggests that the confident military opinions being offered to the French Cabinet were not without some reasonable foundation. But setting aside the euphoria of the French soldiers who shouted 'à Berlin' as they made their way to the front, and the understandable excitement of their leaders, the French high command could not possibly suppose that the campaign was going to be other than hazardous in the extreme. Quite apart from the convincing evidence of the Austro-Prussian War, the War Ministry had had the regular, balanced and accurate reports from Stoffel, the Military Attaché in Berlin, who had repeatedly pointed out the immensity of the task faced by the French leaders by a painstaking comparison of Prussia's military institutions with those of France.

By 1870, many of the French leaders were household names. Françoise-Achille Bazaine was born in 1811 near Versailles, although his family came originally from Lorraine. He enrolled as a private in the French army at the age of

20, and the following year transferred to the Foreign Legion. He saw service first in Africa and then in the Carlist Wars in Spain, before returning to Africa where, by the age of 36, he had risen to the rank of lieutenant colonel. Bazaine went to the Crimea in command of a regiment; and, being very much a protegé of Pélissier, the French commander there, rose to command of a division by the end of the war.

When the Italian War broke out in 1859, Bazaine again commanded a division; he was wounded when he led his men in a charge on the village of Melegnano; at Solferino, it was Bazaine's division that stormed the strongpoint that was the key to the Austrian position. In Mexico in 1863, however, after he replaced Forey in command of the French army operating in support of the Emperor Maximilian, Bazaine was not to enjoy such success. He became a marshal in 1864, and although he safely extricated his army in 1867 when Maximilian's empire collapsed, he was associated with the failure of that rash venture, and was somewhat out of favour at Court (although not in the public esteem; he was very much the favourite soldier of the opposition). His military reputation was such, however, that when before the war broke out it was intended to operate in two armies, he was earmarked to command the Army of Lorraine; in the event he took command initially of the 3rd Corps.

Maurice de MacMahon, born in 1808, was commissioned from St-Cyr in 1827. He served in the Staff Corps until 1840, when he joined the Chasseurs à pied. He reached the rank of general in 1848. In the Crimea, he was sent out to succeed Canrobert in command of the 1st Division, which he commanded in a successful assault on the Malakoff redoubt at Sebastapol. When a messenger was sent to MacMahon as his hard-pressed division hung on to the position they had won, his reply became legendary. 'Tell your general,' he said, 'that here I am and here I stay.'[17] In 1859, MacMahon, who had seen a lot of service in Africa during his career, commanded the 2nd Corps, which was composed entirely of troops from the Army of Africa. At Magenta, his corps carried out the crucial turning movement, an attack upon the town, which was led by MacMahon in person right up to the first houses. Somewhat prematurely, as units of the Foreign Legion moved up, he clapped his hands and shouted 'Voici la Légion. L'affaire est dans le sac!'[18] Ultimately it was, but not until after a bitter struggle in which French casualties were extremely high. On the following day, Napoleon, in the course of an emotional meeting with MacMahon, promoted him marshal and named him Duke of Magenta. MacMahon joined Napoleon and Victor Emmanuel in their triumphant entry into Milan; an accomplished showman, he 'picked up a little girl and rode with her on his saddle through the streets lined by hysterically cheering crowds and beneath the tempest of flowers and petals cascading from balconies and windows.'[19]

Later in the campaign, MacMahon successfully employed a balloonist in reconnoitring Austrian positions as the allies advanced on them; and at Solferino, his corps was again the thick of the fighting. After serving as ambassador in Berlin, he later returned to Africa as Governor General, and came back in 1870 to be assigned to the command of the 1st Corps.

Marshal Edmond Le Boeuf, born in 1809, had succeeded Niel as Minister of War in 1869. He was an artilleryman who had also served extensively in Africa; in the Crimea he commanded the French batteries before Sebastopol. He enjoyed a

Marshal Le Boeuf, French Minister of War in 1870 (Rousset/*Histoire*)

difficult relationship with Ollivier, who inherited him as Minister of War when he formed his Cabinet in January 1870. The two men had very different political views; and Ollivier treated military affairs as a matter for Napoleon rather than the Cabinet, getting no regular reports from Le Boeuf.[20] In July 1870, following the precedent of 1859, the Emperor went off to war in supreme command with the Minister of War to act as his Chief of Staff. 'Such a system could only work well if the sovereign was provided with expert professional advice from a trusted source; but in 1859, and still less in 1870, there was nobody to play Moltke to Napoleon's William.'[21]

General Charles Auguste Frossard, born in 1807, was an engineer. He was particularly close to the Emperor, having been appointed military tutor to the Prince Imperial in 1867. He had seen action at Antwerp and Rome, as well as in the Crimea, reaching the rank of general in 1855. In 1870, a certain amount of ill-feeling was caused when, after being offered the alternatives of commanding either the engineers of the Army of the Rhine or a corps, he was appointed to lead the 2nd Corps.

General L R P de Ladmirault was another commander who had spent long periods in Algeria. An infantryman, he was born in 1808. He was promoted to general in 1848. In 1859, he was twice wounded when commanding a division at Solferino, as a result of which he thereafter found riding extremely difficult. He was a sound, dependable professional soldier whose appointment to command the 4th Corps came as no surprise.

General Pierre de Failly, born in 1810, was another infantryman. He reached the rank of general in 1857; in Italy he commanded a division in Niel's corps. He was best known for his defence of Rome against Garibaldi in 1867, when he won the victory of Mentana. He was appointed to command the 5th Corps.

The 61 year old Marshal Canrobert, assigned to the 6th Corps, was one of France's most distinguished soldiers. He too had seen extensive service in Africa; he reached the rank of general by 1850. In the Crimea, he briefly held the overall command before reverting to command of a division. He had failed to impress senior British commanders there, one of whom remarked that his 'indecision is proverbial,' while another described him as being 'in an excited state of uncertainty' between over alarm and over caution on one hand, and a belief that 'to get out of his apprehended dangerous position he must adopt a proposition that is urged upon him of extreme rashness' on the other.[22] (He was never particularly ambitious nor had an excessively high opinion of his own ability; when in 1870 he was offered the command of the Army of the Rhine, he firmly refused it). Canrobert had competently led the 3rd Corps in Italy in 1859.

Generals Felix Douay, who commanded the 7th Corps, and Charles Bourbaki, the commander of the Imperial Guard, were the youngest of the French corps commanders, both having been born in 1816. Douay had commanded the Voltigeurs of the Guard at the storming of the Malakoff Redoubt at Sabastopol. Bourbaki, who was of Greek descent, was yet another long-serving African; he had been a divisional commander at Solferino in 1859.

Two other prominent French commanders were destined to play especially important roles in the Sedan campaign. General Auguste Alexandre Ducrot was born in 1817, joining the infantry from St.Cyr in 1837. He served extensively in Algeria; during the Crimean War he took part in the Bomarsund expedition, where he commanded a regiment. He reached the rank of general in 1858. In 1860, he served as second in command of the Syrian expedition. He was an articulate, energetic and very outspoken soldier, who had been a strong advocate of many aspects of army reform. In 1866, he wrote to Faure commenting on the 'cowardice and absolute lack of patriotism of the Crown's advisers'[23]; this kind of observation came easily to Ducrot, who complained of Niel that he was 'too clever by half.' He had no doubt that war would come with Germany, and fiercely argued the need for preparation, producing extensive studies for submission to the War Ministry. Upon the outbreak of war, he took up the command of a division in MacMahon's 1st Corps. General Barthélemi Lebrun, one of Le Boeuf's two assistant Chiefs of Staff, was 61 in 1870 and was a noted military artist and writer. He had served as Chief of Staff to the Imperial Guard between 1860 and 1866.

The French higher commanders were on the whole slightly younger than their adversaries. Napoleon was born in 1808; Le Boeuf a year later. MacMahon was sixty two years old and Bazaine fifty nine, which was, in fact, the average age of the French corps commanders at the outset. The study by Richard Holmes of the French Army as it approached the war of 1870 has shown, however, that many French commanders were in indifferent health, a number of whom

> took the field in a state of health which made them a burden to their superiors and subordinates alike. Of the eleven cavalry commanders on August 1, four were in questionable health, and the inaction of the French cavalry may in part be attributed to the poor physical condition of its commanders.[24]

Such lethargy was not confined to the older cavalry generals; there were to be a number of instances of infantry commanders reacting sluggishly to events. Taken

French troops 1870, by Knötel: 1 - Chasseur à Cheval, 2 - Garde Mobile, 3 - Line Infantry, 4 - Artilleryman, 5 - Turco, 6 - Cuirasssier, 7 - Dragoon (Scheibert)

overall however, the physical courage displayed by French generals was certainly not less than that of their German counterparts, and they too suffered high casualties as a result of their boldness.

French strategic planning for a war which senior French officers regarded as inevitable was nonetheless a good deal more rudimentary than that of the Germans, in the absence of a highly trained and organised general staff. Indeed, when Jarras, later to serve as Bazaine's Chief of Staff, took over the post of head of the Dépot de la Guerre in 1867, he was 'stupefied' to discover the lack of operational plans for a war against Prussia.[25] Niel, then the War Minister, had begun to prepare such plans, but they were incomplete when he died and was succeeded in August 1869 by Le Boeuf. Handicapped by the French policy of not creating major formations – divisions and corps – in peacetime, strategic planning was sketchy in the extreme. So far as it went, it was based on a proposed organisation of three field armies; this was a consistent feature of all French planning from 1866 until the outbreak of war itself in 1870. In 1868 the general scheme for the deployment of the three armies contemplated that the 1st Army, under MacMahon, should be based at Strasbourg; that the 2nd Army, to be commanded by Bazaine, should concentrate around Metz and that the 3rd Army, to be commanded by Palikao, should take up a position around Langres. Canrobert was to command the Guard Corps, which would concentrate at Châlons. The first two armies would comprise three corps each, while the 3rd Army would have two. As a basis for strategic planning, this deployment would do well enough; but in fact it was never developed in any greater detail and was no more than an order of battle that was continuously amended to take account of changes of personnel.[26]

There were, however, other more worked out proposals for the operations of the French Army produced by various individuals. The most carefully considered was that prepared by Frossard in 1867. He planned to take advantage of the series of 'positions magnifiques' which he had identified and on which the army could stand to resist a German invasion. He had also based his plan on a deployment in three armies, with a further reserve being collected around Paris. His expectation was of an attack coming through Weissenburg which, after a holding action there, would lead to a decisive battle being fought along the line of the Sauerbach. Meanwhile the army of the Moselle would, he thought, encounter an offensive between Sarreguemines and St Avold, which it could meet in the Cadenbronn position.[27] The defensive positions which he proposed to hold he had in many cases personally surveyed; and it was, at least, an original and thoughtful contribution to the debate on the best way to meet the challenge of war. It was not, however, accepted by all French leaders that a defensive strategy should be adopted. General Auguste Ducrot, who in peacetime was based at Strasbourg, was convinced that the only way to defeat what would otherwise be an overwhelming German assault was to launch a pre-emptive strike across the Rhine. This, he believed, would prevent the South German States from joining Prussia, and enable the triumphant French forces to advance to Würzburg to link up with the Austrians there before turning north towards Berlin.[28]

But it was the outline of Frossard's plan which stood as the basis of French advance planning – until, that is, it became possible in early 1870 to consider the alluring prospect that Austria might really now be ready to join hands with France if war broke out. In February 1870 Archduke Albrecht, Austria-Hungary's most distinguished soldier, came to Paris to discuss the possibility of a triple alliance

'An old trooper' - a characterful study of a veteran French infantryman, by Carl Röchling (Lindner)

between France, Italy and Austria. The outline of the campaign plan that he proposed, much like that of Ducrot, contemplated a joint advance into South Germany towards Würzburg – Nuremberg, which would serve to detach the South German States from the Prussian cause. Then, when the combined armies were concentrated, they could advance northwards. This plan had, at first sight, a lot to commend it; but it soon became clear that most of the immediate risks would have to be borne by France. Following the Archduke's visit, Napoleon called a meeting of Frossard, Le Boeuf, Lebrun, and Jarras to review the plan. In May 1870 they arrived at the conclusion that, as it stood, it was too risky unless absolute confidence could be placed in Austria and Italy being ready to move with France; this, Franz Joseph told Lebrun in Vienna the following month, could not be counted on. In any case Austria would require forty two days to mobilise. Napoleon, however, did not entirely give up on the idea and the possibility was one more of the false hopes that influenced French decision making.[29]

5

Mobilisation and Deployment

The crisis that had so suddenly exploded came upon a Europe almost wholly unprepared. In Paris, Ollivier had on June 30 assured the Chamber that 'in no period has the maintenance of peace seemed better assured,' while in London, Edmund Hammond, the very experienced Under Secretary in the Foreign Office, used similar words in briefing the newly appointed Foreign Secretary, Lord Granville, telling him that he never had during his long experience known 'so great a lull in foreign affairs,' and that he did not know of any pressing questions which would need to be dealt with immediately.[1] But, as the crisis quickly developed, the ugly potential that the incident of the Hohenzollern candidature possessed became very clear. Although there was a pretty general belief on the part of many British statesmen that Bismarck was 'at the bottom of it'[2], it was the response of the French government that gave rise to most anxiety. As has been noted, Lord Lyons had been, as early as July 10, warning Granville that the French were getting excited, and might provoke a conflict.

His judgment was very soon to be proved entirely correct. In England, however, after Leopold's withdrawal, Queen Victoria thought at first that the problem had been entirely resolved and was profoundly relieved about it; she was all the more staggered therefore by the French declaration of war when it came, and

The French Senate celebrates the declaration of war, painting by Conrad (Rousset/*Histoire*)

wrote to her daughter, the Crown Princess of Prussia on July 16: 'Beloved child, I cannot say what my feelings of horror and indeed indignation are, or how frightfully iniquitous I think this declaration of war! My heart boils and bleeds at the thought of what misery and suffering will be caused by this act of mad folly! And just when all that we and Leopold B [the King of Belgium] were asked to obtain to settle the question had been obtained.'[3] Four days later, she again expressed her opinions in the strongest terms: 'no one here conceals their opinion as to the extreme iniquity of the war – and the unjustifiable conduct of the French.'[4]

Although there were some in Britain who took France's side in the dispute, even accepting the French view of the events leading to the outbreak of war itself, the general opinion was that expressed by Queen Victoria. By July 13, Granville was reporting to Lyons: 'My colleagues in the House of Commons are getting very angry and G [Gladstone] wishes me to use stronger language to the French than would in my opinion be useful.'[5]

While the general staffs busied themselves with the mobilisation of their armies, newspaper editors in Germany and France, and in many neutral nations, hastened to mobilise their war correspondents. Greatly improved communications had swiftly developed the importance of their role and their journalistic skills, especially in Britain, which produced some of the most enterprising and successful of the war correspondents. The official attitudes which they encountered in Berlin and Paris were, however, very different, as the *Daily News* reported.

> The leading English newspapers apprehending the historical importance of this war, made preparations for obtaining information on a scale which had never been surpassed in the history of the European newspaper press, and gentlemen of military as well as literary experience offered themselves, to follow and record the movements and operations of the hostile armies. But the French government were slow to authorise the presence of neutral observers within the lines of its armies, and in the end that authorisation was distinctly refused;

and one of the *Daily News* correspondents who gained an interview with Ollivier reported that 'there was a possibility of generals disliking correspondents, and of either arresting them or sending them back to Paris', adding that the real reason was that they objected to writers in their camp because they disliked and resented criticism.[6]

William Howard Russell, the most famous of the war correspondents, had been intended by the editor of *The Times* to be attached to the French headquarters. When, however, the French declined to approve Russell's attachment to the Imperial Staff, plans had to be changed. From the outset, Bismarck had shown himself much more alert to the importance of the world's press than had the French, and as soon as an application was made for Russell to join the German forces, the permission was unhesitatingly granted; and, after some not inconsiderable difficulties, he finally reached the Crown Prince's staff, to which he was to be attached, just in time to miss the battle of Wörth. Meanwhile Archibald Forbes, reporting for the *Morning Advertiser*, although lacking Russell's formidable reputation, was earlier on the scene, reaching Cologne by July 19 in time to witness the early stages of the German mobilisation. He too, like the other correspondents attached to the German forces, enjoyed the benefit of the unstinted

King William at the grave of his parents, 19 July 1870, painting by von Werner (Scheibert)

cooperation and assistance given to him by the German authorities. As a result of this official assistance, and the speed of the communications available to journalists to send back their reports, and of the keen competition between their newspapers, the British public in particular had access to prompt and remarkably accurate (and uncensored) reports from the battlefields. The further consequence was that the performance of Moltke and the other German leaders was reported at first hand, and with, perhaps, rather more understanding and respect.

In addition to the war correspondents, there were accredited to the opposing headquarters a number of foreign military representatives. Perhaps the most distinguished of these were the American Generals Sheridan and Forsyth. Phil Sheridan had been one of Grant's most outstanding commanders during the American Civil War; now President, the latter asked Sheridan to which headquarters he preferred to be attached and Sheridan had no difficulty in choosing to join the German staff, 'for the reason that I thought more could be seen with a successful side.'[7] As with the full cooperation given to the journalists, the Germans went out of their way to make these foreign attachés welcome, and afforded them every facility. Sheridan, arriving at the Royal Headquarters on August 17, was given the opportunity to accompany Bismarck himself the next day to the scene of the impending battle before Gravelotte; and throughout the ensuing campaign that was to culminate at Sedan, he was to be treated very much as if he had been a senior member of the German staff. Sheridan and his military colleagues were probably given rather more careful attention than the large number of distinguished 'schlachtenbummler' – the royal and noble personages who, accompanied by a large staff, felt it necessary to accompany the German armies on their march into France. Bismarck, who never bothered to conceal his contempt for princelings of no political significance (except where they could temporarily be turned to some useful account), was particularly irritated by their presence, which gave the German quartermasters some particularly difficult problems, especially during those phases of the campaign in which the Royal Headquarters moved on a daily basis.

Catering for all these observers was, however, only a small part of the immense and complex task that now faced the staffs of the armies on both sides as the mobilisation and deployment proceeded. As the days went by, the German mobilisation proceeded with characteristic efficiency. This was no more than Moltke had expected; at the outset of the crisis and two days before the start of mobilisation, he had been found by Stiehle sitting on a sofa reading a novel by Sir Walter Scott. Asked how he could be doing so at such a time, Moltke replied: 'Why not? Everything is ready. We only have to press the button.'[8] The contrast with his harassed French counterparts could not have been more marked. In the event the Prussian mobilisation was completed in about a fortnight. It had gone so smoothly that Roon was reported as saying, in an echo of Moltke's confident assurance to Stiehle, albeit with a touch of hyperbole, that 'he had never spent a fortnight so free of cares with so little work to do in his entire public career.'[9]

The Prussian mobilisation plan was comprehensive in the extreme. Based on a detailed assessment of the number of troops immediately available, and the steps required to bring units up to combat strength, 'it determined in advance which troops would be assigned to the field armies, which to depots and which to garrison duty. It determined where all the troops were to be initially posted and supplied detailed instructions regarding matériel, horses transport equipment, uniforms, arms and munitions, and tools.'[10] The French, on the other hand, in spite of a belief that they had gained on this occasion an advantage over their opponents, quickly fell further and further behind, as such plans as had been made began to disintegrate. Le Boeuf's mobilisation plan assumed that the field army would be complete by the fourteenth day. The order for mobilisation was finally sent out on

Prussian troops depart for the theatre of war, by Plinzner (Scheibert)

July 14 and it was just two weeks after this that Napoleon arrived at Metz to take command. The progress of the mobilisation had, however, fallen a long way short of Le Boeuf's expectation. By the time of Napoleon's arrival at Metz, the French troops that had concentrated were less than half the number that it had been hoped would be ready for action. Above all, the logistical problems faced by the whole army were acute, not so much for want of supply as for the want of any effective means of distribution. A stream of anguished protests flowed in from subordinate commanders to the Imperial Headquarters. It was an unhappy beginning.

There was a 'total absence of military forethought on such essential questions as the loading and the unloading of trains, security of the permanent way and the facilities of stations in the concentration area.'[11] It took Marshal Canrobert ten hours to get from Châlons to Metz and on the journey he saw 'the most inexplicable disorder ... all the station officials had lost their heads. Trains full of stragglers from General de Failly's corps were in a siding: they shouted and sang with a deplorable attitude.'[12] At the core of both mobilisation and deployment plans, there was a basic assumption that the war was to begin with a rapid French advance, and the staff on both sides, therefore, shared a belief that it would be maps of Germany and not France that would be required.

The difficulties confronted by French Headquarters had been made very much greater by a sudden and completely unexpected change of deployment plan. On July 11, as the prospect of war was becoming very apparent, the decision was taken to abandon the proposed formation of three armies, and instead to concentrate the field army in one command as the 'Army of the Rhine'. It was a decision which Le Boeuf believed to have been taken for purely political reasons, based on the illusory hope of Austrian cooperation.[13] The eight corps of which the Army of the Rhine was to consist were to be under the overall command of the Emperor, with Le Boeuf acting as his Chief of Staff. The sub chiefs of staff were to be Generals Lebrun and Jarras; General Soleille commanded the artillery. Marshal Bazaine, who had of course been one of the intended army commanders, was particularly offended. He was to command the 3rd Corps, concentrating in Metz; like the 1st Corps (Marshal McMahon) at Strasbourg and the 6th Corps (Marshal Canrobert) at Châlons, his corps comprised four divisions rather than three and his cavalry division had three brigades instead of two. The other five corps were each commanded by generals: the 2nd Corps (Frossard) concentrated at St Avold; the 4th Corps (Ladmirault) at Thionville; the 5th Corps (de Failly) around Bitsche; the 7th Corps (Felix Douay) at Belfort: and the Guard Corps (Bourbaki) at Nancy.

While the French were thus hastily assembling an ad hoc general staff from scratch, Moltke could rely on a team that he had personally assembled and trained to give effect to the detailed plans so carefully drafted over so long a period of preparation. His immediate deputy was the Quarter Master-General, Theophile von Podbielski, who had served in that capacity since before the Austro-Prussian war. The divisional chiefs, or section heads, were Colonels Julius von Verdy du Vernois, Paul Bronsart von Schellendorff, and Karl von Brandenstein. The latter was in charge of the railways section, and it would be upon the performance of his department in carrying out strictly the mobilisation plan that success initially depended. Another key appointment was that of the highly regarded Albrecht von

Stosch as Commissary-General; he had feared that he would get a headquarters post, but he would greatly have preferred an appointment in the field.

The final composition and deployment zones of the German army followed closely the 1868/9 plan. There were, however, to be only three armies. The First Army, under Steinmetz, comprising the VII and VIII Corps, concentrated around Wittlich. Prince Frederick Charles' Second Army, composed of the III, IV, X and Guard Corps, was detraining in a position Neuenkirchen-Homburg. The Crown Prince's Third Army with the V, XII, I and II Bavarian Corps, and the Württemberg and Baden Divisions, was assembling near Landau and Rastatt. Moltke held in reserve for the moment, in front of Mainz, the IX and XII Corps, while it was assumed that the other three corps held back to cover possible Austrian complications were unlikely to be available during the first three weeks of the campaign. Three cavalry divisions were assigned to the First Army, two to the Second Army and one only to the Third Army.

Meanwhile Napoleon arrived at Metz committed to an offensive. It was very clear to the French that only by a rapid concentration and advance would they make up for their anticipated numerical inferiority. The advance, from positions around Metz and Strasbourg and pivoting on the latter place, was intended to be made across the Rhine near Maxau not far from Karlsruhe, and well to the south of Mannheim and the concentration area of the Prussian Second Army. With this immediate offensive in mind, the French deployment was thrown well forward, with a large part of the forces that were early in the field concentrated close to the frontier. Unfortunately, because of their fearful logistical problems, they were without adequate supplies and equipment for the proposed advance. This plan, optimistically decided upon before the concentration was under way, was soon altered, as it became obvious to Le Boeuf and the other French commanders that such an advance was, in the present state of the French concentration, simply not feasible; and it is even clearer with hindsight than it was to them that to have embarked upon the planned offensive would have exposed the French to early and comprehensive disaster. It had by now in any case become quite evident that France could not look for military support either to Austria or to Italy.

Moltke, of course, was unaware of the extent of the problems that confronted the French mobilisation, but he drew some immediate conclusions. He noted on July 19: 'If the French had meant to wait for their operations till their reserves were up they would not have declared war today.' The likelihood of early action on the frontier meant that it was 'important to have a cool and prudent officer at Saarbrücken.'[14] The clear signs of an immediate forward move by the French appeared to confirm that they were doing what had always been expected and endeavouring for both military and political reasons to disrupt the German mobilisation.

> By keeping a careful watch over the enemies movements we obtained unmistakable evidence that the French were moving towards the frontier without previously enrolling their reserves, and without completing the mobilisation in their respective garrisons ....It would not be natural to assume that the enemy would renounce the advantages which belonged to an orderly mobilisation and organisation, without crediting him with a desire of some compensation in the attainment of greater aims.[15]

The obvious motive for the early forward move seemed to be a quick offensive across the Rhine and for this Moltke was entirely prepared, since it had always seemed the best chance for the French to gain the upper hand. He expected this offensive to be launched about July 25, with three corps in the front line comprising 65,000 infantry. They must, he believed, wait for their second line before they could attack Alzey or Mannheim with just under 100,000 infantry, which meant a delay until August 1. By then he would have available at least half as many troops again. Much the same situation obtained further to the south, where the Germans faced an advance by McMahon from the direction of Strasbourg.[16]

As days passed, however, with no sign of the expected attack, the Germans began to realise that after all they might be the attackers and that it would be their maps of France that they would require. Reporting to the King on July 22, Moltke told him that the French had not yet crossed the frontier, but might do so at any moment. On the other hand, he recognised that it was possible that the French might further postpone their invasion. Thinking about it, he now proposed that the Second Army should assemble on the Rhine.[17] This change in deployment meant that the III and X Corps would now detrain at Bingen, concentrating in the areas Kreuznach-Mainz, and the Guard and IV Corps would detrain at Mannheim. The effect would be to postpone for a few days an advance in strength over the frontier, but would mean that if the French did push forward with the offensive that had appeared to be in preparation, the Second Army would meet it in fighting order. Orders to this effect went out on the following day. Meanwhile Moltke took a close interest in the activity of the Prussian cavalry along the frontier, and the damage being done by a number of enterprising Prussian units to bridges and road communications. To Stosch, who had gone forward to Mainz, he telegraphed instructions to be ready for the proposed concentration. 'Desirable to push forward supplies at once to line Kreuznach-Alzey-Worms. Very large magazine Alzey, other points Gaubickelsheim and Monsheim. Ovens to be set up at Neuenkirchen, Homburg, Saarlouis. Pioneers can help the bakers.'[18]

Meanwhile at Metz, pending Napoleon's arrival, Bazaine had been initially responsible for the command of the French forces as they assembled. On July 21, he drew some conclusions of his own from the rather sketchy intelligence that he had so far received as to the Prussian concentration:

> It would appear that the Prussians intend awaiting battle in the neighbourhood of Mainz; they are concentrating troops between that place and Coblenz; their subsistence in that district is difficult; it is generally believed that a war lasting over two or three months will be ruination and destruction. Only the weakly men are allowed to remain with the depots; all the robust men between the ages of 18 and 36 are obliged to march.[19]

By July 27 Le Boeuf had arrived on the scene, and was able to report to the Emperor that 'McMahon's four divisions must be pretty nearly formed at Strasbourg and Hagenau. The Marshal has consequently a considerable military force in Lower Alsace. He can call up Conseil-Dumesnil's Division of Douay's Corps from Colmar. But I consider it of great importance that the railway from Lyon to Strasbourg should be well watched.' Douay's 7th Corps was now placed under McMahon's orders, and Le Boeuf constantly pestered him to speed up his concentration.

At the other end of the French line, the remaining army corps were in a tight huddle between Metz and the frontier, save for de Failly's 5th Corps at Saargemund and Bitsche. The idea of a rapid offensive was fading fast. Arriving at Metz on July 28, Napoleon found his senior commanders without any practical ideas as to what ought best be done. His proclamation to his army on that day still suggested an offensive war. 'Whatever may be the road we take beyond our frontiers, we shall come across the glorious tracks of our fathers. We will prove ourselves worthy of them.'[20] It was now perfectly clear to him, however, that an ambitious stroke towards the Rhine was out of the question, and he substituted for this a modest thrust across the Saar below Saarbrücken by the 3rd Corps, while another moved on Saarlouis. Even this, however, was abandoned in the face of the protests of Bazaine (who was to command the operation) and the other three corps commanders that they were not ready.[21] This recognition of the reality of the situation was reflected in the direction given to McMahon that he was not expected to move for a week.

Without any clear objective, and still lacking any of its reservists, and painfully short of some essential equipment, the various units of the Army of the Rhine spent the closing days of July in edging closer towards the frontier, and closer to each other, and waiting for something to turn up.

At the Royal Headquarters the generally calm atmosphere continued to prevail. Although the German mobilisation had gone without a hitch, the deployment, at least in its early stages, had not been trouble free. Moltke's decision on July 23 to detrain the armies on the right bank of the Rhine, and to move them thence to their concentration areas had also created the kind of problems inseparable from last minute changes of plan. The logistic consequences were considerable, with supply convoys now obliged to move along roads occupied by combat units marching to their concentration areas. As a result, therefore, in spite of their relatively slow progress towards the front, many corps outran their supply trains and thus were not ready for battle as soon as Moltke had intended.[22] But in general the early developments were well within the scope of the situation envisaged by Moltke's 1868/9 plan. As far as could be judged the French had originally concentrated as he had predicted with the object of effecting an invasion of South Germany, although the confused French movements since then made assessment of their intentions extremely difficult. By July 29 it seemed likely that they intended to concentrate on the line Forbach-Bitsche. Moltke had by now a pretty accurate outline of the French order of battle, and their main points of concentration, which he distributed to his commanders on that date, noting that 'encounters between the advance troops of the two sides [had] been more lively since July 27' but that there were still 'no definite signs of offensive intentions on the part of the French'[23] He was already keeping a watchful eye on the possibility that Steinmetz might move forward too soon, and on the same day sent the first of a series of orders to ensure that the First Army was kept on a tight rein. 'King orders First Army not for the present passed the line Saarburg-Wadern with its main forces. Trier to be held if attacked.'[24] The German deployment was well able to take care of most eventualities, and the only criticism that could be voiced of Moltke's plan was that he had left the frontier district wholly exposed to even the most tentative advance by Bazaine. Moltke's review of the situation had, however, correctly shown that in fact the French options were extremely limited, unless a very bold policy indeed was to be pursued.

By July 31, Steinmetz's leading units were on the Saar, while the VIII Corps advanced down the Nahe valley towards Saarlouis. As a result of the decision to detrain on the Rhine, Frederick Charles was still well back with the X Corps at Bingen, the XII Corps at Mainz and with the III and VX Corps somewhat in front of these. The Guard Corps was between Worms and Mannheim, with the IV Corps moving on Kaiserslautern. The Crown Prince's army occupied the triangle Speyer-Annweiler-Karlsruhe. That day, the Crown Prince attended the Sunday church service at Speyer in 'an extraordinarily ugly building', but was comforted by the response of the South Germans to the war, noting that all of them 'regarded the immediate future in a temper of enthusiasm and confidence.'[25] But his army was still by no means ready, and it was still echeloned well back from the frontier.

During the last days of July, there had been constant brushes between small units, particularly of cavalry, as each side strove to collect intelligence about the others concentration. By now, it was becoming evident to Moltke that the principal focus of any French advance would be on Saarbrücken, garrisoned only by one battalion of infantry and three squadrons of Uhlans. Concerned about the safety of this small force, he sent a telegram on July 30 to Goeben in Coblenz: 'Little band at Saarbrücken must not be sacrificed. Support by Second Army at present impossible. No objection to support by detachment from Wadern posted at Sulzbach or Neuenkirchen for it to fall back upon. Not desirable now to damage railway.'[26] As a result of this the pocket sized force was strengthened on July 31 by the addition of two more battalions of infantry; meanwhile French activity continued to increase in front of the town. It was still obvious, though, that the small force there could offer little more than token resistance to any determined French advance on Saarbrücken. It was to this town that Archibald Forbes had made his way, as being the most likely point at which the first clash would come, but in these early days he found the situation unreal. 'It was not easy to realise the wrath to come, as one sat by the table d'hôte, in the sunshiny Rheinischer Hof, clinking glasses with those right pleasant comrades, the officers of the Hohenzollern battalion.'[27] He went on patrols with the German pickets, and witnessed a number of small engagements, while the tiny German garrison awaited the advance of Frossard's Corps which was known to be the other side of the ridge, but which, inexplicably, still failed to advance.

To the south, the German cavalry had been far more active than their French opponents and a good deal more successful in gaining intelligence, especially as to the deployment and state of readiness of the corps of MacMahon and Douay. Much to their surprise, since a French advance had also been expected in this area, it was becoming apparent that no attack was immediately planned. On July 30 Moltke suggested to Blumenthal that the Third Army should advance in the direction Hagenau-Bischweiler; when Blumenthal responded with news that the French were assembling bridging material south of Lauterburg, Moltke confirmed that the Third Army 'should at once advance southwards on the left bank of the Rhine, seek the enemy, and attack him. By this means bridge building south of

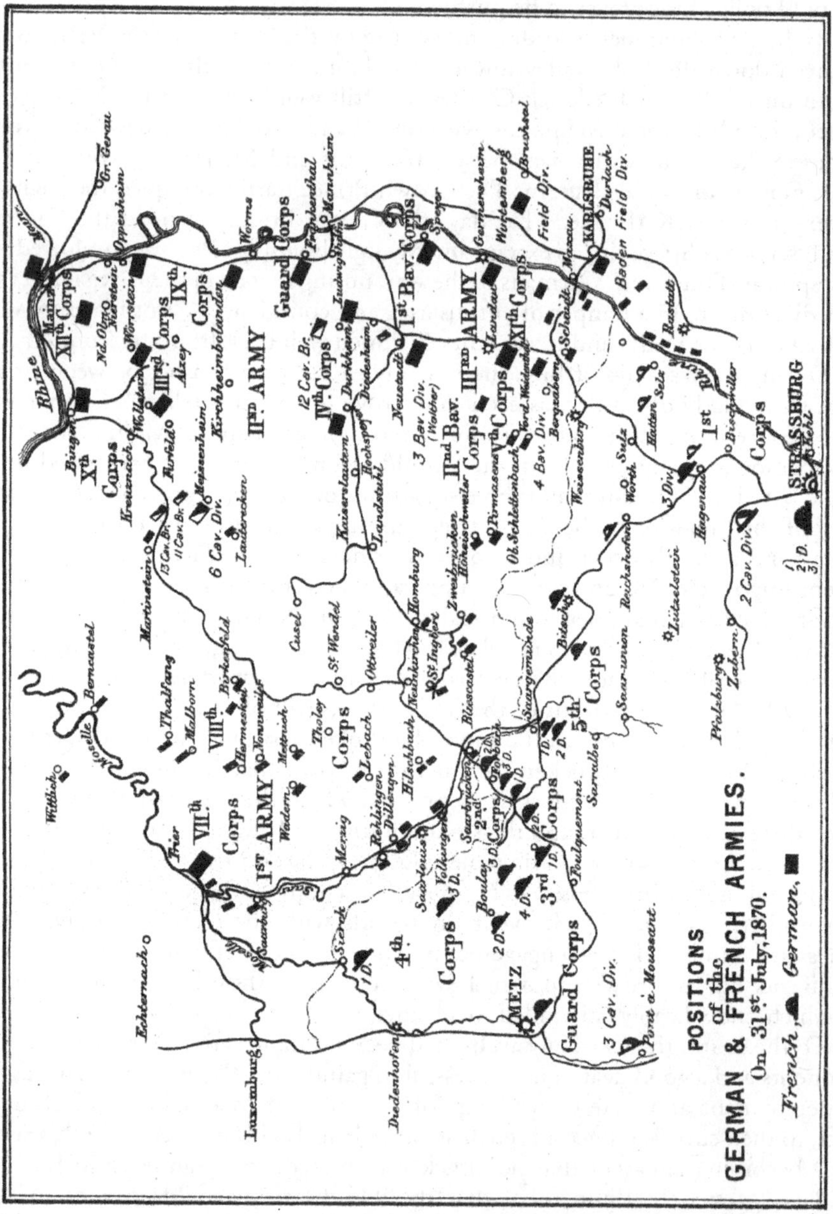

Positions of the German and French armies on July 31

Lauterburg will be prevented and all South Germany most effectually protected.'[28] The response was disappointing; the Third Army was not yet ready to move. A sharp enquiry next day from Moltke as to when it would be ready elicited a reply from Blumenthal that this would be August 3. Moltke was extremely dissatisfied with this response, which arrived during the afternoon of July 31, just before the movement of royal headquarters from Berlin to Mainz. Discussing the matter with his staff as the train rolled westward, he drafted 'a fresh and very decided order to go on.' When he read it, Verdy said to Podbielski that it should not be sent, saying that he knew Blumenthal's staff well in the last war. 'If you wish to create strained relations with them, during the whole of this campaign, send it; but I am perfectly sure that they will feel offended, and, I think, not without some cause.' Instead he suggested that as soon as they got to Mainz he should himself go to the Third Army headquarters at Speyer to convey the need for haste. Moltke, to whom Podbielski referred the question, agreed, and the telegram did not go.[29]

The royal train was extremely crowded, carrying the King, Bismarck, Moltke, Roon and their staffs; it had been suggested that perhaps the bulk of the General Staff might go in another train, but Moltke would have none of this. Even during the railway journey he might have need of any of his officers, and he insisted that they must all travel with him. One task which his staff had on the thirty seven hour journey was to take his mind off graver matters by playing whist with him, a game he much enjoyed, but which he played very badly. As Verdy recorded, he would 'look his neighbour for some time straight in the face with his great eyes saying: "I must try and find out from his face whether he has the card" … not only the player in question, but all the rest would end by bursting out laughing.'[30]

On August 2, a forward movement was finally ordered by French Imperial Headquarters, when the decision was taken to advance on Saarbrücken. Since the operation involved no less than six divisions, there could be no doubt of its success, for what that was worth; it resulted in the occupation of the heights dominating the town, although not the town itself. The retreat across the Saar of the small German force, now under Count Gneisenau, was unimpeded after it had put up a defence brisk enough to give the French war correspondents something to write home about. And the fourteen year old Prince Imperial, who had accompanied his father, wrote home of his experiences facing the Prussians. 'They still had two or three companies in ambush behind a bridge and they were firing on any horsemen who showed themselves. Papa chose to look all the same, and we heard several bullets. A splinter of shell was picked up quite near the Emperor.'[31] Over in Saarbrücken Forbes admired the courage of the defenders. They 'fought with a desperate valour, and were as cool under fire as if they had been at their dinner.' He was less impressed with the French failure to follow up their advance; they missed a great chance, he thought, due to 'their own inconceivable unreadiness, and to the imbecile inaction of their leaders, assignable to ignorance, treachery, divided councils.'[32] But in Paris, nonetheless, this forward movement was reported as a major victory. Moltke and his staff, newly established at Mainz on August 2, were unmoved; the real battles were to come, and very soon.

6

The Opening Battles: Weissenburg and Wörth

The first encounter was much closer at hand than either side realised. Away to the right of the French armies, MacMahon was trying to get his forces together. He had pushed forward towards the frontier the lst and 2nd Divisions of his own lst Corps, putting both under the command of Ducrot. He then proceeded to give orders direct to the 2nd Division commanded by Abel Douay; so too did Ducrot, and the unfortunate Douay began what was to prove a fatal day in receipt of conflicting instructions. In the event, Douay's division came up to the little town of Weissenburg on August 3; the protection of Weissenburg was regarded as essential as it was here that the bread was being baked for all the forces under MacMahon's command.

Unluckily for Douay, the leading division of the Crown Prince's army was bearing down on him. The advance of the Third Army had finally got under way, in part as a result of Verdy's visit to the Crown Prince's headquarters on August 1 following a hectic and complex journey across the lines of movement of the Germany troops. There, although not without some grumbles from Blumenthal who complained that 'the instructions given from Headquarters as regards the general idea are very defective, for as far as the Third Army is concerned, nothing whatever has been said of the role it is to play,'[1] Verdy succeeded in getting orders

Crown Prince Frederick William, commander of the German Third Army (Scheibert)

issued for the army to cross the frontier on August 4 along the line Weissenburg-Lauterburg. Blumenthal, meanwhile, promised to write to Moltke to set out his own thoughts. When he got the letter Moltke was reassured; in his tactful reply, which no doubt took account of Verdy's report of Blumenthal's remarks, he wrote that

> the intentions explained in your letter of yesterday quite correspond to the views and intentions of these headquarters. The Third Army is left quite free in the execution of its mission. Direct co-operation with the Second Army is at present impossible owing to the Hardt mountains. Only from here can the accord of the operations of both armies, with due regard to the enemy's measures, be secured.[2]

At the point chosen for the crossing, the frontier follows the Lauter from its junction with the Rhine to Weissenburg and thereafter continues westward into the Vosges mountains, so that the Crown Prince's army was presently advancing along the side of the Vosges into which it to would have to turn to its right if it was to co-operate directly with the other German armies. It was clear both to Moltke and to Blumenthal that it was necessary in the first instance to put paid to MacMahon.

Weissenburg, on the River Lauter, lies between two spurs of the Vosges, that to the north being the Wolfsberg and that to the south the Geisberg. The advance on the town was to be led on the right of the army by von Bothmer's 4th Bavarian Division. There were few roads, and a large part of the front of the advance was on the north side of the Lauter through the thick forest of Bienwald, which meant that considerable care was necessary if congestion en route was to be avoided. In the event it was not. One principal victim of this was the 4th Cavalry Division (Prince Albrecht) which, instead of covering the advance and being placed where it could

Bavarian troops push forward during the Battle of Weissenburg, engraving from the painting by Braun ((Pflugk-Harttung)

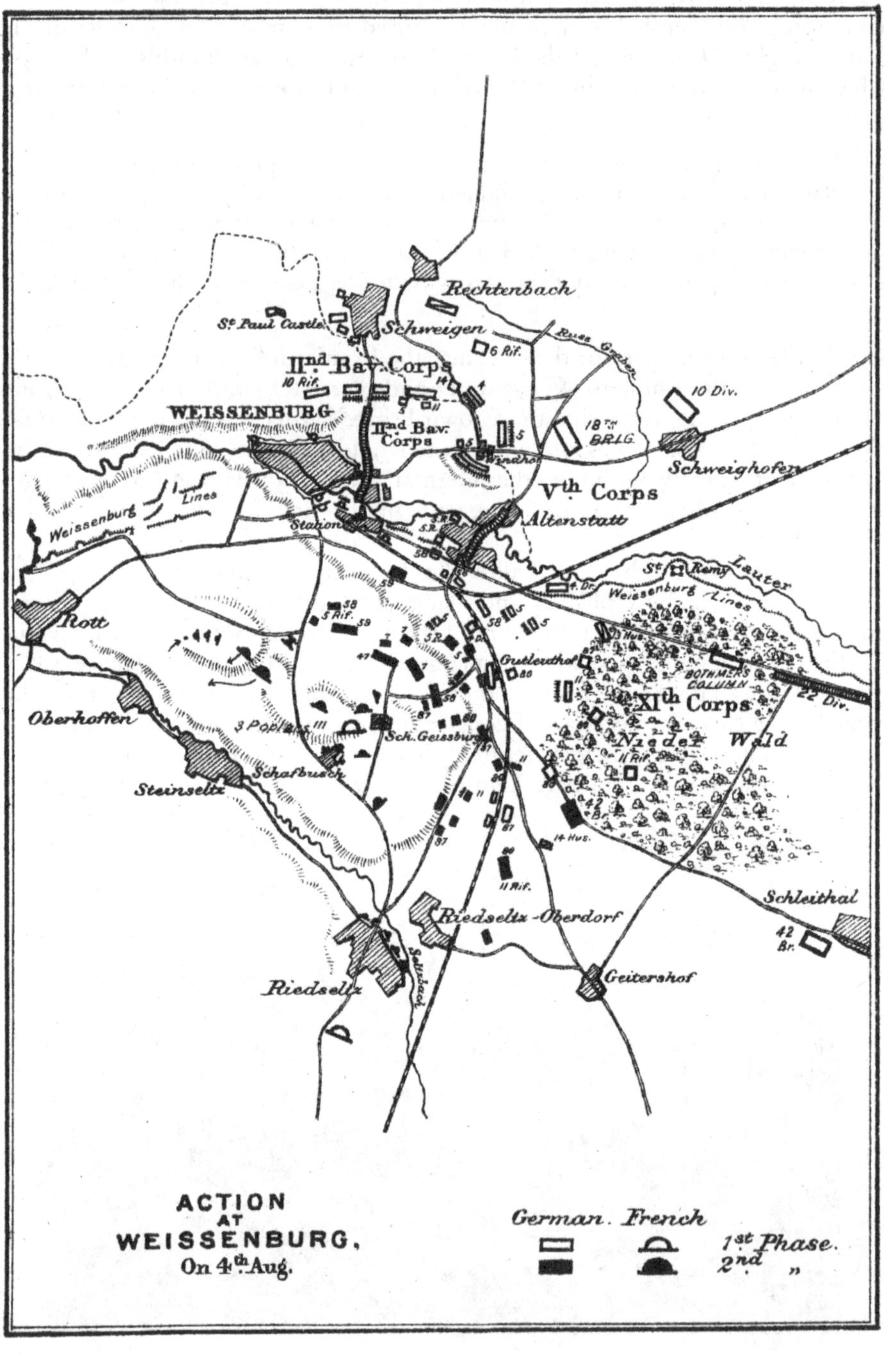

The Battle of Weissenburg, August 4

Bavarian artillery in action during the Battle of Weissenburg, painting by Braun (Rousset/*Histoire*)

seek intelligence of the French movements, was, in fact, well behind not only the leading troops of the advance guard but also the rest of Hartmann's II Bavarian Corps. In the event, this was, after the battle, seriously to prejudice the Crown Prince's assessment of the position.

Douay's difficulties were sharply increased by delays in moving up to Weissenburg, and by the fact that his superiors had given him little idea of the overall situation into which his division was moving. He finally got into Weissenburg late on the evening of August 3. That night, it rained heavily, and by morning movement down the muddy roads was seriously hampered. At 4 a.m., Douay sent out an early reconnaissance. The cavalry pushed forward ineffectually for a mile or so and then, learning from inhabitants that a large number of Prussians were approaching, returned at 7.30 without making any effort to check this intelligence. Meanwhile, at 6 a.m. Douay was belatedly warned by MacMahon to expect an attack by large enemy forces.

Douay's instructions from MacMahon had been to put the bulk of his division into Weissenburg and the valley of the Lauter, a disposition which would have exposed them to the enemy command of the high ground north of the river; Ducrot, on the other hand, had ordered him to leave a battalion in Weissenburg and occupy the Geisberg ridge with the rest of his force. In the event, when, by 8 a.m., the Bavarians reached Schweigen and pushed forward their artillery to the Wolfsberg, they were in a position by 8.30 to open fire on those troops already in Weissenburg itself. The attack took the French entirely by surprise. Douay was at his headquarters to the southwards and it was Pellé, commanding the 2nd Brigade, who ordered infantry and artillery forward to support those already in the town. Bothmer's division made slow progress as it advanced towards the western exit of the town, and was further delayed by an apparent threat to its right. For a while, the French artillery were able to force the German artillery back, but the arrival at Schweighofen, to the east of the town, of the advance guard of Kirchbach's V

The Geisberg Château following the Battle of Weissenburg, 4 August 1870 (*Illustrierte Kriegs-chronik*)

Corps enabled the Bavarians to attack again soon after the head of Bose's XI Corps began to move up on Kirchbach's left.

By 10.30, as Bothmer began his fresh attack on Weissenburg, it was very plain to Douay that if he did not retreat soon, he would be cut off. However, just after giving orders for a retirement from Weissenburg, he was killed by a shrapnel bullet when an ammunition limber blew up; the command passed to Pellé, but he did not become aware of this for another hour and a half. By now, in any case, it was impossible to extricate the troops in the town without some reinforcement to cover their withdrawal. Soon after noon, Pellé pulled back first Septeuil's cavalry brigade, and then his artillery leaving three battalions on and around the Geisberg where Commandant Cecile was in command. Cecile organised his troops for a desperate defence in a strong position but, as it became clear that his force would be surrounded there, attempted to break out, but was killed before his force had gone fifty yards. At 3 o'clock, the beleaguered garrison finally surrendered. South of the Geisberg, an attempt was made to make a stand at Schafbusch, but the huge numerical superiority of the Germans soon forced back the remnants of Douay's division. Meanwhile, the garrison of Weissenburg itself had received the order to withdraw too late and by the time they attempted to do so, the town had been surrounded. After a number of attempts to escape, these too surrendered. As the fighting drew to a close, Kirchbach, close to the firing line, was wounded by a Chassepôt bullet in the neck, and von der Esch, his Chief of Staff, took over command.

It was now that the absence of the 4th Cavalry Division most seriously embarrassed the Crown Prince, in that touch with the enemy was entirely lost. In fact, the wreckage of Douay's division streamed away south westwards having sustained losses of over 2,000 men. The only pursuit was by a cavalry regiment that followed up the enemy as far as Soultz, and then returned. All that was known at the headquarters of the Third Army was that the enemy had not taken the Hagenau road; but whether the retreat was towards Bitsche or Wörth was unclear. The importance of this was that it might have given some indication of where the rest of MacMahon's forces might be found. Orders were given for extensive reconnaissance patrols, in an effort to clarify the position.[3]

That evening as he rode round the battlefield, the Crown Prince was deeply moved, not only by the success of his army, but by the scenes that met his eyes. He was shocked to find how many officers had been killed or wounded in the fighting, due probably to over- eagerness on their part. He came upon the body of a dead French commander still attended by his faithful dog; met a group of excitable French doctors whose baggage had been swept off in the rout; and saw so many wounded that when he returned to his headquarters, he was overwhelmed with grief.[4] He had won the first important engagement of the war, although it had not, from the German point of view, been without serious tactical mistakes, not the least of which was the impetuous nature of the attacks made upon strong enemy positions. On the other hand, in one vitally important particular, it was already clear that lessons had been learnt from the war of 1866; 66 guns came into action against 18 French guns in preparation for the decisive infantry assault.[5]

MacMahon and Ducrot had watched the battle from the top of the Col de Pigeonner. They can never have been in much doubt of the outcome, for which their muddled thinking was largely responsible. MacMahon, however, still aimed at checking the Crown Prince, even by attacking him, once he had got his army together. Indeed, if he could get the bulk of the 7th Corps northwards into the position at Wörth, and some support from de Failly's 5th Corps presently around Bitsche, he would have a force which, in total, was not greatly inferior to that of the Crown Prince. In fact, the bulk of the 7th Corps had been delayed far to the south near Belfort, largely as a result of the operations of a detachment under Colonel von Seubert on the upper Rhine that had been formed to give some reassurance to the South Germans.[6]

On August 5 in sultry, thundery weather, the Crown Prince pushed on. The laggard 4th Cavalry Division now moved south and west from Weissenburg, and its reconnaissances located a strong French force at Wörth, with some infantry at Hagenau. This information still did not sufficiently locate the principal concentration of the French, so the Third Army's movements were such as to cover the possibility that MacMahon had either gone southwards towards Strasbourg or west towards the main body of the French army. By nightfall on August 5, Hartmann's II Bavarian Corps had moved through Klimbach on Lembach. Kirchbach's V Corps marched directly towards Wörth while Bose pushed through Soultz on the left with the XI Corps. Behind these, von der Tann's I Bavarian Corps was closing up in the rear together with Werder's detachment.

MacMahon had, in the meantime, also been given control of de Failly's 5th Corps although this was still strung out from Saargemund through Bitsche. Conseil-Dumesnil's division of the 7th Corps had joined him in the Froeschwiller-Wörth position, to which he now brought the whole of his own lst Corps. He did not expect to be attacked there until August 7 at the earliest, by which time he ought to have had a large part of the 5th Corps there as well, the assistance of which

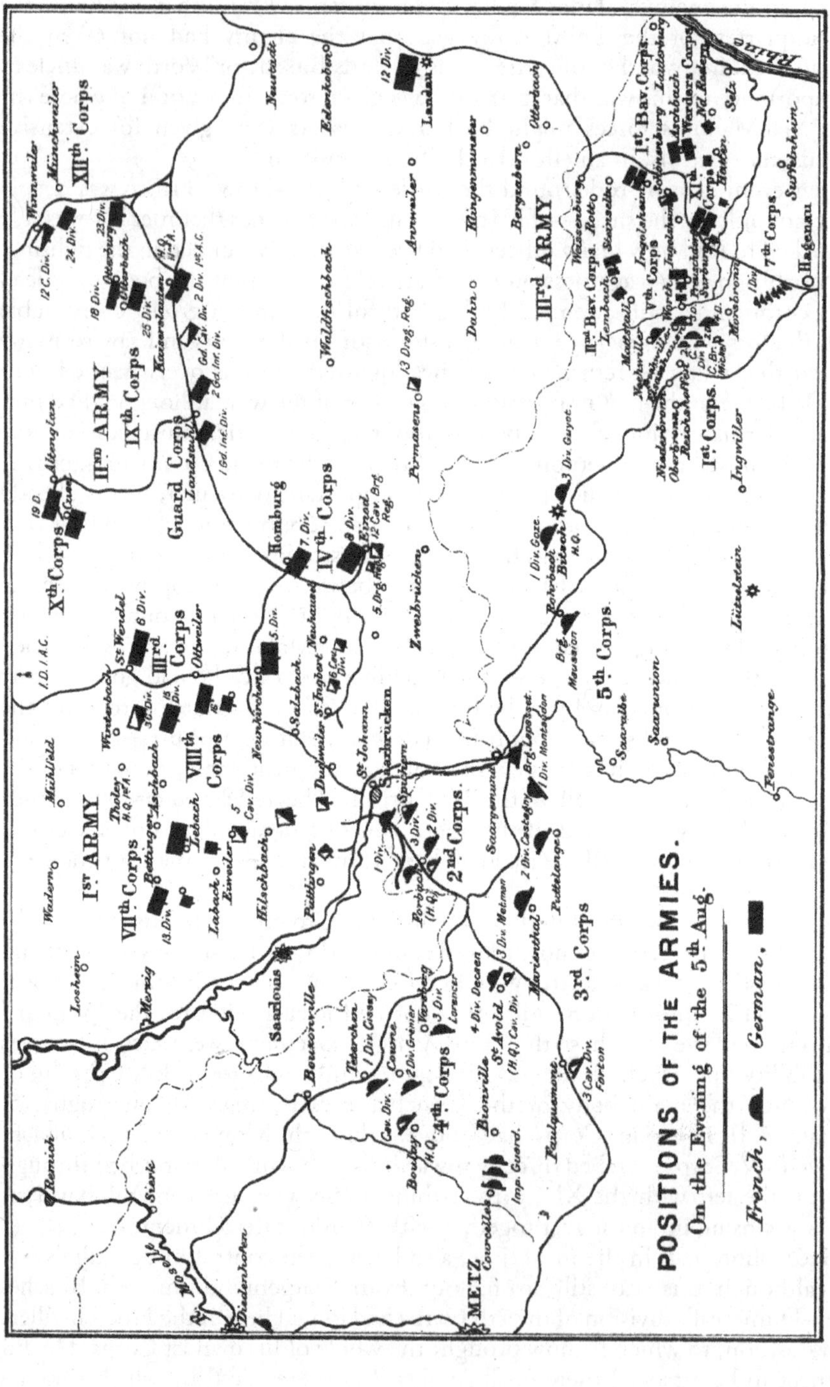

Positions of the armies on the evening of August 5

Marshal MacMahon, commander of the 1st Corps, Army of the Rhine, and later commander of the Army of Châlons, painting by Princeteau (Rousset/*Histoire*)

he requested from de Failly on the afternoon of August 5. The tardy movement of de Failly in his support was in part explained by the latter's mistaken belief that he must protect the railway and the gap which separated MacMahon from the rest of the Army of the Rhine; as a result of the German advance the railway was now useless, and the best way to preserve MacMahon's ability to link up with Bazaine was by reinforcing him so that he could hold the position he had taken up.[7]

The defensive position at Wörth which the Third Army was now approaching was frontally very strong, rising up to the west from the swampy valley of the Sauerbach. The western slopes of the valley commanded the eastern along the whole of the position, and the meadows on either side of the stream offered very little cover. The country town of Wörth lay in the centre and in front of the position, the key to which was the high ground behind the village of Froeschwiller at the highest point of the plateau. Altogether the position was three and a half miles long and MacMahon had immediately available some 48,000 men for its defence. The tardy movements of de Failly in coming up in support meant that no part of the 5th Corps had yet arrived.

Ducrot occupied the left of the position in front of Froeschwiller with his left flank refused. Raoult's 3rd Division was to the east of Froeschwiller overlooking the valley, with Pellé in reserve behind his right rear. Lartigue's 4th Division was on the right looking towards Gunstett and Morsbronn, while Conseil-Dumesnil was in his rear with Michel's cavalry. Perhaps the greatest threat to the French position, however, was that MacMahon, not for the last time in his military career, was in two minds as to what to do. He began the day in debate with Ducrot as to the advisability of withdrawing into the Vosges, and got as far as preparing orders to this effect when the fighting broke out. Although close to a large enemy force of

Prussian infantry storm through Froeschwiller, by Zimmer (Klein)

whose advance he was perfectly aware, he had not, however given much thought as to how he was to retreat from the position he presently occupied. His options were to go through Bitsche, retiring directly on the main body of the French, which he might not be able to do if the Germans were across the Saar; or to go through Hagenau towards Strasbourg directly away from the main body; or to fall back on Saverne through Bouxviller. Nor had MacMahon really done all that he might to strengthen the Wörth position, having had few field works constructed and even leaving intact some bridges over the Sauerbach.

By late in the afternoon of August 5, the headquarters staff of the Third Army were satisfied that they were facing a substantial enemy force in position in the vicinity of Froeschwiller, and the orders for the army next day called for a change of front westwards. Apart from this, it was to be a rest day, which the troops, after a long march in the intense heat, badly needed.[8] Like MacMahon, Blumenthal had not expected the battle to take place until August 7, for which he 'had prepared a good scheme for the turning of the enemy's right flank.'[9] The plan was for Hartmann and Kirchbach to remain their positions, while Bose wheeled to the right and von der Tann moved westwards in support, leaving Werder alone facing southwards while the cavalry remained in the centre of the army at Soultz.

Blumenthal may have thought this to be a good scheme, but when the overall position is considered, the orders which he gave seem curiously tentative. The bulk of the French force was, as the Germans well knew, close at hand, yet half the German troops were ordered to stay put while the others came up into position. MacMahon's belief that he had a day to spare was, in fact therefore, well founded; it was once again to be the impetuosity of junior commanders in getting their troops involved that was to take the decision as to the fighting of a battle out of the hands of the principals.

At Mainz, meanwhile, Moltke was still largely in ignorance of what was going on; early on August 6 he sent an irritable telegram to Blumenthal: 'Till now not the smallest detail of the action at Weissenburg has reached the King, nor any approximate statement of our losses, while French newspaper accounts are already known here. Omission to be repaired at once'[10]

By then, however, there was already more news to report; fresh fighting had broken out on the Third Army's front. The 20th Brigade, the most forward unit of the V Corps, was commanded by von Walther, who was engaged in a personal reconnaissance of the French line at 4 a.m. on August 6 when he heard unusual noises. These suggested to him the French might be retiring, but it had been raining heavily all night and was very misty in the valley, so he sought leave to push forward troops to see what was going on. He got no reply from Kirchbach, and at 7 a.m. pushed forward a battalion which succeeded in getting one company into the village of Wörth before being fired on by French artillery. The village itself remained unoccupied but Walther, clear that the French were still in position on the heights above the valley, now withdrew.[11]

At much the same time to the south, Lartigue probed forward towards Gunstett to ascertain the German strength there, and ran into the advanced guard of the XI Corps as it moved up into the positions prescribed in the orders issued the day before.

While this was going on on the northern sector of the front, Hartmann had been moving his troops forward in response to an instruction the day before that he should be ready to support Kirchbach if the latter was attacked. The sound of artillery fire led him at once to suppose that this situation had arisen and he pushed his 4th Bavarian Division forward towards Froeschwiller. One of its brigades, the 7th, got lost for a while when it mistakenly moved towards Neehweiler; the other ran into an Algerian regiment in Froeschwiller wood which held them up. When the missing brigade arrived, it delayed long enough for the French to deploy additional troops to prevent any further advance. By 10 a.m., the French were able to counter-attack and force the Bavarians back through the wood and across the Sauer; at this point, by an unlucky chance, Hartmann got verbal instructions to break off the battle and withdraw. What had happened was that a copy of an order sent by Third Army Headquarters to Kirchbach to break off the action, in ignorance of the true position, was passed on to Hartmann; Kirchbach, by the time he got the order, was already so committed that he had no choice but to ignore it, but it meant that later when Hartmann was called on to support the V Corps, his troops had to do all over again what they had done in the morning.[12]

In the centre, Kirchbach's Chief of Staff, von der Esch, felt obliged to do something since fighting was now going on both to his left and to his right, even though Walther's reconnaissance which had started it all was now safely withdrawn. Accordingly, he brought up the corps artillery and between 9.30 and 10.15 massed it in the centre opposite Wörth. This quickly dealt with the French artillery, which in the face of 108 guns pulled out after three quarters of an hour. Meanwhile, the competent Kirchbach, who had by now arrived on the scene (in a carriage, as a result of the wound he got at Weissenburg), gave orders for the occupation of Wörth itself and the heights beyond, committing 20th Brigade in an attack in two columns across the Sauer. To the left, Bose's XI Corps was itself

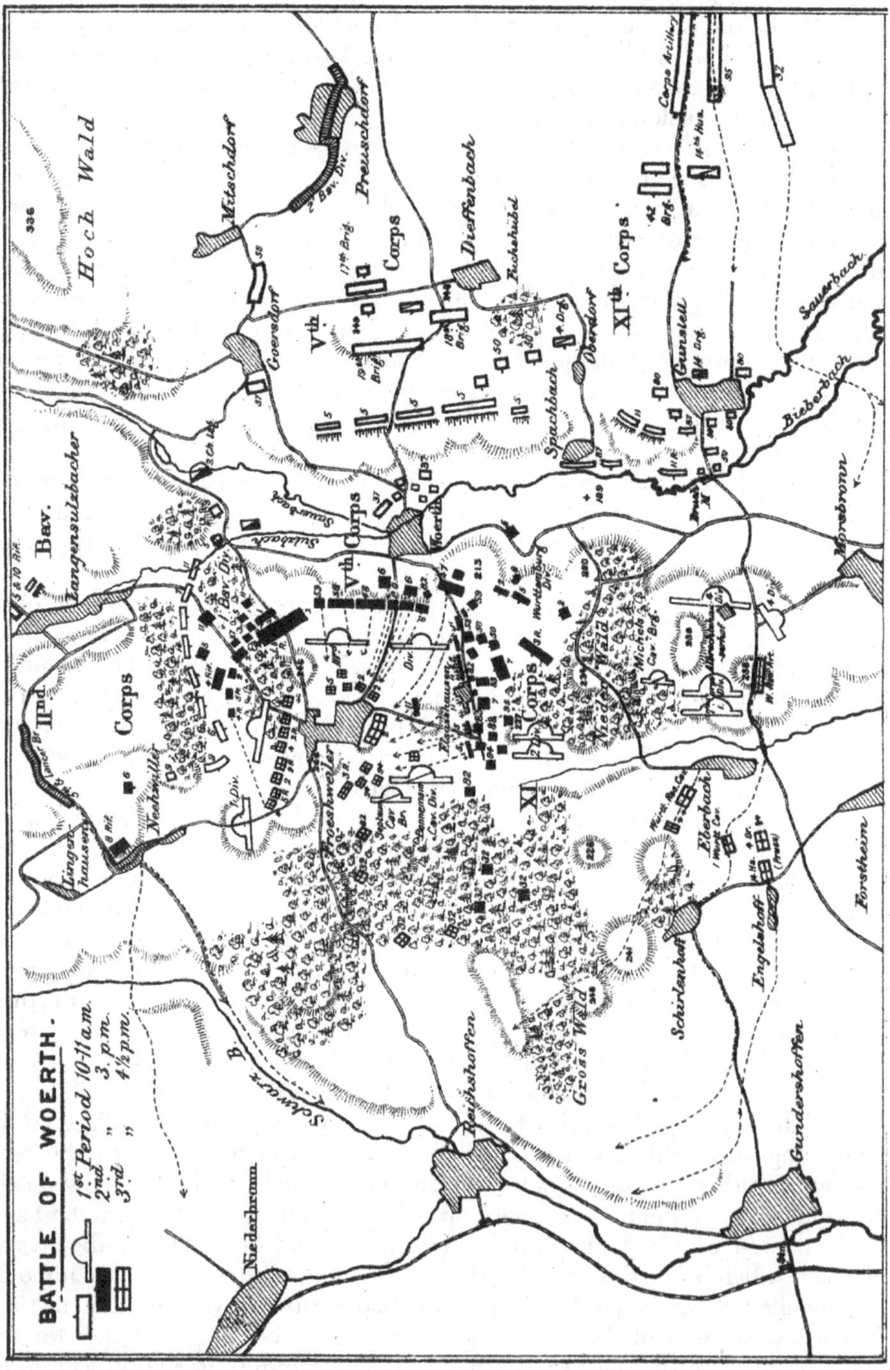

The Battle of Wörth, August 6

becoming more heavily engaged as five battalions in two columns went over the river. Strongly supported by artillery fire from a line of massed batteries on Gunstett hill, they were at first successful, but a counter-attack by the 3rd Zouaves, Ist Chasseurs and 3rd Turco regiments drove them back.

Kirchbach had at 10.30, after ordering Walther's attack, received firm instructions from the Crown Prince not to continue the fight and to 'avoid everything that may induce a fresh one.'[13] This was the message which, when repeated to Hartmann, had led the Bavarians to fall back.

Kirchbach, however, resolved to continue the battle, feeling that an order dictated at 9 a.m. had by now lost all relevance, and that to abandon the action would be costly in terms both of morale and casualties. He sought support from Hartmann, who protested that on the basis of the written order he had received to break off the action he could not help; and from Bose, who also was at first unable to offer immediate aid. A further application to Bose, who had ridden forward to assess the position, led to his agreeing to help the V Corps by attacking in front with the 21st Division (von Schachtmeyer) and on Lartigue's right flank with the 22nd Division (von Gersdorff). Confusion prevailed for a time as to the objectives assigned to the various units which were broken up among three advancing columns, and one brigade commander, von Schkopp, blithely ignored an instruction that would have strengthened the frontal assault at the expense of the flanking movement, a decision that was to have an important bearing on the outcome.

The frontal attack, supported once again by the cruelly effective fire of the massed batteries on Gunstett hill, was soon successful, and pushed Lartigue back until the Albrechtshauserhof was taken. This lay opposite Gunstett, above Morsbronn, which was itself quickly taken by the turning movement led by Schkopp. It was now Lartigue's turn to appeal for help but, unlike his immediate adversaries, he got none. MacMahon had none to offer, he said; Lartigue must stand firm. Help was on the way from the 5th Corps, he added, more in hope than expectation. Lartigue had to do something, so he asked Michel, whose Cuirassier brigade was at hand, to charge the enemy advancing from Morsbronn. Michel was at first reluctant but then assented. His splendid cavalry suffered a fate quite as disastrous as Cardigan's Light Brigade at Balaclava. There was, in fact, a grim echo of Nolan's response to Cardigan on that occasion; when Michel asked Lartigue what was his objective, the latter simply pointed to Schkopp's infantry debouching from Morsbronn. When Michel launched his brigade, it was enfiladed by infantry well placed in vineyards, hop gardens, ditches and sunken roads. Most of the survivors of these hazards were cut down in Morsbronn village itself. Nearly all the rest were taken prisoner save for one group of cuirassiers who encountered a squadron of German hussars in the Eberbach valley west of Morsbronn. The two small forces met and faced each other at ten paces. A few pistol shots were exchanged, a few men fell; and then each party rode off. Other groups of survivors of Michel's brigade ran into the hussars as well as infantry behind Morsbronn, and appear to have sustained even heavier losses. For all practical purposes, the brigade had ceased to exist. It had, however, gained a little time for Lartigue who was able to retreat westwards on Schirlenhoff and Gundershoffen.

Bonnemains' Cuirassiers falter at Wörth, by Speyer (Bork)

The collapse of MacMahon's right was complete by 2 p.m. In the centre, the Crown Prince and Blumenthal had arrived at Dieffenbach and were seeking to get a grip on the battle. The first order that they issued at about 1 p.m. was an effort to put the brakes on Kirchbach until von der Tann could arrive, but they soon accepted that the impetus of the battle was out of their control and issued further orders to support the V Corps who, at 2 p.m., launched a further attack from Wörth and Spachbach. Half an hour later, by which time von der Tann was engaged to his right, Kirchbach committed the rest of his corps. Heavy fighting followed in which Ducrot, opposed by Hartmann's Bavarians, was called on by MacMahon to send reinforcements to the hard pressed French centre. Even this was not enough; Elshasshausen fell, and MacMahon was left with no choice but to retreat from a position which was now untenable. Fresh German troops from Werder's detachment were pressing forward, and the battle was clearly lost. Once again the French had to resort to a desperate effort to gain time. Eight batteries of reserve artillery near Froeschwiller were sacrificed, moving forward at the gallop and deploying across the Morsbronn road facing Elsasshausen, coming into action within a few hundred yards of the advancing German infantry, and suffering heavy casualties.[14] The French cavalry was also called upon for a further sacrifice to cover the retreat. Bonnemains' Cuirassier Division was at the foot of the long slope between the Wörth-Morsbronn road and the Grosswald, about 1000 yards west of Elsasshausen. As in the case of Michel's charge 'the ground for the attack was extremely unfavourable, as the numerous ditches and stumps of trees, as high as a man, impeded the movement of bodies of horse, and the infantry found cover in the fenced hop plantations and vineyards.'[15] Neither of Bonnemains' brigades could break through; met with 'an annihilating file fire' and sustained gunfire from the German artillery, they were thrown back with shattering losses. The lst Turcos, an Algerian regiment badly damaged at Weissenburg, was also thrown forward in an endeavour to retake Elsasshausen in which they suffered further dreadful

The Prussian 47th Infantry Regiment storm the heights beyond Froeschwiller, painting by Carl Röchling (Rousset/*Histoire*)

casualties. The Germans now closed in on Froeschwiller, but in spite of the now customary support of massed batteries of artillery, it was not until 5 p.m. that the village fell into their hands. Ducrot collected five battalions at the entrance to the Grosswald, holding back the advance for a few minutes: soon, however the French fell back in disorder down all three roads available to them, the bulk of the broken army retreating in the direction of Saverne while Ducrot retreated by way of Niederbronn and some other units took the road to Bitsche. The latter was covered by Guyon L'Espart's Division of the 5th Corps which arrived at Niederbronn at 4 p.m., too late to influence the outcome of the battle and to do anything but to join the retreat.

The casualties had been heavy, the total French losses exceeding 20,000, while those of the Germans were about 11,000. As night fell on a calm, still summer's evening, the exultant Germans paused to consider their own losses. Bose had been wounded twice, his Chief of Staff, von Stein, taking command; and as at Weissenburg, there was a high proportion of casualties among the officers. The final victory had, in the end, been won by the tenacity of the German infantry, but it was only made possible by the total dominance of the artillery, which had been employed at short range in very advanced positions.[16] For the Crown Prince and his staff, it was a deeply satisfying moment, even though the battle had been fought against their wishes and conducted without reference to their orders. Riding over the battlefield that evening, the Crown Prince came upon the V Corps, and recorded that his meeting

> was so affecting that I was moved to tears. Generals, officers, men all dashed up to me, the bands struck up *Heil dir im Siegerkranz* and the *Hohenfriedburg March*, and the hurrahs of the brave fellows drowned any possibility of my ex-

> pressing my gratitude, which today more than ever stirred me to the bottom of my heart.[17]

Later, he encountered a dejected Colonel of Cuirassiers, overcome at the completeness of the French defeat, and did his best to cheer him up.

Moltke was still fretful about the lack of prompt reporting from the Third Army, and 3.30 a.m on August 7 sent an urgent telegram of inquiry: 'Till now only one telegram, dated 10.15pm reached here from Soultz. Important data lacking. When the battle? In what direction enemy retreat?'[18] When he received further news, however, he was generous in his appreciation of the Third Army's success. Next day he wrote to Blumenthal:

> Hearty congratulations on your brilliant success. Your first telegram of yesterday evening not arrived here, so learned only early this morning that battle was at Wörth and that enemy was retiring on Bitsche. Telegraphed at once to Second Army that MacMahon can perhaps be caught near Rohrbach by cavalry and left wing of Second Army, in case he takes the direction of Saargemünd, which the French still hold.[19]

He went on to outline his view of the immediate situation and his thoughts as to the best way of exploiting the victory. He also sent Major von Holleben to the Third Army headquarters to give Blumenthal a personal briefing. Blumenthal, whose capacity for self satisfaction was almost unlimited, was unimpressed,writing sourly in his diary:

> The same old story! Congratulations upon the victory; satisfied with everything; also much good advice to carry out plans which have been carried out long ago. Still, a sort of impatient feeling is apparent, as though we ought to be getting along more quickly, whereas we have pressed our men to the utmost – in fact, too much.[20]

There were times when Blumenthal's overweening belief in his own military judgement got in the way of his understanding of Moltke's strategic intentions. A few days later, as the German armies closed together in pursuit of the retreating French, he petulantly confided to his diary: 'I cannot conceal from myself that General von Moltke has manoeuvred us into a pretty mess, and I think that he has incorrect notions of what troops are capable of, and of what they can be called upon to do and still retain their organisation.'[21]

For MacMahon, whose casualties had included Colson, his Chief of Staff, there was nothing left to do but to report the defeat to the Emperor and to pull back his shattered corps as best he could. The defeat had been too comprehensive to enable him now to conform in any way to the movements of the main body, which had itself been involved in a crucially important confrontation some forty five miles to the west.

7

The Opening Battles: Spicheren

While MacMahon and the right wing of the French armies had been thus engaged, significant events had occurred on the left. When, on August 5, MacMahon had been given command of the 5th and 7th Corps in addition to his own lst Corps, Bazaine had been placed in command of the 2nd, 3rd and 4th Corps, while the Imperial Guard and the army reserves remained under the orders of the Emperor. During the days that followed the advance on Saarbrücken, the French had been extremely uncertain as to what might be the movements of the enemy. On August 4, it had been thought possible that the Germans would advance a part of their forces without waiting for the rest to come up. Le Boeuf wrote optimistically to Frossard, the commander of the 2nd Corps, on that day that the 'affair at Saarbrücken and the reconnaissance towards Saarlouis have apparently evoked an offensive movement on the part of the enemy'[1] and went on to look forward to the prospect of a battle fought with marked local French superiority. Later, the French thought that perhaps Steinmetz was further to his left than was in fact the case, between Saarbrücken and Zweibrucken, which led to their attention being distracted towards the prospect of an advance between Saargemünd and Bitsche. It was in this state of uncertainty that, now nominally under Bazaine's

General von Steinmetz, commander of the German First Army (Rousset/*Histoire*)

command, Frossard applied to Le Boeuf for permission to pull back from Saarbrücken to the heights between Forbach and Saargemünd. He was told that he might do so on August 6, but Frossard, aware of increased activity in his immediate front, did not wait and fell back on the evening of August 5 to his new position on the Spicheren heights which he occupied with Laveaucoupet's division.

The position was a strong one and was one of the 'positions magnifiques' which Frossard himself, surveying the area before the war, had earmarked as suitable for a defensive battle. In the centre stood the Rotherberg, 'conspicuous at a distance by its glowing red hue, projecting like a bastion from the enemy's front'[2] which dominated the whole of the valley. The position in fact ran from the Saar, south of St. Arnual as far as the railway between Stiring-Wendel and Forbach. The heights which the oncoming Germans would face sloped steeply to the northward and rose well above the string of lower hills immediately south of Saarbrücken. Although to the west of the position the country was flat, the French left was covered by the Stiring copse and by the village of Stü provided a strong defensive position. The position on the heights had been strengthened by the digging of shelter trenches and gunpits. The right of the French position was covered by the Giferts Forest and the Stiftswald. Frossard had two other divisions; that of Vergé was posted in the Stiring Valley, while Bataille's division was kept in reserve at Oettingen to enable Frossard to keep an eye on his left flank, which could be seriously menaced by a German advance from Völklingen.

Bazaine's own 3rd Corps was near enough to offer some support to Frossard Bazaine himself had, like Frossard, become alive to the prospect of a German attack in the Saarbrücken area. Since Bazaine was in any case senior to him, and was now responsible for Frossard's corps as well as his own, it is difficult not to sympathise with Frossard's view that if he was to become engaged in a major battle, Bazaine should move his corps forward and take over the conduct of the battle personally. Bazaine, however, like Le Boeuf and, indeed, everyone else on the French side, knew very little about the movements of the German army and was left merely in a state of uneasy awareness that something was about to happen.

For his part, Moltke was entitled to feel a similar uncertainty about the movements of the German armies. The headstrong and wilful temperament of Steinmetz was already testing Moltke's patience and giving rise to serious difficulties as the First and Second Armies moved up to the frontier. Steinmetz had been edging much further to his left south-eastwards than Moltke had ever intended. Frederick Charles asked Steinmetz to shift to his right to allow the Second Army to develop its advance but Steinmetz was not prepared to budge, relying on the fact that on August 4 at noon, he had received a laconic message from Moltke ordering him to remain his existing position in the triangle Tholey-Lebach-Ottweiler. At 3pm on August 4 Steinmetz sent off an insubordinate telegram to Moltke, which the latter only received five hours later. In it he complained: 'Do not understand the strategic idea of giving up position on the Saar, for which no grounds in military situation; explanation desired in order to be able to play my part correctly in future … I am afraid the French will see in our new position an advantage won by them.'[3] Moltke replied promptly both by telegram and by a patient letter on the following day restating his objective of the battle of encirclement as clearly as possible.

> I quite agree with Your Excellency as to the importance of the army commanders having an insight into the motives underlying the King's orders issued to them .....As was already explained at Berlin – I think to your Excellency in person, but certainly to your Chief of Staff and Quartermaster General – the mission of the First Army, apart from protecting the Rhine province in the first instance is considered to be to take a most decisive part against the enemy's left flank in the battle.

He added, pointedly, that 'the cooperation of all three armies can be directed only by His Majesty.'[4] This reached the First Army headquarters only at 2.30am on August 6; in the meantime, the impetuous Steinmetz had sent an outspoken complaint direct to the King at 1.30am on August 5, to the effect that the forward movement of the Second Army would mean that it 'pushes itself before the First, and as I have received no directions for the further advance I have no guidance for rightly coming into action.'[5]

The position of the First Army was by now giving rise to extremely serious traffic difficulties on the roads, and Moltke sent a curt and direct order at 12.30pm on August 5 to Steinmetz to vacate the St. Wendel-Ottweiler- Neunkirchen Road.[6] He also sent a further letter to Steinmetz in answer to the latter's attempt to go over his head to the King, bluntly restating his order that 'it is appropriate for the First Army to remain today and tomorrow substantially in its present position, and merely to clear off entirely from the road St Wendel-Ottweiler-Neunkirchen, which is indispensable for the movement of the Second Army.' And again he peremptorily reminded Steinmetz of his obligation to do as he was told: 'His Majesty expressly reserves the order for an operation of this kind.'[7] This should have made the position plain enough even to a commander as self willed as Steinmetz, but even Moltke's marble calm was shattered by the First Army commander's further rejoinder, on which he scribbled a number of angry annotations. Against Steinmetz's suggestion that his objective should have been to facilitate the advance of the Second Army by drawing the enemy's troops on his own, Moltke noted: 'Would have exposed First Army to defeat.' Against the explanation that Steinmetz had not been able completely to clear the road to Neunkirchen 'because the troops that had to be transferred from here towards the west would have come upon places already filled with other troops,' Moltke could write only '??'. But it was the announcement that Steinmetz was moving not only westwards but also southwards that most upset Moltke, since it was in direct conflict with the instructions he had given, and entirely perverted his strategic intention for the following day.[8] Moltke, in his own history of the Franco-German War, written many years later, confined himself to the deadpan comment that 'the protrusion to the south-eastward of the First Army towards the Saar, which had not been intended by the supreme command, had brought its left wing in upon the line of march laid down for the Second and detachments of the two armies had to cross each other at Saarbrücken on the 6th.'[9] Steinmetz, who had, in the meantime, had the I Corps attached to him as well, now proceeded to issue orders for the advance of his army both westwards and southwards, in pursuance both of his determination to avoid being elbowed into a supportive position and of his instinctive concern to involve his army as quickly as possible in the thick of the fighting. He still chose to believe that the Second Army's role would be to operate towards Nancy, and in spite of Moltke's reminders behaved as if a much greater freedom was to be his than was ever in Moltke's contemplation.

Having taken the greatest care in the course of his concentration to keep his assembling forces well back from the frontier, Moltke had no intention of now allowing either the First or the Second Army to be caught on its own emerging from the forests and beaten in detail. It was his concern to avoid any risk of this that caused the issue of the original order to the First Army to halt where it stood. Looking back at the policy of the Royal Headquarters, the Official History again restated that its intention was not to issue directives on a long-term basis, but to give the army commanders only a general guide as to operations, and not otherwise limit their independence.[10] However, direct orders might need to be given on a day to day basis because of the critical situation. This had always been Moltke's way: back in 1866, before that campaign had even begun, he had set out his philosophy in a private letter to Blumenthal. 'Do not infer from my telegram of today that it is the intention, once the operations of the army have begun in the face of the enemy, to restrict them by instructions from above. My whole endeavour would be directed to preventing this.'[11] As Moltke's experiences with Steinmetz were now demonstrating, however, it was a policy that could led to real difficulty in the event of a headstrong army commander becoming carried away.

Cavalry reconnaissance on August 5 suggested that the French were now falling back from their position on the Spicheren heights. On the basis that the French were now pulling back from the Saar and probably as far as the Moselle, Moltke that evening gave orders to the First Army that 'as the enemy appears to be retiring from the Saar the passage at the frontier is now open; at the same time you should cross the Saar below Saarbrücken, as the road to St. Avold through that town belongs to the Second Army.'[12] In the event, this telegram did not reach Steinmetz until after the battle fought on the next day and both Steinmetz and Frederick Charles moved forward in accordance with their previous instructions. This inevitably meant that the left of the First Army and the right of the Second Army must become entangled when they reached the frontier at Saarbrücken.

It was the movement to its left of the VII Corps, commanded by von Zastrow, that was to bring on the battle. As the First Army moved up to the line of the Saar, inclining towards Saarbrücken rather than Saarlouis, on its left flank the VIII Corps, moving up from St. Wendel and Ottweiler, moved into the Second Army's path. The cavalry reports previously referred to now led von Kameke, the commander of the 14th Division, to the firm conclusion that the abandonment of the heights above Saarbrücken meant that the French were indeed falling back and he asked Zastrow, his corps commander, if he might cross the Saar to occupy the heights. Zastrow replied only that he should use his own judgment; Kameke needed no more encouragement, ordering his advance guard under von François to act accordingly.

Meanwhile, von Goeben, whose VIII Corps constituted the left of the First Army, had ridden forward ahead of his corps to reconnoitre along the Saar. It had been his intention to cross at Saarbrücken, a plan which Steinmetz had approved, but which Goeben shelved when he encountered François' troops already on the road for that town. He confirmed, however, that he would move up in support of the 14th Division if he were needed. François pushed on; after crossing the Saar he occupied first the nearest of the heights above the town, the Exercise Ground hill, and then on his left sent two battalions to climb the Reppertsberg. At this stage, the only French response consisted of artillery fire from the Rotherberg, and none of the German commanders expected any major battle to develop, still supposing the French to be in the process of retiring. The battle that in fact ensued has been described by one German commentator as coming 'as a complete tactical surprise to the Germans. That this was so must be attributed absolutely to the improper use which already, on the days preceding, had been made of the numerous cavalry of the First and Second Armies.'[13]

There were now three German corps heading for Saarbrücken, albeit very strung out along the roads to that place. Apart from Zastrow, whose corps was being pulled forward by the eager Kameke, and Goeben who was letting them through, the III Corps (Konstantin von Alvensleben) had also been ordered forward by the Second Army, in order to occupy Saarbrücken, and von Stülpnagel, the commander of 5th Division of that Corps, received orders to clear the First Army units off the road. By now, however, the situation had already begun rapidly to change, and François was given immediate support by one of Alvensleben's brigade commanders, von Döring, who had himself ridden across the Saar to take a look at what was going on. Seeing, sometime before 10 a.m., French infantry moving forward, he ordered up his 9th Brigade to reinforce François, reporting to Stülpnagel what he was doing. When news of this reached Alvensleben, he in turn ordered the whole of the rest of his corps to move forward.

Meanwhile Goeben, mindful of his promise to François earlier, was also reacting to the increasing rumble of French gunfire, and he too responded by ordering up the rest of his corps. The limited number of roads, and the fact that they converged on Saarbrücken, inevitably meant that as individual units of different corps came up to the battlefield, they quickly became totally intermingled.

The German artillery had got swiftly into position, François getting three batteries on to the Exercise Ground hill and another towards the Reppertsberg, but it was almost midday before the main action developed. Kameke sat on his horse in Saarbrücken urging forward the infantry columns as they came up. As they approached the heights, the eager infantry were able to see for themselves for the first time the position that they were to assault. Two battalions were pushed forward on the right towards Drathzug, while Colonel von Eskens pushed forward with two battalions on the other flank towards the Giferts Forest. By 1 p.m. sufficient progress seemed to have been made by these protecting flank attacks, and François now led two battalions of the 74th Regiment forward from the Exercise Ground hill upon the Rotherberg itself. A murderous fire from the French defenders caused heavy casualties. For a while they were pinned down on the lower slopes, but seeing progress apparently being made to left and right, Kameke again ordered François to storm the Rotherberg.

Led by François the 74th Regiment scrambled up the almost sheer face of the Rotherberg and seized and held a position along the crest, evicting the French infantry from the shelter trenches there. They sustained further heavy casualties, among them François himself who, hit by five bullets, died as he was urging on a company of the 39th Regiment as it too reached the heights. Further advance was, for the moment, impossible and it seemed for a while that Kameke's boldness had exposed his division to a terrible and needless defeat. On the right of François' brigade as it clung to the edge of the Rotherberg, von Woyna's 27th Brigade was committed to a bitter struggle around the old coal pits and in the outskirts of Stiring-Wendel, but part of his brigade had been diverted as it came up and thrown into the battle on the edge of the Rotherberg. Further help was close at hand. One after another, fresh German units arrived and were committed piecemeal into the battle. On the right, Zastrow pushed forward Glümer's 13th Division through Völklingen and Klein & Gross-Rossel, threatening Frossard's left and thereby potentially his line of retreat. Through Saarbrücken itself came Goeben's leading troops and, arriving on the Reppertsberg at about 3 p.m, he now took over control of the battle from Kameke. Finally on the left, Alvensleben's troops began to come up and these were diverted into the struggle for the Giferts Forest. Here a position was won looking across the narrow valley at the French positions on the Spicheren ridge. For the moment, no further progress was possible. As the battle wore on, the three German corps commanders met and held a hasty council of war by the roadside near the Galgenberg. It seemed to them that the progress already made indicated a victory, and a telegram to this effect was despatched to Royal Headquarters.[14]

On the right, Glümer's advance through the valley towards Forbach increasingly began to menace Frossard's left flank. Although his position on the heights was unbroken and as late as 7 p.m. Laveaucoupet's division, after beating off an attack by Alvensleben, was able again to advance and counter-attack, Frossard was coming to regard his position as untenable. Any further delay in pulling back might mean that the door through Forbach would be slammed shut. As the Official History recorded, 'at nightfall the French troops retired from the plateau at all points under cover of a brisk fire of artillery which was once more

The Prussian 48th Infantry in the Pfaffenwald, at Spicheren, by Röchling (Lindner)

General von Stiehle, Chief of Staff of the German Second Army (Pflugk-Harttung)

opened at half past seven o'clock from the numerous batteries on the Pfaffenburg.'[15] It was at about this time that von Steinmetz rode up to the Spicheren heights. On his right at Stiring-Wendel, where the advance of Bataille's division had relieved the pressure and enabled the French to recapture the southern end of Stiring copse, brisk fighting continued as von Woyna's 28th Brigade, encouraged by the French retreat from the heights, again attacked. Gradually, the defenders of the village pulled back, and the fighting died down.

Through the night, Frossard's troops trudged back from the battlefield, meeting as they did so fresh units coming up too late to influence the outcome. Their retreat was not disturbed. Steinmetz's orders were to regroup, and the darkness of the night and the difficult ground in any case made it extremely difficult to interfere with Frossard's retirement.

The important German victory that had been gained reflected no great credit on the higher command. It was most certainly not a battle for which Moltke's strategy had made provision – as he wrote in his own history of the war, a decisive action on that day 'certainly had not been anticipated.' Not for the last time in the campaign, the battle was brought on by a belief that the adversary was in retreat, and that

> if we wished to hold him fast or at any rate not to lose his touch, action was necessary. This was felt instinctively, so to speak, by everyone; and as it was no longer a question of days, but probably of a few hours only, the leading troops lapsed into action of their own will and without loss of time. This conduct was in perfect accord with the views of those in authority, although at the moment the resolution was taken no orders had been received from that quarter.[17]

Neither Steinmetz nor Frederick Charles knew what was going on. Alvensleben was to write candidly that 'it was not the Prussian General, it was the

The storming of the Spicheren Heights - the 9th Company of the Prussian 39th Infantry Regiment, led in person by General von François, painting by von Werner (Scheibert)

Prussian soldier that defeated the enemy.' And apart from the great courage and determination of the Prussian infantry, who were prepared to accept savage losses to take an enemy position, the victory was due to the crushingly effective use made of the German artillery in spite of all the difficulties of the terrain. As at Wörth. abandoning entirely the concept of an artillery reserve, which it was correctly

Prussian artillery makes its appearance on the Rotherberg, Spicheren, by Röchling (Lindner)

The Battle of Spicheren, August 6

believed had materially diminished the effectiveness of artillery against the Austrians four years before, the Germans now concentrated it as quickly and as far forward as possible so that it was brought into action in overwhelming force. To this the French had no adequate reply, and again and again during the early battles the speed and strength of the German artillery response saved a desperate situation.

In addition, the policy of letting the artillery march in rear of the infantry was abandoned in favour of keeping well to the front, and instead of moving slowly on the march and coming into action at the gallop, the artillery now moved at a trot, ensuring that it was able to take a decisive hand in the battle at an early stage. All in all these changes in artillery tactics gave Moltke an advantage which was to prove overwhelming in the first encounters of the war.[18]

Although the circumstances of the battle prevented any effective pursuit of Frossard's corps because the upper hand was gained only at the end of the day, the effect of the battle was crucially important. The Official History noted the consequences.

> The moral value of a victory extends far beyond the limits of the battlefield. It bears its significance on its face. The entirely unlooked for intelligence of a simultaneous defeat in Alsace and Lorraine came like a thunderclap in the sunshine upon the over-confident capital of France; even in the Imperial Headquarters all resistance was renounced for the moment. Thus in the course of the following week the whole land as far as the Moselle, fell into the hands of the Germans.[19]

8

Borny-Colombey

During August 6 Napoleon had received a stream of reports from Frossard which encouraged him to suppose that the latter was successfully fighting a defensive battle on the Spicheren heights. At the end of the day, however, while still awaiting news of the final outcome of that battle, he received a terse and disastrous report from MacMahon; 'I have lost a battle; we have suffered great losses in men and material. The retreat is at present in progress.'[1] Later that night, the reports of Frossard's retreat from his position at Spicheren came in. It was a shattering double blow.

Napoleon's first response was, however, positive. The following morning, Sunday August 7, he called for his train to take him up the line to St. Avold, where it was proposed that the army should now concentrate. When, however, he reached Metz station, he learned of the fall of Forbach and that St. Avold itself was now menaced by the German advance. The problem posed by the two simultaneous defeats was, most immediately, that of reuniting the severed parts of the French army. MacMahon was in full retreat and this had, to some extent, opened the road from the frontier to Paris to the oncoming army of the Crown Prince. On the left flank, it might be possible to assemble the 5th Army Corps to hold off the German advance. Canrobert's corps was on the point of moving by railway forward from Châlons to Nancy. Napoleon's first thought was to order a general retreat of the whole army on Châlons and in pursuance of this object, Canrobert was ordered to stay where he was and to pull back those of his troops who had begun to move off for Nancy. Frossard, who had fallen back on Saargemund during the night of August 6/7, marched on towards Puttelange; the remaining corps also pulled back, and Napoleon wired Eugénie to say that his troops were in full retreat, and that nothing could now be thought of beyond the defence of the capital. The correspondent of the *Daily News* arriving in Metz that Sunday morning 'immediately perceived that something was going wrong' when he found an officer whom he knew and who belonged to Ladmirault's corps; 'the news he gave me was sufficient to justify the terror and panic one read in everybody's face.'[2] All around him he saw convincing evidence of the complete breakdown of French morale and in the chaotic surroundings of Metz on that day, he and other journalists only narrowly escaped being shot as spies.

MacMahon's decision to fall back from the battlefield of Wörth towards Saverne meant that any attempt to reunite the whole French army in reality had very little chance of succeeding in any position further forward than Châlons, and the Emperor's first decision was in this sense entirely sound. The effect on the French of their defeats in early August was to cause all the units of the Army of the Rhine to fall back towards the line of the Moselle and, as they did so, to assemble in two separate groups, which of necessity became the disunited armies of Metz and of Châlons respectively. MacMahon might, momentarily, have had an opportunity of preventing this division of the French army had he chosen to retreat through Bitsche rather than Saverne, but it would have been a line of retreat that exposed him to a good deal more risk and, in the event, he conducted his retirement so skilfully as to break off contact with the Crown Prince's army almost entirely. Losing touch with the enemy was, indeed, just about the only immediate plan being pursued by the French army. It was an object that was materially assisted by the inevitable confusion that had afflicted the successful German armies in the course of their victories on August 6, and by the need for rest for many of the units involved in what had been two very vigorously contested engagements. At the headquarters of the Third Army, there was a strong conviction that the French were retreating through Reichshoffen towards Bitsche. Contact, however, having been effectively lost, it was some time before it was appreciated that this was not so, and MacMahon, marching away as briskly as he could, first to Sarrebourg and thereafter to Luneville, was soon able to put a good deal of distance between himself and his adversary. The Third Army followed in the general direction of Saarunion-Sarrebourg but, for the moment, MacMahon was effectively off the board of play, and had taken with him not only his own Ist Corps, but also most of the 5th Corps which was still under his orders, as was Felix Douay's 7th Corps. This had remained, however, firmly based upon Belfort, apart from a fruitless advance towards Mühlhausen, followed almost at once by a retreat to its starting point. The Crown Prince, therefore, was not seriously impeded in his advance, first to the line of the Saar which he reached on August 12, and thereafter as he pushed on towards the Moselle, which he reached between Nancy and Blainville on August 15. It was only then that he received information of MacMahon's retreat on Châlons.

Moltke, meanwhile, was still with the Royal Headquarters back at Mainz; he moved with it to Homburg during the morning of August 7. He was, for the moment, much more concerned with the movements of the French left. That Sunday had dawned with a thick mist over the battlefield of Spicheren substantially reducing visibility and hampering reconnaissance. In any case, the principal units of Steinmetz's army that had been engaged the day before were obliged to spend most of the day reorganising. Moltke ordered them, however, to clear the main Saarbrücken-St. Avold road which he assigned to the Second Army. Late on August 7 he issued orders 'that the First Army tomorrow remains halted with the VII and VIII Army Corps in its present position between Völklingen and Saarbrücken, and holds the heights of Spicheren against attack, if attack there be.' Any further advance must, he said, await the gathering by cavalry reconnaissance of sure information as to the enemy's movements.[3] The Second Army was also ordered to halt; but since he at this time assumed MacMahon to be retreating through Bitsche on Saargemund, Moltke was anxious that Frederick Charles should move his IV Corps under Gustav von Alvensleben to his left on Rohrbach. Should MacMahon in the event be caught moving along the road, the III Corps was to take Saargemund from the north.

Steinmetz, meanwhile, had given grounds for further offence, addressing an angry telegram to Frederick Charles on August 7 complaining that the Second Army was taking his ground. A copy of that telegram having reached Moltke, he drafted a firm remonstrance to be sent to Steinmetz over the King's signature, although it appears in the end not to have been sent. In it he restated both the original directions given to the First Army and its disobedience of them. He concluded by saying: 'I must therefore reject as unfounded the expostulations to the Second Army conveyed in your telegram, and expressly recognise that the Second Army was led forward precisely according to my intentions, and I have expressed this to General of Cavalry Prince Frederick Charles.'[4]

MacMahon's departure meant that Moltke now had only the left of the Army of the Rhine immediately before him, consisting of four corps, and these were engaged in a retreat to a position on the French Nied. This movement was being conducted following a decision to adopt a compromise plan that would leave the French left wing in front of Metz while MacMahon continued to fall back. Back in Paris, Eugénie, Ollivier and the rest of the government had been horrified by Napoleon's initial response to the battles of Spicheren and Wörth. It was clear to them that the effect upon the population of such a lengthy retreat might be extremely serious. Ollivier wanted Napoleon to return at once to Paris, but Eugénie would have none of this. She was determined to maintain the general morale and issued a proclamation to the French people in ringing tones. 'Let there be but one party among you, that of France; one single flag, that of national honour. I am here in your midst. Faithful to my mission and to my duty, you will see me in the forefront of danger to defend the flag of France.'[5] Receiving Ollivier's telegram setting out the views held in Paris, Napoleon reversed his decision and gave orders that the left wing should remain before Metz.

On August 9, responsibility for the left wing was assigned again to Bazaine; inevitably, these repeated changes in the command structure continued to cause confusion. In response to public pressure, Bazaine was, in fact, made Commander in Chief on August 12, by which time, largely as a result of what was believed to be a serious threat from the north to the left flank of the Army of the Rhine, the forces under his command had begun to fall back from the position that they had been taking up along the French Nied. In fact, there was no such threat. Steinmetz, who had been greatly offended by the rebuke which he had received for his unauthorised initiatives before Spicheren, was now moving forward very cautiously indeed and, as a result, his First Army stood some way behind Frederick Charles. He had, however, now been strengthened by the arrival of the I Corps under Manteuffel who was coming up on the right of the army, heading for the Nied. The size of the German armies was itself now acting as a brake on their progress; 'the roads were sodden from continuous rain and it was perfectly impossible to move alongside them.'[6]

On August 9 Moltke moved his headquarters to Saarbrücken. As he drove there in his carriage, he passed columns of troops who had not yet been engaged as they moved up to the front. Verdy was with him.

> The road hither is very pretty, and its beauty was much enhanced for us by passing on the way the marching columns of the Saxon Corps and the camps of the XI Corps. The latter lined for some ten miles both sides of the road, over 30,000 strong. My ears are still buzzing with the hurrahs and the strains of the military bands, as we drove directly behind the King.[7]

That evening, considering the reports coming in from his cavalry patrols, it seemed to Moltke that the French were now falling back behind the Moselle or possibly along the line of the Seille. He accordingly gave instructions that all three armies should move forward in pursuit, although allowing the First and Second Armies a rest day on August 10. It was essential, however, that he keep his forces well in hand; for this reason 'as the left wing cannot reach the Saar till August 12 the Corps of the right wing must make proportionately short marches.'[8]

Moltke's frustration with the failure of Army staffs to keep him fully informed flared up again next day, when he sent a pointed message to Steinmetz.

> It is reported from other sources that Your Excellency has today moved your headquarters from Völklingen to Lautenbach. No official report of this or of the movement of the First Army today, or of the changes, if any, contemplated for tomorrow in the positions of the First Army, has yet been received; such report still awaited.[9]

His patience with his unruly subordinate was by now running out.

Steinmetz, however, was unabashed by such reproaches. On August 10 he fired off a further letter of complaint to Royal Headquarters, again claiming that troops of the Second Army were trespassing on roads assigned to him, and asking that his trains might be united at St Avold and thereafter move along the road through Falkenberg. Demarcation disputes of this kind were by now occupying a lot of Moltke's time. In reply to Steinmetz on August 11 he again pointed out the necessity of sticking to the routes indicated.

> The occupation of Buschborn by the 35th Regiment does not correspond with the orders of His Majesty for the advance of the army, and this must at once be set right. It is quite impossible to march otherwise than on the roads by which the corps to which they belong are themselves advancing. How inadmissible it is to depart from this practice is shown by the confusion which prevailed yesterday on the road to Forbach.[10]

In spite of his reproof the previous day, Moltke was still not being told of the movements of the headquarters of the First Army or its intended dispositions; a further sharp letter went to Steinmetz on August 11, reminding him of the obvious and fundamental requirement that 'daily reports are to be sent so that His Majesty can at any moment dispose of the corps, which becomes more necessary as the armies come nearer to the enemy.'[11]

The smallness of the villages through which they passed made it necessary for the troops constantly to bivouac and this and the changeable weather led to considerable health problems. As Moltke was discovering, the very strictest discipline was necessary to prevent the roads being clogged by the advancing troops. It was also necessary to forbid unnecessary destruction of railways, and a stern warning to this effect was issued to all three armies on August 11.[12]

The continuing uncertainty as to French intentions obliged Moltke to move with caution. Frederick Charles was coming to the conclusion that the French concentration behind the Moselle might be preparatory to an unexpected counter stroke and wrote on August 11 to Moltke to record his views of this possibility.

> It seems as if this union of masses of the enemy would lead to a battle. I don't think it likely that the enemy will break out from his good position and attack us, though that would better appeal to the French character than their strict de-

> fensive so far. This defensive of his has been a failure; conceivable now that he tries an offensive. For this to me improbable case I shall prepare myself in such a way that if possible he will not be able to fall upon the several corps before the Second Army has been so far united (i.e. except parts of IV and II) that they can all fight together.[13]

He at least understood Moltke's strategy, suggesting that while the Second Army gripped the French, the First Army should be in a position to envelop the French left. In his response Moltke, who had moved to St Avold, and was by now aware of Bazaine's appointment, commented on the possibility that the French might launch an assault, and the orders that he had issued to take account of this. 'They are based upon the view expressed by Your Royal Highness, that a new leader of the army will rise to the vigorous and correct resolve of a sudden offensive while our army corps are dispersed from Saarlouis to Zabern; but they take into consideration only the possibility directly before us of an attack on the III Army Corps.'[14]

In fact, however, the earlier evidence that the French intended to make a stand in front of Metz was followed during the day by some indications that they were, after all, in retreat upon the fortress itself; and the discovery that the position on the French Nied had indeed been abandoned now suggested that the French army was in full retreat across the Moselle. On this basis, on the afternoon of August 12, believing that such a retreat was indeed the correct response for the French army in its present situation, Moltke issued fresh orders to all three armies. The First Army was now directed towards. Metz on the line Tennschen-Pange, while the Second Army moved to the line Buchy-Chateau Salins, sending outposts to the Seille. The Third Army was to move forward on Nancy-Luneville. Moltke envisaged that the cavalry of the First Army would move forward to the Moselle between Metz and Thionville. At the same time the main thrust of the Second Army's advance was effectively shifted leftwards to secure the crossings over the Moselle at Pont á Mousson and Marbache – a move which put the Second Army's left in touch with the Third Army. The subsequent consequences of this order were to be of immense significance for the fate of Bazaine's army. Moltke and Frederick Charles saw considerable possibilities in a pincer movement north and south of Metz by the cavalry of the First and Second Armies, but Steinmetz evidently did not, for the orders he issued his cavalry were a good deal less emphatic.

Indeed, considering the remarkable reputation that the German cavalry quickly acquired during the war, especially the fear and respect in which the Uhlans were held, some of the reconnaissance in the early stages of the campaign was surprisingly ineffectual. The way in which contact was lost with both Frossard and MacMahon after the battles of August 6 has been justly criticised. During the following days, however, a number of daring exploits contributed to the alarm that even a small party of Uhlans was able to create. As a result, Moltke quickly became very much better informed about his opponent's movements. So far, however, the extent to which Steinmetz's cavalry in particular were held back materially hampered the development of Moltke's plans to advance towards, and then across, the Moselle between Thionville and Metz. On August 12 Moltke himself rode forward from St Avold with some of his officers to reconnoitre, but the French were still too far off for him to see anything of them.[15]

The difficulty now confronting Bazaine was that following the early defeats, the French had no realistic or coherent strategy to pursue. It was significant that, from the outset, Napoleon's reaction had been one of concern with the safety of Paris. Various alternative solutions involving a more adventurous policy had been rejected as inconsistent with the security of the capital, and yet the army before Metz was neither strong enough nor well enough positioned to have any great prospect of holding up the Germans for long without help. The only assistance immediately available was Canrobert's 6th Corps, which finally arrived in Metz on August 11 and 12, and that, by itself, was by no means enough. The right wing, by now far away in Châlons, could offer no early prospect of relief. In Saarburg Blumenthal, who was still concerned about the demands made upon his troops, was reflecting on the situation of the French army, observing that it was so demoralised that it would not make another stand, but would fight only when driven back on Paris. To some extent, his comments were not far from the mark: 'I fancy that there may not be another fight. In fourteen days there will be neither an Emperor nor an army.' He was well satisfied to have 'received a very charming letter from General von Moltke, from which I gather that the King is very much pleased with us.'[16]

The new line occupied by the French on August 11 in front of Metz was almost directly under the protection of the forts to the west of the city, and was by no means a bad position. It was however very vulnerable to envelopment by an advance on a broad front, which it was now evident that the Germans were making. As a result, there followed a number of days of anguished indecision on the part of Imperial Headquarters, torn as it was between the fear of being surrounded, and a great reluctance to abandon the security which seemed to be offered by the fortress of Metz itself. On the evening of August 12, Napoleon told Bazaine that, if there was no German attack on the next day, the army should move, but Bazaine did nothing about it, and spent the morning of August 13 engaged in matters of detail. The reports of German cavalry movements which reached Napoleon increased his alarm, and at noon he firmly told Bazaine to retreat at once. But even now Bazaine remained irresolute; the bridges would not be ready until next day, he wrote, and in any case the Germans were so close that a retreat would be dangerous; and he does seem to have contemplated an attack on Steinmetz in order to drive the Germans back. The launching of such an offensive appeared to Napoleon to be extremely damaging to the prospect of a safe retreat, and that night he forbade it. In consequence, it was resolved that next day the army should indeed retreat on Verdun; but before they could leave their positions to the west of Metz, the matter had been taken out of their hands.

The First Army's advance was presently led by von der Goltz's brigade of Zastrow's VII Corps, and pushing forward, it had encountered the 3rd Corps (now commanded by Decaen) in position before Vallières and Borny. In fact, the orders issued by Moltke, (whose headquarters had now moved to Herlingen), to the First Army for its operations on Sunday, August 14 were to stay put on the French Nied 'and to observe by pushing forward advanced guards, whether the enemy retires or advances to the attack.'[17] These orders followed a report from Sperling, Steinmetz's Chief of Staff, who had ridden forward to the First Army's outposts to see for himself the enemy's position; he concluded that it was unlikely if not impossible

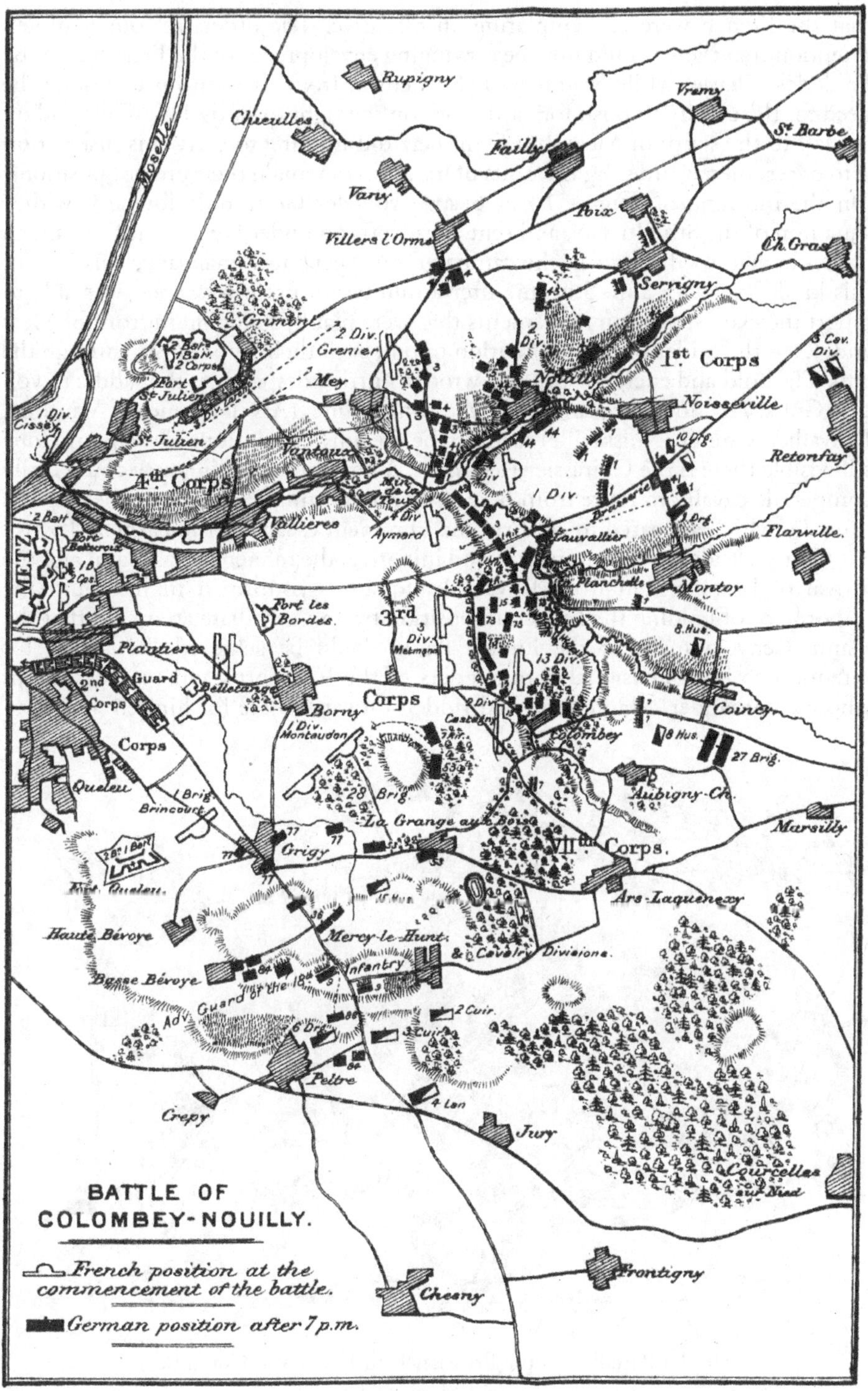

The Battle of Borny-Colombey, August 14

that the French were contemplating an offensive. The orders set out Moltke's intention that there should now be a swinging envelopment of the French right by Frederick Charles while Steinmetz held them in front. It went on to restate the need for the cavalry to push forward, both on the right towards Thionville and on the left to the south of Metz, but Steinmetz did nothing to carry this instruction into effect, merely ordering the units of his army to remain their present positions. On the morning of August 16 at 6 a.m. von der Goltz rode forward, with a squadron of the 8th Hussars, and sent ahead a troop under Lieutenant Stumm, an officer he had used earlier in the campaign on special reconnaissance missions of this kind. By 10.45 a.m. Stumm, after a number of narrow escapes, was able to report the extensive troop movements that were plainly going on in front of Metz and, later, the evident French intention to pull back their whole army through the city. The bold and energetic Stumm wrote a hurried despatch in the saddle to von der Goltz. 'A slow retirement of the whole line (Ars Laquenexy, Vantoux, Lauvallier, Coincy, Noisseville) seems to be the only conclusion. The enemy alone still visible there is the Cuirassier Regiment. A detachment of infantry could easily compel the cavalry to retire from here.'[18] As the morning wore on, further reports came in, which appeared to confirm the imminent escape of the French. To von der Goltz, a leader of determination and initiative, the inference was plain; and the arrival of Brandenstein from Royal Headquarters confirmed in his mind the importance of holding the French in position by an immediate attack, so that the planned envelopment of the French flanks could be achieved. Reporting his intention to both divisional commanders of the VII Corps and to the I Corps whose commander, Manteuffel, had ridden forward to see for himself at 2 p.m.

The 1st Battalion of the Prussian 13th Infantry at Colombey, by Knötel (Pflugk-Harttung)

what was going on, he launched his brigade at 3.30 p.m. in an immediate attack intended to halt the French retreat. The position which the French still occupied was very strong, overlooking a deep valley through which ran a little river with steep banks; and the French, in addition, had the advantage of a very large numerical superiority. It was Decaen's 3rd Corps that was still in position here, although already preparing to follow the corps of Frossard and Ladmirault in their withdrawal across the Moselle.

Von der Goltz's immediate advance took Château Aubigny, after which he pushed on towards his principal objective of Colombey. After taking this village and beating off a counter attack, he was held up by strong French forces in the woods beyond, and thereafter could do no more than hang on to the ground that he had gained. He was, however, quickly supported first to his right by Manteuffel's corps and then, not long after, by the arrival of the rest of the VII Corps.

Before the battle began, Steinmetz had refused Manteuffel's request for permission to advance, and Zastrow likewise had no intention of attacking. However, as at Spicheren, the sound of the opening German barrage was all that Steinmetz's subordinates required to make up their minds, and the arrival of the support that von der Goltz needed quickly extended the front of the battle. Manteuffel, coming up on the right through the Montoy valley and Nouilly, was himself soon pinned down, and Ladmirault's corps, which had returned to strengthen the French left, was able to resist the most determined German assaults. On the other flank, the rest of Zastrow's corps to fought hard to get up from the valley on to the higher ground towards Borny, while at Peltre von Wrangel's division of the IX Corps from the Second Army was also prompted to advance, and pushed towards Grigy. Fierce fighting became general all along the line but by nightfall, a stalemate had been reached at all points. The Germans had sustained heavy casualties (over 5,000) and the French had also suffered badly, Decaen being among those killed; the total of French casualties amounted to about 3,500. That night Steinmetz, who arrived on the battlefield at about 8pm, ordered both Manteuffel and Zastrow to withdraw from the battlefield to avoid the possibility of French artillery attacks. It was an instruction with which they refused to comply, preferring to respect the feelings of their weary but exhilarated troops who had fought so hard all day rather than the orders of their army commander who had not intended to fight a battle at all. Steinmetz's reaction to the battle was recorded in a history of the First Army's operations. 'He could not but express disapprobation that so serious an action had been engaged in without orders from higher authority, and that it had been permitted to develop to such an extent, when the role of the First Army was essentially defensive.'[19] After his own proceedings earlier in the campaign, there was a decided irony in this demand for obedience.

Back at Herlingen, Moltke was in complete ignorance of what was going on, as Verdy recorded:

> During the afternoon we heard the sound of cannon now and then in a northern direction. It could only have been part of the First Army engaged with the French before Metz. But we only became sure of its meaning when Brandenstein and Winterfeldt, who had been sent thither, came back at night.[20]

The Prussian 53rd Infantry at Colombey, painting by Hünten (Scheibert)

Although the battle had ended with the French once more engaged in the retirement on which they had embarked in the morning, von der Goltz's opportunism had imposed a serious and, as it was to turn out, a potentially fatal delay on the French withdrawal. By the time the German higher commanders arrived on the scene, the battle was over. Von der Goltz was still anxious about the way his unauthorised attack would be viewed, but Verdy, who met him on the battlefield on August 15, was quick to reassure him 'that his course of action had eminently furthered the objects aimed at; for the delay which the battle had caused to the French was favourable to our projected operations and would facilitate their execution.'[21] The contrast between the skilful professional opportunism of German commanders like von der Goltz and the cautious inaction of their French opponents was remarked by Moltke; 'there shone forth, along with their ready acceptance of personal responsibility, the eager mutual helpfulness of all the commanders within reach of the battlefield.'[22] On their visit to the battlefield on the morning of August 15, Moltke and the King, with a large part of the headquarters staff, had an opportunity for personal discussions with both Steinmetz and Manteuffel. As they rode forward towards Metz, Verdy noticed that they had gone well beyond the line of cavalry outposts. 'I rode up to General von Moltke and drew his attention to the fact that our gracious Sovereign was moving forward in the direction of the enemy without protection. Moltke directed me to ride on, but in such a manner as not to attract notice.'[23] Verdy rode on until he came in sight of Metz, 'wrapped in a bluish haze, out of which rose the gigantic outline of the cathedral.' In front of the city, he saw no French troops outside the fortifications, but beyond it saw strong columns moving up the heights on the far side of the Moselle. Moltke accordingly ordered Steinmetz to halt in his present position, and send forward cavalry only to watch French activity in the fortress of Metz.[24]

Bazaine had on August 14 been even more disconcerted than Steinmetz by the unexpected battle. After assuming the overall command of the French army, he had at once become involved in the considerable logistical problems presented by the withdrawal of 90,000 men through the few narrow roads available. The plan determined upon was for Napoleon to go to Châlons, while Bazaine withdrew the army from Metz and fell back on the fortress of Verdun where, it was hoped, contact might be established with the forces of MacMahon, and the risk of encirclement in the Metz position thereby avoided. When firing broke out to announce von der Goltz's unexpected assault, Bazaine angrily refused to order a counter-attack, saying that he would not have a battle and that the retreat must continue. Nevertheless, he had to fight; and soon, characteristically, was in the thick of it, his shoulder being struck by a shell fragment. Later that night he made his way through the streets of Metz, crowded with retreating troops, to Longueville, a couple of miles outside the city, which was the point Napoleon had reached and where he proposed to stay that night. He greeted Bazaine enthusiastically, saying 'vous venez de briser le charme.'[25] Bazaine, who was suffering some pain from his wound, suggested that because of it he should give up the command. Napoleon refused to consider such a thing, adding, however, that there were to be 'above all, no more reverses; I rely on you' – an injunction which can only have served to inhibit the cautious Marshal still further. The orders given for the retreat reflected his great anxiety that his whole force be kept as closely concentrated as possible, and the army moved out of the city along one road and at a very slow pace. Given his awareness of the serious threat to his line of retreat posed by the German crossings of the Moselle south of Metz, his failure to press on faster was astonishing, and was shortly to expose his army once again to another opportunist stroke by an eager German commander.

9

Mars La Tour

To the south of Metz Frederick Charles had been pushing carefully forward, closing up to the Moselle crossings. On August 15, Moltke sent urgent orders to him arising out of the events of the previous day. Before visiting the battlefield of Borny, Moltke had notified Frederick Charles of the victory: with an eye to the steps to be taken to exploit it, he reserved the disposition of the III Corps. Following his visit to the battlefield, Moltke sent at 11am from the First Army headquarters at Flanville a brief report to Frederick Charles: 'French completely thrown back into Metz and probably by now in full retreat towards Verdun,' and released III Corps to the disposal of the Second Army. At the end of the afternoon, on his return to his headquarters at Herlingen, Moltke sent off full instructions to all three armies in the light of the new situation:

> The conditions in which the I, and VII Army Corps and parts of the 18th Division won a victory yesterday evening quite excluded pursuit. The fruits of the victory can be reaped only by the vigorous offensive of the Second Army against the roads from Metz both by Fresnes and Etain. It may be left to the commander of the Second Army to conduct that offensive according to his own judgement with all the means at his disposal. to Verdun.[1]

In deference to Moltke's first order Alvensleben's III Corps was ordered to halt by Frederick Charles until the position was clarified. This order crossed with a report from Alvensleben, who had already resolved to push his corps forward to the

Marshal Bazaine, commander of the Army of the Rhine (Rousset/*Histoire*)

Moselle, since no threat was now to be feared from Metz; but the reference to his corps in the original order to the Second Army caused the order for his advance to halt at Cheminot to be repeated. Once the order releasing the III Corps to the Second Army had been received Alvensleben, once again, set his corps in motion for the Moselle crossing at Novéant (apart from his artillery, which crossed at Pont à Mousson). Behind him followed the IX Corps, while to his left came Voigts-Rhetz's X Corps heading for the crossings at Pont á Mousson. The 5th Cavalry Division, which was operating under the orders of Voigts- Rhetz, was sent forward to cross the Moselle and scout towards the Metz-Verdun road which was going to be a vital line of retreat for Bazaine. After reaching that road, the orders to the division's commander, von Rheinbaben, required him to turn north towards Metz but, unfortunately, he lacked the imagination to permit one of his brigadiers, von Redern, to cut the Verdun road itself. Facing him, and in fact well ahead of the bulk of the French army still filing slowly out of Metz, was Forton's cavalry division. Rheinbaben had been told by Voigts-Rhetz to move in strength 'to try to bring the enemy to a halt.'[2] If he had displayed rather greater initiative he could have inflicted a decisive defeat on the French advanced guard. He had succeeded in concentrating the whole of his division and was opposed only by Forton and, behind him, units of two more cavalry divisions. Forton was one of a number of French cavalry commanders who were handicapped by age or uncertain health; his failure to push on and clear the road, which was later much criticised, was due largely to the fact that he 'was incapable of commanding his division; he suffered from piles which made riding agony.'[3] Finally, ahead of the III Corps and to its right, the advance patrols of the 6th Cavalry Division remained in close touch with the fortress of Metz itself; but some of their reports which were received by Alvensleben, and which indicated the true position of the retreating French army were, however, wholly discounted by him.

It was evident to Moltke that a good deal of responsibility would fall on the III Corps if the retreating French army was to be intercepted, but as Verdy noted, its commander was seen as more than equal to the task. 'General von Alvensleben enjoyed such a high reputation as a leader of troops that he was looked upon as capable of coping with the most difficult situations. Thus our expectations as to what would happen where he was were indeed wound up to the highest pitch.' So that Alvensleben might hear at first hand what was expected of him, Bronsart was sent off that evening to the headquarters of the III Corps. Reflecting Moltke's belief that the decisive moment was approaching, Verdy added that 'the prolonged halt of the French at Metz gives room for the hope that the leading columns of Prince Frederick Charles advancing by forced marches will be able to inflict on them considerable damage today or tomorrow.'[4]

Bazaine's greatest anxiety as his army toiled up the steep road out of Metz was that the Germans might fall upon his rear. French staffwork during the war had been thoroughly undistinguished but now, when it mattered more than ever, it was if anything rather worse. By nightfall on August 15, the head of the army, apart from the cavalry, had got no further than Rezonville. This was the 2nd Corps, behind which came the rest of the army echelonned back to Metz, where Ladmirault's 4th Corps had made no progress at all. The contact by Forton and others with the German cavalry can have left Bazaine in no doubt that he would

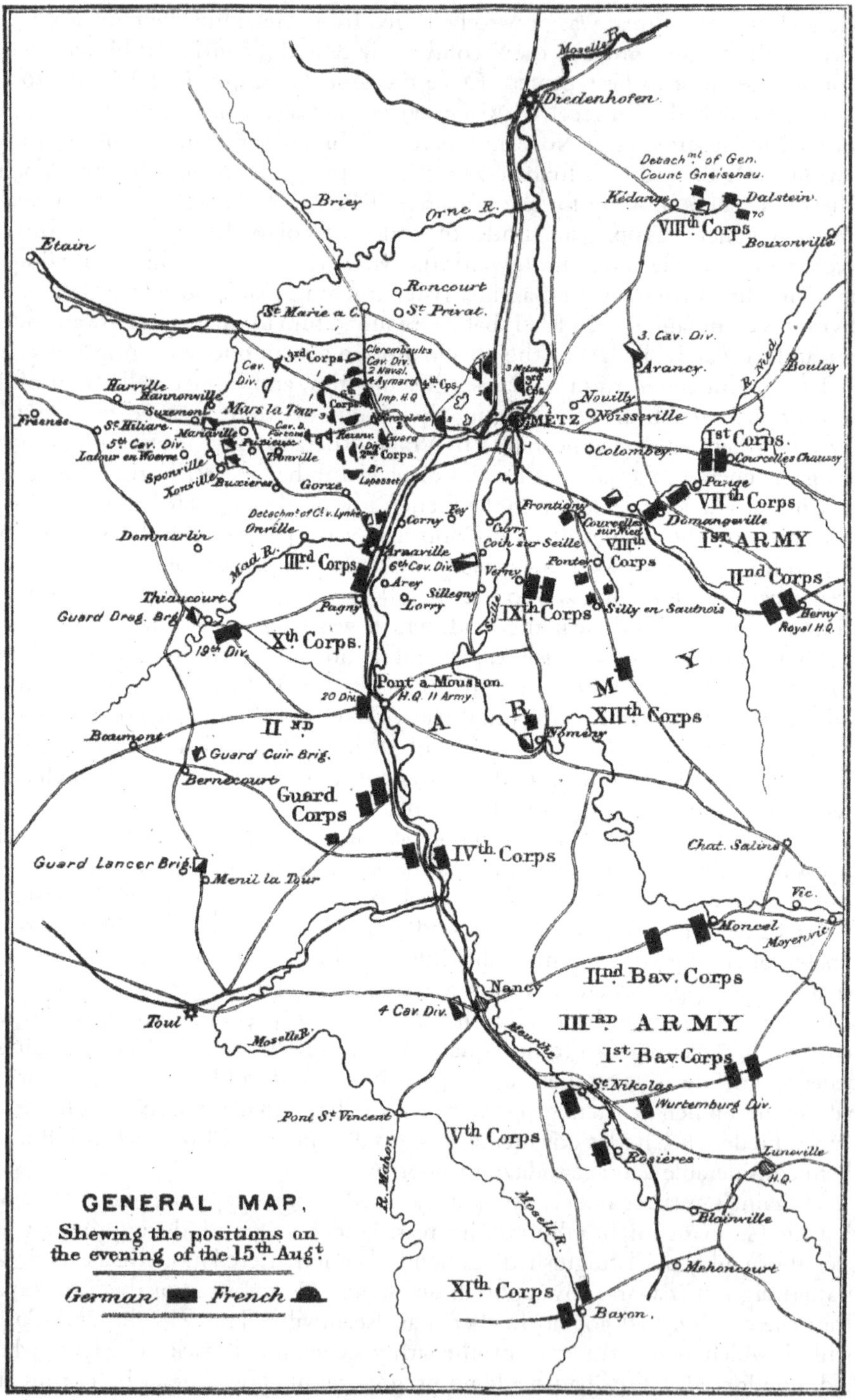

Positions of the armies on the evening of August 15

French Grenadiers of the Imperial Guard, on the morning of the battle, painting by Petit-Gérard (Rousset/*Histoire*)

experience some difficulty in pushing down the Verdun road, but he remained more concerned to keep his army together against other as yet undeveloped threats. This contributed to his willingness to accept proposals from his corps commanders, especially Ladmirault, that they should delay their movement away from Metz. That night, Napoleon finally decided to leave the army, and next morning Bazaine took his leave of him at Gravelotte surrounded by the lancers and dragoons of the Guard. There the haggard and dejected Emperor again urged upon Bazaine the need to get the army to Verdun as soon as he could. Then he clattered off with his escort down the wooded road to Conflans with the Prince Imperial and Prince Napoleon, on their way to Verdun and Châlons.

If Bazaine knew very little about the position of his enemy, Moltke was for the moment in not much better state. Rheinbaben's timorous handling of Redern's brigade had ensured that not much in the way of hard facts had been elicited about the position of the main French army, which was supposed by Frederick Charles by now to be heading briskly for the Meuse. This general ignorance of the position of the French was quite needless. A shoemaker travelling from Metz to Verdun had been picked up by an Uhlan patrol, and reported accurately that all the villages between Metz and Vionville were crowded with over 100,000 troops, that Napoleon had been with the army earlier, and that Bazaine was at Gravelotte. Sent back to headquarters, the shoemaker slipped away, and this crucial intelligence was never received by the higher command.[5] And other cavalry reports, indicating the great strength of the enemy on the plateau west of Metz, pointed pretty clearly to the real position of Bazaine's army and that it was retreating by the more southerly of its escape routes. As we have seen in his orders issued on the evening of August

15, Moltke had emphasized the need for a 'vigorous offensive' on the part of the Second Army, and he had gone on to give Frederick Charles a free hand as to how to carry it out.[6]

Frederick Charles had already that morning indicated that he intended to cross the Moselle the next day, and even before receiving Moltke's order had given Alvensleben's III Corps the task of reaching the Metz-Verdun road on August 16, while to Voigts-Rhetz's X Corps the objective assigned was St. Hilaire. On August 16, therefore, the Second Army pushed forward towards the line of the route to be taken by the French army, which had that morning resumed its retreat. Meanwhile Le Boeuf had succeeded to the command of the 3rd Corps following the fatal injury to Decaen at Borny-Colombey. So little was the general sense of urgency that his troops were allowed to put up their tents again, since it was not expected that they would have to move off until the afternoon. For the moment it was only the French right wing, which had lagged behind on the previous day, which moved forward. Ahead of the main body of the army, the French cavalry was bivouacked around the villages of Vionville and Rezonville. The most advanced unit of all was Murat's Dragoon Brigade of Forton's division at Vionville; but, quite untroubled by any concern for the whereabouts of the enemy, this was peacefully engaged in the task of cooking breakfast and watering its horses at the shady pool outside the village. Here it was discovered by the advance units of Redern's brigade, leading Rheinbaben's division, who were allowed to approach without detection within rifle range of the French camp. The first shells that burst there at 9.15 a.m. from the German horse artillery caused instant confusion and Murat's dragoons fled in disorder towards Rezonville. A French historian described the scene.

> Immediately there was a panic in the streets of Vionville. The men mounted their horses and pushed up the road, which was encumbered with wagons and

Marshal Canrobert, commander of the French 6th Corps, Army of the Rhine (Rousset/*Histoire*)

loose horses. The officers, in spite of the heavy fire, tried to stop their men, but only succeeded with great difficulty; finally they managed to restore order in a few troops, and these served as a rallying point to the remainder; they now returned to the plateau of Rezonville.[7]

One cynical French sergeant there, on being told that Murat's brigade was returning from reconnaissance, remarked to his captain that 'it appears they are returning rather fast'. The surprise was complete, but however dramatic its effect, the advantage gained by the Germans was less than might have been achieved had an attack been made by the German cavalry itself, instead of by the horse artillery. As it was, the French cavalry collected itself after a time and was, before the end of the day, again ready for action, while the French infantry were unaffected save to be alerted to the threat from the oncoming Prussians. In consequence of this they advanced now towards Vionville. Frossard pushed Bataille's division forward towards Buxières, occupying Flavigny and Vionville, while Vergé advanced on the heights above Gorze. To his right, Canrobert also put the 6th Corps in motion from its position to the west of Rezonville.

Behind the German cavalry, Alvensleben was coming northward as quickly as possible, urged on by his belief that it was a French rear guard that lay ahead and which was covering the French retreat out of Metz along the northern route. His right wing, Stülpnagel's 5th Division, reached Gorze at 9 a.m. and soon pushed on up to the heights towards which Vergé was advancing. Heavy fighting developed as the French tried to throw the German troops off the plateau before they could strengthen their hold. Döring, the commander of the 9th Infantry Brigade, was killed as he rode forward to the left of his brigade which was in serious trouble, and a defeat was only averted by a timely bayonet charge towards Flavigny by the advancing troops of the 10th Brigade. The retention of the ridges south of Flavigny

General Konstantin von Alvensleben, commander of the German III Corps (Rousset/*Histoire*)

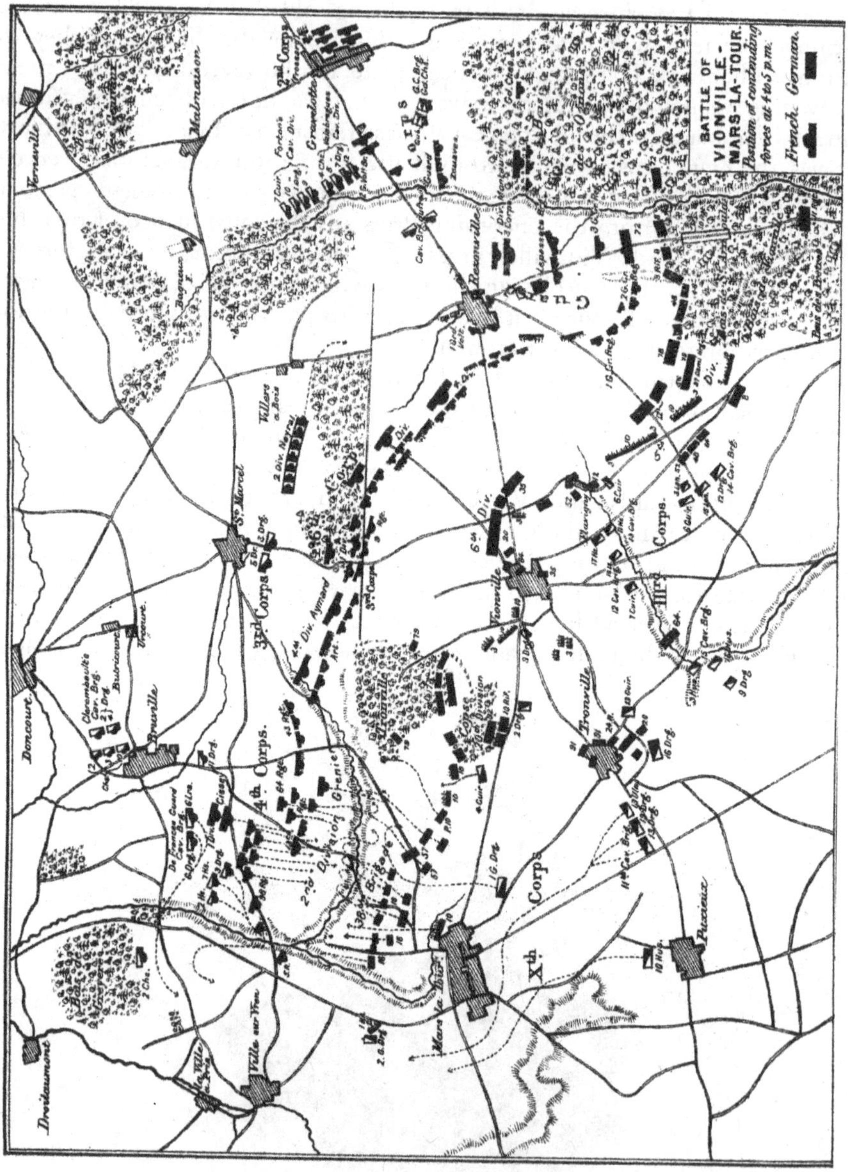

The Battle of Mars la Tour, August 16

was crucial to the German position, confronting as it now did the developing strength of two French army corps. Stülpnagel rode up and down the front of his hard-pressed division, which had lost many senior officers who had fallen in the fierce fighting which continued all morning. Luckily for him, the advanced troops of the X Corps were coming forward and these began to deploy to Stülpnagel's right in the Bois de Vionville.

To the west, Alvensleben himself had been riding with von Buddenbrock, the commander of the 6th Division. Assessing from the reports received from Stülpnagel that the French were falling back in a northerly direction, Alvensleben directed Buddenbrock to move past Mars la Tour upon Jarny – in other words, right across the front of Bazaine's army as it marched westwards towards Verdun. Alvensleben rode on ahead to Tronville to meet Rheinbaben and to find out the position of those in contact with the French. By mid morning it had become clear that the objective of Mars la Tour-Jarny was inappropriate and Buddenbrock wheeled to the right to attack the French positions at Vionville, where Bataille was now supported by Lafont de Villiers' division from the 6th Corps. Vionville was taken by 11.30. Buddenbrock, moving north of the village as far as the Roman road, ran into the rapidly deploying units of Canrobert's Corps. Tixier's division could now move forward from St. Marcel, and on this part of his front as well Alvensleben was in danger of being overborne by heavy numerical disparity. In particular, the deployment of the French artillery along the higher ground of the Roman road threatened Buddenbrock's troops in Vionville. To strengthen his position, the latter ordered an advance from the village towards Flavigny, which fell after such heavy and confused fighting that even the Official History found it impossible to describe it in detail.

> In this advance over the almost bare plateau against the broad front of the French there instantly kindles an obstinate contest, in the blood-bedewed variations of which unity of command is speedily lost. The watchfulness of the subordinate commanders and the bravery of individuals take its place. Guided by the formation of the ground, the enemy's sweeping fire, and the momentary inspiration of the officers, the company columns at full intervals are moved hither and thither and intermingled ... Vain would be the attempt to reproduce a true picture of this wild struggle in all its details.[8]

Throughout the morning Alvensleben's position was greatly strengthened by the promptness with which the artillery of his corps reached the front and deployed, often well ahead of the infantry. Alvensleben had by now, not surprisingly, been obliged to commit the whole of his reserves, engaged as he was with the corps of both Frossard and Canrobert. His conviction that he had only a fast disappearing French rear guard to pursue had given place to a clear understanding of the true position of his corps which was now very exposed indeed. For his part, however, Bazaine, who had been interrupted at breakfast by news of the attack on Murat's cavalry, was throughout the day disturbed by the notion that what the Germans were really trying to do was to get round his left and cut him off from Metz. But for this he might have been quicker to realise the weakness of Alvensleben's position and to punish the latter's overbold advance much more severely. Even so, with only the hope of support from the X Corps later in the day which had been promised him by Caprivi, its Chief of Staff, who had

General Frossard, commander of the French 2nd Corps (Rousset/*Histoire*)

come up at the start of the day to see what was going on, (and to urge the cautious Rheinbaben forward) Alvensleben had a long and anxious struggle ahead of him.

By noon, the capture of Flavigny by units of the 5th and 6th Divisions, approaching from different sides, and acting quite independently, because 'the preparations of the 6th Division for the attack on Flavigny were quite screened from the view of the 5th Division by the intercrossing valley'[9] led to the first of the dramatic cavalry strokes that were to characterise this battle. Frossard asked for, and obtained, cavalry reinforcements and at 12.30, with Bazaine murmuring 'we must sacrifice a regiment', a regiment of Lancers was ordered to attack the 10th Brigade, east of Flavigny which was now in flames. It was followed by a Cuirassier regiment. Despite all the courage and determination of the cavalry, the charge was wholly ineffective, being beaten off with very high casualties. Bazaine, riding forward to assess the situation and becoming involved in the positioning of a battery of Guard horse artillery, was himself caught in the counter-attack of the German Hussars. Throughout the encounter, however, he remained entirely composed, although fortunate not to be killed or captured. All that day, Bazaine was to be in the front line, constantly exposed to enemy fire and closely involved in tactical details. All day he concentrated on the need to win the battle in which he was presently engaged; and apart from his continuing anxiety about being cut off from Metz, he appears to have had no more considered strategical objective than to fight it out where he stood.

Alvensleben's greatest weakness was on his left, which was increasingly threatened by the advance of Canrobert's corps which, albeit rather tentatively, was now beginning to push forward. Painfully aware that his one priceless asset was time, at 2 p.m., he in his turn looked to his cavalry for help, ordering von Bredow's

12th Cavalry Brigade, of which two regiments were immediately available, to attack Canrobert's artillery along the high ground above the main road. Moving up the lower ground north of Vionville, Bredow, without pausing, wheeled to his right and charged at the head of his brigade, with the 7th Cuirassiers on the left and the 16th Lancers on the right. It was an attack that belonged to an earlier era when the stopping power of rifle fire was not so great, but nonetheless, against all the odds, Bredow was able to ride over the first line of the French batteries near the Roman road. The French artillerymen were cut down, and the survivors of the brigade rode on into the valley leading down to Rezonville. The commander of the 7th Cuirassiers described the breakneck charge:

> We penetrated into the first battery, of which but two guns succeeded in firing. The battery commander and all the men were cut down. Conscious of the prime necessity of overthrowing as many of the enemy as possible between the wood and chaussée, the regiment, under a flanking infantry fire from the wood threw itself upon a second battery and an infantry column. Whatever of this battery did not reach the shelter of its infantry was cut down. According to the instructions given by Major General von Bredow, we were not to stop at the first line to take prisoners, but to charge the second line at once.[10]

North of Rezonville, Forton's division had been formed up. Bazaine ordered him to counter-attack with support from Valabrègue. Fierce and confused fighting ensued, at the end of which Bredow's men cut their way out and fell back through the artillery lines which they had previously overrun, rallying behind Flavigny. Four hundred out of the eight hundred men taking part in the charge had fallen; but Canrobert's advance had been checked and the pressure for the moment was off. Von Bredow himself was lucky to escape, as the regimental history of the 20th Infantry Regiment reported.

> Under the powerful influence of this drama, the fight seemed for a moment to come to a standstill. This wild cavalry charge is watched with strained attention. Now come a scattered crowd of Cuirassiers past our position, then we see in their rear a senior officer, soon recognised as General von Bredow, who is pursued closely by French Cuirassiers. The French are every moment gaining on the General, whose horse is exhausted; they must soon overtake him, when a soldier of the llth Company, running forward, shoots the leading French officer as he raises his sword to cut the General down. Our men cheer, and the French retire.[11]

During Bredow's charge, the infantry had secured a stronger position on the edge of the heights above the main road; the effect of the charge had been enormous. Hohenlohe reflected that

> the charge of 800 cavalry against 40,000 men is not only a deed of valour of the first rank, equal in every way to the most celebrated and famous deeds of all wars, old and new, but it also obtained at an extraordinarily small sacrifice a success of rare importance and was by no means an objectless ride to death, like Cardigan's charge at Balaclava, though many critics have tried to make it out to be so.[12]

Meanwhile Frederick Charles, who had shared Alvensleben's original view about the French position, was on his way north to the battlefield. There was not much he could do to influence events. He arrived about 4 p.m. and went to

Prussian artillery during the Battle of Mars la Tour, from a watercolour by Knötel (Scheibert)

Flavigny, towards the right of the line; but it was at the other end of the line that the next serious threat was to develop.

Alvensleben's left was covered by von Barby's 11th Cavalry Brigade which was watching the enemy at Bruville and and St. Marcel. For a while the French activity on this part of the front was confined to artillery fire, but at 2.45 p.m. Grenier, with the first of Ladmirault's divisions, moved forward from Bruville and forced Barby back towards Tronville. In the Bois de Tronville, the three battalions defending the woods faced overwhelming odds and were gradually pushed back by heavy infantry pressure supported by concentrated artillery fire. In order to hold Alvensleben's left, they fell back on the village of Tronville itself and it was there, at last, that significant reinforcement was received, when at 4 p.m. von Kraatz's 20th Division arrived on the scene. Voigts-Rhetz himself, in receipt of constant messages from his Chief of Staff, Caprivi, who had remained up at the front, had himself ridden forward ahead of his corps, and when Kraatz arrived, he directed him at once to retake the Tronville copses. Meanwhile the original line of march prescribed for the X Corps on St Hilaire had led Schwartzkoppen to bear away with the 19th Division to the west. It was not until the afternoon that the direction of his division was changed and Schwartzkoppen took the main road to Mars la Tour, reaching Suzemont around 3.30. Soon after 5 p.m., he joined the attack on the French right by launching the 38th Brigade at the Bruville heights while Kraatz's Division reoccupied the Bois de Tronville. This attack, however, fell not on the French right but ran straight into Grenier's front. Without artillery support, and charging into a quite unexpected ravine, in places nearly fifty feet deep, the attack failed disastrously. The French counter-attacked, and for the moment the whole German left was threatened. The situation was saved only by yet another cavalry charge. Three squadrons of von Auerswald's Ist Guard Dragoons and two squadrons of the 2nd Guard Dragoons were launched in a desperate assault on the advancing troops from Cissey's division. Appalling casualties were sustained (one of them being Herbert Bismarck, wounded in the thigh) but the charge nonetheless broke up the French attack and enabled Schwartzkoppen's shaken infantry to disengage.

Rheinbaben, meanwhile, was himself preparing an attack by Barby's Brigade, starting immediately to the south of Mars la Tour. Seeing this, and to protect his own right, Ladmirault himself prepared to send forward six regiments of cavalry. On each side, regiment by regiment of the available cavalry was drawn into the battle. Heavy casualties, especially among regimental commanders, were again sustained by both sides. Barby moved around the west of Mars la Tour. The main impact of his assault was immediately to the east of Ville sur Yron. With the aid of the chance arrival of a lone squadron of dragoons commanded by Captain von Trotha arriving from the north west, the German cavalry was in the end successful. It was, the Official History remarked, 'the most important cavalry engagement of the whole war.'[13] The moral effect was even greater. Ladmirault gave up all hope of turning the German left, and thereafter stood on the defensive while Voigts-Rhetz, in order to secure the position beyond doubt, strengthened his line on the heights between Tronville and Mars la Tour.

On the German right, however, the battle continued well into the night. Bazaine, still convinced that Moltke was trying to get round his left and menace his communications with the fortress of Metz, pushed up heavy reinforcements behind Frossard and Canrobert, concentrating the additional strength available to him opposite the Bois des Ognons. Frederick Charles himself, now getting reinforcements as the corps of Goeben and Manstein arrived on the battlefield, ordered a final attack on Rezonville, where Bazaine had drawn up a powerful artillery line of 54 guns which engaged the German artillery in a fierce duel until late in the night. As twilight fell, Manstein's troops pressed forward and in the gloom drove back the French on Rezonville, while even later two brigades of cavalry broke up a French infantry position in front of Rezonville, albeit at the expense of heavy casualties. Frederick Charles also ordered a renewed attack on the left by Voigts-Rhetz which was, however, having regard to the exhausted state of his corps, quite out of the question. By 9p.m. the battle had drawn to a close, 'Deep silence then reigned over the broad expanse upon which since 9 o' clock that morning death had been reaping so terrible a harvest. The hot summer's day was succeeded by a cool night, and after almost superhuman efforts the warriors snatched a short rest in their bivouacs.'[14] In the course of the battle the French losses had been of the order of 17,000 men. The Germans had lost over 16,000, or nearly a quarter of their total strength. But Bazaine's retreat had been headed off and, as the rest of Frederick Charles' army moved north, any resumption of the movement on the southern road to Verdun was now quite out of the question.

Bazaine, who had to the end of the day distinguished himself by his personal courage, returned to the inn at Gravelotte to consider his position. All day he had over-estimated the strength of the enemy immediately opposed to him. Any renewal of the battle next day on the line of the Mars la Tour road seemed to offer him little hope of success. His exhausted troops, whose units had become completely intermingled, had bivouacked on the battlefield. For many of his staff,

The Zieten Hussars (Prussian 3rd Hussars) at Mars-la-Tour, by Knötel (Pflugk-Harttung)

indeed, the day seemed a considerable victory. But it was not a view that Bazaine shared: 'notre situation,' he said, 'n'est pas brillante.' Wearily after dinner he prepared his orders for the next day. To Jarras, his Chief of Staff, he appeared almost to be asleep. To the Emperor he sent a report of the battle, saying that he was falling back on Metz to restock with ammunition and supplies, and would probably now have to take the northern road. The orders he issued were to fall back on the fortress: 'the great expenditure of ammunition which has taken place and also the fact that we have not supplies for many days, prevent us from continuing the march which has begun. We shall therefore fall back at once to the plateau of Plappeville.'[15] When he had finished dictating his orders, he asked his staff 'if anyone thinks there is something better to be done, let him say so.'[16] Metz appeared to offer temporary security for the army; and no-one dissented.

As a result of the battle the Germans had gained a remarkable strategic advantage, thanks to the strong nerve and clear sighted appreciation of the situation, first of Alvensleben, and later of Voigts-Rhetz, and the courage and devotion of their soldiers, which enabled them to impose their will upon the enemy. Alvensleben identified the key point in his contribution to the battle. 'At the crisis of an illness the place of the doctor is by the bedside of the sick man. In this case the sick man was the road from Vionville to Mars La Tour.'[17] The closing attacks ordered by Frederick Charles were noted by the Official History as showing the enemy 'that the Prussians had both the ability and the firm will to triumph in the yet undecided struggle.'[18] Writing many years later, Moltke did not take such a favourable view of Frederick Charles, of whom he never had a particularly high opinion.

> It was clearly most inadvisable to challenge by renewed attacks an enemy who still outnumbered the Germans; which .... could not but jeopardise the success so dearly bought .... Notwithstanding all these considerations an order from Prince Frederick Charles's Headquarter issued at seven o' clock, commanded a renewed and general attack on the enemy's positions.[19]

Perhaps Moltke was indulging his personal dislike of the Red Prince, as Forbes thought; but, with the benefit of hindsight, the Second Army had little to gain by these renewed attacks, since Bazaine's belief that he must retreat to save his army was by then well established, and even if Ladmirault, as he later claimed, was anxious to renew his attack on Voigts-Rhetz, it was highly unlikely that he would get very far with it.

Moltke had moved his headquarters during the day to Pont à Mousson, arriving during the afternoon. As soon as he got there he received the first reports of the fighting at Mars la Tour. It was too late to reach the battlefield in time to be of any influence on the outcome, and in any case, as Verdy noted, 'any dispositions to be made there fell moreover within the province of Prince Frederick Charles, who was on the spot.'[20] So Moltke had to content himself with studying the stream of reports reaching his headquarters which all indicated that the fighting was extremely fierce, with heavy casualties. In the light of the first information reaching him, by 5pm Moltke felt sufficiently clear about the situation to order Steinmetz to get his two available corps over the Moselle behind the XI Corps 'in order to press the enemy northwards away from Châlons and Paris ... the further direction of the VIII and VII army corps must be regulated by the G.O.C First Army with no other considerations than that they may reach the enemy as quickly as possible.' Mindful of the recent past, he added that 'to restore the deployment of both armies for the further advance is reserved for the general headquarters.'[21] It seemed evident however that the French retreat had been intercepted; but it was not until Bronsart returned and 'reported on the particulars of the battle with that calm self control which never forsook him' that the whole picture became clear.[22]

A recent study of the battle has concluded that this was the one day

> when the French were presented with the opportunity of defeating – indeed, of destroying – the chief instrument of the German military machine, and of making good their escape. Whether that would have influenced the final course of the war is a matter for speculation. What is certain beyond argument is that the war – and with it the future of Europe – was decided at Mars la Tour on 16th August 1870.[23]

Bazaine's failure to brush aside the relatively weak German forces that were opposed to him in the early part of the day did indeed cost him the chance of extricating his army. As Colonel Ascoli has pointed out, what Bazaine's real intention was as he gloomily prepared his orders on the night of August 16 is very uncertain, since the account he gave to the Commission of Inquiry in 1871 that he would wear down his adversary by fighting 'one or perhaps two defensive battles in positions which I felt to be impregnable' is at odds with his evidence to his court martial that he was effectively trying to buy time for the deployment of the Army of Châlons.[24] It was to be the irony of the latter's fate that it was itself to be destroyed in an attempt to rescue Bazaine.

10

Gravelotte

Reviewing the information brought to him at Pont á Mousson by Bronsart, Moltke saw clearly that the situation as it had developed represented a tremendous opportunity to turn Bazaine irrevocably away from his route to Verdun and Châlons. He had no fear of the outcome of renewed fighting, pointing out in a letter to Stiehle at Second Army headquarters that 'the more the III Army Corps has in front of it the greater will be the success tomorrow when we shall have available against the enemy the X, III, IX, VIII, VII army corps and possibly also XII.'[1]

What was important was to get up to the front line to see things for himself. Very early in the morning of August 17, therefore, the King with Moltke and the rest of the Staff rode north from Pont á Mousson, reaching Flavigny about 6 a.m. There they remained for the rest of the day, in close touch with the troops that had fought the day before. Verdy accompanied Moltke when he rode on to the north along the Rezonville road.

> The air was boiling hot, the ground hard, and everywhere the traces were seen of yesterday's bloody fight. The village nearest to us had only been evacuated by the French during the night or early in the morning. Beyond it, on one of the ranges of hills running parallel with Metz, were distinctly visible the white lines of small tentes-d'abri which marked the presence of considerable French forces.[2]

Moltke conferred with Goeben, who had come up ahead of his corps; but it was clear that not much could be done to resume the battle that day, and that the French for their part intended no offensive move. The weather was clear and dry; Verdy recorded that there was insufficient food for the whole headquarters staff, many of whom became fatigued in the intense heat. One of those was Count Kutusov, the Russian Military Attaché who, falling into an exhausted sleep, was taken for a dead French officer by a couple of pioneers, who promptly embarked on the task of burying him. It was a spectacle which Bronsart and Verdy much enjoyed before they felt obliged to intervene.

The exhausted state of the German cavalry accounts perhaps for the lack of reconnaissance that day. At all events, Bazaine was able to break off contact with his enemy (except at the western end of the German line) without any close monitoring by German patrols, and the position to which he was retreating did not become immediately apparent. What was clear, however, was that he was going back towards Metz and Moltke had no difficulty in concluding that the Second Army, pivoting on the First Army, should advance in a great wheel, first north and then northeast, to follow the retreating French. Verdy suggests that Moltke was anxious to renew the battle on August 17. Since Bazaine was engaged in a movement to put his army more or less where Moltke wanted it, this has generally been discounted and certainly as soon as he had reached the battlefield, Moltke took no steps to re-establish contact with the enemy, expressly forbidding

Prince Frederick Charles, commander of the German Second Army (Pflugk-Harttung)

Steinmetz to embark on any aggressive operations. In any case, the decision that the French should be attacked on the following day was made by noon, and the orders were issued as early as 2 p.m. The timing of this has attracted considerable comment: Hönig in particular noted that it was due to the great age of the King, who had been on the battlefield since 6.00am following a lengthy ride from Pont á Mousson and was proposing to return there for the night. Nonetheless, although critical of the reasons for the orders going out so soon, (albeit very tactfully) Hönig observes that 'in no other instance had Moltke's great designs been so clearly expressed in an order as was the case here.'[3] This order, which was issued from Flavigny at 1.45 p.m., read as follows:

> The Second Army will start tomorrow, 18th, at 5.00 a.m. and will advance in echelon (from the left) between the Yron and Gorze streams, (roughly speaking between Ville Yron and Rezonville). The VIII Corps is to join on to this movement on the right wing of the Second Army. The VII Corps will at first have the task of securing the movement of the Second Army against possible enterprises from the direction of Metz. Further decision of His Majesty will depend on the enemy's measures. Reports to His Majesty are to be sent for the present to the height south of Flavigny.[4]

At the time of this order, Moltke certainly knew that the French were pulling back from Rezonville through Gravelotte. Such reports as he had from further north, out of sight of the headquarters, were conflicting; although pointing to a retreat on Verneville, they gave no indication of the French movements beyond that place, and Moltke himself allowed that as an alternative to concentrating on Metz, the French might be 'retiring by the two roads which still remained open, by Étain and Briey.'[5] His conclusion that this course might be adopted by the French was based on a belief that a concentration on Metz would be strategically quite wrong.

Moltke's order was, according to Hönig, deliberately imprecise. It gave no statement as to the assumed position of the French; it gave no battle objective to Frederick Charles; it gave no instructions as to the employment of cavalry; above all, it gave orders direct to two of the corps of the First Army without giving a reason for this unusual step (although by now Moltke's mistrust of Steinmetz was considerable). On the other hand, it ensured that the German army would be moving forward, their exposed right flank being covered by Steinmetz, able to act in whatever manner the actual position of the French dictated. What Moltke could see was that the French retreat after August 16 had immensely strengthened his strategic position, but it is open to doubt that his army commanders saw it so clearly and the operational decisions which they took on August 18 were by no means what Moltke intended or the situation demanded.

Steinmetz was greatly enraged by the order as 'wanting in consideration' in depriving him of direct control of two thirds of his army, and he proceeded thereafter to behave as if this had not happened.[6] His annoyance can have had no beneficial effect on his impetuosity on the following day. At all events, Steinmetz, still cross, reported on the night of August 17 the movements he had ordered for all three of his corps on the basis of what he considered the considerable danger to the VII Corps from the direction of the valley of the Moselle. Moltke would have none of it. His firm response next morning at 4 a.m. was to reinforce his previous instructions; direct orders would be given during the day on the battlefield. He explained that if 'the enemy's army throws itself into Metz, a right wheel will be made by our army. Direct support of the First Amy will if required be given by the second line of the Second Army.'[7] After sending this order, he set off from Pont á Mousson.

In any case, as the Germans moved forward, Steinmetz was not in the right place to act as a pivot for the advance. Obsessed with the notion of a threat down the Moselle valley, he did not pursue, on August 17, the advance of the VII corps up to Gravelotte, leaving it instead in the narrow Mance valley. Next morning, still sulking, he did not make his appearance until 8 a.m. on the plateau south west of Gravelotte. Frederick Charles, on the other hand, rode out of Mars la Tour at 5.30 on August 18, quite sure that the French had gone north to Conflans – something they could only have done if they had been confident that they were not very closely pursued. His aim was, therefore, simply to march north in concentrated masses rather than long columns and decide later 'whether it will be eventually necessary for the Second Army to make a wheeling movement to the right or to the left.'[8] The quality of the intelligence available to him of the enemy movements was not, however, assisted by a decision that the bulk of his cavalry should be kept in the rear. He also did not improve matters by pulling the Guard Corps across from his extreme left to his centre; since the XII Corps was moving north via Mars la Tour, it thus delayed the march of the Guard Corps. Moltke was, later, rather inaccurately and unfairly critical of this move. On the right of the Second Army, nearest the French positions, marched the XI Corps while the III and X Corps followed close behind. The II Corps was coming from much further back and would reach the battle later in the day.

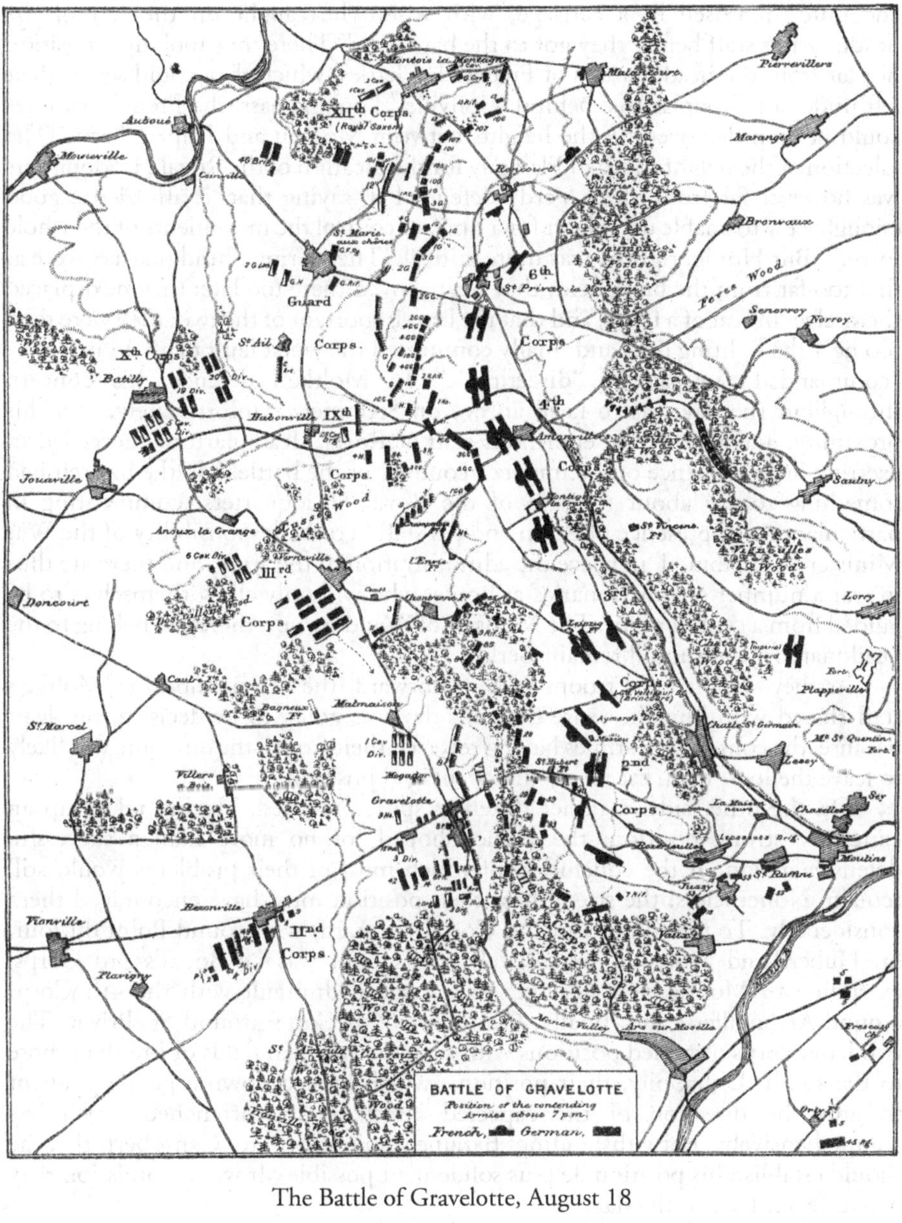

The Battle of Gravelotte, August 18

It was another glorious day with a cloudless sky and the prospect of excellent visibility. By noon, the temperature had risen to 86°F. Royal Headquarters, coming up from Pont á Mousson, arrived at Flavigny at 6 a.m. Verdy might well not have been in the party having, to his horror, overslept, waking to find the quarters occupied by the staff strangely quiet. As he was beginning to panic, he encountered Stosch in a carriage, with whom he caught up the rest of the headquarters staff before they got to the battlefield. There they took up a position not far from the headquarters of Frederick Charles, which they could see to their left under a tall poplar tree behind Vionville.[9] Looking east, the French batteries could be seen deployed on the heights between Moscou and Leipzig farms. The selection of the height south of Flavigny for the location of the Royal Headquarters was however far from ideal. Verdy defended it, saying that 'it afforded a good enough view to enable us, at least for a time, to control the movements of the whole force.'[10] But Hönig, rightly, was more critical: 'The German headquarters were at first too far from the battlefield; they next arrived there too late; they next placed themselves in rear of a flank, and that the least important of the two; they were then too near the fighting line, and finally committed the worst fault of all, in that they "commanded" instead of "directing."'[11] In Moltke's defence, his concern throughout the day was to keep an eye on Steinmetz. Unfortunately, even his proximity, and that of the enormous staff at Royal Headquarters, succeeded in exerting little influence on Steinmetz's conduct of the battle. Moltke himself had something to say about the size of the Royal Headquarters, commenting in particular on the presence of Roon and his staff. To the responsibility of the War Minister he attributed 'in peace the administration of the army, and there are thus in war a number of functionaries at home, who will only allow themselves to be guided from a central point. The Minister of War does not, therefore belong to the headquarters, but should remain Berlin.'[12]

As they watched the troops moving forward, the key members of Moltke's staff shared with him the sense that this day was going to be decisive, not least because, the contending armies having reversed their fronts, the outcome was likely to leave the loser in an especially disadvantaged position.

On the other side, a rather different spirit prevailed. Having taken up an extremely strong position, the French hoped for no more than a successful defensive action, at the conclusion of which most of their problems would still remain. Nonetheless, the strength of their position must have encouraged them considerably. To the south, the 2nd Corps (Frossard) was around Point du Jour, St. Hubert and Moscou; immediately to its right was Le Boeuf's 3rd Corps, extending to Montigny la Grange; then came Ladmirault with the 4th Corps around Amanvillers; and, finally, Canrobert's 6th Corps around St. Privat. The two latter corps occupied positions with much more open fields of fire than those to the south. Unhappily, their positions, which looked down a gentle gradient towards the direction of the expected attack, were entrenched much less comprehensively, notwithstanding Bazaine's injunction to Canrobert that he should establish his position 'le plus solidement possible'. It was an omission they would regret later in the day.

Having thus provided for his subordinates a position that was, with one major flaw, tactically extremely well chosen, Bazaine evidently was disposed not to interfere in their conduct of the ensuing battle. He posted his reserve, Bourbaki's Guard Corps, at Plappeville, thus reinforcing his left, a further reflection of his anxiety that Moltke aimed to drive him away from Metz. In consequence, the weakness of Canrobert's exposed right flank, in the air north of St. Privat, went unsupported.

Bazaine's mind was still entirely dominated by the security that the fortress of Metz would appear to afford his army. It was its relation to this source of strength that determined his objectives in falling back after Vionville-Mars la Tour. On the one hand, he was determined not to lose touch with Metz while, on the other, he was anxious to take up a position that would give him some hope of later regaining his freedom to manoeuvre. Beyond this, he seems to have had no plan. Jarras, his Chief of Staff, saw him as simply waiting for chance to give him an opportunity. The problem was, as Hönig pointed out, that Bazaine could only attain both his objectives by ensuring that his right wing was not defeated, and his initial deployment laid so heavy an emphasis on the left and the protection of his links with Metz that his other objective became unattainable.[13] And Bazaine displayed little interest in the possibilities for a counter-stroke that his flank position in relation to the German line of advance might have been intended to provide. When Le Boeuf reported the northward movement across his front of Frederick Charles' Second Army, which was clearly evident by 9 a.m. from the clouds of dust visible from the French positions, he appears not for a moment to have entertained the idea of a forward move.

For some hours the undisturbed progress of the German deployment continued. The only sign of hostilities was the continuing outpost activity in front of the First Army, and the uncertainty at Royal Headquarters as to French intentions persisted as late as 9.30 a.m.[14] At that time, observations of troops visible on the heights in the direction of Metz suggested the possibility of a northward movement, probably towards Briey, and Moltke so informed Frederick Charles.[15] In the meantime, preparations began for an advance by Manstein's IX Corps through Verneville. Subsequently, however, it became clear that the French remained in great strength in the First Army's front. By 10.30 a.m., Moltke concluded that the French proposed to stand and fight between Point du Jour and Montigny la Grange, and he ordered Frederick Charles to move his left wing, comprising the XII and Guard Corps, towards Batilly where they would be placed to prevent any resumption of a French movement on Briey or to attack Amanvillers.[16] The order contemplated a simultaneous assault by both armies, and this instruction was confirmed personally by Moltke to Sperling, Steinmetz's Chief of Staff. The 10.30 order was, of course, quite incorrect in its assumption that the French right flank could be turned by a movement on Amanvillers, and as soon as reports began to indicate that the French right extended beyond that place, Frederick Charles sought, at 11.30, to postpone the attack of Manstein's IX Corps until the XII and Guard Corps got into position. He was too late. Acting on the earlier orders received, and tempted by the opportunity to surprise the French who had deployed no outposts, Manstein's artillery began the battle shortly before noon, shelling French positions due east of Verneville. This step Manstein took in spite of the fact that it was clear from Verneville that he would not strike the French right flank, which clearly extended to the north; but the tactical opportunity seemed too good to miss. As soon as Manstein's artillery opened fire, Moltke sent a stern warning to Steinmetz: 'the fight we now hear is only a partial engagement in front of Verneville, and does not imply a general attack by the First Army, which ought not to show large masses of troops but only artillery to prepare for attack later on.'[17]

Manstein's decision was gravely mistaken. His attack fell chiefly upon Ladmirault's 4th Corps and the right of Le Boeuf's 3rd Corps. The latter was largely entrenched on the crest of the plateau with a force pushed forward to the Bois de Genivaux. The 4th Corps was not entrenched nor had it taken the opportunity of fortifying the farms in its front.[18] Although certainly surprised, Ladmirault quickly recovered, pushing his infantry forward and bringing artillery rapidly into action. As a result, Manstein's artillery soon found itself in a very exposed position and began to suffer heavy casualties both from artillery and also from rifle fire from the French skirmish line. Even when the infantry of the 18th and 25th Divisions came up, the French pressure did not slacken and the advance quickly ground to a halt as the French took full advantage of the wide and open fields of fire their positions gave them as well as the advantage in range which the chassepôt possessed over the needlegun. The 18th Division was split, the advance guard of three battalions moving towards the Chantrenne farm on the edge of the Bois de Genivaux and the next three battalions being directed to support the exposed artillery which stood on a spur south of the Bois de la Cusse. In fact, this force was driven back into the shelter of the woods, and was too late in any case to prevent one German battery being overrun by a French infantry assault that followed a most destructive spell from a mitrailleuse battery which had caused heavy casualties among men and horses. Only two guns were saved. For a while, however, the French took possession of the rest, although only able to get two of them back from the position, the other two being retaken later in the day. When Manstein was able to bring up the 25th Division, this too was thrust into the Bois de la Cusse. Its artillery took up a position on either side of a railway cutting and concentrated its fire on St. Privat but its infantry was, for the moment, quite unable to gain ground.

Meanwhile, Moltke's injunction to Steinmetz proved to be of little avail. The first to move was Goeben, whose troops were about Villers aux Bois and Rezonville. He had since 2 p.m. on the previous day been detached from the First Army, and now took the VIII Corps into action as soon as the sound of artillery was heard from the north. Goeben remained independent throughout the battle and, in fact, received no further orders from headquarters whatever.

At 12.15, he ordered his 15th Division to move up from Villers aux Bois to a jumping off position in the Mance Valley. By 12.30, Steinmetz could restrain himself no longer, ordering the artillery of Zastrow's VII Corps to open fire. The artillery formed a gun line to the south of the Gravelotte road and this was extended to the north by Goeben's artillery. Together this formidable artillery force, in position at first some 2,500 to 3,000 yards from its targets and, later, from somewhat closer positions, quite overmatched the French artillery which was, in any case, ineffective at this range. In consequence, the German artillery was able thus to prepare the infantry assault largely undisturbed. In fairness to Steinmetz, the use of artillery alone would have been consistent with Moltke's instructions; but he had no intention of leaving it at that.

The French position to be attacked by VII and VIII Corps was of immense natural strength, rising between 200 and 300 feet above the bed of the Mance ravine and it had been, in addition, artificially improved. The key points were the fortified farms of Moscou and Point du Jour, which had been linked by a system of trenches. In front of them, by the bridge over the Mance, was the walled farm of St. Hubert. The French right was held by Le Boeuf's 3rd Corps, which extended as far as La Folie where it was already engaged with Manstein's attack. Le Boeuf's left was composed of the divisions of Metman and Aymard. To his immediate left was Vergé's division of Frossard's corps, and then came Bastoul's division positioned to the southeast of Point du Jour (Laveaucoupet's division had been detached to garrison Metz). Finally, Bazaine held his extreme left with Lapasset's brigade from the 5th Corps, on the line Rozerieulles-Ste Ruffine-Moulins.

The 15th Division's attack was, in the first instance, obstructed by the strip of wood that linked Bois de Genivaux with the Bois de Vaux, the far edge of which was occupied by the French. On the right, von Wedell's 29th Brigade was not held up for long and by 2 p.m., had evicted the French from the wood opposite Point du Jour. To the left, however, von Strubberg's 30th Brigade experienced much greater difficulty, before pushing through the wood and on up the slope toward St. Hubert. By now some 116 guns were in action behind them as the German infantry fought its way forward. It was the artillery that silenced the defenders of St. Hubert long enough for the farm to be taken with a rush at about 3 p.m. Further to the right, the gravel pits south of St. Hubert had also been taken. The capture of St. Hubert prompted an assault, at first successful, upon the quarries of Rozerieulles. At the same time, however, on the other flank of the 15th Division, attacks towards Moscou made little progress.

Meanwhile, Steinmetz, paying close attention to these developments, could see that Goeben's advance was making progress. In a state of some considerable excitement, he rode over to Goeben at Gravelotte, believing that the French were pulling back troops perhaps to reinforce their distant right, and accordingly convinced that the moment had come for a decisive thrust. The discussion between them was brief. The hot-tempered and impetuous Steinmetz presented a marked contrast with the calm and thoughtful Goeben, who was able to learn little of what Steinmetz proposed to do, although he was shortly to be very much affected by it. In his fixed belief in the French retirement, Steinmetz decided to bring up part of the VII Corps' artillery and Hartmann's lst Cavalry Division, directing them to cross the Mance and take up a position south of the Gravelotte road, while he ordered the infantry of the VII Corps to advance. 'A more extravagant movement has rarely been attempted in war, or one less justified by the evident facts of the situation as well as by the results' wrote one historian of the campaign;[19] and for Hönig 'in short, Generals von Steinmetz and von Zastrow destroyed here in a few hours the glory of the whole of their great lives.'[20] Hearing the orders now issued by Steinmetz, the German officers concerned could hardly believe their ears. Steinmetz's arbitrary manner and overweening self-confidence was too well known to allow an argument, but von Zimmermann, the commander of the artillery of the VII Corps, passed the word privately to his subordinates to waste time, believing

General von Fransecky, commander of the German II Corps (Rousset/*Histoire*)

that he would thereby save his troops. For many of them, he succeeded; but not for all, as Hönig recorded.

> Since 1866, General von Steinmetz had regarded himself as infallible. It was, therefore, scarcely worth while for anyone to have an opinion, since throughout the zone of command of General von Steinmetz there was allowed to be but one opinion, his own. Such a general of necessity produced on the people around him the effect of a nightmare, while to Moltke he seemed a surly army leader, troublesome, difficult to manage, and a hindrance; and so he was indeed![21]

The movement was utterly disastrous; four batteries followed by several regiments from the lst Cavalry Division came forward and were at once subjected to a violent artillery barrage as well as to heavy mitrailleuse and rifle fire. One battery was forced back at once; and after sustaining heavy losses, the cavalry turned about and retreated to Gravelotte. Displaying immense courage, the other batteries held their position. The cavalry retirement affected the infantry, however. The French had not, in fact, been preparing to withdraw as the obstinate Steinmetz had convinced himself but had, instead, a reserve at hand, and seeing the disastrous outcome of the cavalry and artillery advance, launched a local counter-attack which retook the Rozerieulles quarries. In the ensuing retreat, Steinmetz and his staff came under heavy fire, and crowds of retiring German infantry took refuge in the Mance ravine. The time was by now about 5 p.m. and for a while there was a lull in the battle. Not surprisingly, the situation gave rise to mounting tension at the Royal Headquarters, from which even Moltke was not immune. When the

King became impatient at the lack of progress, Moltke's pent up feelings burst out, as Waldersee observed.

> After some time the King was again indignant and expressed himself to Moltke complaining of the troops and of their not gaining ground. Moltke replied with equal heat: "They are fighting for Your Majesty like heroes!" "I am the best judge of that," the King retorted. Whereupon Moltke gave spur to his horse and dashed forward down the incline towards Gravelotte.[22]

Thus far at any rate, the French could regard themselves as having achieved a distinct tactical success in this part of their front. It is, however, perhaps putting it rather too high for Professor Howard to suggest that 'the whole German position on this front was at the mercy of a strong well-timed French counter-attack';[23] to be effective, such a counter-attack would need preparation and would need to overcome the still immensely superior German artillery, to say nothing of the fresh troops not yet committed. Steinmetz's failure for the moment, however, left him uncertain what to do next. Although he could have pursued an attack against the extreme left of Bazaine's position by attacking Lapasset's brigade, he reported to Moltke at 4.15 merely that "the battle in the front was indecisive; and that in order to obtain success in this direction an attacking force against the right wing of the enemy would be necessary.'[24]

To this message, Moltke gave no response. What he lacked at this time was any clear information as to the progress of Frederick Charles. At 2 p.m., Royal Headquarters had moved up to Rezonville from Flavigny, and later (in the belief that Steinmetz was advancing on the plateau) had moved up to just south of Malmaison where it remained for the rest of the battle. There, Moltke and his staff

The Crown Prince of Saxony during the Battle of Gravelotte, painting by Zimmer (Scheibert)

found that matters were not going as well as they had imagined, and it was at this point that Brandenstein returned with news from the Second Army. In that part of the front, the movements of the Germans had led to a much more rapidly developing situation; but at least Moltke was able to learn that Frederick Charles was acting in accordance with the spirit of his intentions.[25]

By 2 p.m., the Crown Prince of Saxony had identified Roncourt as the extreme right of the French position and in consequence swung wider through Auboué with his 23rd Division, while one brigade of the 24th Division advanced on Ste. Marie aux Chênes. Meanwhile, the Guard Corps had reached Habonville. Frederick Charles had ordered a combined attack on Ste. Marie, and the village was taken by 3.30. Thereafter, the German artillery (that of the XII Corps north of Ste. Marie and that of the Guard Corps between St. Ail and Habonville) was able to concentrate on St. Privat, which was now clearly seen as the key to the French right. The French gunners could do nothing in reply. As the infantry of the XII and Guard Corps moved up, the X and III Corps were coming up behind. The lull in the fighting that had occurred on the German right coincided with that on the left, but here the French could not congratulate themselves on any tactical success. The strength that the Germans were developing in front of Canrobert and Ladmirault boded very ill indeed for the security of Bazaine's right.

In each sector of the battlefield, however, events were now to take another dramatic turn. On the German right, the II Corps under von Fransecky was approaching by way of Rezonville and Gravelotte. This corps was placed under the orders of Steinmetz, following the report made by his capable Quarter-Master, von Wartensleben, to Royal Headquarters at Malmaison. The spectacle of this powerful reinforcement moving forward prompted the French to try to forestall a

Prince August of Württemberg, commander of the Prussian Guard (Rousset/*Histoire*)

German offensive by a counterstroke from Moscou and Point du Jour. The French artillery, which had been largely quiescent for some time, burst out afresh and the French infantry poured down the hill towards the Germans. The one remaining German battery under Gnügge was, however, still in its position below St. Hubert, and although the observers at Malmaison feared that it had been swept away in the assault, when the smoke cleared it could be seen still in action. The French attack had not been properly co-ordinated between Frossard and Le Boeuf, and in spite of a temporary success on the part of the French 55th Regiment from Vergé's division,[26] it was stopped short of the woods and the assailants soon fell back to their start line. In the meantime, Goeben had four battalions from the 32nd Brigade in hand, and pushing up from the Mance ravine, they joined the already overcrowded garrison of St. Hubert in time to see off the last of the French counterstroke, although otherwise unable to add anything to the German effort (except, unwittingly, to be the cause of some temporary but severe chaos when part of a regiment of Hussars following them up to the front line panicked and rushed pell-mell to the rear).

The arrival of the II Corps gave rise to another moment of disagreement between Moltke and the King. Fransecky and his corps had marched all the way from Pont á Mousson and were keen to go into action. It was believed at Malmaison, by the King at any rate, that the Germans were a good deal more established on the heights than was, in fact, the case, and he overruled the protests of Moltke, who subsequently, although very obliquely, reported the dispute in his account of the war. 'It would have been more proper if the Chief of the General Staff of the army, who was personally on the spot at the time, had not permitted this movement at so late an hour of the evening', adding that it 'could hardly be

General Ladmirault, commander of the French 4th Corps (Rousset/*Histoire*)

expected' to be decisive.[27] In fact, his disapproval was total; and when the King insisted on the attack, he turned and silently walked away from the King, pretending to be otherwise occupied. The point was not lost on observers of the scene. It was a rare demonstration of public dissent on Moltke's part; and he removed himself from Royal Headquarters for the rest of the battle.[28]

Moltke's recognition of the pointlessness of the proposed assault was not, therefore, enough to save the II Corps from the consequences. Nor could Fransecky, who now found himself under the orders of the choleric Steinmetz, and who saw the impossibility of the task, do anything about it. It was, in fact, even more hazardous than supposed, because the terrain meant that the II Corps must advance up the Gravelotte road, and the orders given by Steinmetz compounded this by directing a frontal assault on Point du Jour. Darkness was falling as the II Corps advanced. The German artillery was no longer able to dominate the battlefield for fear of shelling its own troops. In all the confusion, as the leading troops of the II Corps came up, they opened fire on a body of troops near St. Hubert which it was believed, incorrectly, had fallen to the enemy. There were by now 59 companies collected at St. Hubert. These held their position but the troops to the south upon whom the fire fell, panicked and broke, followed by stragglers who, during the day, had collected in the Mance ravine. The whole disorganised stream fled to the rear. The II Corps could make no headway and there was little it could do but hold the line.

Further north, however, things had been going better for the Germans. After the lull at about 5 p.m., the Saxons were beginning to envelop Roncourt from the direction of the Bois D'Auboué and the position of the French was now becoming extremely hazardous. At this point, the Guard Corps was moving up from St. Ail

General von Manstein, commander of the German IX Corps (Rousset/*Histoire*)

The Prussian assault on St Privat (Pflugk-Harttung)

towards St. Privat, a movement that prompted a further advance by Manstein on Amanvillers with the 3rd Guard Brigade, which was now under his orders, and the 49th Brigade. It was an attack which suffered heavy losses from French rifle fire, and achieved very little. As usual, however, the artillery was well forward; 'wherever the infantry passed to the decisive assault, the artillery, as at Gravelotte, advanced absolutely into the line of skirmishers and supported the sister arm, fighting with it shoulder to shoulder.'[29]

Meanwhile, observing the Saxon advance from the north and northeast which appeared to be developing well, Prince August decided, at about 5.15, that the moment had come to attack St. Privat. He was tragically wrong. Von Pape, commanding the lst Guard Division, sought to point out his error, drawing attention to the fact that St. Privat had not yet been reduced by artillery fire. The Prince argued with him, rejecting Pape's claim that the Saxon artillery had been silent for an hour. Horrified at the projected attack, Pape continued to protest, suggesting that the Prince should go a little way and see for himself. 'No, I will not,' snapped the Prince. 'Do as you're told. You always want the last word'.[30] With that, Pape turned to execute an order quite as futile as some of those given by Steinmetz at the other end of the line. The Guard moved forward up the slope to St. Privat, suffering enormous losses from the French who were shooting down from positions with unbroken fields of fire. The attack was pinned down some 500 yards short of its objective, and no further advance would be possible until the Saxon presence was felt. In the 4th Brigade, only one field officer remained unwounded.[31]

The effect of the Saxon advance was, fortunately, not long delayed. By 6 p.m., the Saxons had made their way from Montois to the rear of Roncourt, and the progressive collapse of the French right began. Occupied as he was by the threat from the Guard Corps, Canrobert had no troops to spare to strengthen his extreme right flank. Bourbaki, with the Imperial Guard which was acting as Bazaine's

The Hessians attack the farm at Champenois during the Battle of Gravelotte, painting by Röchling (Rousset/*Histoire*)

reserve had, somewhat earlier, sent off Picard's division towards Ladmirault; but Bourbaki had no prospect of reaching Canrobert with the rest of his force in time to be of help since it was, by 7 p.m., behind Bois de Saulny. In consequence, Canrobert felt obliged to begin to pull back the troops on his extreme right.[32] At first the retirement was effected in good order under the cover of artillery fire from the direction of the Bois de Jaumont but when, at 7.30, St. Privat was stormed by the Saxons from the north and the Prussian Guard from west and south, Canrobert's position became untenable and disorganised masses of French troops fell back towards the Moselle.

The effect on Ladmirault's 4th Corps was immediate. Frederick Charles ordered a fresh assault by Manstein's IX Corps on Amanvillers supported by a brigade of the III Corps that was now ready to hand; but it soon proved unnecessary as Ladmirault's troops also reeled back from the positions they had defended so effectively all day.

Bourbaki meanwhile, appalled by the spectacle of the disintegrating French right, turned Picard's division about, which was preceded by its artillery and rejoined his main body at Plappeville, having made no useful contribution to the outcome of the day. The battle, even if the commanders in chief on either side did not yet know it, was lost and won, and its outcome was of immediate and enormous strategic importance. Bazaine now had no choice but to pull back. He did so with apparent equanimity, sitting quietly down to dinner at 7 p.m. and apparently thinking that all that had happened was that the French retreat would have to take place a day early. He was, perhaps, relieved that at any rate his worst fears, of a German thrust to cut him off from Metz, had not been realised.

Dejected French prisoners following Gravelotte, painting by Dupray (Rousset/*Histoire*)

On the other side, Moltke was profoundly unhappy. After watching the final and unsuccessful attacks on Point du Jour, he rode gloomily back with Verdy to rejoin Royal Headquarters, unaware of Frederick Charles' success and grimly determined to fight again next day. When they rediscovered the Royal party at Rezonville, Verdy had his head bitten off by what he described as 'a superior officer' for protesting at the latter's advice to the King, which he had overheard, that there should be no renewal of the attack next day.[33] Moltke firmly put a stop to this kind of advice. When news came at midnight of the victory of the Second Army, the staff at Royal Headquarters were finally able to settle down for the night at Rezonville, some of them in cramped and uncomfortable lodgings and others in the open air, in the knowledge that, however dearly bought, Moltke's object had been achieved. Bazaine was securely shut up in Metz.

The casualties, especially on the German side, were appalling, amounting to 20,163 killed and wounded, of which the Guard Corps alone sustained 8,932. On the French side no such accurate figure exists but their total losses were estimated at more than 13,000.

That the German armies should have been in a position to fight this battle in these positions at all was due directly to the calm and clear-headed strategy which Moltke had followed since the frontier battles. It was the necessary completion of the work begun at Vionville-Mars la Tour. Even before August 16, Moltke had entirely had the upper hand in his personal duel with Bazaine, and all that now remained was to employ the superb German troops to slam tight the door of the prison into which Moltke had manoeuvred his adversary. But the lack of tactical skill displayed by some of Moltke's subordinates exacted a fearful price for his decisive strategic victory. Not least of the mistakes was the over-eagerness to start the battle, a tendency that had been apparent on a number of previous occasions in the campaign already. Moltke, anxious to achieve a simultaneous attack, was absolutely opposed to the piecemeal commitment of units that, in fact, took place.

Blame for the errors must certainly be assigned to Frederick Charles for his muddled thinking (and muddled deployment) at the outset of the battle (although he substantially redeemed this once he had divined the true extent of the French position); to Steinmetz for an obstinacy and irresponsibility that has the power to shock even a century later; to Prince August for a similar and breathtaking lack of judgment; and to the King, for his blinkered insistence on the hopeless assault of the II Corps. Beyond this, however, there can be nothing but praise for the courage of the German troops. Sometimes well led, sometimes badly, they displayed a skill and courage that richly deserved a victory and that, in the end, is what they achieved – a victory that confirmed the decisive outcome of the fighting of the previous week, and set the stage for the drama of Sedan.

11

The Army of Châlons

On the morning after the battle of Gravelotte-St. Privat, Moltke lost no time in taking the crucial decisions that were now to lead to the decisive conclusion to the campaign. He had spent the night at Rezonville and, while still unaware of the success of Frederick Charles on the left wing, at 8.30 that night had ordered the Chiefs of Staff of the various corps engaged in the battle to assemble at Caulre Farm the following morning at 5 a.m. By the time that meeting was held, the extent of the German victory was becoming clearer. At the meeting, Stiehle, Frederick Charles's Chief of Staff, set out what needed to be done that day to ensure that Bazaine was securely shut up in Metz. It was time now for Moltke to consider the strategy to be adopted in the new situation.He had now achieved the principal objective which had informed all his day to day decisions during the campaign so far, which was to prevent the Army of the Rhine falling back on the support of the rest of the French Army.'On the German side the view had predominated from the beginning that it must lie in the interests of the French to effect with the least possible delay the junction of the Army of the Rhine with the rearward military forces.'[1]

Any attempt by Bazaine to achieve that junction was now very much more hazardous, but in the orders which Moltke issued as early as 11 a.m. that morning, he addressed the possibility 'that the French army which has been thrown back upon Metz might risk the attempt to break through to the west.'Although he moved with impressive speed in deciding upon the strategy now to be pursued, he knew he must also take account of the practical and logistical problems faced by his troops after a gruelling series of battles.

> After the events of the last few days it is needful and possible to give the troops sufficient rest and to bring up reserves to fill up the gaps caused by our losses.It is also requisite that the armies should keep abreast during the further advance towards Paris, in order to be able to confront in sufficient strength the new formations which are assembling probably at Châlons.[2]

The issue of the orders was a remarkable demonstration of Moltke's speed of decision and the efficiency of his staff.Hohenlohe points out that the Royal Headquarters could not by then have been able to assess the casualties sustained the day before.

> Under these circumstances it is surprising that the Supreme Command should have been able to distribute the available forces so correctly for the two principal objects of operation, and that as early as 11 a.m on 19 August, not only the requisite and most important strategically decisions had been taken for the further measures, but that the necessary orders to that effect should also have been prepared and issued.[3]

Moltke assigned to Frederick Charles the task of besieging Metz, giving him the whole of the First Army together with four corps from his own army (the II, III,

Members of the Army of Châlons in camp, by Pallandre (Rousset/*Combattants*)

IX and X Corps), a reserve division under von Kummer, and the lst and 3rd Cavalry Divisions. Placing this entire force under the command of Frederick Charles had the additional benefit of solving the problem of what to do about the irascible Steinmetz who was, within three weeks, provoked into a quarrel and sent home to the governorship of Posen.

A new Army of the Meuse was formed, comprising the Guard, IV and XII Corps with the 5th and 6th Cavalry Divisions, and placed under the command of the Crown Prince of Saxony, of whom Moltke had formed a very high opinion.To this army, in conjunction with the Third Army, was assigned the task of dealing with what was left of the French forces outside Metz. Moltke, with the initiative firmly in his hands, intended to lose no time in following up his advantage.For the moment, the Third Army was ordered to halt for the present at the Meuse because Moltke intended that it should not get too far ahead of the Crown Prince of Saxony's army in their joint westward advance.

That afternoon, Moltke drove back to Royal Headquarters at Pont à Mousson with Verdy and Winterfeld. Moltke was even more taciturn than usual, speaking only three times on the journey. Seeing a young dead NCO of the llth Regiment, he remarked 'this was the bravest of the brave'. Later he reflected: 'I have learned once more that one cannot be too strong on the field of battle'. And finally, as they drove in the evening sunshine into Pont à Mousson, he mused, 'what would be our feelings now, if we had been beaten?'[4]

The staff of the new Army of the Meuse was at once organised and, as Chief of Staff, Moltke chose Major General von Schlotheim. He had hitherto been commanding the Hessian Cavalry Brigade, but had served as Chief of Staff of the Elbe army in 1866. His task was to get his army on the road westward as quickly as possible, preceded by the cavalry who must now seek out the remaining French forces. No time was lost and, on August 20, all the units of the Army of the Meuse were on the move.

At the headquarters of the Third Army, news of the outcome of the Battle of Gravelotte had been awaited anxiously throughout the night of August 18/19.It was not until 5 a.m. that news was brought to the Crown Prince by Major von Hahnke, who during August 18 had ridden up to Royal Headquarters to see what was going on, and during the night came all the way back. The Crown Prince, who had himself been restrained with difficulty by Blumenthal from going to witness the battle, again 'was irresistibly drawn to join the King' but, again, accepted that he must stay with his own army.[5] Blumenthal received instructions from Podbielski that the Third Army must stay where it was, an instruction that, in the light of his previous complaints, rather unreasonably irked him because he felt that the Third Army should now push forward 'else the morale of the army will suffer,' in contrast to the views of his Royal master who 'wished to concentrate and move backwards one march.'[6]

Next day, they both drove out from Nancy up the Moselle valley to Pont à Mousson. Blumenthal found the King 'intensely strained' and 'quite nervous'[7] while the Crown Prince noted that he was 'quite cut up by the frightful losses.'[8] Both of them observed the contrast with Moltke. Blumenthal, who had of course been in conflict with Moltke on more than one occasion and usually confided his disagreements with Moltke to his diary, found that he 'was cold and calm, as always, and was not troubled with cares, a state of mind I cannot share with him.'[9] Rather more generously, the Crown Prince observed that Moltke 'remains always entirely unperturbed, confident, clear-headed and firmly resolved to move forward on the main objective – Paris.'[10] During the discussions at Royal Headquarters on this day, the outline of Moltke's plan for the westward advance was explained and the Third Army was given another day's rest as part of Moltke's plan that it should not be more than one day's march ahead of the Crown Prince of Saxony. It was generally supposed that the decisive battle might be fought in the Châlons area, to which it was assumed the assembling French forces were being directed. Before leaving Pont à Mousson the Crown Prince had the opportunity of a discussion with Bismarck whom he found 'moderate minded' and 'speaking very reasonably.'[11] Next day, Blumenthal enjoyed 'a blessed day of rest'[12] at Vaucouleurs, while to the north the Army of the Meuse continued to move westwards, with the IV Corps at Commercy, the Guard Corps at Woël and Hannonville and the XII Corps at Jeandelize. The cavalry divisions were already sweeping far ahead with, on the right, the 5th Cavalry Division at Étain, the 6th at Fresnes, the Saxon Cavalry Division at Hennemont and the Guard Cavalry Division at St. Maurice sous les Côtes.

As the various corps of the Third Army in position along the Meuse prepared for their advance, their staffs reflected on the likely course of the decisive struggle that lay ahead. At the headquarters of the two Bavarian corps, 'plans of the camp of Châlons, which had casually been taken away in remembrance of days spent there, were now brought out.'[13] The terrain over which the campaign was now to be fought was well suited to an army seeking to bar an advance on Paris from Lorraine. In the south, the gentler slopes were separated by many rivers and streams; the heights were often wooded. Further north, on the edge of the hilly region of the Argonne, the forests were denser; the Argonne stretched twenty to thirty miles westwards, and here, in wet weather, movement off the roads was often extremely difficult. Further west still, the great rivers of the Seine, the Marne and the Aisne, running through deep valleys, gave further opportunities for a sustained defence. To the north-east, the extended valley that runs west from Longwy is broken by the rivers Chiers and Meuse; at Mézières the Meuse bends northwards into the thick forest of the Ardennes, while further east the Belgian frontier runs through the forests and hills barely half a dozen miles from the two rivers. Across the country into which the Germans were now to advance, the main roads ran principally southeast-northwest; some of these were obstructed by the French possession of the fortresses of Toul and Verdun. And the east-west railways that ran Nancy-Châlons-Paris and Metz-Mézières-Reims were, for the same reason, closed to the Germans.

On August 16, Napoleon had bidden farewell to Bazaine, saying: 'To your charge I commit the last army of France. Think of the Prince Imperial,' and added that the army should get on to the road to Verdun with all speed. After an adventurous journey by road, he himself reached Verdun at about 1 p.m. and then travelled by train to Châlons, although the only rail transport that could be found for him was a third class carriage, and he did not arrive at Châlons until the early hours of the following morning.

On August 17, there was a Council of War so that the French leaders might take stock of their position. Into the camp at Châlons had been pouring all the available field troops left to the Second Empire. MacMahon, with his own 1st Corps, and Conseil-Dumesnils division of 7th Corps had, after the Battle of Wörth, fallen back westwards at first by road to Saverne, a retreat which he continued to manage with sufficient speed and skill to avoid further contact with the Crown Prince's army. On the evening of August 7, his force reached Sarrebourg, into which also now marched de Faillys 5th Corps. By August 10 MacMahon, ignoring all suggestions that he might move north to rejoin the main army around Metz, had reached Luneville. From here part of his troops went direct by rail to Châlons and the remainder, marching safely out of range of the Third Armys cavalry, went to Chaumont and then by rail to Châlons.

Towards Châlons also proceeded in due course the rest of Felix Douay's 7th Corps. One division of the corps had been stationed at Belfort, where it had succeeded in reducing itself to a chaotic shambles. It first advanced to Mulhouse where it encountered no opposition; then, on receiving the news of the battle of Wörth, it retreated precipitately on Belfort once more. There, it was in due course on August 12, joined by the remaining division of 7th Corps, and they remained there for four days until ordered to join the Army of Châlons by rail, although they did not, in fact, catch up with the army until August 22 at Reims after a prolonged, exhausting and uncomfortable journey. In addition to these three corps, there was also formed at Châlons a new 12th Corps, the command of which was at first assigned to General Trochu, who was one of the central figures in the anguished discussions which took place on August 17.

Those present at the meeting had, of course, no idea of the real outcome of the battle of Vionville-Mars la Tour, although there were, as usual, persistent rumours of a French victory. The problem which they faced at this conference was extremely intricate, involving political as well as military considerations. It was plain to all that the future of the Army of Châlons was closely linked with the stability, even the survival, of the Imperial regime, and the decisions finally taken were with this in mind. Napoleon, who was suffering acutely from the effects of the journey the previous day, sat silent and benumbed while the generals argued about what to do. The prime mover of the decision-making process that day was Prince Napoleon, and it was his view that finally prevailed because he enjoyed a good deal of popular esteem. It was agreed that General Trochu was to be appointed Governor of Paris and that he should return at once to the capital, taking with him the rowdy and disaffected Gardes Mobiles de la Seine, whose conduct daily depressed still further the morale of the army. Napoleon, to whom his cousin remarked at one stage of the discussion that 'you abdicated the government at Paris; at Metz you have now abdicated the command of the army,'[14] was also to return to Paris.Finally, MacMahon would, as soon as it was finally concentrated, march the Army of Châlons itself to the capital and there accept battle under the walls of the city. Napoleon's doubts as to the wisdom of his cousin's policy were overcome by MacMahon's firm conviction that a retreat on Paris was the correct military decision (as well as his reassurance that Napoleon could count on Trochu's loyalty).

MacMahon's appointment to the command of the Army of Châlons was more or less inevitable. He had been considered as a possible commander of the Army of the Rhine, as had Canrobert. MacMahon's defeat at Wörth, however, had disqualified him for that appointment, and Canrobert refused outright to accept it, so that Bazaine, although junior to both of them, was duly appointed. MacMahon was, however, now the most senior candidate still at large and he readily accepted command. Faure was appointed as Chief of Staff, and the energetic Ducrot succeeded to the command of the Ist Corps.Lebrun was appointed in Trochu's place as commander of the 12th Corps.

The Army of Châlons was, apart from the problems of its concentration, which were now more or less overcome, and its relatively low morale, not an inconsiderable fighting force. The new 12th Corps included Vassoigne's division of marines, who were troops of the highest quality; and although the Ist Corps had been badly mauled at Wörth, the 5th Corps and 7th Corps were largely intact.

The firmness of decision that had finally emerged from the conference on August 17 was not, however, to continue for long. In Paris the ministry of Emile Ollivier had fallen on August 9 (although not before he had meditated a coup d'etat against the opposition) after he had been assailed in the Chamber by deputies both from the Left and from the Right. Eugénie, who was not sorry to see the back of the Liberal ministry, at once appointed a new ministry headed by the 74 year old Count de Palikao (who, as General de Montauban had led the French forces in China in 1860, from whence he derived his Oriental title). Palikao assumed in addition the portfolio of Minister of War. The Empress and Palikao, when informed by telegram of the plan arrived at by the Châlons conference, were appalled. The reappearance of Trochu at midnight on August 17, who was as an Orleanist a decidedly suspect figure at these critical times, and the prospect of the return of the rebellious Gardes Mobiles, were regarded by both Eugénie and Palikao as developments not likely to be helpful in maintaining the regime. They were still more concerned, however, with the prospect of the retreats of the Army of Châlons on Paris which Palikao was quick to condemn as appearing as 'a desertion of the Army of Metz'. Eugénie was equally hostile to the suggestion that Napoleon himself should return to Paris, a move which she saw as threatening both his life and that of the dynasty. After lengthy and agitated discussion, a telegram was sent firmly advising both Napoleon and MacMahon to remain at Châlons, and Eugénie followed it up on August 18 with a letter couched in terms so peremptory that her secretary begged her, unsuccessfully, to moderate its text.

Meanwhile, the official communication from Bazaine of the outcome of the battle of Vionville-Mars la Tour, sent off from Metz at 11 p.m. on August 16, had reached Châlons on the afternoon of the following day. Bazaine reported that the army had held its ground in a hard day's fighting but that he was forced to fall back in the direction of Metz to resupply the army and that, having regard to the German positions in his front, he would probably have to take the northern route to Verdun. Napoleon, perhaps reading between the lines, responded to this message by asking Bazaine to tell him the true position 'so that I can act accordingly.' In the face of all these pressures, Napoleon was by now completely irresolute. His first response was a decision that neither he nor the army should go to Paris; but he changed his mind again, and on the morning of August 18, told MacMahon that he would start next day. Within an hour or two, he yet again changed his mind, and gave in to Palikao. This left MacMahon with the responsibility, and he endeavoured that day to seek instructions from Bazaine, who was nominally his superior. Unhelpfully if realistically, Bazaine replied that MacMahon's operations were 'at the moment entirely outside my zone of action.'[15] This, unfortunately, was the last direct contact with Bazaine's headquarters and MacMahon was now entirely on his own, dependent on irregular and unreliable intelligence of Bazaine's intentions and movements, and continually in receipt of pressing advice from Palikao. Next day, still hopeful of some guidance from Bazaine, MacMahon set out in a message to him the position as he saw it. 'If, as I believe, you are forced very shortly to retire, I do not know, owing to the distance which separates us, how I can hasten to your help without uncovering Paris. If you judge otherwise, let me know.'[16] But to this not unreasonable analysis, MacMahon got no reply. His position was unenviable, and now in his turn he vacillated under this pressure just as Napoleon had done.

In the absence of any really reliable information, but plainly now contemplating a move towards Bazaine, he telegraphed Palikao on August 20 to report his dilemma:

> the news received seems to indicate that the three armies are placed to intercept Bazaine by the routes through Briey, Verdun and St. Mihiel. Not knowing the direction of Bazaine's retreat, although I am ready to march tomorrow, I think I am going to remain camp until aware of the direction taken by Bazaine, be it north or south.[17]

Palikao could not give much help, replying that his only news was that on the evening of August 18 Bazaine was on a line between Amanvilliers and Sussy.

It became clear during these anxious days that the German cavalry was pushing forward, and there could be little doubt that it was followed closely by the main body of the Crown Prince's army. In this event, the camp of Châlons would be far too exposed a position in which to remain, and the news on August 20 that German cavalry was now only 25 miles away, finally compelled MacMahon to take the decision to break camp and set out for Reims. This was of its nature a compromise between the plan to retreat on Paris that had provoked such hostility in the government, and any more aggressive manoeuvre directed towards the oncoming Germans. In heavy rain, the Army of Châlons marched out towards Reims, leaving behind it a cavalry division whose mournful duty was to destroy the stores and equipment in the vast camp.

Palikao and the Council of Ministers did not share MacMahon's doubts as to the correct course of action. Any hesitation on his part in doing his utmost to relieve Bazaine could bring down the regime. The Army of Châlons must accordingly go to Metz, and to press this point upon its doubtful commander, Palikao sent August Rouher, the President of the Senate, to Reims on August 21st to see him.

He brought with him Palikao's latest scheme. This was a plan whereby false despatches were to be planted on the Crown Prince with the object of luring him forward to Paris while MacMahon slipped past to the north and marched directly to the relief of Bazaine. Just how long Palikao thought that the Germans might be deceived by this scheme is unclear; and the speed of march of the French armies so far in the war, had been, even at its briskest, unlikely to keep MacMahon for long out of harm's way. When, however, Rouher arrived at Reims, he found MacMahon in a more resolute frame of mind, having been convinced by the first day's march that no practical alternative to a retreat on Paris now existed for his army. He was also pretty well informed about the position of the Germans, although the advance of their cavalry, moving several days ahead of the main body, suggested to him that the Crown Prince was closer than he really was.[18] In the ensuing discussions, it was the Marshal who was the more persuasive, and Rouher was moved to co-operate in the drafting of the necessary proclamation to explain to the Army of Châlons to tell his soldiers what was proposed, in which the Marshal was to say 'My most ardent desire was to bring help to Marshal Bazaine; but this enterprise was impossible.'[19] This done, Rouher returned to Paris to cope with the predictable reactions of Palikao and the Empress.

Like most of the apparently firm decisions taken by the French during the preceding days, this one lasted only a few hours before it too went back into the melting pot. Quite apart from the response in Paris to what was proposed, there was another crucial development which brought to an end the last opportunity in which MacMahon and the Army of Châlons had in their hands the option of the only movement that could ensure their safety, at least temporarily. The decision that was now to be taken was to prove the crucial step that set MacMahon on the inexorable path that led to Sedan.

On the night of August 22, Bazaine's latest message arrived via the general commanding at Verdun, reporting on the outcome of the battle of Gravelotte and dated August 19. It arrived after the issue of the orders for the retreat on Paris but its influence was immediately decisive. After a brief description of the battle of

August 18, as a result of which he said his troops needed two or three days rest, Bazaine announced that his intention was to fight his way out 'via Montmédy to the Sainte-Menehould-Châlons road if it is not too strongly occupied; if it is I shall go on through Sedan and Mézières to reach Châlons.'[20] In the face of this clear evidence that Bazaine was about to march out towards a junction with him, MacMahon at once accepted that the proposed movement on Paris must be abandoned in favour of an advance towards Bazaine. Fresh orders to this effect were at once issued for the advance to commence next day and a message was sent to Bazaine to the effect that the Army of Châlons would, in two days, reach the Aisne. Shortly after this, there arrived from Paris the predictably outraged reaction of Palikao to Rouher's report of the projected retreat on the capital, but the decision to march to the east had, in any case, by now already been taken. Later during the night of August 22, a further message from Bazaine arrived, dated August 20, which repeated the information given in the earlier message but added the qualification that he would take the route proposed only if he could do so 'without compromising the army.'[21] Afterwards, MacMahon was to assert that this message was never given to him and that if he had received it, it would have convinced him that the right course was, after all, to fall back on Paris. Stoffel, who was now serving as Chief of the Intelligence Staff of the Army of Châlons, said that MacMahon had, indeed, received the message but had discounted its significance.[22] The point is not unimportant, for it was MacMahon's decision on August 22 from which directly flowed all that was to follow; and his performance before and after this message was certainly not such as to suggest that if he had seen it, it would have provided him with sufficient backbone to defy Palikao's express orders.

With the encouraging news from Bazaine now to hand, Palikao had firmly conveyed to the Emperor the views of the ministers.

'The decisions taken yesterday evening must be abandoned. No decree, no letter, no proclamation must be published. An aide de camp from the Ministry of War is leaving for Reims with all the necessary instructions. Not to help Bazaine would have the most deplorable consequences in Paris. In the face of such a disaster, it would be believed that the capital could not defend itself.'[23]

Napoleon was not disposed to argue, replying that they would be leaving next day for Montmédy; and, approving a decision that was to have important consequences, added: 'I accept Wimpffen in place of de Failly'[24] – the latter's performance having been seriously criticised from the early days of the war. Although his Emperor accompanied the army, MacMahon does not seem to have been much affected by any advice which his sick and lethargic sovereign might have offered. In the face of the explicit instructions which he received to march to Bazaine's relief, there was little he could do, short of resigning, but to comply. From his position, on August 22, the proposed march on Metz was perhaps in any case not necessarily entirely hopeless. He had, of course, wasted two days; he supposed the Crown Prince's army now to be approaching Vitry which was certainly correct, but that was well to the south and by very swift marching, he could confidently expect to reach the Meuse crossings between Stenay and Dun well before his adversary, wherever he actually was. If his cavalry were to screen his movements, he could be across the Meuse and well on the way towards Bazaine before he could be caught. As intended, the latter was to break out to the north of Metz through Thionville towards Montmédy. Indeed, it was not impossible that an opportunity might then arise for a convincing victory over a part of Moltke's forces which would by then be widely scattered. But the essential element in all of this was the speed with which the Army of Châlons was capable of marching and this, unfortunately, proved quite inadequate. Nor, in the event, were the French able to make effective use of their cavalry to conceal their intentions from the enemy.

12

MacMahon's Flank March

By nightfall on August 23, the whole of the Army of Châlons had closed up to the line of the River Suippe. Its most southerly unit, just north of the camp of Châlons, was the cavalry division of Bonnemains, while its most advanced unit at Monthois was the cavalry division of Margueritte. As the French moved up towards the Suippe, the magazines at the camp of Châlons had been set on fire.The Bavarian Official History considered the irony of the scene.

> The French corps during their march saw heavy clouds of smoke floating over the neighbourhood which they had been taught to regard as the school of future victories. As is shown by the journal of a superior officer who fell somewhat later, the sight of this destruction raised curious reflections in the breast of many an earnest and thinking man, curious reflections on this nursery of victory on the chalky plains near Mourmelon.[1]

To the self-imposed handicap with which the initial delay had burdened the Army of Châlons was now added a further difficulty, when it was discovered that serious supply difficulties must compel MacMahon to stick to the railway at least as far as Rethel, where severe food shortages could be made good. By August 24, Bonnemains' cavalry division had also moved up towards Rethel, passing behind the army; and around this city, where MacMahon had his headquarters, were the 12th Corps and the 5th Corps. The lst Corps was marching northeast and had reached, that night, a point about eight miles south of Rethel while the 7th Corps

The Army of Châlons on the march, painting by Chaperon (Rousset/*Histoire*)

had reached Contreuve to the southwest of Vouziers. Margueritte's cavalry division remained close to Monthois.

Regrettably, the next day saw relatively little progress on the part of the French. Instead of using his cavalry to scout to the south in search of his enemy, MacMahon moved Margueritte's division up to Le Chesne, leaving the 7th Corps, by now at Vouziers, as constituting the extreme right flank of the Army of Châlons. Bonnemains' cavalry division remained at Rethel, from where the 5th and 12th Corps had also made little progress, while the lst Corps had only got as far as Attigny on the Aisne. Continuing supply difficulties still retarded the progress of the French, especially on the part of the 7th Corps. MacMahon was by now painfully aware that his window of opportunity was shrinking visibly.

The contrast between the state of mind of the hapless MacMahon, writhing in a personal struggle between professional conviction and extreme moral pressure, and the icy determination of Moltke, could hardly have been greater. At Pont à Mousson, all the preliminary reports received from the German cavalry indicated clearly that Châlons was to be the point of concentration, not only for the corps of MacMahon and de Failly but also of the new units apparently now being assembled. On August 21, in an order of striking brevity, Moltke issued instructions to the Army of the Meuse and to the Third Army to take up the position Sainte-Menehould-Vitry by August 26. The Third Army's position would continue to be about a day's march further westward, with the intention of confronting the French in a position from which they could be attacked both in front and on the flank. The Crown Prince at Vaucouleurs was concerned that, in order to surround Châlons, he would be obliged to move with his columns at wide intervals, but the general feeling that the next phase of the war would be decisive was expressed by Blumenthal, who wrote that 'we are going to march straight on Paris and that is God's will.'[2] It had now become very cold for the time of year, and on August 23, when the forward march began, rain fell heavily.

On the day before Gravelotte, Royal Headquarters had been joined by two more distinguished visitors in the persons of Generals Sheridan and Forsyth from the United States. On August 19, Bismarck took Sheridan on a tour of the battlefields of Gravelotte. On the way back Sheridan had an opportunity of seeing Bismarck in action as an impromptu traffic policeman.

> Our route led through the village of Gorze, and here we found the streets so obstructed with wagons that I feared it would take us the rest of the day to get through, for the teamsters would not pay the slightest heed to the cries of our postillions. The Count was equal to the emergency, however, for, taking a pistol from behind his cushion, and bidding me keep my seat, he jumped out and quickly began to clear the street effectively, ordering wagons to the right and left. Marching in front of the carriage and making way for us till we were well through the blockade, he then resumed his seat, remarking, 'This is not a very dignified business for the Chancellor of the German Confederation, but it's the only way to get through.'[3]

Sheridan thereafter travelled with Royal Headquarters and continued to spend a good deal of time in Bismarck's company.

On August 22, the whole headquarters moved forward from Pont à Mousson to Commercy, remembered by the King as the town where he had been quartered as long ago as 1814, as the Allies advanced on Paris. When Sheridan and Forsyth reached the place they 'found that quarters had already been selected far us and our names written on the door with chalk.'[4] This kind of administrative efficiency enabled the Germans to overcome the continuing difficulty of accommodating the large entourage of schlachtenbummler. On the way to Commercy Busch watched curiously as Bismarck, walking uphill to ease the burden on the horses, led the way with Abeken, 'at the head of the procession for a quarter of an hour in great wide top boots which in size and shape reminded one of those one sees in portraits from the Thirty Years War.'[5] It was not just at Royal Headquarters that there were large numbers of visitors; on the same day, away to the south at Ligny, where the Third Army Headquarters were billeted, the Crown Prince 'came upon a whole gathering of Englishmen' on the castle keep and commented irritably in his diary: 'God knows I have no room for any more lookers-on, important as it is at the moment to have numbers of Englishmen at headquarters' – a reflection that showed that the Prussian concern with public relations had in no way abated.[6]

During August 23, as the German cavalry patrols spread out and moved forward in pouring rain, rumours began to trickle in to Moltke's headquarters that the French might be pulling out of the camp at Châlons, a development which became more likely as cavalry reports came in that all the villages east of there were clear of the enemy. It was obviously essential to obtain the fullest possible information about MacMahon's movements, and Moltke wrote to Blumenthal to bring him up to date.

> It would meet His Majesty's intentions if the cavalry divisions remained in front of the army the whole time and also on August 26. According to the reports received here it is not improbable that the enemy's army assembled at Châlons is marching away from there. In that case it is desirable to ascertain by the cavalry, pushed on and beyond and also to the north of Châlons, the precise direction of the enemy's march.[7]

By this date Moltke's staff had been able to prepare, from the interrogation of prisoners and a careful examination of all the intelligence that had been collected over the previous days, a detailed order of battle of the Army of Châlons, which it was able to circulate to all the units moving forward in pursuit of MacMahon.[8] During the day, the Germans made an attempt to seize the fortress of Toul, which had been unsuccessfully assaulted by the IV Corps a week before. Rather than accept the delay of bringing up heavy siege artillery, the corps artillery of the VI Corps was moved up to support an attack by the Bavarian infantry. The first summons to surrender was refused; in spite of a three hour bombardment that set the town on fire a further summons was also rejected. Since it seemed evident that the fortress could not be reduced by field artillery alone, the Germans gave up, contenting themselves with masking it with Landwehr troops.[9] By nightfall on the 23, apart from the reconnaissance towards Châlons, the German cavalry was scouting forward on a line Vitry-Revigny-Mondrecourt-Verdun, and both armies were making good progress. The Army of the Meuse had now closed up to that river, with the IV Corps across it at Commercy, while the Third Army was led by the V Corps which lay between St. Dizier and Ligny, and the XI Corps which was at Montiers sur Saulx. The II Bavarian Corps was between Tronville and Ligny, while the I Bavarian Corps was some ten miles behind at St. Aubin. The VI Corps was in the rear at Gondrecourt.

On August 24, first reports came in from the cavalry, now scouting over forty miles ahead of their corps, in confirmation that the great camp at Châlons had indeed been abandoned by the enemy; half a squadron of dragoons rode into Mourmelon and found that although considerable destruction had been wrought there by the burning of the main magazine, there were still large stores of provisions, tents and heavy guns. Another indication was an intercepted letter from a French officer suggesting that MacMahon intended to march to the relief of Metz. All of this led Moltke to point out to the Saxon Crown Prince the need to keep a close eye on Reims, and he suggested that the Reims-Longuyon-Thionville railway should be broken at several points in case this indeed proved to be the axis of future operations by MacMahon and Bazaine.[9]

At noon on August 24, as the German advance continued under cold overcast skies, Moltke arrived at the Third Army's Headquarters at Ligny for a discussion with Blumenthal and the Crown Prince. He had been pressing them continually to push cavalry as far forward as possible to locate the French, and the question that was very much in their minds as they sat down to review the position was whether MacMahon would really attempt to relieve Bazaine. Podbielski, who attended the conference, was the first to suggest that in spite of the appalling military risks involved, the French would make the attempt on political grounds. He suggested that the further advance should, therefore, bear off towards the right.[10] Blumenthal thought that the French march on Reims suggested that 'they mean to take up a

General von Podbielski, Quartermaster General of the German armies (Rousset/*Histoire*)

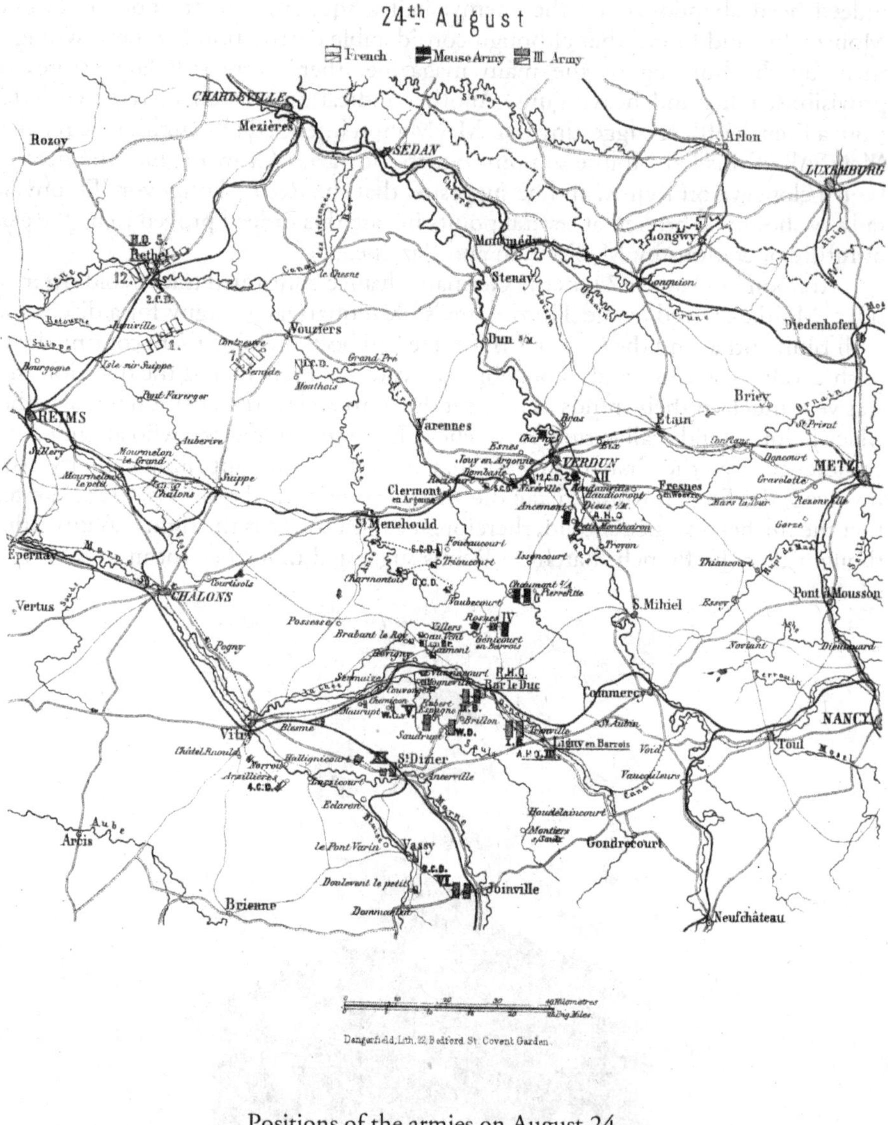

Positions of the armies on August 24

position to a flank which we cannot pass and one from which they will be able if necessary to relieve Metz. The idea is not a bad one.'[11] Moltke was the least convinced of all that MacMahon would put his head in a noose by setting out for Metz. To him, all the indications were that MacMahon still intended to cover Paris either directly or by a flank position such as Blumenthal suggested. For the moment, it was decided to continue the march westwards, but the reports of the French movements persuaded the Crown Prince that at the least they should accelerate their advance to be ready for all eventualities. That same afternoon, one of the many newspapers which the German cavalry seized upon and forwarded to headquarters, brought information that MacMahon was, indeed, now at Reims with an army of some 150,000 men. By the evening of August 24 it had begun to rain again as Royal Headquarters moved forward to Bar le Duc. When he arrived there Moltke drafted an order based on the discussions at the Ligny conference which would push the two armies forward in such a direction to give him the option of wheeling towards Reims, or carrying on towards Paris, as circumstances dictated; but the news that MacMahon had reached Reims meant that it was now unnecessary, and he held it back.[12]

That night Hohenlohe was quartered on a priest, whose curiosity about the German intentions led him to suspect that his host might be in contact with the French army. When the priest asked if when they got to Châlons the Germans would take the train to Paris, Hohenlohe's brigade major replied gravely that they were afraid that the railway officials had run away, and they should find no one at the booking office to sell them tickets. The priest's reply reassured Hohenlohe about his possibly sinister motives. 'Ah oui, il pourrait y avoir des difficultés.'[13]

With the aim of removing a further obstruction to the line of his advance, Moltke had ordered that the Saxon XII Corps should, on August 24, seize Verdun by a coup de main – again, as in the case of Toul, in order to avoid the prolonged delay of bringing up siege artillery. In spite of a heavy bombardment the result was, however, the same, the commandant of the fortress indignantly rejecting a demand for its surrender. In the face of such determination, the powerful defensive works of the fortress decided the Saxons against an infantry assault. Masking Verdun with one brigade, the Saxons pushed on to the west.[14]

Forbes, who had now caught up again with the Royal Headquarters after an abortive trip to find the Third Army, watched the King arrive there and later saw him emerge from his quarters to smoke a cigar and listen to the Bavarian regimental band play. Forbes thought that the Bavarian helmet was, compared with that of the Prussian soldiers, most ugly, and that their pale blue uniforms quickly got 'seedy.'[15] Sheridan took rather a different view, noting that the Bavarians 'were trim looking soldiers, dressed in neat uniforms of light blue; they looked healthy and strong but seemed of shorter stature than the north Germans.'[16] Verdy, who had accompanied Moltke and Podbielski to the Third Army to attend the Ligny conference, was also struck by the uniforms he saw there. 'The headquarters of the Crown Prince were gay with many colours. There were to be seen there, besides the uniforms of the various arms of the North German troops the light blue infantry and the light green light cavalry uniforms of the Bavarians, as well as the darker ones of the Wurttembergers. Conspicuous, too, was the English scarlet; its wearer was Lieutenant General Walker, the British military plenipotentiary.'[17] The unity of the Germans was very striking. As Busch remarked, observing the Bavarian troops marching before the King 'who after the war of 1866, or even three months ago, would have thought it possible?'[18]

During August 25, the reconnaissance reports reaching headquarters were eagerly devoured. They confirmed MacMahon's march to Reims but gave no indication of its later movements. Moltke remained cautious about French intentions. Quite apart from the continuing uncertainty as to the enemy movements, he was concerned that the logistical consequences of any change of plan would be considerable.

> It is always a serious matter to exchange, without the most pressing necessity, a once settled and well devised plan for a new and unprepared scheme. It would have been unwise and unskilful hastily to alter the whole direction of the advance because of rumours and information which might later probably turn out to be unfounded. Endless difficulties must result from such a course; the arrangements for bringing up baggage and reinforcements would have to be cancelled, and aimless marches might impair the confidence of the troops in their commanders.[19]

Accordingly, while leaving the Army of the Meuse to advance westward, the Third Army was, for the following day, ordered to move only slightly to its right with its right wing at Givry and its left at Changy. The Third Army's reconnaissance suggested that MacMahon had halted at Reims so any more drastic change of direction was, for the moment, postponed.

Throughout August 25, the German cavalry pushed further and further to the west and northwest. The 5th Cavalry Division, acting on Moltke's instructions to the Army of the Meuse, sent one regiment, the 17th Hussars, to break the railway west of Montmédy, burning a wooden railway bridge near Stenay. The rest of the division went on towards Sainte Menehould, while the 12th Cavalry Division moved on Varennes without encountering the enemy. The 6th Cavalry Division, meanwhile, had some momentary excitement when a battalion of Gardes Mobiles appeared, marching from Vitry towards Sainte Menehould, en route to Paris. After a confused encounter, the whole of the battalion was taken prisoner; losses on both sides were light, although later in the day a number of French prisoners were killed or wounded in an abortive escape attempt while they were being marched off.[20] While this was going-on, the 4th Cavalry Division also had a success to record; appearing before Vitry, which had now been left with a garrison of only 300 National Guards, its summons to the commandant to surrender was, under the threat of a bombardment, successful in obtaining an immediate capitulation.[21]

That afternoon, Moltke sat down and reflected on the position. Although still finding it difficult to believe that his opponent could take such a risky step as to march northeastwards towards Metz, the straws in the wind increasingly pointed to this possibility.

For his private use, therefore, he worked out a table of marches which he reckoned would take the three corps of the Army of the Meuse, together with the two Bavarian corps, to the area of Damvillers east of the Meuse in three days, and there be well placed to fight MacMahon in a position of some advantage, if indeed he had got over the river. Moltke reckoned on being able in addition to bring the III Corps and the IX Corps, which constituted Frederick Charles' reserve at Metz, through Étain and Landres, which would have given him a total of 150,000 infantry with which to bar MacMahon's progress.[22]

Forbes had now convinced himself that Vitry and Châlons would be the line of march of the Third Army, so in another attempt to join the Crown Prince he set off in that direction and thereby entirely missed the next stage of the campaign. This time he got himself so far detached that he did not catch up with the army until August 31.[23]

During the evening of August 25, at Bar le Duc, Verdy and the junior German staff officers were in high spirits, after supper singing the 'Wacht am Rhein' and other songs, when their entertainment was suddenly interrupted by an orderly officer, who

> suddenly came rushing in with the words "General Moltke requests the attendance of the Chiefs of Sections; four other officers are to be ready to ride off at once!" In a moment our exuberant spirits vanished, we had to return to serious business again. Swords were buckled on quickly; "The enemy is on the march," we conjectured. "But in what direction?" was the question, as we rushed into the office close by. We were right, he had marched. The cavalry division of Prince Albert had dashed into the camp at Châlons, had found it empty, and the French retreating towards Reims. Later intelligence said, "the enemy is already past Rethel." It seemed astonishing to all of the staff that MacMahon could be marching to the relief of Metz. Against such an attempt indeed nothing could be said theoretically; but a flank march of the French round our right wing was practical only if their troops were quicker in marching than our own, and we ourselves – blind.[24]

Moltke sent out orders at once directly to the individual corps. 'The corps will not march tomorrow according to previous orders, but will cook a meal in good time and await further marching orders.'[25] Blumenthal, when he got the news during the night, was at first dubious, since the reports came from 'newspapers and sources of such like description which are quite unreliable' but as confirmation came in, he too accepted that MacMahon was trying to get round to the north.[26] Verdy was sent off to the Crown Prince of Saxony 20 miles away, and endured a hair-raising journey in the dark, arriving before dawn. There he woke the Crown Prince and Schlotheim who 'determined, as was done also, almost at the same time, by the Royal Headquarters, not to wait for further intelligence, but to set the troops in motion at once in a more northerly direction.'[27]

For Moltke, the decision had still not been easy. In any circumstances, to plunge into the hilly and heavily wooded Argonne and thus disrupt the careful supply arrangements made on the basis of a march on Paris, was a risky move. To take the decision on the basis, not of reports of the enemy's whereabouts coming directly from his cavalry reconnaissances but of newspapers, speeches and overseas telegrams, which was all he had to go on, was a considerable gamble. 'Erst wägen, dann wagen' was his motto; and once his mind was made up he and Podbielski sought out the King and obtained his authority. The great wheel to the north had begun.

While Moltke was thus reaching a conclusion, and acting on it, MacMahon was still at Rethel. On August 26, he moved forward in an easterly direction. Although the 7th Corps remained around Vouziers, covering the right flank, on the left flank the 12th Corps made progress to reach Tourteron. In the centre, the 5th and lst Corps were echelonned between Le Chesne and Attigny, preceded by Margueritte's cavalry division at Oches and followed in the rear by Bonnemains' division. Douay had sent one brigade of his 7th Corps under General Bordas towards Grand Pré, but he here encountered the advanced patrols of the 5th Cavalry Division which, originally advancing from St. Menehould on Vouziers, had now been directed on Grand Pré. Bordas at once withdrew from that place into the impassable Bois de Bourgogne, telling Douay that he was retreating on Buzancy in the face of superior forces. There, however, where another brigade from the 7th Corps had advanced, the appearance of one squadron of Saxon cavalry also provoked an immediate retreat upon the main body at Vouziers. Douay was convinced by these reports that he had the enemy on top of him and did not, therefore, attempt to move out of his position between Chestres and Falaise in which he prepared to defend himself, on the higher ground to the east of Vouziers. Meanwhile, though, Bordas had now discovered his mistake and that he only had some detachments of cavalry in front of him. Accordingly he went back to Grand Pré and reoccupied the town. In. spite of this, however, his divisional commander, Dumont, ordered him to retreat on the main body at Vouziers. As the rain fell steadily, Douay's corps remained in its position and prepared for an imminent attack. Back at Tourteron late that night, MacMahon got the news and decided that he must concentrate next day with his whole army on the line Vouziers-Buzancy. While the French were in this manner entirely uncertain about their immediate opposition, accurate and detailed reports of the French movements in the area had on the other hand promptly been made to the German headquarters.

That night, Napoleon, convinced by the presence of the ubiquitous German cavalry of the hazardous position of the Army of Châlons, resolved to send the Prince Imperial away. Napoleon was careful not to consult Eugénie about the decision, and on the following morning, 'father and son, useless adjuncts of a lost army, parted at Tourteron; Louis sad and bewildered yet docile as became a soldier, Napoleon labouring to disguise his thought that they were embracing for the last time.'[28] The Prince Imperial and his escort went off to Mézières, while Napoleon moved with MacMahon's headquarters to Le Chesne.

On August 26, MacMahon had despatched a message warning Bazaine of his difficulty in moving further east without news of him. This was the day on which Bazaine had planned to execute an operation whereby his forces would advance to the east of Metz, in order to compel the Germans to concentrate on that side of the city and so facilitate the link with MacMahon. The appalling weather conditions, however, caused the advance to be halted. The decision to undertake such an operation appears to have been taken without any information as to MacMahon's movements. According to the evidence before his court martial, Bazaine did not get news of MacMahon and the advance of the Army of Châlons until August 29 (although one member of his staff was later to claim that he had had the news on August 23). The conference of generals called to discuss the situation concluded that the insufficiency of available ammunition precluded any further attack on that day.[30] As the rain teemed down, Bazaine rode back to his quarters, remarking as he passed a body of troops on the road: 'Well, they wouldn't bite today', a reference which could as well have been intended to mean either his generals or the enemy,

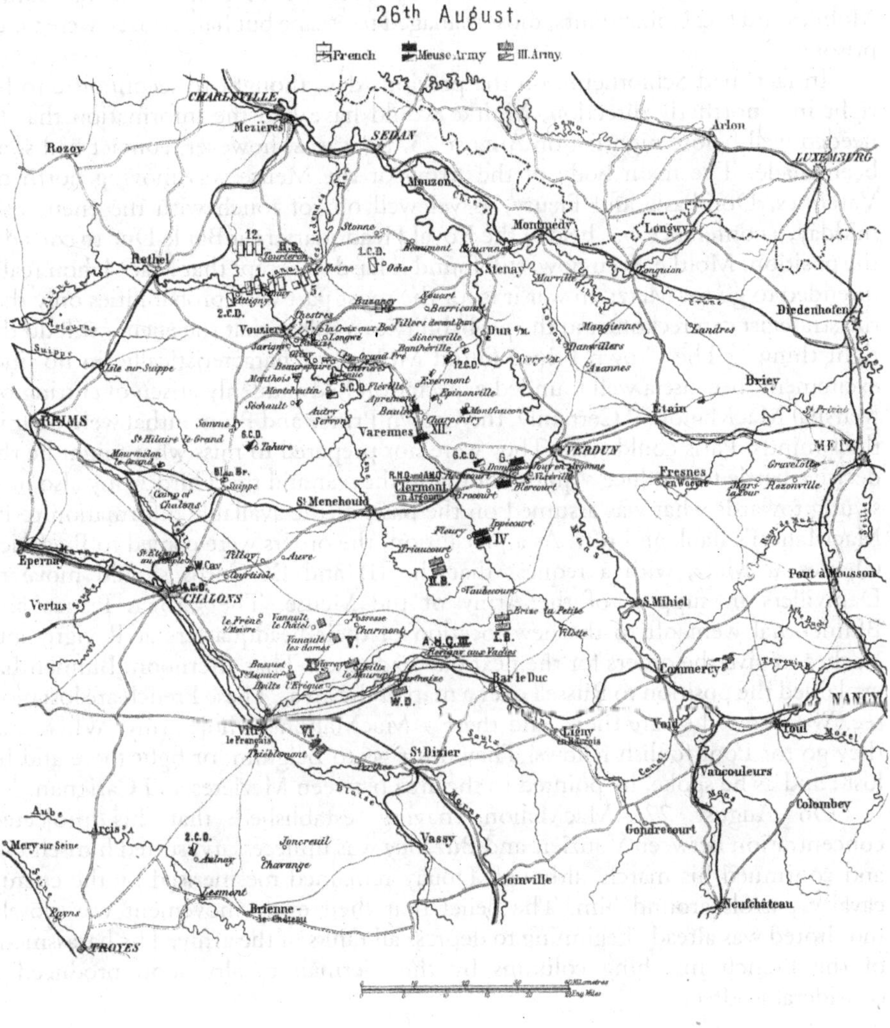

Positions of the armies on August 26

who had not been tempted by the French advance into making any substantial alteration in their positions.

All through August 26, the German cavalry had searched assiduously along the whole front for MacMahon. Their boldness inevitably exposed them to the occasional setback, however; in Épernay, some twenty miles west of Châlons, a party of forty Uhlans despatched there to wreck the railway were forming up in the marketplace when they were attacked by overwhelming numbers of Gardes Mobiles and local inhabitants; most managed to escape but half a dozen were taken prisoner.

In fact, had Schlotheim, on the previous day, thought to reconnoitre to his right in a northerly direction, Moltke would have had the information that he needed well before nightfall on August 25. As it was, however, contact had soon been made. The main body of the Army of the Meuse was moving north on Varennes, Dombasle and Fleury, as yet well out of touch with the enemy. At midday, a conference was held at the Royal Headquarters at Bar le Duc to consider the position. Moltke, even now, still found it hard to accept that MacMahon really intended to go for Metz; 'in war it is for the most part with probabilities only that the strategist can reckon; and the probability as a rule is that the enemy will do the right thing.'[31] The Crown Prince found Moltke uncharacteristically 'in no little excitement, because a well founded expectation had suddenly arisen of cutting off Marshal MacMahon.'[32] Certainly, the Crown Prince and Blumenthal were clear in their minds. Paris could wait. They were not prepared to miss what might be the decisive battle to produce a quick ending to the war and the Third Army also now swung towards what was assumed on the basis of the available information to be MacMahon's flank and rear. As a precaution, the orders were copied to Frederick Charles at Metz, with a request that the III and IX Corps should move to Damvillers in support of the Army of the Meuse. The Crown Prince and Blumenthal went off to the new location of their headquarters at Revigny aux Vaches to give the orders for the next day's advance. That afternoon, Blumenthal explained the position to Russell over a map of the area. 'These French are lost, you see. We know they are there, and there – MacMahon's whole army. Where can they go to? Poor foolish fellows! They must go to Belgium, or fight there and be lost'; and as he spoke, he pointed to the area between Mézières and Carignan.[33]

On August 27, MacMahon, having established that his projected concentration between Vouziers and Buzancy was unnecessary, sorted himself out and continued his march, although Douay remained mesmerised by the enemy cavalry patrols around him. The belief that their every movement was closely monitored was already beginning to depress all ranks of the army. The harassment of the French marching columns by the German cavalry soon produced a considerable effect.

> The result of all this was indescribable fatigue for the enemy's infantry. They reached the end of their march, as night fell, utterly tired out, and neglected from very weariness the most ordinary precautions as to outposts around their miserable bivouacs, while our infantry, quite near to them but without their knowledge, was comfortably housed in villages.[34]

MacMahon did not, however, correct the egregious error of locating the bulk of his cavalry to the left and rear of his main body, a mistake which was, in part, responsible for his own almost total and continuous ignorance of the German movements, and for the ease and thoroughness with which the German cavalry were able to follow the movements of the Army of Châlons.

On the rare occasions when the French cavalry were employed with more enterprise, they were scarcely a match for their opponents. On August 27, at Buzancy, Brahaut's cavalry division of de Failly's 5th Corps had moved to cover the concentration of the corps at Bar. Two squadrons of Chasseurs had been posted south of the town; encountering these, the advanced guard of the Saxon 24th Cavalry Brigade at once attacked, upon the personal instruction of the brigade commander, the enterprising Major General Senfft von Pilsach, and drove the Chasseurs back into Buzancy. There, however, the main body of French cavalry came into action and forced the Saxons to retreat, until a brilliantly executed flank attack by Captain von Wolffersdorff, with a lone squadron, again drove the French back. The action finally ended when a battery of Saxon horse artillery came into action, the fire of which was so effective that the French attempt to counter-attack again was shattered, and the Chasseurs 'withdrew in such haste through Buzancy that the 3rd Squadron of the 18th Lancers, which was now likewise advancing, was unable to reach them.'[35] A commentator writing on the relation between guns and cavalry twenty five years later noted this as 'perhaps the most characteristic, or even the only, purely horse artillery and cavalry action in the whole war,' and suggested that the experience contributed to de Failly's failure to employ his cavalry effectively to cover his corps at Beaumont three days later.[36] The French cavalry proved equally ineffective in checking ambitious individual patrols. Also on August 27, one enterprising German cavalry officer, Lieutenant von Ziegler, rode nearly ninety miles around the 7th Corps, and thus located it as being definitely at Vouziers.[37]

MacMahon moved Margueritte's division forward to Beaumont in an attempt to get news of Bazaine, because he was now becoming distinctly uneasy. The panicky over-reaction to the appearance of the German cavalry reflected the mounting anxiety of the French about their obviously hazardous situation. Blumenthal reckoned that MacMahon should attack at once; 'the most unfavourable turn affairs could take would be that MacMahon should throw himself now his whole strength upon us;'[38] and certainly the German armies were, at that moment, somewhat vulnerable as they swung northwards into the forest of the Argonne. Verdy and his colleagues wrestled with the staff problems that were created because 'a quarter of a million of men facing west on a front of some 70 miles, i.e. four or five days march, had suddenly to wheel round on their extreme right and front north' -problems which led to the Argonne being 'heartily cursed' in spite of its scenic charms.[39] Moltke shared Blumenthal's view about MacMahon's options. It

> seemed as though in the French army less attention was paid to the repulse of an attack than to the evasion of one, and to the unobserved attainment of Montmédy the point of rendezvous with the other army. When the movement of the Germans from southward could no longer be doubted, it would certainly have been best for the French to take the vigorous offensive in that direction

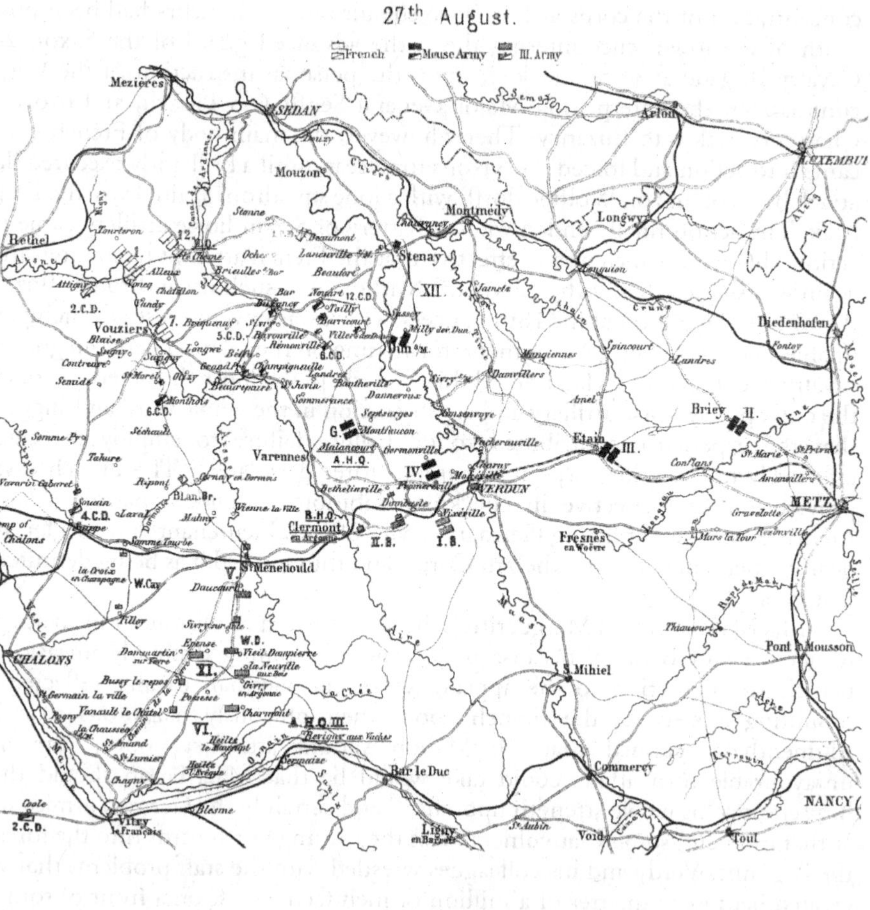

Positions of the armies on August 27

with intent to defeat them or at least to sweep them out of the vicinity of their own line of march.

Moltke noted, however, 'that the German cavalry formed an almost impenetrable screen. The Marshal could not know that his enemy was echelonned from Vitry to Varennes, a distance of more than 37 miles, and was not at all in form to attacking just then in serious earnest.'[40] And late on August 27 Moltke felt sufficiently confident to countermand the orders to Frederick Charles to send two corps from the army around Metz.[41]

Throughout August 27, the continuous contact with German cavalry patrols emphasised still further to MacMahon the risks that he was taking; and when reports of German infantry on the Meuse ahead of him were received, he concluded that his last hopes of successfully getting through to Metz had evaporated. Accordingly, at his headquarters at Le Chesne, he now issued orders for a left wheel to the north intending his army to move on Chagny, Vendresse and Poix with Mézières as the objective. He then dictated to Colonel Stoffel, his Chief of Intelligence, a report to Palikao. In this telegram, he recorded that there were two armies threatening him, one on the right bank of the Meuse, the other moving on the Ardennes.

> I have no news of Bazaine. If I advance to meet him I shall be attacked in front by a part of the First and Second German Armies which, favoured by the woods, can conceal a force superior to mine, and at the same time attacked by the Prussian Crown Prince cutting off my line of retreat. I approach Mézières tomorrow, whence I shall continue my retreat, guided by events, towards the west.[42]

Just as he was about to have the telegram sent off, his Chief of Staff, Faure, came in; he read it, and correctly predicted that if it went off then, his intentions would be overruled by Paris; he strongly advised that MacMahon should not send it. 'You can transmit it tomorrow, when we are already on the road to Mézières', said Faure. MacMahon, however, insisted that it be sent and, by 1.30 a.m. the following morning, he received the inevitable response from Palikao.

> If you leave Bazaine in the lurch, revolution will break out in Paris and you yourself will be attacked by the enemy's entire forces. Paris is well able to protect itself from without, the fortifications are complete. Your rapid junction with Bazaine appears to me of paramount necessity ... everyone here feels the importance of relieving Bazaine, and your movements are watched with the greatest suspense.[43]

Palikao went on to say that the Crown Prince had faced front to the north but that MacMahon had at least thirty six hours in hand over him and possibly forty eight; that reinforcements were on the way; and so on. MacMahon knew, or ought to have known, what nonsense all this was but characteristically, and in spite of the urgent advice of the Emperor, he countermanded his orders for the retreat. 'The Marshal's will broke down under this strain. He could not bear the thought that men might in future point to him as one who had deserted a brother Marshal.'[44] Although fresh orders went out to the four French corps at once, it was too late to prevent the start of the movement

> As, however, the corps had commenced the march to Mézières on the morning of August 28 before their receipt, while the carriages sent on ahead had to be brought back, the columns of march crossed at several places. Along the roads sodden with pouring rain the wearied troops, wet through and disheartened, did not reach their destinations until late in the evening.[45]

The die was cast, or almost. At Stonne on that same day, August 28, the Emperor made a last and very determined attempt to dissuade MacMahon from carrying out Palikao's instructions. He pointed out that they were not, in fact, orders. MacMahon was, he said, free to act as he thought fit. He should reconsider his position to go on. But then to Stonne came a further telegram from Palikao couched in sterner terms. 'In the name of the Council of Ministers in the Privy Council, I request you to succour Bazaine, profiting by the 36 hours advantage you have over the Crown Prince of Prussia.'[46] It was enough. 'Je vous demande,' wrote Palikao and, in the face of this, notwithstanding all that Napoleon could say, MacMahon preferred to suppress the instincts of his military common sense in the comfort of carrying out an explicit order.

It is difficult not to feel some sympathy for MacMahon. The pressures put upon him were strong and conflicting. But the fact remains that almost until the last moment, he had a chance of escape. He was not incapable of seeing that to plunge on was to court utter catastrophe; but, in the end, that was what he did, hoping, presumably, that something would turn up, perhaps that Bazaine would break out or perhaps that the Germans would in some way make an irremediable mess of the opportunity he was giving them. This last was perhaps the least likely of

The action at Nouart, by Pallandre (Rousset/*Combattants*)

the events that might occur to save him, and it was at Stonne on August 28 that MacMahon finally ensured that the Army of Châlons would be exposed to complete destruction.

The course of the campaign might, however, have been somewhat different if, in its march to the north-east, MacMahon had been able to push his marching columns on faster. If Douay in particular had pressed on towards the crossings at Dun, he might well have got there before the most advanced German army corps which, after the right wheel began, were the XII Corps and the Guard Corps. These, as the Bavarian Official History points out, could not have got to Dun before the evening of August 27 and Douay might well been able to hold that crossing until reinforced by Ducrot with the 1st Corps while the other two corps crossed the river at Stenay. As Helvig went on to observe, 'the success of the whole move towards Sedan depended on the correct and rapid employment of the two days, the 27 and 28 of August.'[47] and on the second of these days, Douay again wasted most of the day at Quatre Champs awaiting orders that were delayed because the first officer carrying them from MacMahon was captured by the German cavalry. By nightfall on August 28, Douay had still not reached the line of the Bar, bivouacking for the night at Boult aux Bois. De Failly had reached Belval and Bois des Dames with, to his rear, Margueritte's cavalry division at Sommauthe. Lebrun's 12th Corps was between Stonne and La Besace, while Bonnemains' cavalry division remained to the south-west of Stonne. Finally, Ducrot, with the lst Corps, was on the road between Le Chesne and the bridge over the Bar.

Blumenthal had been awakened at 4.30 on the morning of August 28 at Revigny, to receive fresh orders to move to the line of the Tourbe.[48] He then moved on himself to Sainte- Menehould, where his headquarters were to be for that day, where he got news that the enemy was in retreat, probably on Le Chesne. All day, the Third Army pressed northwards in continuous rain. Blumenthal, as usual, regarded it as crucially important to get every man under cover. Royal Headquarters were at Clermont on this day and Sheridan, who was extremely comfortably billeted for the night on a local apothecary, went to visit Bismarck, who he found to have been not so lucky, having been assigned to a very small and uncomfortable house. There Sheridan found him 'wrapped in a shabby old dressing gown hard at work.' Bismarck explained to Sheridan what was going on, describing MacMahon's advance as 'a blundering manoeuvre which cannot be accounted for unless it has been brought about by the political situation of the French.'[49] Moltke, after some uncertainty during the day as a result of conflicting cavalry reconnaissance reports, was now satisfied that he knew what MacMahon was trying to do, and that he knew the best way to deal with him. 'The German cavalry had strict orders, while watching the French as closely as possible, not in any way to check or press them,'[50] and it was in the execution of these instructions that the Saxons evacuated Nouart in the face of the French advance towards the Meuse crossings. By nightfall, the XII Corps was moving up the right bank of the Meuse and held the crossings at both Dun and Stenay. The Guard Corps was at Bantheville and Romagne. As usual, the German commanders were extremely solicitous of the welfare of their troops, as Hohenlohe related:

> It seemed absolutely necessary the Guard Corps should bivouac in its position with the two villages Romagne and Bantheville on the Anthon brook before its

> front. But a tremendous storm of rain fell during the march into position, which wetted everything through and soaked the ground. Relying on the trustworthiness of the advanced cavalry, which would in any case bring information of the approach of the enemy soon enough to allow the position to be occupied in time, the General in command was able to permit the infantry to take advantage of the shelter of the two villages named above. As a matter of fact, the whole corps found shelter against the abominable weather in the vast dwelling-houses, stables, and barns.[51]

The IV Corps was some five miles south at Montfaucon. The I Bavarian Corps had reached Varennes and the II Bavarian Corps was at Vienne le Château, while the V Corps was across the Tourbe between Cernay and Malmy. The Württemberg Division had reached the line of the Tourbe with the XI Corps in the rear of the Bionne at Courtimont. It was still, therefore, only the German cavalry that was in contact with MacMahon, and they continued to watch his every move. On the right, the 12th Cavalry Division had pulled back from Nouart, while the Guard Cavalry Division was stretched between Buzancy and Remonville. The 5th Cavalry Division had moved to its left between Monthois and Grand Pré while on the road north of the former town and beyond Vouziers the 6th Cavalry Division began to scout round the rear of MacMahon's army.

At 9.00pm Moltke received a report from the Lancer Brigade of the Guard Cavalry Division at Buzancy which suggested that the French, rather than trying to get away to the north, were pushing on to the Meuse. This was further confirmation for Moltke of MacMahon's intentions. At 11pm on August 28 he issued from his headquarters at Clermont instructions intended to make sure of his prey.

> The appearance of strong bodies of the enemy's infantry at Bar near Buzancy suggests that the enemy means to try to de-blockade Metz ... In order not to challenge the enemy to an attack before sufficient forces have been assembled it is suggested to HRH the Crown Prince of Saxony first of all early to collect the XII Guard and IV Corps in a defensive position about the line Landres-Aincreville.[52]

13

Beaumont

For Blumenthal, August 29 began very badly. Having spent the previous evening redrawing the plans for next day, he retired to bed, only to be woken at half past twelve with the new orders issued by Moltke. As usual he made an irritable note in his diary.

> Everything was again altered. We had to work out the scheme, and then write and issue orders, which lasted us till three o'clock in the morning. According to my way of thinking, it is an immense error to keep continually making changes with every new report which comes in. The information is for the most part unreliable, or exaggerated and misinterpreted, and continuous alterations create a sort of nervous uncertainty which soon communicates itself to the troops.[1]

The orders for the Third Army were to move forward to be ready for a major battle on August 30, but provided that 'a further offensive against the road Vouziers-Buzancy-Stenay is reserved'; Moltke added in his own hand that 'an advance at once to seize the Buzancy road from weaker enemy forces is not excluded by the above orders.'[2] On his way from Clermont to Grande Pré via Varennes during the morning of August 29, Moltke sent direct orders to the

General von Blumenthal, Chief of Staff of the German Third Army (Scheibert)

leading corps of the Third Army, slightly revising their instructions in the light of the continuous information coming in from the German cavalry.

The Crown Prince of Saxony took steps to concentrate the XII Corps the next day, bringing it over the Meuse at Dun, and pushing forward the 12th Cavalry Division towards Nouart, supported by an advanced guard of the corps. All along the line as dawn broke, the German cavalry patrols trotted forward; Moltke's object for the day was not to fight any sort of decisive battle but to clear up all doubts as to what the French were actually doing.

For that day, MacMahon had actually prescribed that the French army should continue its movement to the north east. For the two corps furthest from the enemy, the march objectives for the day were fairly easily achieved. Ducrot pressed on with his lst Corps to Raucourt, after enduring a good deal of harassment from the German cavalry, which made a nuisance of itself all day. Lebrun, preceded by Margueritte's cavalry division, crossed the Meuse at Mouzon. For the other two corps, however, the day went not so well. Douay with the 7th Corps, whose orders were to march to La Besace, also had to put up with repeated interference from the German cavalry; and although there was no heavy fighting, in his case the constant prodding sufficed to delay him seriously, and he bivouacked for the night at Oches and St. Pierremont, four miles south of his objective.

It was, however, for the 5th Corps that August 29 was most disastrous in its consequence. During the previous night, de Failly had been ordered that he should, on the following day, make for Stenay. He moved in two columns, his right led by Brahaut's cavalry division, followed by Lespart's division marching on Beauclair; and his left, comprising Goze's division and Maussion's brigade, on Beaufort. As had been the case throughout the French march north-eastwards, the French cavalry remained closely in touch with the main body rather than scouting southwards in the direction of the oncoming enemy.

Unknown to him, however, de Failly was even further out of luck than usual. Late the night before, MacMahon at Stonne had received information of the occupation of Stenay by the Saxons, so he gave up the idea of crossing there, intending to cross further north at Remilly and Mouzon and then to push east and southeast through Montmédy to Metz. Orders were accordingly drawn up for de Failly to move next day on Beaumont instead of on Stenay; they also continued full details of all the recent movements of the French Army. These orders were entrusted to a staff officer, the Marquis de Grouchy, who was sent off escorted by a body of Chasseurs. Unluckily, however, he ran into one of the German cavalry patrols led by a Lieutenant von Plessen, and, in the ensuing skirmish, was captured. As a result, de Failly set off as originally planned for Stenay; and Moltke was provided with some interesting and very up-to-date intelligence about the forces opposed to him.[3]

At 8 a.m., the Crown Prince of Saxony sat down with his corps commanders at Aincreville to review the latest reconnaissance reports. Mindful of Moltke's concern to let the French march on, but anxious to get the clearest possible information about their movements, he sanctioned an advance up to the Buzancy-Stenay road, the Guard moving up towards Buzancy. It was preceded by its cavalry division, which scouted out towards the Le Chesne-Beaumont road, while the Saxon cavalry division was to move off through Nouart and Oches, backed up by

The French are surprised at Beaumont, by Speyer (Bork)

the advanced guard of the XII Corps. The evidence was accumulating, however, that the French were close at hand and in some considerable strength.

De Failly, however, was not so well informed. His cavalry screen, pushed forward only a little way ahead of the main body of his corps, were startled suddenly to encounter strong German forces at Nouart. Von Seydlitz, commanding the advanced guard of the XII Corps, which consisted of the 46th Infantry Brigade with the lst Cavalry Regiment and some artillery, had pushed forward his infantry in support of his cavalry patrols to occupy the village of Nouart. When the French cavalry crossed the Wiseppe just north of the village, it began to climb the slopes up to the Bois de Nouart to the northwest. The Saxon infantry moved out of the village towards the wood and dispersed the French cavalry, whose reports of the engagement at once determined de Failly to abandon his advance towards the Meuse and to get Lespart's division into a defensive position between Bois des Dames and Champy. Following up the successful repulse of the French cavalry, Seydlitz pushed his infantry across the Wiseppe to occupy a string of copses on the other side of the stream, from where, if required, an assault could be launched on the principal French position. The engagement continued for about four hours, until 4 p m, but the corps commander, Prince George of Saxony, who had come up to see for himself, and whose main body was now close at hand, was himself very conscious of Moltke's desire not to bring on a premature battle; and at about 3 o'clock he gave orders for the action to be broken off, and for the advanced guard to fall back to the heights above Nouart.[4]

Coincidentally, de Failly himself ordered a retreat, having just now come by a copy of the missing order that prescribed Beaumont as his objective for the day. During this prolonged engagement, the Saxons sustained 363 casualties and the French about the same. The Saxons had, however, succeeded in their limited objective which was to impose further delay on the march of de Failly's corps. The French retreat on Beaumont was closely observed by the Saxon cavalry who encountered stiff resistance as the French slowly retired northwards covered by two brigades and by artillery fire.

The sound of the fighting at Nouart was audible to Prince August who, with the bulk of the Guard Corps, had reached Buzancy. At this time, it was evident that a French force of approximately corps strength was passing only two miles in front of his leading units and Prince August, anxious to get involved either by attacking that force or by moving towards Nouart to reinforce the Saxons, reported to the Crown Prince of Saxony, who firmly told him not to get involved; the object of the day was to reconnoitre and hold the enemy, not to attack him. Douay, still harassed by the cavalry, was able to continue his march towards La Besace, although he was further delayed by mistaking de Failly's corps for an enemy force much further forward than he expected; he was obliged to halt for some time until their identity had been cleared up. Meanwhile de Failly's exhausted troops trudged northwards during the night and his rear guard, in fact, only reached the encampments to the south of Beaumont at 5 a.m. the next morning.

All that day, Moltke's greatest anxiety was that MacMahon, instead of blundering on into the trap that had by now been set, would, before it was too late, turn about and head westwards as fast as he could; it seemed now that this might have happened. Riding past the columns of the Ist Bavarian Division as they marched northwards, he gave orders that the division should move to its left on St. Juvin rather than Sommerance, 'because on the following day the operations would probably be continued in a westerly direction.'[5] When he encountered the Crown Prince and Blumenthal as they arrived at Senuc, where their headquarters would be for the night, he greeted them with the news that the French appeared to have got away.[6] Moltke's disappointment was profound. The Crown Prince and Blumenthal drove with him to Royal Headquarters, which was located at Grand Pré, speculating that the appearance of the Germans in such strength advancing northwards had led MacMahon to give up his advance on Metz. The Crown Prince read with interest an intercepted letter from a French officer commenting on MacMahon's deficiencies (his 'dispositions were good for nothing') and which added that the Emperor 'follows the army about, devoid of all consideration, and nothing but a burden to it, himself in a mood of discouragement.'[7] By the time they got to Grand Pré, however, Moltke's anxiety that the French might have made their escape had begun to evaporate. De Grouchy's capture gave 'complete confirmation of the movements of the French army as they had been conjectured',[8] and all the other reports coming in suggested that the position into which MacMahon had now got himself was one from which in fact he could scarcely hope to extricate himself. Once he had settled down at Grand Pré, Moltke reviewed the position. From right to left, he had the XII Corps still around Nouart, the Guard Corps at Buzancy and, in their rear at Remonville, the IV Corps. The Third Army had made sufficient progress during the day to be able to take part in any operations next day. The I Bavarian Corps was between St. Juvin and Sommerance, while the II Bavarian Corps was to the south of Cornay. To its left, around Grand Pré, was the V Corps and the Württemberg Division, while the XI Corps was on the road between Vouziers and Monthois. The VI Corps, some way back, had reached Vienne le Château. The concentration of his two armies had proceeded so successfully that Moltke concluded that on the next day he could afford to broaden his front and to advance to what might prove a decisive battle. The information that had been gathered during the day placed the French between Le Chesne and Beaumont, and it was upon this line that he determined to advance, with the left of the Third Army directed on Le Chesne – a movement which would, in fact, take it well to the west of MacMahon's actual position.[9]

That night at Royal Headquarters, the Germans could still hardly believe their luck. Sheridan dined with the King. 'The conversation at table was almost wholly devoted to the situation, of course, everybody expressing surprise at the manoeuvre of the French at this time, their march along the Belgium frontier being credited entirely to Napoleon.'[10] Bismarck as usual went off by himself for a walk around the little town, thereby causing Busch some anxiety for his safety. 'He went about the narrow streets of the town freely in the twilight without a companion, in lonely places where he was quite liable to be attacked.'[11] Busch was sufficiently worried to set off after him and try and keep him in his sight.

Moltke's understanding of the situation was greatly assisted by the information brought back to Royal Headquarters by two key members of his staff. Brandenstein, who had visited the XII Corps, reported that 'the presence of two French corps at St Pierremont and Bois des Dames appeared certain and that there were also hostile troops at Beaumont'. And Bronsart returned to say that Germont and Autruche had been abandoned by the French. These reports were further confirmation that MacMahon was taking a north easterly direction.[12]

A large part of the success on which the Germans could now begin to congratulate themselves was due to the use made in this campaign of the German cavalry. This was in striking contrast to the persistent habit of the German commanders, in the early days of the war, of holding back their cavalry behind the infantry and artillery. As a result, the encounter battles on the frontier had been fought, to a considerable extent, in great ignorance of the positions actually occupied by the French; and this was still largely true at Gravelotte. This had, in fact, given an opportunity to the French cavalry which, if they had been used with more enterprise at that stage of the campaign might, in the absence of their German counterparts, have been able to gather much important intelligence about German movements and even to hamper those movements. In the event, though, they were themselves completely wasted. In these last few days of August, the German cavalry, displaying a continuous initiative which exercised a profound effect on French morale, had herded the dispirited Army of Châlons across the rainsoaked countryside, watching its every move, and denying to MacMahon any useful information at all about Moltke's movements. By the evening of August 29, the Germans were able to 'foresee that if fate had not destined it otherwise and great mistakes were not committed or misunderstandings and misconceptions did not creep in, that this, the last French army, had brought itself into a position from which it could not escape without disaster.'[13]

Russell, at the Crown Prince's headquarters, recorded the scene that night.

> A last look before I turned in … revealed a beautiful sight: all the stars of heaven seemed to have settled on the face of the earth, and as far as the eye could sweep, the watch-fires burned on the hillside, valley and rolling plain – near at hand, lighting up the figures of the soldiers in their bivouacs and justifying Rembrandt at every flash, and far away gathering closely into asteroids and nebulous clouds which closed in the horizon. Some 80,000 men are resting all arounds us on their arms, and yet no sound is heard except the neigh of a horse now and then, or the voice of a sentry challenging.[14]

Early on August 30, MacMahon rode down to de Failly's camp south of Beaumont, feeling by now extremely anxious about the position of his army. After a brief discussion with de Failly – there is no record of what passed between them – he rode off to Oches to the camp of the 7th Corps. There he found that the northward march had begun, Conseil Dumesnil's lst Division having already set off to Stonne while the 2nd Division was preparing to leave. In conversation with Douay, MacMahon was forthright. 'You will have 60,000 men upon your hands, this evening, if you do not succeed in getting beyond the Meuse', he said.[15] He added that Douay should get rid of his baggage convoy and cross the river at all costs, suggesting that Villers devant Mouzon would be the place to cross. This visit over, MacMahon, heavy with misgiving, rode off again to the north.

That morning had dawned with much improved weather. Verdy looked out of his window at Grand Pré. 'After the rainy days of last week, the morning sun shines out again merrily, and brightens the comfortable little room which I occupy here. The clear sky points to a hot day, and hot it will probably be in more senses than one.'[16] Meanwhile at Senuc, Blumenthal had endured another broken night. 'The orders from the King's headquarters came to me in the night again, and tore me out of my first and sweetest sleep. It was very much against the grain that I got up and spent hours and hours of the night working with head in hand.'[17] But the excitement of his staff was mounting as what was plainly going to be a decisive battle approached. The tension communicated itself to Russell.

> There is a good deal said of men being "cool under fire". One has seen men very cool under it, but I have never met with one yet who is not a little excited before he goes into action. It may be pleasurably so. Still there is a glisten in the eye, and a heightened colour in the cheek, and a timbre in the voice, not derived from internal coolness. Our staff is tremendously civil. We go about exchanging lights and even cigars; men look into their holsters and see what there is to support life upon, and happy is he who has a nice sausage end and a hunk of bread and some hard boiled eggs.[18]

Bismarck, however, was not one of those who thought that August 30 would lead to any decisive action. He drove off with Busch from Grand Pré to Buzancy, rebuking Busch on the way for returning salutes of officers who passed the carriage, explaining that 'the salute was not to him as Minister or Chancellor but simply to his rank as general, and officers might take it amiss if a civilian took their salutes as including himself.' They stopped at a Prussian battery and spoke to the officers, who shared Bismarck's doubts about what lay ahead that day. Bismarck remarked: 'This reminds me of a wolf hunt I once had in the Ardennes, which began just here.

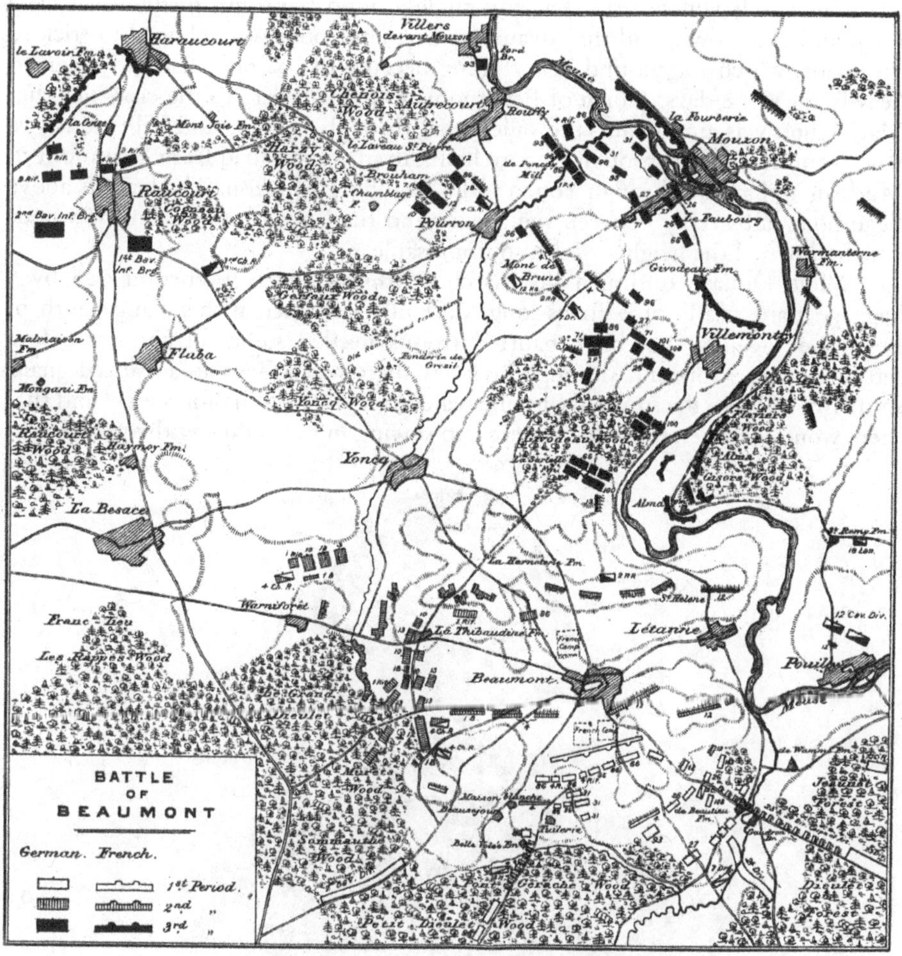

The Battle of Beaumont, August 30

We were for many long days up in the snow, and at last heard that they had found the tracks of a wolf. When we went after him he had vanished. So it will be today with the French.'[19]

The main objective of the day's advance was the town of Beaumont, which lies in a dip some six miles south of Mouzon. The spire of its church, visible from afar, stands out. Rather more than a mile or so south of the town the thick woods came to an end. On the northern slopes above the town were further encampments.

The woods which formed a semi-circle around the south of the town were thick and overgrown, and the advancing German troops were obliged to stick to the roads, which they found heavy going because of the rain that had fallen so heavily for some days. North of Beaumont, four roads lead to the crossings that MacMahon was aiming at – the valley road through Letanne and Villemontry, a road from Beaumont through La Sartelle Farm, the main road from Beaumont to Mouzon and a road through Yoncq to Le Faubourg Mouzon. The heights above Beaumont fall steeply between the Meuse and the Yoncq brook, and the woods which crowned the heights were also impassable.

While Douay continued his march northward, heavily encumbered by a baggage train nearly nine miles long, de Failly remained in his camp south of Beaumont, feeling that his exhausted troops needed some further rest before setting out for Mouzon. Although he knew there was a German advanced guard some five miles to the south of him, he believed it was heading for Stenay and that there would be, therefore, no objection to staying in camp during the morning.

General Gustav von Alvensleben, commander of the German IV Corps (Pflugk-Harttung)

Moltke's orders had put both his armies in motion very early on August 30, the Army of the Meuse, moving to the east of the Buzancy-Beaumont road, being required by 10 a.m. to cross the line Fosse-Beauclair, while the Third Army was to start early enough to be able to support the Army of the Meuse with at least two corps advancing in the direction of Buzancy and Beaumont. The advance of the Army of the Meuse was to be led by the IV Corps and the XII Corps, with the latter moving up along the left bank of the Meuse while the IV Corps, which had had to set out very early in the morning, rested briefly at Fossé and Nouart before moving from those places on Beaumont.

These movements were intended as far as possible to be co-ordinated to enable a joint attack to be launched as soon as the enemy had been encountered, but the XII Corps was delayed and it was Alvensleben's IV Corps which was the first to reach the edge of the woods overlooking de Failly's camp south of Beaumont. The sight that greeted von Schöler, the commander of the 8th Division, when he reached the front seemed scarcely credible. It was about noon. The camp about 800 yards away was tranquil, with cavalry horses picketed, the artillery teams absent watering and such soldiers that were visible busy cooking or engaged in other routine tasks. Schöler was in a quandary. With the advanced guard of his division, he had outstripped the rest of his corps which was itself ahead of the others. Should he wait? While he was considering the problem, he was joined by his corps commander, Gustav von Alvensleben who, like his brother at Mars la Tour, had to take an immediate decision about the commencement of a vital battle. His mind was soon made up for him by sudden signs of movement in the camp below. Since the presence of his force appeared to have been discovered, Alvensleben hesitated no longer. 'He therefore, at 12.30 p.m., caused the batteries of the advanced guard to open fire on the camps, in which the troops were now hastening to arms. Like a startled swarm of bees dense bodies of tirailleurs hurried to meet their bold assailants and overwhelm them with a hail of bullets.'[20]

Although the French had been taken entirely by surprise, as had been the case at Mars la Tour they recovered very quickly. By 1 o'clock, they were in a position to mount a counter-attack, having already imposed heavy casualties on the advanced guard, especially by rapidly bringing into action artillery south and west of the town, and on the heights above. All the while the battle continued, however, fresh German troops were coming up along the road through the wood bringing with them part of the corps artillery which strengthened the position which Schöler had established along the edge of the heights overlooking the French camp. To Schöler's right, von Schwarzhoff's 7th Division had been advancing towards the Belle Tour farm. Schwarzhoff had intended to deploy the whole of his division, and then wait for the rest of the German forces to get into position on either side of him, but as he was engaged in this process he heard Schöler's artillery open the battle to his left and at once pushed forward to take part in the fighting which was by now intense. By 1 p.m., three and a half battalions of the 8th Division, and three of the 7th Division were hotly engaged with the enemy, supported by eight batteries. Alvensleben had made his way to Schwarzhoff's headquarters at Belle Tour and sent out reports to Prince George's XII Corps on his right and von der Tann's Ist Bavarian Corps on his left in order to co-ordinate the assault on de Failly. In spite of severe difficulties, Alvensleben's artillery had got quickly to the front. 'The columns of the IV Corps were painfully dragging themselves through the forest on two very narrow and very bad roads. Only seven battalions and a half had reached that edge of the forest which it was desired to occupy, the rest were still in the woods. And yet 48 guns were on the spot to commence the action.'[21]

De Failly's surprise had been total, although it is difficult to see why. The outposts and patrols that should have alerted him to the proximity of the German advance quite failed to discover any sign of the enemy, and this in spite of the fact that the Germans were confined to the roads. Some confusion exists as to whether, at the moment of the assault, the sudden movement in the camp was due to a belated awareness of the enemy as a result of a report by a peasant, or whether an order had been given to fall in preparatory to marching off to Mouzon. It was now, for de Failly, vital that his retreat to Mouzon should not be hampered by the German assault, and it was his desperate awareness of this that accounted for the ferocity of the attacks which his infantry made upon the Germans. At one point they penetrated the German position to within 50 yards of their artillery before being driven back. The gun line which was formed along the northern slope behind Beaumont was gradually extended, and poured a heavy fire on the Germans. The advance of Schwarzhoff on his right, however, enabled Schöler's leading battalions to take first the camp site, and then the town of Beaumont itself, which they occupied before the last retreating French troops had left the town, many of whom were taken prisoner. In the camp, the confusion the Germans found was the most striking evidence of the completeness of the surprise. Verdy, who had spent a large part of the morning before the battle by getting hopelessly lost on his way to find the Crown Prince of Saxony, inspected the camp after its capture, where he found extensive confusion.

> The horses of the battery, still coupled together, lay dead or wounded; three guns had been put out of action, while many of the wagons could not be horsed. All the officers' luggage lay about, the trunks open just as they had been used; the carriage with the military chest and medicine carts were upset, the knapsacks were all ranged in order.[22]

The food that the hapless 5th Corps had been in the act of preparing when Schöler arrived on the scene provided lunch for the IV Corps as they marched through and, later, a more careful search of the camp found boxes of sardines, truffled sausages and paté de foie gras, which the German staff greatly enjoyed. Sheridan, too, riding through the camp 'noticed on all sides ample evidence that not even the most ordinary precautions had been taken to secure the division from surprise.'[23]

As usual, the German artillery deployed quickly and immediately engaged in a successful duel with the French artillery on the hillside above Beaumont. The latter, heavily outnumbered, resisted for a while in a position which ran along the heights from above La Thibaudine farm to a point above Letanne. By 3 p.m., the French guns had fallen silent and they withdrew in succession into the hills and woods above Beaumont. By 3.30, Alvensleben was ready to begin the advance of his corps northwards from Beaumont in pursuit of de Failly's retreating units. To his rear he was now supported by the Guard Corps which had closed up on the IV Corps. After de Failly had disappeared into the woods beyond Beaumont, he had,

The French 88th Line Regiment defend the Givodeau woods, at Beaumont, by Pallandre (Rousset/*Combattants*)

since there was nowhere else to make any effective stand, fallen back towards Mouzon and, he hoped, the protection of the River Meuse, although posting for a while a rear guard on the hill above Yoncq in order to gain some time to establish a defensive position along the Meuse. Lebrun, on the far side of the river, had, on learning of the opening of the battle, thought to send help to de Failly in the shape of the infantry brigades of Cambriels and Villeneuve, and Béville's Cuirassier Brigade. This understandable attempt to help his colleague was at once countermanded by MacMahon who rode up just as the movement was getting under way. Concerned though he might be for de Failly's corps, he certainly did not want any other part of his army caught on the wrong side of the river.

De Failly, in the meantime, had, by his headlong retreat, succeeded in breaking contact with the enemy. He had been obliged to split his forces into two parts passing one either side of the Bois de Givodeau. His left, with the artillery moving up the road to Villemontry, fell back upon the heights above that village, and there occupied a very strong position from which they were supported by Lebrun's troops and artillery on the right bank of the Meuse. When, in due course, von Montbé's 23rd Division came up with the position above Villemontry, it at once launched an attack, but at first all attempts to shift the French failed.

On the left of the German advance, von der Tann's I Bavarian Corps had been almost up with Alvensleben when Schöler launched his attack upon de Failly's camp, and were getting into position to attack La Thibaudine farm when they were distracted by fire from an unsuspected French force on the Beaumont-La Besace road. The encounter occasioned the French, however, still more surprise. These troops were a brigade from Conseil Dumesnil's division of Douay's corps which had set off early in the morning from Oches, covering the immense baggage train of the corps. The brigade's route was changed by MacMahon when he rode by it on his way north after his visit to Douay, and when the head of the column reached the point where the road forked, it took the wrong turning towards Beaumont. A staff officer galloped after the errant brigade and caught it as it crossed the Yoncq. It was at this moment, however, that contact was made with the Bavarians, and there ensued a brisk conflict. For a while, the French seem to have been attempting to break through towards the east, extending their front southwards to Le Grand Dieulet wood, so that at that time they were at right angles to the main French position, which was at that time along the heights above Beaumont. Von der Tann, concerned to cut off the retreat of the French brigade, ordered his 3rd Brigade to move to the left of the 4th Brigade which was acting as his advanced guard. Upon the Bavarians advancing through the Bois des Murets, the French were quickly forced back in disorder. A brief attempt to hold a position along the banks of the Yoncq soon dissolved, and they retreated northwards on the west bank of that river, pursued by the shells of the advancing Bavarian artillery.

Throughout the afternoon, the Germans pushed forward along the plateau leading towards Mouzon. In their turn, however, they were seriously hampered by the impenetrable Bois de Givodeau, which delayed Schwarzhoff's 7th Division as it trudged northwards in pursuit of the vanished enemy. It was followed closely by Schöler's 8th Division, while on its right, the XII Corps had experienced considerable difficulties, at first in the swampland of the Wamme west of Beaumont, and then, having extricated themselves from this, in the Meuse valley, where they were assailed by French artillery fire from the right bank. After a while they swung to their left, climbing up the plateau and following Alvensleben's corps into and around the Bois de Givodeau. By this time, Alvensleben had debouched from the woods, but had abandoned the task of trying to dislodge the French from the heights above Villemontry, a task which he now left to the Saxons as they came up.

To his left front, Alvensleben found that the French had occupied a position on a height known as the Mont de Brune, about a mile from Faubourg du Mouzon.[24] The French artillery in this position in fact faced eastwards, as the principal threat was assumed to be coming from the direction of the Bois de Givodeau but, in reality, supported on the extreme left by a mixed Bavarian brigade which von der Tann assembled from the available troops around La Thibaudine, the Germans were now approaching from the direction of Yoncq.

By 5.30, sufficient strength had been collected around the foot of the Mont de Brune for an attack from the southern side to be launched by von Zychlinski's 14th Brigade which, in spite of heavy fire and considerable casualties, succeeded in taking the crest of the hill, capturing ten guns and driving the French in headlong flight towards Mouzon. With this position lost, de Failly's last chance of covering the Mouzon crossings had gone and the three battalions that had stormed the position pressed rapidly forward towards the town.[25]

Since daybreak, MacMahon had realised that the only course he could follow was to get the whole of his army across to the security offered by the right bank of the Meuse. Now, seeing the débacle that threatened if the crossings were taken, he resorted to the desperate expedient of a cavalry charge. Not for the first, nor the last time in this war the courage and dedication of French cavalry was to be sacrificed in an attempt to make good the infantry's retreat. There still remained on the left bank of the Meuse north of Faubourg de Mouzon the 5th Cuirassier Regiment which had been part of Béville's brigade that Lebrun had ordered across the river earlier in the day and which, having already crossed, was left there by MacMahon when he prohibited Lebrun's advance to de Failly's assistance.

The regiment's charge fell upon the leading company of the 27th Regiment commanded by Captain Helmuth. Displaying great coolness, he ordered his men not to close ranks or to form a square but to stay where they were and to hold their fire. With what Moltke later described as 'a noble contempt for death,'[26] the French regiment charged up to the scattered infantry until, upon Helmuth's order, they opened fire at close range, inflicting frightful losses. The Cuirassiers' commanding officer, Colonel de Contenson, was shot down only 15 yards from the German infantry. A few of his men got close enough for hand to hand combat and the resourceful Helmuth himself was attacked by a Cuirassier NCO, but very soon the whole mass of cavalry was driven back pell mell towards the Meuse and, with no bridge to cross, many drowned as they attempted to swim to safety.[27]

In Mouzon itself there was chaos. De Failly was now obliged to abandon the Villemontry position, which had remained untaken until the turning of his right by the fall of the Mont de Brune exposed the French troops there to the risk of being cut off from their line of retreat through Mouzon. The troops from above Villemontry were hurriedly pulled back into the town and joined there the confused throng of troops, horses and equipment that struggled to get across the only bridge. By nightfall, all that could cross had done so and the whole of Faubourg de Mouzon and the western end of the bridge itself was in German hands.

To the west, Douay had fared a little but not much better. Shorn of St. Hilaire's brigade, which had managed first to lose itself, then encountered the Bavarians and then retreated precipitately northwards up the Yoncq valley, the rest of the corps marched on. The collapse of the 5th Corps, however, soon made it clear that Villers devant Mouzon was not going to be practicable as a crossing point. In any case, the bridge there soon came under fire from the Bavarians advancing northward after they had reached Pouvron. Douay posted a rear guard north of Raucourt in order to hold off the advancing Ist Bavarian Division of von Stephan while he took the rest of his corps further down stream towards Remilly. The position at Raucourt was soon taken by the Bavarians just as darkness fell.

The confused and headlong nature of Douay's retreat had brought his corps close to panic; and they found at Remilly that the floodwaters of the Meuse (which had been dammed in order to create lakes to strengthen the southern defences of Sedan) were too deep to allow the fords to be used. The corps was thus confined to using one bridge, the planking of which was covered by the waters. Both the cavalry and artillery experienced great difficulty in inducing their horses to cross such an obstacle, and progress in getting the corps over the river was extremely slow. When, during the course of the night, Douay learned of MacMahon's orders for a general concentration on Sedan, he took that part of his corps that had not got across the river further downstream, crossing finally at Torcy, where he was obliged, at about 3.30 a.m. the following morning, to call on the garrison of Sedan to open the gates to his battered command.

Moltke and the King, with Royal Headquarters, had watched the battle until night fell from the Vaux en Dieulet heights near Sommauthe. Returning that night to Buzancy, as all the nearer villages were full of wounded, Moltke was irritated by

> the great inconvenience of inadequate lodging for hundreds of illustrious guests and their suites, when, for once in a way for military reasons, headquarters were established in a small village, instead of a large town. Shelter for those officers whose duty it was to prepare the necessary orders for the morrow was only found late at night, and with considerable difficulty.[28]

Verdy, who had spent the day with the Crown Prince of Saxony, encountered chaotic conditions on the road back to Buzancy and, at the very entrance of the village, found four rows of wagons that had become jammed fast and over which he had to climb before reaching the staff office at 1.30 a.m. where he found Moltke and the rest of the staff preparing orders for the next day.[29]

It had been a battle that MacMahon had had no intention of fighting. As Moltke remarked in typically dry understatement: 'by the result of this battle the French army had been driven into an extremely unfavourable position.'[30] This very important strategic victory had not been won by the Germans without suffering considerable loss. Their casualties in killed and wounded amounted to some 3,500, mostly from the IV Corps upon which had fallen the bulk of the fighting. The French put their loss in killed and wounded at about half this number but, in addition, some 3,000 prisoners, mostly unwounded, fell into German hands, together with 51 guns and a considerable quantity of wagons, ammunition and other equipment. Perhaps more importantly, the morale of the Army of Châlons, which had been steadily deteriorating, had been dealt a further dreadful blow (but, apparently, not all the French were utterly cast down; it was reported that on the evening of August 30, with the Germans just the other side of the river, a ball was held by French cavalry officers at Douzy for the ladies who had come in the hope of watching a victorious battle. If true, it demonstrated a French sang-froid even exceeding that of Wellington who when he visited the Duchess of Richmond's ball at Brussels, was a good deal further from the front line).

The position into which the French had been driven prompted Moltke to suggest to Bismarck that some steps ought to be taken about the situation that might develop if MacMahon was driven across the Belgium frontier. During the afternoon, Bismarck telegraphed instructions to the Minister of the North German Confederation in Brussels, von Balan, to warn the Belgian government that the frontier might be crossed by French troops and that, if they did, they should be at once disarmed.

That night, soon after he got to Buzancy, Moltke issued a general order.

> Although until now no report has come in showing at what spot the fighting of the separate corps ended, it is clear that the enemy everywhere retreated or was beaten. The forward movement is therefore to be continued tomorrow as early as possible, and the enemy to be vigorously attacked wherever he stands this side of the Meuse, and to be squeezed into the narrowest possible space between that river and the Belgium frontier.

Moltke added that the Crown Prince of Saxony must prevent MacMahon from getting away to the east while the Third Army should push forward against the enemy's front and right flank. 'If the enemy should pass onto Belgian territory without being at once disarmed, he must be pursued thither without more ado.'[31] He had no intention of giving MacMahon the slightest chance now of getting away.

14

August 31

General Emmanuel Felix de Wimpffen had been Governor of Oran when the war broke out. Anxious to secure an active command in the campaign, he had been energetically lobbying the War Ministry from Africa. He had long enjoyed a high reputation in Imperial circles and the pressure to replace de Failly as commander of the 5th Corps after what was seen as his failure adequately to support MacMahon at Wörth provided the opportunity to appoint Wimpffen to a key post. Among other things, de Failly had been quite unjustly blamed for the separation from his corps of its reserve artillery, which Palikao recorded as having been left behind at Chaumont without orders;[1] and, by August 22nd, the decision had been taken that Wimpffen should replace him. Ordered by telegraph, accordingly, to report for duty, the latter arrived in Paris on Sunday, August 28 where he had lunch with Palikao. Whether or not he was then offered the command of the 14th Corps, which was at that time in course of formation in Paris, is a matter of some dispute. He recorded later that it was an offer made to him, which he declined; Palikao on the other hand recalled that what was discussed was the possibility that Wimpffen might replace Lebrun in command of the 12th Corps.[2] It had been Lebrun who remarked of Wimpffen that he had 'an unlimited confidence in his own capacity',[3] and he certainly responded with a good deal of assurance to Palikao's complaints about the situation at the headquarters of the Army of Châlons. 'Send me to the army', he said. 'I shall impart the needed boldness and decision.' Palikao was impressed; next day just before his train left for Rethel, Wimpffen was handed a secret order from Palikao, to the effect that in the event of anything happening to MacMahon, he was to succeed him in command of the army. Equipped with this, and with some very unsatisfactory maps, which he obtained from the War Ministry, he set off to his new command. At Rethel, he left the train and rode off to Mézières with a small escort assigned to protect him from German cavalry patrols, but which panicked when coming under fire from what turned out to be a party of francstireurs. From Mézières he went by train, on August 30, to Bazeilles, riding on towards Mouzon, where he encountered the first units of his new command as they streamed back in disorder from the battlefield of Beaumont. At Amblimont,

> he met crowds of various corps streaming back from the battle, who cried loudly for bread and made known their state of depression and exhaustion, whilst their leaders appeared helpless and indifferent. In consequence of the utter want of discipline among the troops the General had some difficulty in halting a number of men, even after he had pointed out to them that they were not pursued.[4]

In the confusion, he lost his personal baggage. Trying to help bring order out of chaos, he collected together a number of units and disordered parties of individual troops drawn from all four corps and led them back to Sedan. It was not an encouraging start.

During the events of August 30, Ducrot's lst Corps had been the least affected by the Battle of Beaumont. Two of its divisions had been, during that day, at Carignan where it had enjoyed the company of the Emperor and his suite. The rest of the corps was at Douzy. In the course of the day, MacMahon ordered Ducrot to cover the retreat of the rest of the army, remarking to Bossan, Ducrot's aide de camp, that he did not yet know what he would do, but that in any case the Emperor should leave at once for Sedan.[5] Given the alternative lines of march of the army, either westward towards Mézières or eastwards to Montmédy, Ducrot had no difficulty in deciding how it would be best for his corps to be disposed. The movement to the east to the relief of Metz was, he saw, now quite impossible; in the other direction there were supplies, there was Vinoy with the 13th Corps, and there was just about enough space to manoeuvre between the Meuse and the Belgium frontier. Unhesitatingly, therefore, Ducrot ordered that the divisions of Wolf and L'Hériller should remain at Douzy, while his other two divisions were posted on the heights above Blagny. This done, he went off to interview his Emperor and tell him what was going on around Mouzon. Napoleon could not believe his ears. 'Mais c'est impossible! Nos positions etaient magnifiques!'[6] Urged by Ducrot, who was carrying out MacMahon's instructions, that he should take the train to Sedan, Napoleon refused, insisting on staying with the corps covering the retreat. He was unimpressed by Ducrot's suggestion that the Imperial suite would hamper the retreat. Later that night, though, Napoleon changed his mind and went off to Sedan by train without telling Ducrot that he was going.

During the night, Ducrot had heard nothing further from MacMahon. Pondering what must now be done to save the army, he had a discussion with Margueritte, whose cavalry division was the other side of the River Chiers opposite Carignan, and who immediately agreed with Ducrot that the only practicable step would be for the army to retreat on August 31 through Illy, and thence west to Mézières.[7] With this in mind, Margueritte began at once to move his division to the right bank of the Chiers. Next morning, Ducrot, still without news from MacMahon, reported to him his plan to march on Illy through Francheval and Givonne, and gave the necessary orders to Wolf and L'Hériller. They, however, had, in the meantime, received orders direct from MacMahon when he passed through Douzy to move straight to take up the positions allotted to them at Sedan along the valley to the south of Givonne. Ducrot, meanwhile, looking across the Chiers valley from the heights above Francheval, could see the Germans moving up to Douzy, a sight which reinforced his view that there was no time to waste. He was accordingly horrified when at last at 4 p.m. he received orders from MacMahon to the effect that the lst Corps should take up the defensive positions assigned to it to the east of Sedan. 'I gave you the order that you should retreat from Carignan to Sedan and in no way to Mézières where I have no intention of going', he complained; this greatly irritated Ducrot, who had in fact received no such order.[8] Quite apart from this, however, Ducrot regarded a deployment of the army in defensive positions around Sedan, rather than a concentration upon Illy in preparation for a move westwards, as quite disastrous and it was with 'un véritable désespoir' that he now ordered the Ist Corps to Sedan.

Outwardly at any rate MacMahon was more cheerful. On the evening of August 30, when giving orders to Lebrun for the retreat of the 12th Corps by

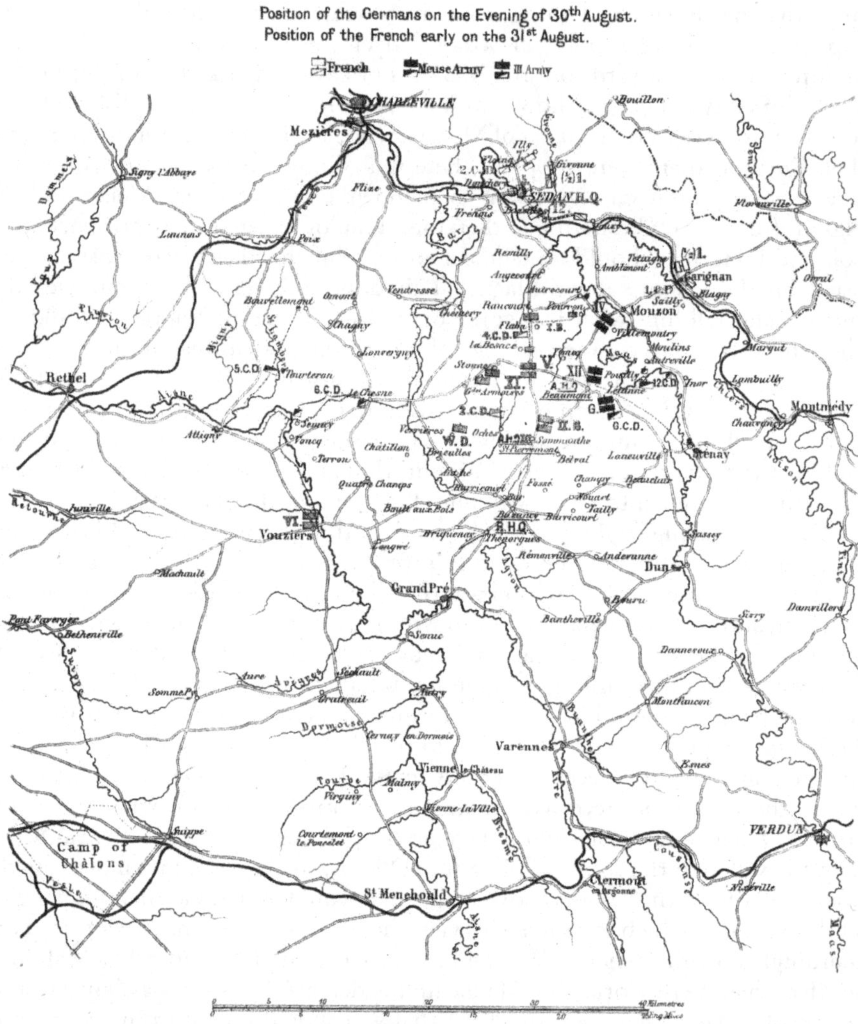

Positions of the armies on August 30/31

Douzy upon Sedan, he was reflecting upon the situation. 'We have had a bad time, but the situation is not hopeless. At the most the German army before us cannot exceed in numbers 60 or 70,000 men. If they attack us so much the better; we shall be able doubtless to fling them into the Meuse.'[9]

His decision to go to Sedan seems to have been prompted only by considerations of supply, and not to have been part of any settled decision as to what he might do next. After the war, he testified to the Parliamentary Inquiry that the move was dictated solely by the need for food and ammunition, and not with any intention of accepting battle at Sedan. Certainly, although the position had some defensive possibilities, it was no place in which to stay if the Germans were close at hand. His conversation with Lebrun appears to confirm that he thought himself to be opposed by only about three German army corps, of which one was on the right bank of the Meuse, and that he had time to rest and refresh his army before the next move. Nothing much was done to assess the strength of the advancing German forces and if, as he later told Douay his intention was to manoeuvre in front of the enemy, MacMahon did remarkably little to find out how far that would be possible.

Napoleon had turned up at Sedan during the night of August 30/31, and MacMahon had lost no time in telling that he should go at once to Mézières, where Vinoy was arriving with the leading units of the 13th Corps. Napoleon, however, once again, rejected the advice and insisted on staying at Sedan.

At Imperial Headquarters on the morning of August 31, Wimpffen reported to MacMahon who received him without enthusiasm. Napoleon was depressed and emotional, taking Wimpffen's hand with tears in his eyes and asking him what he thought was the reason for the disastrous outcome of the battle of Beaumont.[10] Neither the Emperor nor MacMahon, however, told Wimpffen anything about the situation or what their plans were. Wimpffen asked that orders now be issued for him to take over the 5th Corps but, getting no response, finally went off to find the headquarters of the corps and there told de Failly that he come to supersede him as its commander. The coolness of his reception by MacMahon no doubt contributed to Wimpffen's decision not to disclose the commission he held to succeed MacMahon if the need arose.

In the meantime, Vinoy had sent an officer of his staff, Captain de Sesmaisons, to report to MacMahon the arrival of his leading troops at Mézières. De Sesmaisons had had an adventurous journey by train from Mézières to Sedan, being fired on by German horse artillery from the heights above Frénois. When he got to headquarters, he reported his observations of German columns moving northwards on Donchéry.

Napoleon at once gave orders to de Sesmaisons that Vinoy should concentrate the whole of his corps at Mézières, instructions which he confirmed by telegram. In view of the proximity of the Germans, he arranged for de Sesmaisons to have a horse, and showed him personally the route that he should take back to Mézières, adding that the army would retire in that direction the following day. He told de Sesmaisons that this would be a safe route to take, since this was an entirely new road from St. Menges through St. Albert and Vrigne aux Bois and had not been marked on the map and, accordingly, would be unknown to the enemy. It was a remarkable commentary on the comparative efficiency of the two general staffs that, unknown to Napoleon, the German maps did indeed show the road. During this visit de Sesmaisons also saw MacMahon, and both he and Napoleon emphasised their belief that the Germans could not have sufficient forces to cross the river at Donchéry to disrupt a French retreat on Mézières.

While de Sesmaisons was at headquarters, Douay arrived, anxious to obtain reinforcements to enable him properly to defend the whole of the position assigned to the 7th Corps along the ridge from Floing up to the Calvaire D'Illy. MacMahon agreed that he should have reinforcements adding, in confirmation of what he had been telling de Sesmaisons, 'but I do not want to shut myself up in lines; I wish to be free to manoeuvre'. 'Monsieur le Maréchal, tomorrow the enemy will not leave you the time', said Douay, who returned to his own headquarters profoundly uneasy. Later in the day, when he heard from an old soldier who lived in the neighbourhood that the Germans were now getting across the river at Donchéry, Douay ordered his troops to entrench the position between Floing and Illy. When Douay reported this enemy activity to headquarters nothing more was done to reconnoitre these movements, which seriously threatened any prospect of the Army of Châlons escaping westward. [11]

At 5.30 p.m, MacMahon held a Council of War. By then, although evidence was accumulating from all sides of the extent and the strength of the German advance, MacMahon seems to have accepted the possibility that he might have to fight a defensive battle. The orders for the next day, however, were merely to the effect that it should be a rest day for the whole army.

For the movement on Mézières to be practicable once the Germans got across the river at Donchéry, an immediate retreat down the roads to Mézières on the right bank of the Meuse was essential. Any German bridgehead at Donchéry must be liquidated or, at the least, contained and any other German crossings of the river must be prevented. The bridge at Flize had been destroyed by a battalion despatched by Vinoy from Mézières. The bridge at Donchéry had, however, fallen unbroken into the German hands. This was due to the initiative taken by the German cavalry from Frénois. The shelling of Sedan station by the German horse artillery so alarmed the station master that, knowing that there was a ration train in the station yards, he ordered it away to Mézières. This contained some four fifths of the provisions for which MacMahon had come to Sedan, and which were thereby denied to him. On the train, there travelled also a company of engineers with orders to blow the bridge at Donchéry; but this plan entirely miscarried when the engine driver, fearful of the shells fired from the other bank of the river, stopped long enough only to drop the engineers, and went on his way again to Mézières before the explosives could be off-loaded. The seizure of this bridge by the Germans necessarily further restricted the time and space available to MacMahon. To get even a part of his army away, Vinoy would have to be ready to cover the crossings at Charleville-Mézières, and a phased withdrawal from the positions to the east of Sedan would be necessary while other units held off the advancing troops of the Saxon Crown Prince. Throughout the day, this remained a possible though hazardous option, but in spite of what had been said to de Sesmaisons, nothing at all was done to prepare for it.

Moltke's orders issued during the evening of August 30 had reflected some uncertainty as to the final positions his troops had reached. Unlike MacMahon, however, he had a pretty clear idea of where his enemy was and no doubt at all about what he was going to do. And his subordinate commanders had, in any event, made their own preparations to anticipate his instructions. As dawn broke on August 31, the commander of the 24th Cavalry Brigade from the 12th Cavalry Division, Major General Senfft von Pilsach, took a squadron of lancers forward from Pouilly towards Mouzon to reconnoitre the French positions on the right bank of the Meuse. It was soon plain to him that the French were pulling back towards Douzy and Carignan and, in thick fog, he trotted forward unopposed to Mouzon. With only one officer and four men, he rode into the town, accepting the surrender of numerous French stragglers before crossing the bridge to the left bank of the Meuse to report that the French had gone.[12] An infantry battalion was at once sent over the river to garrison the town.

Meanwhile, the main body of the German cavalry was exploring the country between the Meuse and the Chiers, which they reported as being clear of the enemy. Evidently, however, the French were still in some strength on the right bank of the Chiers, although by noon the leading units of the Guard Cavalry Division were riding through and beyond Carignan in pursuit of Ducrot's retreating corps. The cavalry continued to harass the French as they pulled back, while behind them the infantry divisions of the Guard Corps and the XII Corps crossed the Meuse at Pouilly and Létanne respectively and then pushed on northwards in pursuit of the enemy. The Guard Corps moved on the right through Vaux and Sailly while the XII Corps, on the left, passed through Moulins and Mouzon. Meanwhile, the IV Corps, on the left bank of the river, remained in its positions west of Mouzon. As the cavalry bustled up the tail of Lebrun's retreating 12th Corps, they could see in the distance Ducrot's lst Corps falling back from Carignan through Francheval, where it operated as the last rearguard of the Army of Châlons as it concentrated at Sedan.

During the day, the Crown Prince of Saxony faced little opposition as he firmly shut the door to the east. When the Guard Corps reached Francheval and Pourru aux Bois, the last road to Metz was cut. During the day, the Guard Corps marched more than 30 miles to get to these positions and once there, Crown Prince Albert allowed them to bivouac for the night. The XII Corps, meanwhile, marched on, its advanced guard reaching Douzy about 3 p.m.[13] During the rest of the afternoon, it closed up to the Chiers with, on the right, 23rd Infantry Division between Tetaigne and Lombut and, on the left, the 24th Infantry Division at Brevilly and Douzy. Meanwhile, the IV Corps, which had had a hard fight the day before, remained in its positions at Mouzon, acting as the pivot on which the righthand side of Moltke's trap swung shut.

On August 30, the only unit of the Third Army to have been actively engaged in the Battle of Beaumont was von der Tann's I Bavarian Corps. During the day, the rest of the Third Army had continued its march to close in on MacMahon. On the extreme left of the army, the 5th and 6th Cavalry Divisions had moved, respectively, from Attigny upon Tourteron and from Vrisy upon Le Chesne and Semuy. In the centre of the army's advance, the V and XI Corps, with the Württemberg Division, had moved northward in the general direction of Stonne followed at some distance in the rear by the VI Corps which, during August 30, marched from Vienne le Chateau to Vouziers.

It had seemed to the Crown Prince and Blumenthal that the French position at Stonne was likely to be fairly strong, and that the proper course would be to wait until they had two corps available to attack it; but soon after Alvensleben began his attack on de Failly's troops at Beaumont, it was evident to Moltke that the longer the French remained in the Stonne position, the worse it would be for them. Accordingly, he ordered the Crown Prince not to press the enemy too hard with Kirchbach's V Corps which had by now got into line at Oches; and then, at 3 p.m. on August 30, it was seen that the French were retreating. (This was Douay's rearguard finally getting under way). Kirchbach accordingly pushed the V Corps forward to La Besace. Behind him, Gersdorff's XI Corps, which had set off from Monthois, was now arriving in front of Stonne, having crossed the path of the Württemberg Division which was heading northwest towards Verrières. By nightfall on that day the Crown Prince's army had closed up alongside the Army of the Meuse and, with the exception of the cavalry screen and von Tümpling's VI Corps away to the left, the whole of his army now stood between the Meuse and the Bar and was at Moltke's disposal for the operations planned for August 31.

For that day, the principal objective of the Third Army was, of course, to cut off any westerly retreat by the French and to close up to the River Meuse at Sedan itself. It had been Prince Albrecht's 4th Cavalry Division that had been the first unit to reach the river, occupying the heights above Frénois early enough in the day to shell de Sesmaisons' train as it steamed in from Mézières. Meanwhile, the XI and V Corps were directed on Donchéry, capturing the vital bridge there during the afternoon and crossing it with the cavalry and infantry units which had led Douay to begin entrenching his positions above Floing. To the left of these two corps, the Württemberg Division continued its march north-westwards towards Flize to operate as a flank guard of the army.[14] During the day, it made contact with patrols from Vinoy's 13th Corps operating from Mézières. Southwest of the Württembergers, the 6th Cavalry Division (commanded by Duke William of Mecklenburg-Schwerin) had reached the River Vence at Poix; after destroying the railway there it pushed forward, encountering a mixed force of infantry and cavalry, which it drove back to Mézières. Rheinbaben's 5th Cavalry Division, meanwhile, began its day at its overnight camp at Tourteron, later probing towards Reims with a hussar regiment. On the extreme left, in echelon along the River Aisne, the VI Corps had a brigade at Amagne and another at Attigny with a division at Semuy guarding against a threat to the left flank of the German operations that did not really exist.

For von der Tann and the I Bavarian Corps, the task for August 31 was to follow the French and to take up a position near Remilly and, after some delay due to the late arrival of orders from Army Headquarters, the advanced guard moved out from Raucourt at 8 a.m. Von der Tann, realising that he would be called upon to get across the Meuse, brought up his pontoon train, while his senior engineer officer went forward to reconnoitre four crossing points. Von der Tann himself rode forward with his advanced guard, and soon received news of large scale French movements towards Sedan on the right bank of the Meuse. The French movement was covered by several batteries of artillery, which opened fire on von der Tann as he deployed above Remilly, and he quickly brought up his own corps artillery to the heights above Remilly. By about 11 a.m. he had ten batteries in action, firing partly on Bazeilles and partly on the French columns moving towards Bazeilles from Douzy, which were soon compelled to change course and march in a more northerly direction. At about noon, the Bavarian gunners saw the French beginning to make preparations to blow the railway bridge near Bazeilles.[15] It was obvious that if the bridge was to be preserved for use next day, there was not a moment to lose. Von Stephan, commanding von der Tann's Ist Division, at once ordered up the 4th Jäger Battalion. Captain Slevogt, who was in command of the leading company, saw that some of the arches of the bridge were already filled with powder barrels, and just as the French engineers prepared to lower more barrels under the far end of the bridge, the Jägers dashed forward and drove off the French. They seized the powder barrels and emptied them into the Meuse and then took up positions on the right bank of the river. As fresh troops came up in support, the riflemen, intoxicated with their own success, established themselves on the railway embankment and drove back the French battalion that came forward at this point and then pushed on to Bazeilles. The resourceful Captain Slevogt was among the many officers killed, but in spite of the heavy casualties, the riflemen continued to advance and succeeding in entering the village. Seeing this successful advance, the 2nd Battalion, on the other side of the Meuse, also crossed the river in support.

Von der Tann, on the heights above Remilly, was furious, having had no intention of crossing the river until the Crown Prince of Saxony should have advanced far enough to co-operate in an attack on the enemy. At 2 p.m., von der Tann gave orders that two pontoon bridges should be built across the river near Aillicourt; but he still made no effort to support the riflemen fighting in the outskirts of Bazeilles, believing that if he did, the whole corps would probably be drawn by degrees into a purposeless struggle. Finally, to his relief, the riflemen were seen retiring from Bazeilles towards the railway bridge and Aillicourt, where they were ordered merely to hold the bridgeheads that had been gained. By 5.30, the fighting on this sector had ended for the day. The Bavarians could see from their positions above Remilly the advanced guards of the XII Corps, which had halted for the day at Douzy. The artillery duel across the Meuse had forced Lebrun to move his rearmost division out of range of the Bavarian guns, going north to cross the Givonne at Daigny. During the artillery exchanges, a number of houses in Bazeilles caught fire.

As night fell, therefore, the Germans had secured the vital crossings at Remilly and Aillicourt, where the Bavarians were already in contact with the enemy at Bazeilles; and at Donchéry where by nightfall the advanced guard of the XI Corps had established itself, pushing forward outposts beyond the town into Vrigne-Meuse and Rigas Mill. In Donchéry, an important item of intelligence was gleaned.

> According to the statements of the inhabitants empty trains had been despatched to Mézières up to within a short time before, for the purpose of bringing troops from that place to Sedan, a piece of information which was opposed to the previous idea that the enemy intended to move away westward and was therefore at once reported to army headquarters.[16]

Positions of the armies on the evening of August 31

This was confirmed by an examination of the books of Donchéry railway station. Gersdorff, the corps commander, had ridden forward into the town to join his advanced guard and ordered a pontoon bridge to be built west of Donchéry while blowing up the railway bridge to the east of the town. The rest of his corps bivouacked at Cheveuges. Both rail and telegraphic communication between Mézières and Sedan had now been cut off. Further west, the Württembergers had driven the French out of Flize and occupied an outpost line between Elaire and Chalandry in order to prevent any interference from Vinoy at Mézières.

15

Sedan: The Battlefield

A dozen miles from the Belgian frontier, Sedan stands on the River Meuse which follows its twisting path around the south and west of the town before turning back to form the Iges peninsula. Once, the city had a considerable role to play in French history. Before being absorbed into the Kingdom of France, the Duchy of Bouillon and the Principality of Sedan had preserved their independence as the 'sovereign states', and were justifiably regarded with deep suspicion by the rulers of France. They served as a convenient haven for those plotting against the French throne, as well as a sanctuary for Protestant men of learning, which gave the city the title of 'the Geneva of the north'. The Duc de Bouillon, who on his wife's death was granted title to the sovereign states by Henri IV, was an inveterate intriguer against the Crown; so was his second wife, and so was his oldest son, whose participation in a conspiracy against Richelieu and Louis XIII finally led to the handing over of Sedan in exchange for his life. But it was the second son who was to reflect most fame on the city of his birth; Henri, Vicomte de Turenne was to become Louis XIV's most brilliant commander and one of the outstanding figures of French military history.

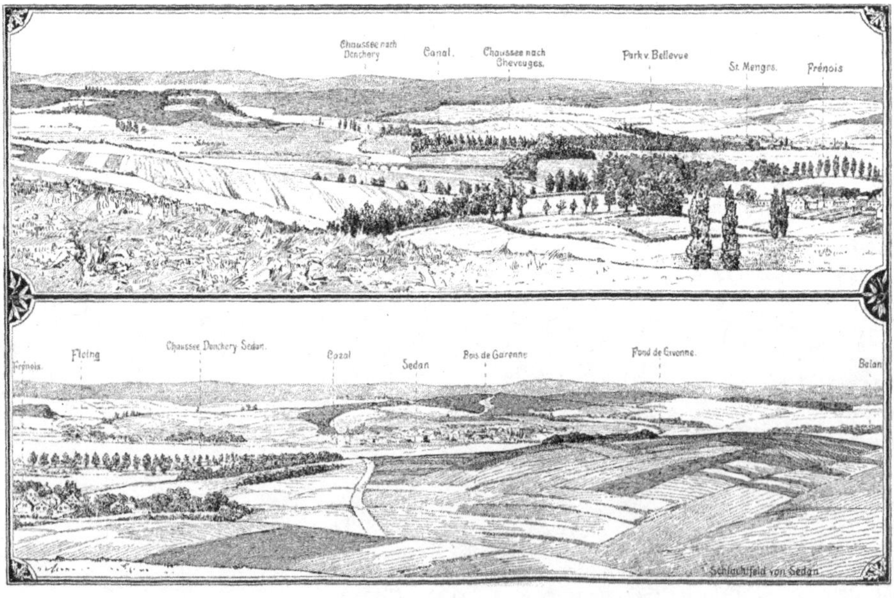

The battlefield of Sedan, from the heights near Frénois, from a sketch by A. von Werner (Pflugk-Harttung)

The centre of Sedan is dominated by its citadel; by 1870 its military significance had long since faded, and the city itself was a quiet backwater of about 20,000 inhabitants. It had, though, only some half a century earlier experienced foreign invasion, having been for three years after Waterloo occupied by Prussian troops. As a defensive position, it offered some short-term advantages but, in general, left much to be desired; by August 31, however, it provided the Army of Châlons with probably the only available point at which it could hope to concentrate and regroup. The principal geographical feature of the battlefield is the River Meuse itself and this, together with the little River Givonne which flows into the Meuse from the north, rising in the hills near the Belgian frontier, defined the shape of the battle. The Meuse meanders northwest from Mouzon, covering the city of Sedan to the south and west. The Official History noted that the broad valley of the Meuse 'mostly within cannon range of the fortress is enclosed at many points between high banks, while by damming the river it was completely laid under water along the whole extent between Sedan and the west side of Bazeilles.'[1] Then comes the sweep first north and then south around the Iges peninsula before the river swings westward again past the little town of Donchéry. Opposite Sedan itself, on the left bank in a smaller loop of the river, had grown up the suburb of Torcy, on the outskirts of which stood the city's railway station. The railway ran southward on the left bank of the river to Bazeilles and then crossed towards Carignan; northward from Sedan its route took it across the base of the Iges peninsula before crossing to the right bank to run through Donchéry.

The eastern side of the French position was formed by the valley of the Givonne, which runs into the Meuse just east of Bazeilles. On either side of the valley, the ground rises steeply, offering a good defensive position along its western side, from which 'an effective fire could be brought to bear upon almost every point of the opposite field of approach.'[2] Along the length of the valley lie scattered clusters of buildings and small villages. Just above the village of Givonne itself, the river there is joined by a smaller stream and the valley bends somewhat to the west. This part of the position was, in fact, not immediately covered by MacMahon,

The suburbs of Sedan, from an oil sketch by Bracht (Pflugk-Harttung)

since it was assumed that so dense was the forest and broken ground through which an enemy must approach that it could not be traversed.

There were defensive heights, too, to the northwest of Sedan, running from the village of Floing to join the valley below Illy, which was the northernmost point of the French position. Here the ground is a rugged undulating upland, the highest point of which is a little south of the Calvaire d'Illy. Upon the slopes which run down towards Sedan from this point lies the Bois de la Garenne. The northwest face of the French position offered particularly good defensive possibilities. 'Continuous ranges of hills separated by broad depressions formed several parallel ramparts of defence towards the northwest; yet from the very commencement the French had limited themselves to the occupation of the southernmost, which project from the Bois de la Garenne between Floing and Cazal.'[13]

At the base of the Bois de la Garenne runs a defile called the Fond de Givonne, through which runs the main road from Sedan to Bouillon. From this tight defensive position there radiated only a limited number of escape routes – northwestwards towards Mézières, between the head of the Iges loop and the Belgian frontier, the main road to Bouillon, the roads eastward along the Chiers and the southerly exit from the city at Torcy.

MacMahon positioned his army to cover the obvious approaches. Douay's 7th Corps held the heights from Illy to Floing. Douay had been, from the outset, extremely apprehensive about the position he was to hold, and pressed anxiously for reinforcements to secure the key point of his line, the Calvaire d'Illy. The information given to him the previous afternoon that the Germans were preparing to cross the river at Donchéry, had sharpened his fears. His decision to entrench the position between Floing and Illy was a step that he had previously avoided because of the exhaustion of his men. He posted a strong force at St. Menges, covering the road to Vrigne aux Bois and Mézières. Behind the 7th Corps stood three cavalry divisions commanded respectively by Margueritte, Bonnemains and Amiel.

Ducrot's Ist Corps was posted along the line of the Givonne valley while on his left, Lebrun's 12th Corps occupied Bazeilles and the heights immediately above that village. To the rear and behind Ducrot's left, to the west of Givonne village, lay the cavalry division of Michel. Finally, the battered 5th Corps, of which Wimpffen had now taken command, was held in reserve, partly in the old camp under the walls of the Citadel, and partly behind the position occupied by Douay's corps.

The swampy area south of Sedan had, by September 1, been flooded and the Meuse itself thus provided most of the defence of the southwest of MacMahon's position. Opposite the city, above the villages of Frénois and Wadelincourt, the wooded hills rose towards the Bois de la Marfée. There were wooded hills, too, rising steeply from the eastern side of the Givonne valley and these, which masked apparently impenetrable heights through which the Germans could not be expected to come, probably contributed a good deal to MacMahon's fatal underestimate of his enemy's strength, and his overestimate of the security of his own position.

While the Army of Châlons was thus settling down in its defensive positions, away to the southeast on August 31 the Army of the Rhine was embarking on another attempt to escape from its prison. On August 29, Bazaine had received the news previously referred to that MacMahon was on the move towards him. The information, in fact, came to him in a message from Turnier, the commandant of Thionville: 'General Ducrot,' ran the message, 'is in command of MacMahon's corps: he must be on this day, the 27th, at Stenay on the left wing of the army, General Douay on the right wing at the Meuse. Be in readiness to march at the first gun.'[4] This seemed positive enough, even for Bazaine; and he next day gave orders for the issue of iron rations and for preparations to be made for an advance. Later that day an earlier message from MacMahon himself came in, announcing his movement on the Aisne – 'where I shall act according to circumstances in coming to your aid.'[5] On the assumption that MacMahon had been moving towards Metz since August 27, Bazaine expected to meet him quite close to that city. His plan was to advance on the right bank of the Moselle between the river and the Saarlouis road. That part of his army currently on the left bank of the river was to cross the bridges below the fortress at 6 a.m. on August 31, and it was hoped that the entire army would be concentrated on the right bank by 10 a.m. On the right of the German troops in position on the front selected for the attack, on the Moselle from Malroy to Charly, was the 3rd Reserve Division (von Kummer), which included some Landwehr units brought up to relieve regular troops needed for the advance on Paris. In the centre, the 1st Infantry Division (von Bentheim) covered the position running from Failly to Noisseville; while on the left, on a front facing northwestwards stood the 2nd Infantry Division (von Pritzelwitz). Upon these three divisions, under the command of Manteuffel was to fall the whole strength of the Army of the Rhine, which would receive powerful support in its attack from the guns of the fortress.

Evidently the French did not intend to rely heavily on surprise. 'Considerable uproar and the incessant clanging of military bands in the positions of the invested army had attracted the attention of the Prussian watch posts as early as the evening of 30 August', as the Official History noted.[6] This was repeated during the early hours of the following day and a great deal of French activity was observed from the German positions. Bazaine's aim was to achieve a victory on the right bank driving the German defenders northeastwards while he advanced northwards towards Thionville. Frederick Charles had no difficulty in divining what Bazaine was up to, and in order to frustrate this manoeuvre he ordered, early on August 31, that the II Corps should move off towards St. Privat. But, in the afternoon and evening, a fierce assault fell on Manteuffel's troops before he could be reinforced. Manteuffel fought tenaciously in his most forward positions and in these he held off the assault of Ladmirault's 4th Corps between Failly and Noisseville; however, the assault of the 3rd Corps under Le Boeuf was more successful and, sweeping through Noisseville it turned north on Servigny, while on Ladmirault's left the 6th Corps pushed forward into the outskirts of Failly. The French had gained ground significantly, and as he retired to bed that night Bazaine, who had spent the day in the front line with his troops, might for the first time for a very long time, have felt some satisfaction and even some hope for the future. But, incomprehensibly, at 5 a.m. next morning he was to be found drafting orders remarkable, even for him, for their extreme timidity. He cautiously prepared two messages for use later in the day; one announcing a modest success and the other a retreat back into Metz. In the event, it was the latter telegram which had to be used. Manteuffel had seen the danger of Le Boeuf's thrust from Noisseville on Servigny; and early on September 1, reinforcements now having reached him, he threw forward his troops supported by a powerful artillery line. The village of Noisseville was defended by Bastoul's division; overwhelmed and unsupported by the rest of the French army, most of which was close at hand, at 11 a.m. on September 1, Bastoul fell back. Thereafter, the threatened breach in the encircling lines was closed and Bazaine's weary troops found themselves back once more within their siege lines. Losses in the battle on the German side amounted to nearly 3,000 men killed and wounded, while the French had lost slightly more than 3,500. While this battle was proceeding, more spectacular events were occurring at Sedan; but it was the battle at Noisseville which effectively sealed the fate of Bazaine's army.

Neither the attempted breakout nor its dispiriting outcome was, of course, known to MacMahon and his staff, as they prepared for the next move of the Army of Châlons. Nor, on the night of August 31, were they well informed about the dispositions of the enemy facing them, while Bazaine, naturally, knew nothing of MacMahon's real situation. Frederick Charles, on the other hand, was kept closely informed of developments. At 10 p.m. on August 31 Moltke wrote to tell him of the events that had followed the battle of Beaumont, and foreshadowed what was to come.

> The enemy's army is trying to march off on the right bank from Sedan to Mézières. A thrust forward through Donchéry, which is already in our possession, will begin very early in the morning .... In these conditions a serious disturbance of the army before Metz by parts of the army of MacMahon does not seem probable.[7]

While the French troops had been coming up to take up their defensive positions around Sedan, the Germans had been steadily pushing on with the task of shutting off the various escapes routes available. Some units did, in fact, manage to escape, such as Brahaut's cavalry division. But for the most part, the French were glad to have found a position which looked as if it might for the time being be defensible. The contrast between MacMahon's irresolution and Moltke's implacable determination had already been evident throughout the campaign, but never was it more apparent than on August 31.

That day too Napoleon issued what was to be his last General Order. It was not an outstandingly inspiring document.

> Soldiers! The commencement of the war has not been fortunate and I desire therefore, disregarding all personal prejudice, to relinquish the command of the armies to those marshals, whom public opinion especially designates for this duty. As yet not one success has crowned your efforts; I understand however, that the army of Marshal Bazaine is re-organised under the walls of Metz, while that of Marshal MacMahon was only slightly attacked yesterday. There is therefore no cause for your spirits to droop. We have prevented the enemy from penetrating to the capital, and all France is rising to expel the invader. Under these cogent circumstances I have, while worthily represented by the Empress in Paris, preferred the role of the soldier to that of the sovereign. From nothing will I shrink to save our country. There are still, God be thanked, brave men, and –

should there be cowards – the Articles of War and public scorn will be their punishments.

Soldiers! Prove yourselves worthy of your old fame.

God will not forsake our country if every man does his duty. Napoleon.[8]

Throughout the day, as the German columns pressed on to give effect to Moltke's plans, the reports coming in to his headquarters made it clear that MacMahon had abandoned the left bank of the Meuse and was concentrated around Sedan. Since to accept battle in that position appeared to him to be extremely imprudent, and he invariably assumed that his opponent would make what he judged to be the most dangerous move, Moltke continued to make his own plans on the basis that MacMahon was preparing either for a rapid retreat to the west towards Mézières or possibly by an attack towards Carignan. Of the two, Moltke thought the Mézières route more likely, as he indicated to Frederick Charles, although there were some indications pointing the other way. Accordingly, he took steps to cover either eventuality and by late afternoon was fairly well content that he had the situation well in hand. It would be for the Crown Prince who, that day, took up what Blumenthal described as a very indifferent quarter in a brewery,[9] to prevent the escape through Mézières, and the advance of the Third Army had proceeded far enough to ensure that this was the case.

The Crown Prince's headquarters were at Chémery, and it was through this village that Royal Headquarters passed on their way to their quarters for the night at Vendresse. Moltke and Podbielski took the opportunity for a brief but vital conference with Blumenthal. With the maps spread out before him, Moltke could see the extent to which his movements had been successful, and he allowed himself a measure of self-satisfaction. 'Now we have them in a mousetrap,' he said.[10] The Official History merely reports laconically 'a short conference at Chémery between Generals von Moltke, von Podbielski and von Blumenthal, upon the situation of the campaign and upon future proceedings.'[11] Blumenthal in his diary, however, observed Moltke as 'rubbing his hands with a sardonic smile on his face,' and it is hardly surprising that even these cautious hard-headed professionals were exultant at the position that they had achieved. The future proceedings which they were considering had been agreed upon some days before; and it was not at once thought necessary to issue any special orders for September 1 because the order of August 30 from Buzancy had already laid down the basic plan; and the details, at least as far as the army of the Crown Prince of Prussia was concerned, had been settled at Chémery.[12] At 9 p.m. on August 31, Blumenthal duly issued his orders for the next day in accordance with his discussions with Moltke. On the left, Gersdorff with the XI Corps and Kirchbach with the V Corps were to push on through Donchéry towards Vrigne aux Bois. The Württembergers were to cross the Meuse at Dom le Mesnil and to position themselves to act either as a reserve, or to obstruct any advance Vinoy might make from Mézières. In the centre, Hartmann, with the II Bavarian Corps, was to occupy the high ground on the left bank of the Meuse opposite Donchéry, and to hold the position stretching eastwards below the Bois de la Marfée between Frénois and Wadelincourt. Finally, on the Crown Prince's right, von der Tann's I Bavarian Corps had, as its principal task, to connect with the Army of the Meuse and to move forward in concert with that army. Behind these army corps, the cavalry divisions were posted close up to cover any eventuality, although it was perhaps already clear that their role on the following day was not likely to be a significant one.

Sheridan, accompanying Royal Headquarters to Chémery, watched with interest as some of the Crown Prince's troops marched past the King. 'They moved in a somewhat open and irregular column of fours, the intervals between files being especially intended to give room for a peculiar swinging gait, with which the men seemed to urge themselves over the ground with ease and rapidity. There was little or no straggling, and being strong, lusty young fellows, and lightly equipped – they carried only needleguns, ammunition, a very small knapsack, a water bottle, and a haversack – they strode by with an elastic step, covering at least three miles an hour.'[13]

Meanwhile, however, a key member of Moltke's staff had seen what, in fact, was probably the tail end of Ducrot's corps crossing from Francheval to the west side of the Givonne valley, and which he took to be a general withdrawal towards Mézières. This piece of intelligence brought to him by Brandenstein went some way to confirm in Moltke's mind that a breakout towards Carignan was no longer probable, and that the real problem was more likely to be at the other end of the line. The intelligence reports that troops were moving into Sedan from the direction of Mézières, still did not lead Moltke to assume that MacMahon was committed to the supreme folly of standing and fighting in the Sedan position. For this reason on receiving Brandenstein's news he wrote at once at 7.45 p.m, to Blumenthal to stress the importance of getting some troops over the Meuse that night so that they could attack at daybreak.[14]

Looking back, Moltke wrote many years later of MacMahon's situation that he

> could scarcely have realised that the only chance of safety for his army, or even for part of it, lay in the immediate prosecution of his retreat on the lst of September. It is true that the Crown Prince of Prussia, in possession as he was of every passage over the Meuse, would have promptly taken that movement in flank in the narrow space, little more than four miles wide, which was bounded on the north by the frontier. That nevertheless the attempt was not risked was only to be explained by the actual condition of the exhausted troops; for on this day the French Army was not yet capable of undertaking a disciplined march involving fighting; it could only fight where it stood.[15]

In addition to pushing forward the Third Army on the left in this way, Moltke also varied the task to be given to von der Tann; he was now ordered to hold fast the enemy opposite to him, and he was in addition given the right to attack independently of the Army of the Meuse. Von der Tann's corps had already scored a notable success that was to be of great importance on September 1 when securing the all important railway bridge, over the Meuse near Bazeilles, and by following this up by throwing the two additional pontoon bridges over the river east of the railway bridge.

The Third Army passed on to the headquarters of the Crown Prince of Saxony details of Moltke's instructions, and of the latest intelligence received from Brandenstein. This information reached the Army of the Meuse at 1 a.m., and orders were at once issued for the day's movements.[16] They began with a reference to the news of the possible French retreat through Mézières, and then went on to order the Guard Corps to move on Villers Cernay and Francheval, and the XII Corps on La Moncelle. The movement was to begin at 5 a.m. As a result of the new orders given to von der Tann, Alvensleben's IV Corps was now directed to push forward one division in support of the Bavarians, while the other crossed the Meuse at Mouzon and remained in general reserve at Mairy.

While the Germans were in this way preparing for the battle on the basis that the French were trying to get away, their opponents had now completely abandoned any thought of a retreat on Mézières on September 1. Its four corps were, by the night of August 31, securely ensconced in their defensive positions, although the last troops of Ducrot's corps trudged wearily into line as late as 11.30 p.m. The orders which went out from MacMahon's headquarters prescribing September 1 as a rest day for the whole army, in stark contrast to the German activity, appear to confirm that MacMahon was still under the illusion that the Germans were not yet upon him in great strength and even, perhaps, that all his options -to fight, to retreat to Mézières, or to advance on Carignan – would remain open to him. In fact, the two armies were now in very close proximity and, indeed, some of their units were already in contact. The French troops settled down for the night, their morale somewhat restored by the blazing campfires, and the smell of cooking, and by the sound of drums and cymbals. Commandant Vidal, whose battalion was in camp on the Givonne front, and who was very conscious of just how close the enemy were, noted the striking contrast. 'On one side there was insouciance, a noisy gaiety and brouhaha; on the other, foresight, precision, calm and silence! Here, we thought of nothing but eating and sleeping; over there, they thought only of victory! Such was the attitude of the two armies; it was the perfect characterisation of the two nations.'[17]

The Army of Châlons was now assembled in its tight defensive lozenge around Sedan, while opposite stood the very much larger and thus far entirely victorious German army. Whatever may have been MacMahon's confused assessment of his position, to some of his subordinates the real situation was all too clear. Douay remarked gloomily to one of his officers: 'nothing now remains, my dear Doutrelaine, but to do our best before we are overwhelmed.' And as the evidence of German activity began to appear upon all the hills around Sedan, Ducrot commented succinctly to Dr Sarazin, in a pungent counterpoint to Moltke's remark earlier that evening: 'Nous sommes dans un pot de chambre, et nous y serons emmerdés.'[18]

16

Sedan: The First Stages

Well before dawn on Thursday, September l, the Germans were already active. Not surprisingly there was an air of confident anticipation not only among the soldiers but also among the attendant princes, politicians and civil servants. Verdy, who had been work until 1.30 a.m., rose again at 4 o'clock and by 5 o'clock was on the road with Moltke and the Royal Headquarters from Vendresse towards Sedan.

> It was a fine fresh morning, the morning mists still lingered about the mountain valleys, and clung closely about the wooded slopes in thick wreaths. Mixed with the smoke of the bivouac fires they formed in many places enormous and apparently impenetrable banks of clouds, reminding one of those spectacular pieces on the stage, in which some particularly grand stage effect is set off with all sorts of fireworks. Above them we saw the hilltops rising up into the pure air. Our road was free from troops; the two corps who had started during the night were already about to cross the Meuse, only their transport was still in the bivouacs which we passed.[1]

The Crown Prince was even earlier on the road, leaving Chémery at four in the morning in dense fog. He was obliged to caution his enthusiastic troops against

Crown Prince Albert of Saxony (Scheibert)

giving away their position by cheering as he rode by.[2] Blumenthal went with him in his carriage and, at about 6 o'clock, they reached the height above Donchéry that had, the previous day, been chosen as the position for their headquarters. Back in Vendresse, Moritz Busch had also risen early, to write up his diary, but he had no expectation of going with the royal party to witness the decisive victory that was now confidently expected until Bismarck noticed him and told him to get in his carriage.[3] While they waited for the King, Bismarck gave instructions to Abeken; when the latter was distracted by a passing royal personage, Bismarck was sharp with him. 'Listen to what I say, Mr. Privy Councillor, and in God's name let princes be princes. We are talking business here.'Later, in conversation with Busch he remarked of Abeken (in fact only half a dozen years Bismarck's senior), that 'the old gentleman is quite carried away if he sees anything belonging to the Court – but after all I could not do without him.'[4] Soon the King appeared and the whole entourage rolled off northwards. At Cheveuges, the carriages stopped and the King, his staff and retinue mounted their horses and rode on up to the position on the hill above Frénois selected personally by Moltke from which they were to witness the battle, where they arrived at about 7.30 a.m. By now the sun was up and gradually the fog cleared away, first from the hilltops and, later, from the valleys and river. Soon, under a cloudless sky, the whole of the panorama of the battlefield lay before the royal party. Busch described the scene.

> On our hill a brilliant assemblage had gathered; the King, Bismarck, Moltke, Roon, the crowd of Princes, Prince Karl, their Highnesses of Weimar and Coburg, the Hereditary Grand Duke of Mecklenburg, generals, aides-de-camp, marshals of the household, Count Hatzfeldt, who after a time disappeared, Kutusoff the Russian, Colonel Walker the English military plenipotentiary, General Sheridan and his adjutant, all in uniform all with field glasses at their eyes. The King stood. Others, among whom was the Chancellor, sat on a grassy ridge at the edge of the stubble. I heard that the King had sent round word that large groups must not stand together, as the French in the fortress might fire on them,[5]

Back In Vendresse, Archibald Forbes had made a bad start to the day. Unaware of the impending battle, he was posting letters at 7 a.m. when he heard there was fighting in the Meuse Valley; learning incorrectly that the King had gone off to visit the battlefield of Beaumont, he set off in that direction, found no-one, got lost and rode nearly to Mézières, where he found the Wurttembergers pursuing French troops almost into the town itself. Encountering an officer who told him of the battle now raging at Sedan, Forbes rode off at once on the high road until he came to Frénois.[6]

Russell, meanwhile, had also gone astray, becoming detached from the Crown Prince's staff which he was supposed to be accompanying. He rode up towards Sedan, passing columns of German troops as they moved up towards the battlefield, until as the early mist began to clear he reached a ridge from which he could look across the valley of the Meuse towards Sedan itself, which appeared to him 'to be placed in a lake. Its ancient bastions and battlements, spires and steeples, reflected in the placid waters.'[7] From his position, he could see the fighting that had begun around Bazeilles. He turned westwards and rode until he saw a group of officers dismounted looking through their glasses. Thinking it was the Crown

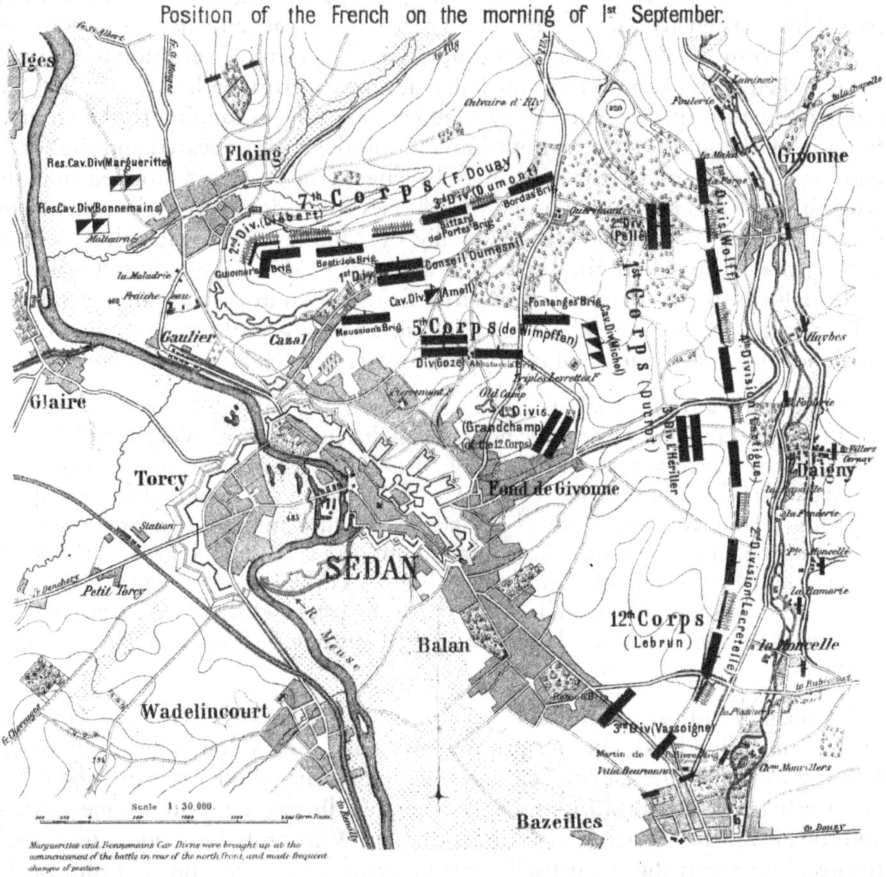

Position of the French at Sedan, September 1, morning

Prince's escort, he galloped briskly towards them until an officer angrily shouted to him to dismount in the presence of the King.

> And, just at that moment, a shot or shell from Sedan whistled through the air and plunged into the bank close to the spot where the King himself, Moltke, Bismarck and three or four of his staff, were standing. This caused an immediate commotion. Whether I was the unlucky cause of the notice taken of us by the French or not I cannot say, but certainly the looks of several of the entourage seemed to imply that I was a criminal of no ordinary magnitude.

Unable to find the Crown Prince and his staff, Russell remained until the middle of the morning with the King's entourage before finally being discovered there by one of the Crown Prince's aides.[8]

In Sedan itself that morning a grim sense of inevitability prevailed. Napoleon was resolved to meet his destiny bravely; with rouged cheeks and a freshly waxed moustache, dressed in a general's uniform covered with decorations, he rode out on his horse Phoebus, accompanied by his staff, from the Sous-Préfecture, with little hope that the battle could possibly be won, and gripped by a personal conviction that for him the day would end in death. Indeed, there seems no doubt that this is what he actively sought; all that day, racked with pain as he rode around the battlefield, he exposed himself with reckless courage.

Meanwhile, MacMahon, still evidently convinced that he had some options open to him, had started the day anxious about the position to the west and had sent two staff officers to ascertain whether the Germans were across the Meuse at Donchéry. As dawn broke, he was still awaiting their report.

Early that morning, the whole of the battlefield had been shrouded in a heavy mist; von der Tann, taking advantage of the limited visibility and of the discretion given to him to attack if it was necessary to do so to prevent the French from retreating, was early on the move. During the night, he and his staff had become more and more convinced that the French would slip away, and he resolved on his own initiative to stop this. It was a decision, as the official historian of the Bavarian forces observed, that 'exercised an unquestionable influence on the course of the decisive battle of Sedan.'[9] With a small staff he went forward at about 2.30 to Aillicourt to superintend the advance. It was still dark at 4 a.m., when the Bavarians began to cross the Meuse, using both the railway bridge seized the day before and also the first of the two pontoon bridges that had been thrown across the river a little upstream. They moved swiftly up the road in an attempt to take the defenders of Bazeilles by surprise. Bazeilles, however, was going to be quite a tough nut to crack. The brigade of Martin des Palliéres (whose commander had been wounded the previous day) which initially formed the village's garrison was composed, like the rest of Vassoigne's 3rd Division of the 12th Corps, of Marine regiments who were to prove brave and capable opponents for the Bavarians. They had moved into the village the night before and had spent the time preparing it for a stout defence. In particular, the stone buildings in the northern part of the village above the Douzy road junction had proved particularly suitable for fortification; and a series of barricades were erected on the main street and in the side roads. In this part of the village, the key point of the defence was a large building known as the Villa Beurmann.

As soon as the Germans opened fire that morning, the remaining brigade of Vassoigne's division (Reboul) moved out from Balan by way of reinforcement; and Reboul took command of the defence of Bazeilles. Evidently the French posted inadequate sentries because, at first, the leading German troops took their opponents by surprise and got into the village without meeting any resistance. They soon, however, ran into the Marines' prepared positions and a savage house-to-house battle developed. Around the Villa Beurmann the fighting was particularly intense, the company attacking this position losing all its officers.[10] At the north end of the village, Major Sauer, whose lst Battalion of the 2nd Regiment had led the advance into Bazeilles, had got a long way ahead of the rest of the Bavarian units attacking the village and occupied a corner house with a handful of men. He was then cut off and the reinforcements for which he sent were unable to break through to relieve this isolated post which, commanding as it did the road into the village, was of crucial importance. Back at Aillicourt, von der Tann was encouraged by news of the approach of the leading units of the Army of the Meuse and was quick to commit further troops to the struggle for Bazeilles. The poor visibility, however, and the nature of the battle had quickly broken up the engagement into a confused melée over which the commanders on neither side could exert much real influence.

Stephan, from his position at Bazeilles station, thought that the village had been more or less occupied and brought up his reserve to attack on his right through La Moncelle, and to clear any pockets of resistance in Bazeilles itself. The French, meanwhile, had launched a violent counter-attack to the west of the village, driving back the Bavarians in this part of the front out of Bazeilles itself and as far as the railway embankment, and capturing in the process Sauer and his men, who were obliged to surrender after three quarters of an hour of desperate resistance. Sauer and the other German captives were taken back to Sedan at 7 a.m., encountering at Balan Napoleon and his staff coming out to the battlefront. They were most correctly treated by their captors, but the civilians in Sedan behaved so badly towards the prisoners that the French escort was much embarrassed.[11]

Stephan's tenuous hold on Bazeilles was now preserved only by the retention of two stone houses at the Douzy road junction. The French attacks on these houses were driven off with heavy loss, but they now took possession of a large house on the other side of the road, from which they could not be budged until two four-pounder guns were brought to point-blank range, finally compelling the French to pull back at 7.45 a.m. When the guns were then moved down through a side street and on to the main street and turned on the Villa Beurmann, however, half the gunners were hit in a few moments and they were hastily withdrawn.[12]

As the morning wore on, both sides continued to feed reinforcements into the battle. Stephan's reserve, which consisted of von Orff's detachment advancing from Remilly, came up to the south and west of Bazeilles and was soon heavily involved; Orff's horse was shot under him and the heavy toll of officers on the German side continued. Meanwhile, the French were reinforced by Carteret Trécourt's brigade from the 1st Corps, which had been brought to Balan, and by part of Goze's division of the 5th Corps which moved up along the Meuse. And the civilian inhabitant of Bazeilles, which was by now on fire in several places, were themselves drawn into the struggle. Claiming that these fired on both wounded and on stretcher-bearers, the German Official History records that 'the Bavarians found themselves eventually compelled to cut down all inhabitants found with arms in their hands.'[13]

To the north and east of Bazeilles, the advance guard of the Saxon XII Corps had been pushing forward on La Moncelle, while Schöler's 8th Division, which was leading the advance of the IV Corps, came up to Remilly. As visibility improved, the German artillery, once again, began to dominate the battlefield. Although for a long time the Bavarian gun line on the other side of the river was ineffectual, the batteries already on the right bank, firing at shorter range, were soon inflicting heavy casualties on the French. Stephan was now supported by the developing attack of von Schumacher's 2nd Bavarian Division, led by Colonel Schuch's 3rd Brigade, which forced its way into part of Chateau Monvillers before being held up by the French tirailleurs beyond. The Bavarian efforts to push forward in Bazeilles itself were still frustrated by the vigorous defence of the Villa Beurmann at the north end of the village. In an attempt to outflank its defenders on their left, Lieutenant Colonel Schmidt pushed forward with the 1st Jäger Battalion into the Monvillers park, but was pinned down after seizing a summer house at the edge of the park. As the bitter conflict continued, 'the three foremost Bavarian brigades became much mixed up in the struggle towards 9 o'clock; the different units were almost entirely dissolved into lines of skirmishers, and even the 3rd Brigade which was the last to come into action only possessed a few unbroken companies.'[14] And as the 4th Infantry Brigade now came forward, it too was in its turn drawn into the battle for Bazeilles. Behind the Bavarians, at about 9 a.m., Schöler began to get his 8th Division over the Meuse to bring it up to von der Tann's support. The latter, as was almost invariably the case with the higher German commanders, had ridden to a point only a few hundred yards from the front line. He found the position of his corps extremely precarious. By now, he had no more reserves and the French resistance was as tenacious as ever; and to his right, in the gap between La Moncelle and the Monvillers park, the French were pouring in heavy reinforcements who stormed forward to the attack German units who, in some cases, had by now run out of ammunition. The French assault was heavily supported by artillery from the heights beyond. Only with the greatest difficulty was the French attack beaten off.

Von der Tann had been the first of the German commanders to move forward, which he did as a result of his liberal interpretation of his orders. To his right, however, as has been seen, the Army of the Meuse was also early on the move. At 5 a.m. the XII Corps had ordered its advanced guard of seven battalions under Major General von Schulz to move forward from Douzy towards La Moncelle, and it set off in the mist and darkness through Lamécourt towards its objective. By 6 a.m. it was heavily engaged with the French infantry in La Moncelle, as well as with a strong force of artillery on the far side of the Givonne.

As soon as Schulz had enough infantry in hand, he launched a successful attack on La Moncelle; and then a bold assault led by Lieutenant Legler and Captain von Beulwitz succeeded in getting over the bridge that crossed the Givonne at La Platinerie. On the far side they seized two houses which served as a bridgehead

General Ducrot (Rousset/*Histoire*)

from which the Saxons could not be expelled, notwithstanding violent French efforts to recapture them.[15]

Immediately in rear of Schulz's force, the rest of the 24th Division was moving up fast; significantly, the corps artillery was next on the road having been pushed ahead of the 23rd Division and the Cavalry Division. Reinforcement was urgently needed; the XII Corps' line now reached as far as Daigny where, in due course, it would connect with the advancing troops of the Guard Corps. These were, however, still some way off. At Daigny, Ducrot now launched an attack, a powerful force from the lst Corps crossing the Givonne and pushing forward to the Bois Chevalier. Schulz had to employ all his spare troops in containing this attack and, as the rest of the 24th Division came up, it too was committed to the struggle. As usual though, it was the artillery that was used to smash Ducrot's attack. A powerful gun line of twelve batteries was quickly built up at the southern end of the Bois Chevalier, firing not only at the French infantry advancing from Daigny but also at the artillery positions of Lebrun's 12th Corps on the heights overlooking La Moncelle.

MacMahon had received from Lebrun, at about 5 a.m., a report of the attack on Bazeilles and he rode off at once to see the situation for himself. Finding that the Marines defending Bazeilles were holding on well, he then repaired to La Moncelle and from the height overlooking the village looked across the Givonne at the Bois Chevalier. While he was doing so, a shell burst nearby and he was hit and, as soon became apparent, severely wounded in the leg. The exact time of his injury is uncertain; MacMahon thought it was about 5.45 a.m. but it was almost certainly later than this. At all events he at once sent word to Ducrot appointing him to the command (in itself a surprise since Ducrot was junior to both Wimpffen and Douay) and was then taken back to Sedan. On route, he met the Emperor and his staff cantering towards Bazeilles.

Ducrot learned of his appointment at about 7 a.m. 'It is very late', he said, 'and the responsibility is very heavy'; but he was at once clear as to the proper course to be followed.[16] Unaware of the extent of the German advance to the west of Sedan, he issued orders at once to retreat on Mézières. 'There is not a moment to lose; we must go back to yesterday's plan' – that is, to retreat at once before the enemy completely surrounded them. And he angrily rejected the suggestion of his Chief of Staff that the retreat could be delayed as all was at present going well. 'Carry out my orders; no more discussion,' he snapped, riding off to see Lebrun. Here, he encountered more dissent; Lebrun, who was on foot, having received a minor injury, was full of his success in pushing back the Bavarians and was at first not at all disposed to accept Ducrot's suggestion that the Germans meanwhile were getting around the French flank.

Finally, however, albeit very reluctantly, Lebrun complied with Ducrot's instructions and gave orders for the retreat; but the execution of these orders brought further command problems for Ducrot. Although he had resolved not to interfere in the conduct of the battle, Napoleon was surprised by the decision to pull back, bearing in mind Lebrun's apparent success on the right, and he sent Captain Guzman of his staff to find out what was going on. Ducrot was firm. 'Tell His Majesty that what's happening on the right isn't important. The enemy amuses us there while he manoeuvres to outflank our wings, and it's behind us towards Illy that the battle will be decided.'[17]

Ducrot's intention was endorsed after the war by MacMahon. Evidently still believing that he had had the choice of moving either east or west, he testified to the Parliamentary Enquiry that the Army of the Meuse and the Bavarians would not have been able to prevent the French moving eastwards. He added that

> the movement upon Mézières prescribed by General Ducrot at 8 a.m. had some prospect of success. In the event of its failure, part of the troops could have escaped through the woods, which cover the greater part of the country between the Meuse and the frontier. In the worst case the army could throw itself into Belgium.

He went on to say that the retreat would have been difficult by 9.00 a.m. but impossible by 11.00 a.m.[18]

When he was satisfied that Lebrun's movement was well under way, Ducrot was thunderstruck to receive a message from Wimpffen. Between half past eight and nine o'clock, Wimpffen had appeared on the scene at Lebrun's headquarters and had announced to him his secret commission to take the command; and he then sent off at once a note to Ducrot to that effect. He had not done so immediately on hearing of MacMahon's injury because he thought that Ducrot, having been chosen by MacMahon to take over, must know the latter's intentions.[19] Ducrot, who after the war engaged in a fierce war of words with Wimpffen, suggested that his announcement of his authority to take command was prompted by the apparent success that was being won at Bazeilles. The

MacMahon is wounded during the early stages of Sedan, by Zimmer (Scheibert)

German Official History, on the other hand, more charitably accepts Wimpffen's own statement that he assumed the command as a matter of duty because of his belief that Ducrot's orders were fundamentally wrong.[20] At all events, Wimpffen's prescription was indeed to reverse Ducrot's orders, and Lebrun's retreat was at once countermanded (Wimpffen claimed that key positions in Bazeilles had been lost because of it but it seems that the retreat order never reached the units concerned,[21] and the German account makes clear that none of the French positions along the Givonne were abandoned until well after Wimpffen took over). Ducrot at once rode over to Wimpffen who was still at Lebrun's headquarters, saying that he had not come to argue about the command, but to tell Wimpffen the true position. Strong words were exchanged between them; Ducrot flourished a map before Wimpffen showing him the danger of a German advance on Illy. Glancing perfunctorily at the map, Wimpffen said impatiently 'yes, yes, that's all very well, but for the moment Lebrun has the advantage and we must make use of it. It's not a retreat we need, it's a victory.' Ducrot's reply was short, and to the point; 'It's a victory you need? Well, tonight we will be very lucky to have a retreat!' and, with this, Ducrot rode off, as he put it, ' la mort dans l'âme' to order the divisions of Pellé and L'Hériller to stay put.[22]

While all this was going on, the French were doing rather well. Lacretelle's division of the 12th Corps, attacking La Moncelle and Monvillers Park, succeeded in forcing the Saxon corps artillery to fall back, and inflicted heavy casualties on the German infantry. It was as well, therefore, for the latter, that Montbé's 23rd

Fierce fighting rages in Bazeilles, a drawing by Röchling (Lindner)

A charge of French Marine infantry during the fighting for Bazeilles and its environs, painting by Sergent (Rousset/*Histoire*)

Infantry Division was now approaching. He was ordered by Prince George to send his 46th Brigade forward to Bazeilles and to reinforce the Saxon batteries east of Monvillers, and to cover their left. The fierce struggle around La Moncelle, and the progress the French were making there, led the 46th Brigade to swing to its right to meet the threat; and soon Montbé himself led another regiment forward to strengthen the position. Prince George had come up to the front line early in the day even before the whole of the advanced guard of his XII Corps was in position, since he believed, like von der Tann, that the immediate task facing the Germans was to prevent the escape of the French. By 7 a.m., it had become very clear to him that the situation was entirely different and that the opposition now in front of his corps was very considerable.

Meanwhile at the end of the French line, Vassoigne was advancing again on the western side of Bazeilles. On the other side of the village, the 4th Bavarian Brigade had become involved in fierce street fighting as it worked its way into the French positions on that side of the village. South of Bazeilles, more German reinforcements were coming up; Schöler's 8th Division from Alvensleben's IV Corps reached Bazeilles station at about 10 a.m., while the 7th Division (Schwarzhoff) had by that time got as far as Lamécourt. These reinforcements, and the effect they had on developments around Bazeilles, materially shifted the balance of advantage towards the Germans; and, further north, the French advance from Daigny was getting into difficulties. Ducrot had noted that the bridge there was of crucial importance as the only crossing point over the Givonne for artillery. The attack, carried out by Lartigue's division, was led by a battalion of Algerian Turcos, followed by Fraboulet's brigade with the divisional artillery. For a while,

General Wimpffen, signatory to the capitulation at Sedan (Rousset/*Histoire*)

the assault made good headway, driving back first the outnumbered Saxon infantry (who were in any case now beginning to run out of ammunition) and then part of the German artillery line. Gradually, however, on this part of the battlefront also, the deployment of German reinforcements shifted the balance. Here, it was the deployment to the north of the extreme right wing of the XII Corps that tipped the scales. Lartigue's troops were rolled back, first towards Daigny, then through the village itself and, finally, across to the other side of the river as the Saxons seized the bridge. Lartigue, up in the front line, had a horse killed under him; his Chief of Staff, Colonel D'Andigné, was wounded; as he lay in a field of beetroot he was startled when a pig came and sniffed at his wounds, and he was a good deal relieved when a couple of shells burst nearby and frightened the pig away.[23] By 10 a.m. Daigny and La Rapaille on the western bank were firmly in German hands.

Napoleon had received the news of Ducrot's supersession by Wimpffen with considerable unease; and he was still more disquieted by the possibility foreseen by Ducrot that the Germans might be getting around the left flank towards Illy. This concern was sharpened when he met, in the Fond de Givonne, a Chasseur officer, who knew the terrain, and who warned him that if the Germans got round Illy, all would be lost. Meeting Wimpffen, the Emperor aired his anxieties. Wimpffen was jauntily confident. 'Your Majesty need not worry. In two hours I will have thrown them in the Meuse', a boast that prompted a muttered comment by one of Napoleon's staff: 'Please God it isn't us that are thrown there.'[24]

Napoleon made his way northwards towards Givonne where a long-range bombardment by the Guard Corps artillery was taking a heavy toll. There, he became involved in the task of deploying three batteries to counter the effect of the German guns. Hohenlohe, whose Guard artillery were on the other side of the valley, saw what happened.

> A battery horsed entirely with greys trotted up from the Fond de Givonne to Givonne itself, and tried to take up its position between that village and the Bois de la Garenne. As soon as it appeared on the hill, the three batteries mentioned above (from the Ist Division of the Guard) opened fire on it. It fell to pieces, as it were, and its ruins remained where they fell. It did not fire a single shot. A second and a third battery met with the same fate.

Accounts given in French sources of this incident suggested to Hohenlohe that on this occasion he had indeed had the Emperor before him.[25]

At La Moncelle, the two houses on the Balan road west of the river, seized with such opportunism earlier in the morning, had been the scene of continuous fighting as the French attacked on all sides. The French advance in the Givonne Valley had made it impossible for a long time for any support to be afforded to the German troops occupying this exposed position. By the time that they had been in that situation for three hours, the ammunition was running low, and it was not until 9 a.m. that some relief got through, first to the nearer house and then to the other. The fighting here was at extremely close range and the casualties on both sides were very heavy. It soon became clear that this advanced position could only be held if there was a general forward movement. After an abortive attempt to drive back the French, Major Leythäuser, who with the regimental colours in his hand had been foremost among the relieving troops, now returned to collect further

The main street through Bazeilles, a photograph taken shortly after the battle (Rousset/*Histoire*)

troops. Bringing forward the 10th Regiment over the river, and supported by further battalions from La Moncelle, he drove the French back and moved up towards the heights above the crossing.[26] To the left of this advance, the 46th Brigade now moved towards Balan and behind them, the advanced guard of the 8th Division now crossed the river. The long struggle of the French to hold Bazeilles was coming to an end, as the advancing Germans now outflanked Vassoigne's left; by 11 a.m. the heights west of La Moncelle had fallen. In Bazeilles itself the Villa Beurmann fell when Schmidt, who had been held up in his position around the summer house, led some detachments of riflemen into the main street of the village; other troops cut down the hedges on the Monvillers Park with their sword bayonets and from there surrounded the villa.[27] With the loss of this critical position, all hope of hanging on in Bazeilles was gone, and the French now fell back from the burning village towards Balan, and to the heights above that place. The Germans were in control of the village by 11 a.m, although in a number of places there were still pockets of fierce resistance. The fire in the village gradually spread until, by noon, the whole place was ablaze, and any further advance had to be over a route cleared by the German pioneers to the north-east of Bazeilles. Throughout these operations the German artillery had succeeded in dominating the French gunners who, by 12 noon, had retreated out of sight behind the heights between Balan and Givonne. Around Bazeilles, the German units, which had become inextricably intermingled during the struggle, began to sort themselves out for the next phase of the battle.

North of the Saxon XII Corps, Prince August's Guard Corps, which comprised the right wing of the Army of the Meuse, was marching forward as fast as possible through Francheval and Villers Cernay towards the battlefield. Pape's Ist Guard Division was in the lead, and its advanced guard reached Villers Cernay by 7.45. Not waiting for the rest of the corps to come up, Pape pushed forward the advanced guard, capturing the village and the heights to the west; and he then came into contact with some Zouaves from Lartigue's Division. All along his front, in fact, Pape met with French pickets to the east of the Givonne but no serious opposition was encountered, and by 10 a.m. the Guards were in sufficient strength to make a dash at the village of Givonne itself, occupying the northern part of the village and driving the tirailleurs that occupied it back towards the Bois de la Garenne. Hohenlohe's artillery was close behind him.

> The heart of every gunner throbbed with joy when he found that all our leaders had but one desire, to bring up their artillery. General von Pape had accompanied the light infantry and Fusiliers of the Guard when they drove the few skirmishers of the enemy whom they found there from Villers-Cernay and the adjoining forest. From the other side of the wood he saw the French grand artillery line, which was firing on the XII Corps from the opposite side of the low ground of Givonne. "Bring me two guns," he cried to me when I met him, "so that I may take that line in flank!" – "You shall have not only two, but ninety", I could proudly answer ... at 8.45 a.m. the artillery of the lst Division of the Guard opened fire'[28]

Meanwhile, the extreme right of the Guard Corps had bumped into some resistance as far north as La Chapelle; but the progress of the main body of the corps, and its all important artillery, was not delayed. The artillery itself was soon in action against the French batteries on the hills to the west of Givonne and Haybes.

The Crown Prince of Saxony had been watching the battle from a hill south-east of Mairy which, although some considerable distance from the front line, gave a good view of the fighting as far north as Dalgny. In this position, he received reports of the struggle along the valley of the Givonne and of the progress that the Guard Corps had made to the north. The earlier indications that only a rearguard remained to hold off the Army of the Meuse while the main body of the French army retreated westward soon gave way to the realisation that a large part of the French army was still deployed along the Givonne. The Crown Prince's object had in any case been to advance to Fleigneux and through Illy to St. Menges, and the discovery that the French intended to stand and fight did not alter his objective, which was to complete the encirclement of the French army by linking hands with the Third Army to the north of Sedan. At 8 a.m. he issued orders to give effect to this intention, after the Givonne position had been taken, notifying von der Tann, from whom he required cover for his left flank as he advanced.[29] By 9 o'clock, Prince August, with the headquarters of the Guard Corps on a hill to the east of Givonne, on which part of the Guard artillery was deployed, could see, looking to the west, the signs of heavy fighting around St. Menges which made clear how far the Third Army had advanced around the far side of the French position.

17

Sedan: The Advance of the Crown Prince

The Prussian Crown Prince on his hill near Donchéry had been able to see little at first of what was going on. He and Blumenthal could hear, though, the roar of artillery from the direction of Bazeilles. By 7 a.m., when the mist lifted, it was evident that von der Tann was engaged in a fierce struggle, and although aware that the Saxon Crown Prince was moving up towards the Givonne Valley it was decided to strengthen von der Tann with part of the II Bavarian Corps by shifting this to the right. One division was to be left on the heights between Frénois and Wadelincourt, whilst the other was to cross the river to Bazeilles. Blumenthal had difficulty in restraining the Crown Prince from moving ever closer to the firing line; he recorded in his diary that it was also his own instinct to do so; 'but I am now old enough to be able to restrain such youthful ardour, and am quite content to find myself looking on at this sort of thing, in calm serenity, from a safe distance.'[1]

Meanwhile, on the left, the XI and the V Corps were making good progress; in accordance with an agreement made during the night between the corps commanders, the XI Corps crossed the Meuse at Donchéry, and the V Corps mainly by a pontoon bridge to the west of that place, making for Vrigne aux Bois in order to block any French movement to the west, and then moving on around the top of the Iges loop of the Meuse, to come in on the French through St. Albert and

Moltke at Sedan, painting by von Werner (Scheibert)

St. Menges. Both corps had set off early, at 3 a.m. and 2.30 a.m. respectively. Still further to the left, the Württemberg Division had at 6 a.m. crossed the Meuse at Dom le Mesnil, heading for Vivier au Court.[2] While the Crown Prince's army was thus moving up to the west of Sedan, it became increasingly clear that, contrary to what had been supposed, the French were not making any attempt to break out in this direction, so that instead of being obliged to fight an encounter battle on the road to Mézières, the Third Army was free to swing round to the east to complete MacMahon's encirclement. With no opposition, the XI and V Corps marched briskly northwards although some confusion was caused when, in the dark, one regiment of the XI Corps inadvertently crossed the line of march of the V Corps.

Hartmann, the commander of the II Bavarian Corps had, as soon as the sound of the guns from Bazeilles became audible, trotted forward with his reserve artillery in time to pick up the orders for his movement to the right. His artillery formed a gun line upon the height east of Frénois, and opened fire on the French in and around Bazeilles in support of von der Tann's attack there. The 4th Bavarian Division with its artillery moved up immediately south of Sedan opposite Torcy, while the 3rd Bavarian Division began to cross the river towards Bazeilles, where it was committed to an assault to the west of the village, before, on von der Tann's orders, moving forward on Balan as the French began to fall back.

By 7.30 a.m., Kirchbach with the V Corps had reached Vivier au Court and Gersdorff's XI Corps to its right had got as far as Vrigne aux Bois, when the Crown Prince sent Major von Hahnke to the commanders of both corps with orders that they should move to the right upon St. Menges.[3] Since both corps had to take the road running between the river and the Bois de la Falizette, some further confusion was to be expected; in the event the XI Corps temporarily mislaid one of its battalions that had gone as far north as Bosseval. The head of the 22nd Division set off again from Vrigne aux Bois, got lost, fetched up at Montimont, and then found itself behind units of the V Corps already using the road defile at the Bois de la Falizette. As Moltke noted, it was surprising that the French had taken no step to defend the 2,000 yards gap between the wooded heights and the river.[4] Had they done so, the logistical problems of the Germans, as they sought to get around the west of the French position, would have been very greatly increased.

In fact, however, while all this was going on, the French remained in apparent ignorance of the Third Army's sweep around their flank, and it was not until a French patrol bumped into a couple of squadrons of Hussars leading the advance of the XI Corps into St. Albert that there was any hostile contact. Following up the retreating French troops, the Hussars reached St. Menges; when Gersdorff brought up his 87th Regiment, the village was swiftly taken by its Fusilier battalion. This was followed quickly by the remainder of the regiment, which took position to the east of the village looking towards Illy. Taking into account the seriousness of the threat which Gersdorff's advance posed, the French reaction was even now sluggish in the extreme. Not only had the door been slammed firmly shut on any escape route out of Sedan to the west and north-west; if Gersdorff was not quickly stopped, the whole of this flank would become indefensible. And, of course, any movement in the direction of Illy by the Germans would expose the Army of Châlons to imminent and complete encirclement. The fundamental difficulties of the position at Sedan had always been evident. What was now becoming clearer was that MacMahon's dispositions had not even made the best of the defensive advantages of the position and, in practice, had increased the difficulties enormously. Neither at St. Menges nor anywhere else along the Meuse at this point was Douay's 7th Corps in a position to hold up the German advance as it developed first by Gersdorff's corps and then by that of Kirchbach. This lack of tactical imagination had been evident all around the French position; to the south, on the other bank of the Meuse, the heights above Frénois and Wadelincourt, and the Bois de la Marfée, were abandoned without even the most token attempt to contest them.

It was at St. Menges that Gersdorff's leading troops now took what proved to be a decisive step, when three companies of the 87th Regiment pushed on south, after taking St. Menges, towards Floing. The rest of the regiment had been left in position east of the village facing towards d'Illy. One of the three companies occupied a small walled copse on height 812 east of the Floing road, while the other two companies under Captain von Fischer Treuenfeld first of all took two outlying farms close to Floing, and then moved on into the north-west part of the village itself, before being driven back into the farm buildings by a French counter-attack.[5]

If he had not done much to bar the German progress thus far, Douay had at least deployed his artillery to advantage along the ridge from Floing to the Calvaire D'Illy. From this position, his guns were able to inflict considerable damage on Gersdorff's corps as it moved forward against the left of his position at Floing; and for a while, the German artillery was heavily outnumbered, sustaining heavy casualties in both men and guns. Gersdorff, who was right up at the head of his corps, having reached the copse on Hill 812 above Floing, acted at once to bring up the whole of his artillery, ordering staff officers to send forward the batteries through the advancing infantry. At 10 a.m., the three batteries in position that were being worn down by the French artillery were reinforced by the whole of the corps artillery; and Gersdorff's gun line now stretched from the St. Albert-Floing road to a position east of St. Menges on the Fleigneux road; by 11 a.m. all the remaining batteries of the XI Corps had come up into line. 'Thus all the 84 guns of the XI Corps had been pushed to the front, and formed an enormous single battery, at a time when so small a fraction of the infantry had passed the defile that it would have been difficult for it to protect this line of artillery.'[6] On the hill at Donchéry Blumenthal remarked to the Crown Prince: 'Now the battle is won, the enemy will either be captured or annihilated.' Although this view was shared by many of the staff, there were still many anxious faces as the day wore on.[7]

The furious artillery duel that followed was crucial to the defence by the 7th Corps of its position. While it raged, Douay launched a number of counter-attacks up the road from Floing, which fell in the first instance on the farmhouses north of the village, which the enterprising Fischer Treuenfeld had hastily prepared for defence. For the next two hours, his two companies fought off a series of continuous French attacks.

Steadily, more and more infantry units came up and deployed, first to cover the XI Corps gun line and then to move forward on Floing itself. The critical importance of yet another position which the French had made no attempt to defend now became apparent. Hill 812 is an isolated knoll with steep slopes on three sides, the northern slope running back to St. Menges being much gentler.

The walled copse that crowned the top of the hill was large enough to offer cover to a substantial body of troops. Since 9 a.m., this had been occupied by the one company of the 87th Regiment that had initially seized it. Behind the copse, on the gentler slope, had stood the three batteries of light artillery which had first opened fire on the Floing ridge, and had been heavily out matched by Douay's guns. The tactical significance of Hill 812 was at once apparent to Forbes when he came up to the battlefield. From across the river he saw it rising

> nearly to an equal height with the high ground ... affording a remarkable position for assailing with advantage the table land on which stood the French; since, crowned with wood, it formed admirable cover for any troops advancing from the west along the low ground, who had full opportunity to make all their dispositions without exposing a helmet.[8]

Observing that Hill 812 was indeed almost on the same level as the position towards which the German attack was now directed, Gersdorff immediately grasped its significance, and he at once ordered all the reinforcements that were coming up to move to the hill, from which he proposed to launch the next stage of his advance. His own corps artillery which had, in fact, experienced some delays crossing the Meuse at Donchéry, had been in position since 10 a.m. and had been joined since 11 a.m. by the rest of the artillery units at his disposal. At the extreme right of the gun line, to the west of the copse on Hill 812, a heavy battery 'suffered such considerable losses from the fire of some well-screened mitrailleuses, that the men and horses from the ammunition wagons had to be brought up to replace the casualties.'9

Now, too late, the French perceived the threat and began to launch a series of counter-attacks to regain the height. There was especially fierce fighting at the corner of the copse nearest to Floing, where Gersdorff's Chief of Staff, Major General Stein von Kaminski had initially collected a small force from various units to protect the guns deployed behind him, and from which he beat off several assaults.

The sight of the apparently unprotected artillery on the slope behind Hill 812 was naturally tempting to the French cavalry; and Margueritte, who with his cavalry division had moved to a position behind Douay's right on the Calvaire d'Illy, was resolved to do something about the German guns that he could see south east of St. Menges. He launched Gallifet with three regiments of Chasseurs d'Afrique towards the small force of German infantry that were deployed in front of the guns;

> swooping down the slope upon the infantry below him, his men and horses soon fell fast, and although they swept through the skirmishers, they were crushed by the fire of the supports and the guns on the hill and the squads of infantry on either side. They endeavoured to ride in upon the flanks, but their bravery was in vain, for nothing could live under the fire which smote them.[10]

Within minutes the controlled close-range musketry of the Germans, and the heavy shell fire from the batteries themselves, had completely broken up the charge, and Gallifet turned away, retreating with heavy losses behind the Bois de la Garenne.

Behind the German guns, elements of Kirchbach's V Corps were also moving up; as with the XI Corps, they were advancing with artillery well to the front. Behind them, inevitably, there was a considerable intermingling of infantry units, which were deployed as soon as they arrived. The gradual extension of the German line northwards towards Fleigneux along the ridge opposite Douay's position on the Floing-Illy ridge was, for the French, a most ominous development. Already some small French units of all arms had begun to trickle northwards towards the Belgium border. As further troops moved forward to St. Menges and Fleigneux, Major von Grote, with five companies of infantry from the 87th Regiment, set off towards the Givonne valley and there encountered a long column of French artillery and cavalry headed for Olly. The French had sought to cover the retreat of this column by posting artillery in a clearing behind the village. After loosing off only two rounds, however, the guns fell to a brisk charge by the German infantry, who pushed on to Olly in pursuit of the cavalry which had scattered on foot into the woods, abandoning several hundred riderless horses. Grote now moved on to the Givonne valley. The last exit from Sedan was closing fast; to the west General Brahaut was picked up by German cavalry with some of his staff in the woods south of Sugny very close to the Belgian frontier.[11]

Even more important than the shutting off of escape routes into internment was the threat to the Calvaire d'Illy which was posed by Kirchbach's extension of his front eastwards. Douay had always been apprehensive about the security of his position and was the more so following the failure of Gallifet's charge; the heavy artillery duel that was continuing as now 144 German guns pounded his positions along the Floing-Illy ridge also alarmed Ducrot who, at about 11 o'clock, sent to know what was the position of the 7th Corps. Getting no answer as the sound of the bombardment increased, he rode over to see for himself, encountering a torrent of retreating men, guns and horses. He then succeeded in picking up a regiment of Cuirassiers; telling its commander he would bring help while it held its position, he rode at speed to find Wimpffen. The latter was south of the Bois de la Garenne; Ducrot told him of the threat to the Calvaire and that his previous forecasts were coming true even earlier than he had expected. Wimpffen was entirely unsympathetic, telling him to hold on with all the troops he could find while he, Wimpffen, attended to the situation in front of the 12th Corps. As Ducrot observed, Wimpffen by this instruction had abandoned all chance of victory; there was no more prospect of throwing the Bavarians into the waters of the Meuse than of launching an offensive on Carignan.[12]

At Kirchbach's headquarters, Verdy examined the French positions on the ridge.

> The impression one gained at the first glance was that the hostile position in front could only be taken by very superior numbers and at a comparatively great sacrifice. But to put out all our strength before communication had been established with the corps of the Crown Prince of Saxony who were wheeling round from the East, did not seem advisable. Once that communication was complete, the iron girdle was firmly riveted, and the issue could no longer be doubtful.[13]

Minute by minute the situation of the French was deteriorating. The smoke rising above St. Menges, which had previously attracted the attention of Prince

August of Wurttemberg and which told him of the progress which the XI and V Corps were making around the far side of the French position, led him now to send forward the most advanced troops of his right wing. In the event, it was the 5th Squadron of the Hussars of the Guard, riding forward from La Virée who first made contact just before noon with the units of the Third Army that had reached Olly. The ring of steel around the Army of Châlons was complete.[14]

But the battle itself was by no means over. Along the north western face of the French position, from Floing to the Calvaire and along its eastern face in the Givonne valley, the French were still offering stiff resistance.

18

Sedan: Floing and Hill 812

Up on the hill above Frénois, the developing situation could be clearly seen. So good was the vantage point that it was very soon evident to the watchers that the final encirclement was close at hand. William Russell observed the spectators.

> The King was dressed in his ordinary uniform, tightly buttoned and strapped; Bismarck, in his white cuirassier flat cap with the yellow band, and uniform. The King spoke but little, pulled his moustache frequently and now and then addressed a word to von Moltke, von Roon or Podbielski, the Chief of his staff. A large telescope was mounted on a tripod, through which Generals Moltke and Roon peered eagerly from time to time towards the east. Moltke, when not looking through the glass or at the map, stood in a curious musing attitude, with his right hand to the side of his face, the elbow resting on the left hand crossed towards his hip.[1]

Moritz Busch, in between trips to Bismarck's coach to help with the deciphering of telegrams, watched the unfolding events in fascination. Bismarck over-heard him, rather over-confidently, explaining the situation as he saw it to the elderly Count Pückler, the Court Marshal. 'If you are developing your strategic ideas, Doctor, it would be better to do it less audibly, otherwise the King will ask, who is that? and I must then present you to him.'[2] So after this, Busch returned to his deciphering. For much of the day, with some of his immediate staff, Bismarck sat, smoking heavily, on a bank at the edge of the stubblefield, and went on with his work while the military and royal personages watched the drama unfold. He chatted from time to time with Sheridan who was wearing his U.S. Army uniform. Among the staff, Abeken was amused by one diversion that distracted Bismarck for a moment. 'A hare was roused the adjutants in a potato-field. The Minister ran after it and brought it to the King, and it remained hidden under Prince Karl's cloak and chair until he had it removed to a distance where the horses could not tread on it.'[3]

On the nearby hill of La Croix Piot, the Crown Prince and Blumenthal for a while became anxious about apparent enemy activity from the direction of Mézières, but later found that the brigade of Württembergers left to watch that town had had little difficulty in repulsing the sortie made by Vinoy 's troops.[4]

By noon, the crisis of the battle was approaching at three points. North of Floing, the build-up of German infantry at and behind Hill 812 was now sufficiently advanced for Gersdorff to feel able to push forward to take the village. At the other end of the ridge, by Illy, the advance of the Guard Corps towards its junction with the V Corps had put the Germans in a position to move against the Calvaire itself. And down at Balan, as the victorious Bavarian and Saxon units sorted themselves out after taking Bazeilles, Wimpffen was gathering himself for a counter-stroke.

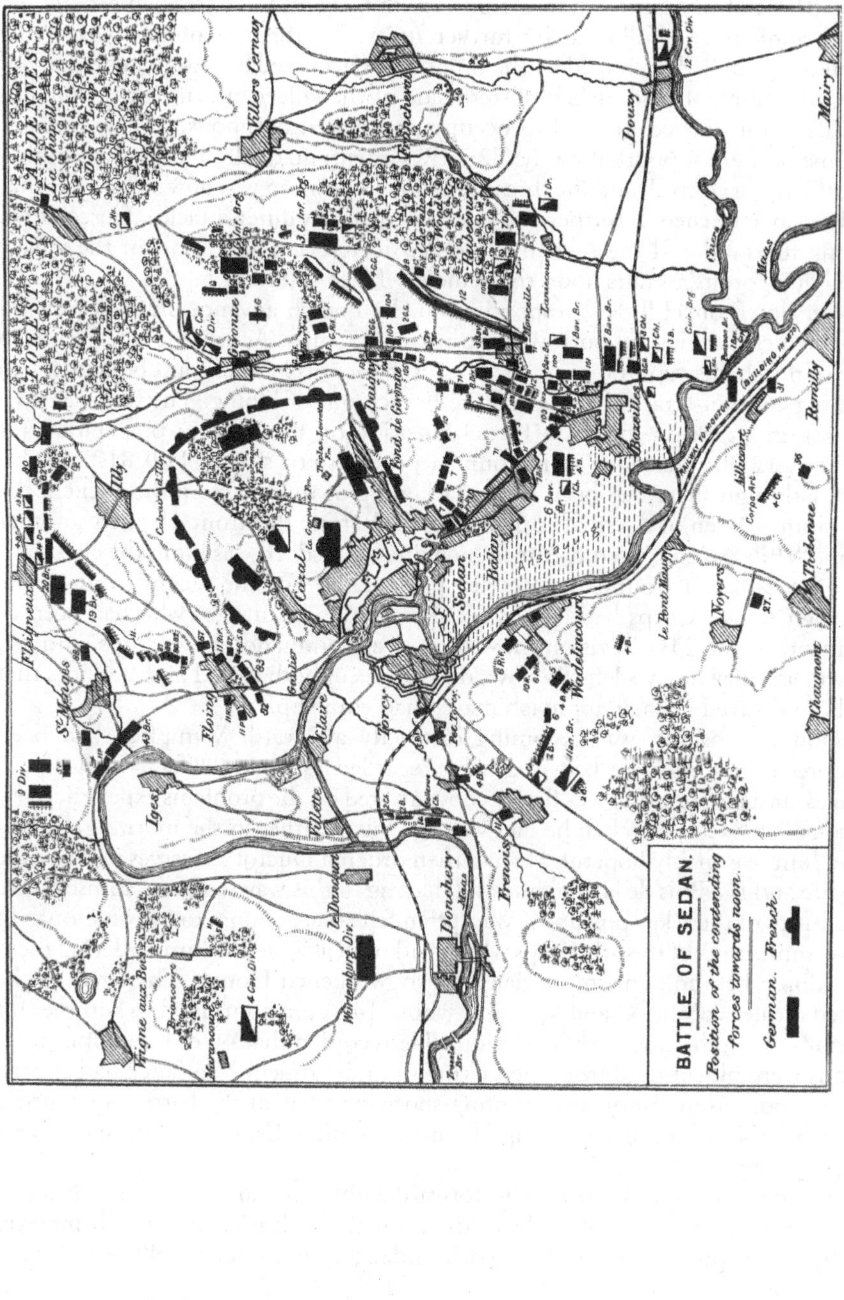

The Battle of Sedan, September 1, towards noon

Fischer Treuenfeld's two companies in Floing had seized a corner house, which proved the key to their hold on the northern edge of the village; and after a number of unsuccessful assaults, the French gave up the attempt to evict them. However, the French still commanded the roads into the village down which any relief could come. At 11 a.m., the first reinforcements moved down from the copse at Hill 812 led by Major von Schorlemmer with two and a half companies from the 83rd Regiment and followed by further units. To the east of the village, the cemetery which had been held by the French was occupied by another company of the 83rd Regiment, and on the western side of the village, a company of the 11th Rifle Battalion moved forward to occupy an isolated farmhouse. These forward movements were supported by the 82nd Regiment; gradually Floing was coming under German control, and the threat to Douay's position was now so obvious that the French launched a further series of energetic counter-attacks. Fierce street fighting followed and the French succeeded in re-occupying most of the village although vigorous assaults upon the cemetery failed to retake it.[5]

Gersdorff, on Hill 812, responding to the French advance, hurried forward reinforcements which he borrowed from the V Corps. Across the open western slope of the shell-swept hill came the 46th Regiment (Colonel von Eberhardt) in a storming counter-attack that cleared the French out of Floing. The way was now clear for an attack on the main French position on the ridge in preparation for which, at 12.30, Gersdorff went round to the eastern side of Hill 812. At this point, although there had been some slackening of the fire from the French, the disposition of senior German officers to lead from the front claimed another victim. While pausing to study the French lines, Gersdorff was hit in the chest by a chassepôt bullet, a wound that was to prove fatal. For the second time in the campaign the XI Corps had lost its leader; von Schachtmeyer, who had been in command of the 21st Division, now took over command of the corps, and got ready to assault Douay's left. By now, those units of both the XI and V Corps that had been delayed in their approach march had come up.[6]

Douay's position was becoming distinctly awkward. Wimpffen had been unimpressed by what he had originally regarded as purely a feint through St. Menges, and his attention was firmly concentrated on the problems experienced by Lebrun's 12th Corps. When he had visited Douay earlier in the morning, he had found him reasonably hopeful. He had then ordered Ducrot's reserves to cover the Calvaire and the Bois de la Garenne and, having in this way reassured himself as to the security of these key positions, Wimpffen felt able, at noon, to call on Douay to release some units of the 5th Corps which had been assigned to him, ordering them to reinforce Lebrun. This move dangerously weakened Douay. The effect of the massed artillery of the XI and V Corps, whose 144 guns continued to hammer his positions along the ridge, was enormous. He recorded that 40 of his ammunition wagons were blown up during the German bombardment.[7] So fierce had it been that by noon ammunition was running short for some of the batteries of the XI Corps, but the effect achieved along the entire length of Douay's position had been overpowering.

At 1 o'clock, Schachtmeyer sent forward eight companies from the 82nd and 87th Regiments towards Illy. Above them on the Calvaire, the French infantry occupying the position were falling back under the continuous shellfire and, for a while, the position was abandoned. Two batteries held on long enough to check any German movement out of Illy, and Douay now addressed himself to the problem of first re-occupying the Calvaire, and then moving forward. Behind the Calvaire, in the Bois de la Garenne, a chaotic situation developed as troops from Ducrot's corps marching up to reinforce the position crossed with the units of Douay had been ordered to send to Lebrun.[8] At this point, the Guard Cavalry took a hand. At 1.30, two squadrons of Uhlans rode up and momentarily seized the position before themselves being compelled by heavy fire from the Bois de la Garenne to fall back again down the Givonne valley. Douay succeeded in collecting together and bringing forward sufficient infantry to take and hold the Calvaire, but he could not get beyond it. But his success here was only temporary; once again, it was the power of the German artillery that proved decisive and, once again, the French infantry on the Calvaire melted away, allowing Schachtmeyer's men to occupy it, preparatory to making an assault on the Bois de la Garenne, into which the increasingly jumbled masses of French infantry had retreated.

Westwards, on the spur above Floing, the French were well dug in, and held a position of considerable strength based on two lines of trenches. For some time, Liebert's division had been successful in discouraging any attempt by the Germans in Floing to move out of the village. Soon, however, the arrival of the troops that had been delayed in marching round the Iges loop began to have their effect. Schkopp, with eight battalions of the 22nd Division, moved down across the meadows beside the Meuse with a view to turning Douay's left flank. Pushing past Floing, he swung round the quarries of Gaulier and moved on the heights, while his right headed for Cazal. Soon after 1 p.m., this advance prompted the German troops in Floing itself to move forward, scrambling up the steep slope towards the French entrenchments. Inevitably, the attacking units became intermingled, and overall control of the attack was quite impossible; but, backed by the inexorable bombardment from the gun line south of St. Menges, the attackers confidently stormed up the hill.[9]

The defenders were, it was quite evident, now beginning to disintegrate under the remorseless artillery pressure at this end of the line, in much the same way as they were at the Calvaire. Ducrot, coming across from his 1st Corps headquarters to see Douay's position for himself, called up Margueritte, whose lst Cavalry Division of light cavalry was now waiting at the edge of the Bois de la Garenne. Ducrot led the division in person up to the position in which it must deploy, and then pointed out to Margueritte the direction he should take. His orders were to attack the German troops assaulting the ridge and then to swing right to roll up the Germans advancing along the front Floing-Illy. Quite apart from the power of the all-conquering German artillery, it must have been evident to both of them that to ask the French cavalry to charge unbroken infantry in such circumstances was suicidal. Nothing daunted, Margueritte rode forward to the crest of the ridge with his staff to reconnoitre, studying closely through his telescope the positions of the German troops at which he was to launch his division, and coming under heavy fire as he did so. Then he turned, and with his escort, rode back at the gallop towards his division; before he had gone far, however, he stopped, not wishing to give the impression of running from the enemy's fire, and with one staff officer turned again to face the enemy. As he did so, he was hit and fell to the ground,

General Gallifet, French cavalry brigade commander (Rousset/*Histoire*)

suffering a terrible and fatal wound which smashed his jaw. Unable to speak, he was got with difficulty upon a horse, and with his staff supporting him in the saddle, returned slowly toward the division.

> The sad procession passed in front of the lst Regiment of Chasseurs d'Afrique. At the sight of their much loved leader, fatally wounded, a sublime outburst of rage and fury passed through the ranks of this magnificent regiment, the chasseurs, standing up in their stirrups, sabres high and flashing in the sun, roared at the top of their voices 'Vive le général! En avant! Vengeons-le!'[10]

Margueritte, bareheaded, still scarcely upright in the saddle, was able to do no more than gesture with one hand to his men to move forward and charge the enemy. Without further orders, the regiment moved off; as they did so, Margueritte's Chief of Staff sent to Gallifet to take command of the division, to which had been added part of Salignac-Fénelon's division from the 12th Corps. The whole force was now launched in a classic, orthodox, and utterly doomed charge upon the advancing German infantry, whose skirmishers had by now established themselves on the edge of the height above Floing. Russell, whose view of the troops involved in the ensuing drama was incomplete, described what he saw in his report to *The Times*.

> The Prussians coming up from Floing were invisible to me. Never can I forget the sort of agony with which I witnessed those who first came out on the plateau

The 3rd Chasseurs d'Afrique at Floing, painting by Walker (Rousset/*Histoire*)

> raising their heads and looking round for an enemy, while, hidden from view, a thick blue band of French infantry was awaiting them, and a brigade of cavalry was ready on their flank below. I did not know that Floing was filled with advancing columns. There was but a wide, extending, loose array of skirmishers, like a flock of rooks, on the plateau ... when suddenly the first block of horse in the hollow shook itself up, and the line, in beautiful order, rushed up the slope. The onset was not to be withstood. The Prussians were caught en flagrant délit. Those nearest the ridge slipped over into the declivitous ground; those in advance, running in vain, were swept away. But the impetuosity of the charge could not be stayed. Men and horses came tumbling down into the road, where they were disposed of by the Prussians in the gardens, while the troopers on the left of the line, who swept down the lane in a cloud of dust, were almost exterminated by the infantry in the village.[11]

The broken ground, the heavy fire from the German batteries, and the steadfast bearing of the German infantry combined to ensure the destruction of the French cavalry. One unit, in fact, reached the group of eight guns which Major von Uslar succeeded in bringing up the hill and there was some brisk hand to hand fighting. Two squadrons of Cuirassiers broke through to Gaulier, where they encountered two squadrons of Hussars. A number of groups got past Floing, and one went all the way to St. Albert, giving the support troops coming up a considerable fright before they were accounted for; and on the extreme right of the German advance, some small groups of Lancers, Cuirassiers and Chasseurs d'Afrique rode over the German infantry, but it was all hopelessly and predictably in vain. For the most part, the German infantry remained unbroken during the half hour in which the French cavalry hurled themselves forward. The longer it

General Margueritte at Floing, painting by Perboyre (Rousset/*Histoire*)

went on, the more desperate became the position of the horsemen. Their casualties were appalling; apart from Margueritte, two other generals, Girard during the charge, and Tilliard earlier, had been killed, and Salignac-Fenelon was wounded. French estimates later suggested that the units concerned lost about half their men. In spite of this, Gallifet's spirit was unbroken. Having taken command, and doing his best to reorganise the shattered division, he was asked by Ducrot to attempt another charge. 'As often as you like, mon general, so long as there is one of us left', he replied, and galloped off to the front of the division. Such determination was not lost on the enemy. Watching the tragic scene from above Frénois as the French cavalry tried again, King William was moved to exclaim 'Ah! Les braves gens!'; Sheridan said angrily: 'I never saw anything so reckless, so utterly foolish, as that last charge – it was sheer murder.'[12] But the heroism of the French cavalry could not long delay the inevitable collapse of the French left, and nor could the brave effort of the French batteries to counter the overwhelming fire of the German artillery. In a further desperate attempt to shore up this part of the line, Ducrot collected up such troops as he could find and tried to lead them forward. For all his charismatic appeal, he could not arouse their élan. Three attempts to launch an effective assault broke down, and soon the advancing German infantry overran the French line and rolled the demoralised French troops back towards Sedan.[13] The German units that had climbed up from Floing moved east and northeast. Von Kontzki's 43rd Brigade, which was part of the force that Schkopp had brought up, pushed on for Cazal. On the left, the advance from Fleigneux finally crossed the Floing-Illy road, notwithstanding the considerable casualties that were sustained as it came forward. This part of the French position was still held in force and had been strengthened here by two rows of trenches, from which the French infantry poured a heavy fire on the advancing Germans. They even launched brief counter-attacks before the victorious infantry of the V Corps swept forward and took the position. Falling back, the French then retreated on the Bois de la Garenne pursued closely by the Germans.

The French troops in Cazal, however, were as yet unbroken and they too attempted to counter-attack, pushing forward energetically once again towards Floing cemetery. The troops of the 46th and 83rd Regiments that held it, however, beat them back again. The French retreated on a farm building higher up the slope, intending to form a defensive position around it. Before they could do so, the German infantry stormed forward with fixed bayonets, seizing the farm and taking 200 prisoners and, with this success, the whole of the ridge that had formed Douay's position was now in German hands.[14]

Kirchbach, still using Hill 812 as the focal point of concentration for the advancing German reinforcements, decided not for the moment to commit his fresh troops, judging that for the present at any rate they were not required. All along the front, the enemy's defences were crumpling up. By 3 o'clock, after a prolonged defence by Liébert's division, Cazal had fallen to the troops from the 43rd Brigade and in the whole front of the XI and V Corps, there remained no position that could effectively be defended; and, in any case, there were no French units any longer capable of offering resistance. By now, virtually the whole of Douay's corps was streaming back towards Sedan itself in an increasingly disorderly rout. Following them up, the German troops were soon approaching the walls of Sedan – not that these had any great defensive value. Verdy, still attached for the moment to Kirchbach's staff, watched the columns of prisoners coming in.

> We saw a winding road leading down from the height, densely crowded with French soldiers, many thousands of them, all men who had surrendered and were coming down under escort ... To our joy we noticed on the way that our losses on this part of the battlefield were comparatively slight; but within the enemy's position the terrible effect of our artillery was again seen in an awful manner.[15]

19

Sedan: The End of the Battle

Even Wimpffen had, by noon, grasped the impossibility of holding his position at Sedan. Still mesmerised by the possibilities offered by an eastwards move, he decided to revert to his plan for a breakout in the direction of Carignan, and with this in mind, gave orders at about 1 o'clock for an assault on the Bavarians, whom he supposed to be exhausted by the morning's struggles to the south-east of Sedan. After taking Bazeilles, the Bavarians had regrouped and then moved forward to Balan, under cover of artillery support that had forced the French guns into the Fond de Givonne. By 1 o'clock the north end of Balan was occupied by the 5th Bavarian Brigade, having taken the village without great difficulty apart from a vigorous resistance offered by the defenders of the adjoining park. Wimpffen's plan was to attack Balan from two directions, intending that Lebrun should assault that village while the right wing of Ducrot's Ist Corps pushed down from the north on Lebrun's left. At 1.15 Wimpffen sent back an urgent message to Napoleon, telling him of the assault that would open road to Carignan.'I have decided to force the line in front of General Lebrun and General Ducrot, rather than be taken prisoner in Sedan. If your Majesty comes to place himself in the midst of his troops they will have the honour to open out a passage for him.'[1] Ducrot, when he heard of the plan, was outraged at the folly of trying to advance down a valley in which the heights on either side would be dominated by the enemy, and compared the absurdity of what he described as an 'entreprise insensée' with the prospects of success that might have been available to his own plan to break out northwest had it been adopted some five hours earlier.[2]

Wimpffen's plan was indeed hopelessly impracticable. Lebrun's 12th Corps was already in retreat into the town of Sedan itself, and only partially now in contact with the Bavarians in Balan. Lebrun himself believed that it was quite out of the question for the available troops to force a way through to Carignan but, in spite of the impossibility of his objective, Wimpffen was, nonetheless, able to get together a number of units in motion towards the advancing Germans. He was not, however, joined by Napoleon. As the day wore on, the outcome of the battle had become increasingly clear to the pain wracked Emperor. When Bazeilles fell to the Bavarians during the morning, he went off first in an attempt to visit Douay to assess his situation but, prevented from doing so by the already large crowds of retreating infantry, he made his way instead into Sedan to discuss the position with the injured MacMahon. He narrowly escaped death when the bridge over the Meuse that he was crossing was hit by German shells but, although an aide was struck, he himself was quite unharmed. After his visit to MacMahon, Napoleon had decided on another attempt to see Douay but was again prevented, this time by the increasing chaos of the traffic jams in Sedan itself. He returned to the Sous-Préfecture, to which later the desperately wounded Margueritte was brought in an ambulance. The Emperor went to see him, taking his hand and saying that he hoped his injuries would not prove too serious. Margueritte wrote a pencilled reply. 'Sire, I thank you. For me, it is nothing, but what will become of the army, what will become of France?'[3] It was while Napoleon was still there in the Sous-Préfecture that Captain de Saint Houen had brought Wimpffen's proposal that the Emperor should place himself at the head of his troops in the breakout attack. Napoleon had no difficulty in rejecting the plan. 'Tell General de Wimpffen that I will not be party to the sacrifice of the lives of several thousand men in order that I may escape.'[4]

At Balan, while Wimpffen awaited Napoleon's reply, the French had, in fact, made some ground. At about 1 o'clock, a preliminary advance on the Bavarian positions compelled some units of the 5th Brigade to retreat and it was necessary for supports from the 6th Brigade near Bazeilles to be brought forward to restore the situation. By about 2 o'clock, however, the Bavarians had achieved this and it was about this time, with no reply from his Emperor, that Wimpffen decided to launch his assault. Accordingly, he advanced with some battalions of Vassoigne's Marines, the 47th Line Regiment and some Zouaves, moving out of the Fond de Givonne towards the heights beyond. On his left, Goze's division moved forward and further beyond that, the division of Grandchamps also advanced, while in Balan itself, Abbatucci's brigade once again attacked the Bavarian positions there. The orders which Wimpffen sent out to the rest of his army to support the advance were, in the chaotic conditions prevailing, received too late. Ducrot, whose Ist Corps was intended to make a forward movement from the north upon La Moncelle and Bazeilles, did not get the orders until after 3 o'clock, while Douay, whose battered 7th Corps was supposed to protect Wimpffen's rear, only got the orders at 2 o'clock. Wimpffen complained later that his problems in getting orders to subordinate commanders were caused by the fact that MacMahon's staff had gone back with their injured commander to Sedan.[5]

Before, however, Wimpffen's advance could get under way, it was already further threatened by developments on the eastern front. The Crown Prince of Saxony had, following the successful outcome of the long struggle in Bazeilles and La Moncelle, determined to move the Saxons to their right as far as Daigny. North of that place, the roads were reserved for the advance of the Guard Corps. Up the Givonne valley, Montbé, whose 23rd Division led the movement, was under the impression that the French had pulled back from the western heights overlooking the river, and was accordingly surprised when he collided with French units still occupying the copse facing Daigny to the west. In fact, Prince George, the corps commander, had seen that the heights were still occupied and had warned Montbé of this, but the messenger had been wounded. The Saxons at once deployed to clear the copse of the enemy and then came under heavy fire from a French position on the heights to the west of Haybes which included two mitrailleuses. Lieutenant Kirchhoff with eleven men ran up the steep slopes on the crest of which was the mitrailleuse battery, and seized the French trenches, taking 35 prisoners. This cleared the way for the Germans to move forward along the road into Fond de Givonne. Supported by artillery fire from the far side of the valley, the Saxons were again counter-attacked by heavy French forces which were, however, thrown back; and flushed with success, the Saxons entered the village of Fond de Givonne, capturing 300 prisoners there. The village, however, was too large for the advanced units of the Saxons to hold it for long and when further French infantry

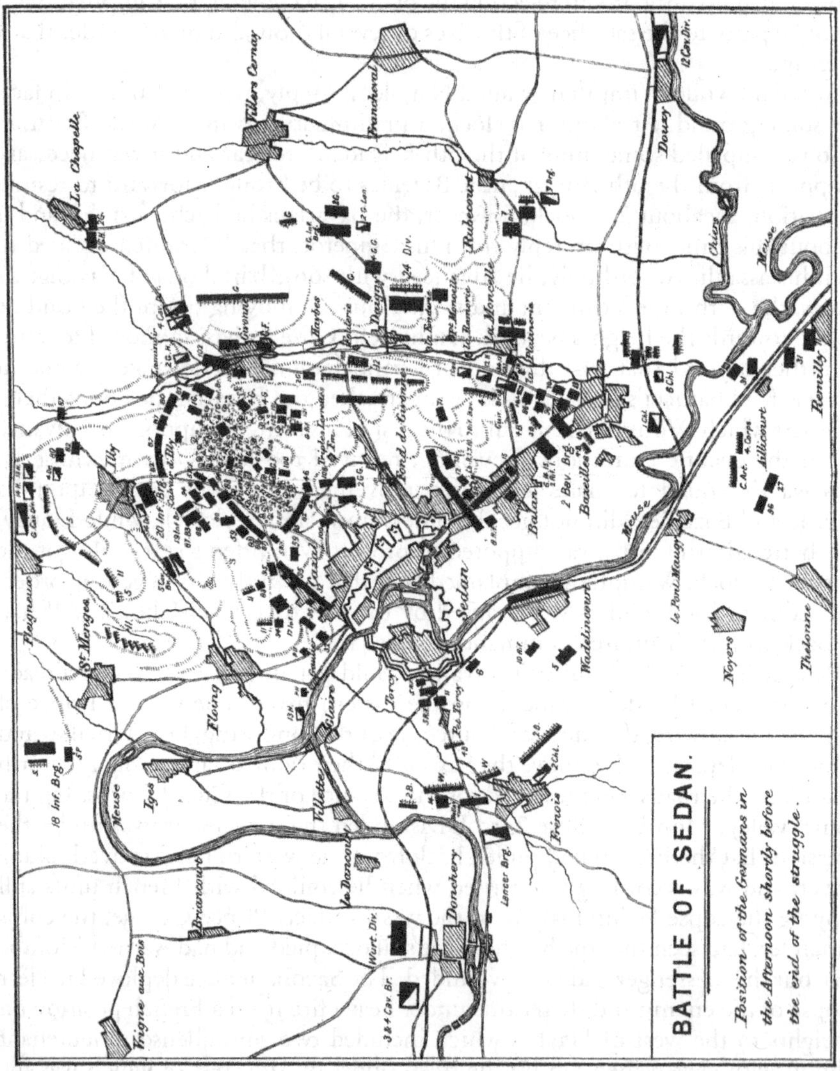

The Battle of Sedan, September 1, afternoon

reinforcements came up, they fell back again to the heights above Daigny.[6] To their right, Prince George brought further units across the river to the plateau. Once he saw that his infantry were securely in possession of the opposite bank he was able to move his artillery through La Moncelle to the western side of the valley, where he joined the batteries of the 23rd Division to form a gun line of 21 batteries stretching from Bazeilles to beyond the northeast of Fond de Givonne. By 3 p.m., although there was still obvious French activity in the Bois de la Garenne, Prince George ordered Montbé to halt, believing that the battle was now as good as won.

Reporting to the Crown Prince of Saxony, he found that his army commander was also now satisfied that no further movement to the north was necessary, in view of the success which had been achieved, and it was upon the Bois de la Garenne that the German attention was now focused.

Into the woods had poured units of Dumont's division retreating from the Floing-Illy ridge, together with some units from Wolff's and Pellé's divisions of Ducrot's corps. Methodically, Hohenlohe divided up the Bois de la Garenne into separate sections, assigning one section to each of his batteries, so that his artillery might leave no part of the French infantry's refuge free from the crushing bombardment, which now broke upon them.

> The first gun of each of these units was to fire at the very edge of the wood, and each of the following guns was to fire in the same direction, but was to give one hundred paces more elevation than the gun on its right ... our superiority over the enemy was so overwhelming that we suffered no loss at all. The batteries fired as if at practice.[7]

The effect of this was soon apparent. 'So annihilating was the fire of the artillery the French were scarcely capable of any organised resistance, when the German infantry towards 3 p.m. moved forward from all sides against the wood.'[8] The advance of the German infantry was aimed at Querimont farm in the middle of the Bois de la Garenne, and as the advancing Germans moved into the wood, thousands of prisoners were taken. Major Feldmann, with four companies, captured 3,000 Frenchmen just south of the farm. In the confused situation within the wood, fresh counter-attacks were launched by the French while the Germans were endeavouring to deal with the huge haul of prisoners, causing some of the latter to seize their rifles again and others to run off, but fresh German reinforcements enabled some 2,000 of these to be brought back to add to the rapidly growing number of French prisoners assembled near Givonne.[9]

Although Wimpffen's advance on Balan had received very little support on its left, nonetheless it did for a while achieve some success. The Bavarians in Balan, now principally comprising the 6th Brigade, were indeed pretty exhausted, many of them having been in action since early in the day, in the course of which they had sustained very heavy casualties. Some of the German units there were running out of ammunition, and it was upon these that fell the principal force of Wimpffen's attack. Preceded by skirmishers, heavy columns of infantry advanced into the northwest of Balan and, in the course of fierce house to house fighting, pushed the Bavarians back. Von der Tann was quickly on the scene, and seeing the strength of the French advance, brought up reinforcements, although the confused street fighting made it difficult to deploy these fresh troops, a problem that was aggravated by the falling back of the units retreating from Balan.[10]

While his forces were thus gaining some ground there, it had been Wimpffen's intention also to try to recapture some of the ground lost in the direction of Daigny and Haybes, and it was the deployment of troops in preparation for this movement which had collided with Prince George's advance up and across the valley at Daigny. Still hopeful, Wimpffen rode back to Sedan to collect up more reinforcements, and it was there that he encountered Lebrun with a crucial message from Napoleon.

The Emperor had been able to see for himself the true state of his army for some hours. An endless stream of demoralised and broken troops pouring into the centre of Sedan added from minute to minute to the chaotic conditions around the Sous-Préfecture. Among the fugitives were a number of the senior commanders. Surrounded by his generals, none of whom could disagree with his conclusion, Napoleon had decided the moment had come to end the slaughter. Ducrot had been among the last of them to reach the Sous-Préfecture, encountering on the way, at about 3.30 p.m., an artillery officer from Wimpffen's staff who told him of the situation of the breakout, and asked that the whole of the lst Corps should now join the assault. Pointing out that he had none of his troops with him, Ducrot made his way into Sedan. There 'the spectacle was indescribable; the streets, squares and gates were encumbered with vehicles, carriages, guns and all the impedimenta debris of a disintegrating army. Bands of soldiers, without rifles or packs were running in and hurling themselves inside the houses and churches.'[11] Ducrot went on to find the Emperor, joining the group of dispirited commanders already surrounding him. Napoleon had by now already given instructions that a white flag be hoisted and sent orders that Wimpffen should cease fire.[12]

When the bearer of this message reached him and told him of the white flag, Wimpffen was furious and flatly refused to countenance it. Indeed, he refused to open the letter of instruction. 'I am not taking any notice of the letter, I refuse to open it,' he said.[13] He insisted that Faure, his Chief of Staff, should go and take down the offending flag. He himself went back to Balan, where his troops were continuing to make progress in their attack upon the 6th Bavarian Brigade, and on his way collected 2,000 or 3,000 men, with these continuing the success so far gained and reaching as far as the church of Balan.

But it was all utterly in vain. Although, by 4.30 p.m, the Bavarians had indeed retreated in the face of Wimpffen's assault, there stood behind them and the Saxon XII Corps to their right the entirely fresh troops of Alvensleben's IV Corps; and no matter what temporary success he might achieve at Balan, Wimpffen had no chance whatever of getting further. And, of course, there was always the German artillery. As usual, with the practised efficiency and speed of response that made them so overpoweringly effective, the German batteries were soon at work preparing for the inevitable counter-attack. And soon, as von der Tann's troops went forward again, they regained the upper hand that they had momentarily lost to Wimpffen's assault. As the French rifle fire slackened, the Germans could see, once again, the white flag flying over the gate to the fortress. This time, in his determination to end the useless killing, the Emperor was to get his way. While Wimpffen had been launching his final assaults, there had been activity elsewhere

Bismarck at Sedan, from a contemporary sketch by Pietsch (Pflugk-Harttung)

on the battlefield. The most critical developments had been in the Bois de la Garenne. The temporary haven of thousands of disorganised French troops had been pounded incessantly by the artillery of the Army of the Meuse while the infantry prepared to attack. The uncoordinated attempts by the French to counter-attack within the wood as the German infantry entered it could not possibly succeed, and out of the southern exits of the wood streamed thousands of fugitives towards Sedan and Fond de Givonne, further disrupting any attempt to advance from the latter place towards the Saxons on the heights above the Givonne valley. The infantry of the Guard Corps followed the retreating French, advancing first into the Bois de la Garenne and then down the road from Illy to Sedan. Fierce fighting around the Querimont farm led to the capture of 5,000 more prisoners together with nine guns.[14] Coming in from the west of the wood, fresh troops of the XI Corps also directed their advance on Querimont. By 5 p.m., the last pockets of resistance in the southwest corner of the wood were liquidated and with this, French resistance in the Bois de la Garenne came to an end, and the only French troops there were the long columns of prisoners, so many in number that they presented a not inconsiderable problem for the scattered German infantry.

Back in the Sous-Préfecture, Napoleon had told Ducrot that he did not understand why the fighting was going on. He had ordered the flag of truce to be displayed and hoped for a personal interview with William. Ducrot told him that he could not count on the enemy's generosity and suggested that a sortie might be

Wounded in the church at Mouzon, during the battle, by Pallandre (Rousset/ *Combattants*)

attempted at night – a suggestion that Napoleon dismissed as having no hope of success.[15]

The end was, however, now at hand. Up above Frénois, the original white flag had been observed. Whatever its display and subsequent removal actually meant, it was obvious that the battle was drawing to a close. Sheridan speculated that Napoleon was likely to be taken in Sedan, but Bismarck dismissed the notion. 'Oh no; the old fox is too cunning to be caught in such a trap; he has doubtless slipped off to Paris.'[16] All the reports confirmed the observations that could be made directly of the battlefield, and it was clearly now merely a matter of bringing the conflict to a swift and merciful conclusion. 'A powerful fire of artillery against the enemy's last point of refuge appeared under the circumstances the most suitable means for convincing him of the hopelessness of the situation, and for inducing him to surrender.'[17] At 4 p.m., therefore, the artillery to the south of the Meuse was again ordered into action, this time directed to concentrate upon Sedan itself. As the Bavarians moved up on Torcy behind this bombardment, the white flag was now seen flying above the Torcy gate. A French colonel rode forward to ask for a cease-fire, and the Bavarians surrounded the gate and awaited instructions.

Meanwhile, Bronsart, with Captain von Winterfeldt, had been sent forward to summon the French commander in chief to surrender. They now rode down to the Torcy gate under a flag of truce, entering the city through the masses of disorganised and leaderless French troops. Bronsart was led to the Sous-Préfecture.

'Les dernières Cartouches', painting by de Neuville (Rousset/*Histoire*)

To his amazement, expecting to see MacMahon, he was shown into the presence of Napoleon. The Emperor had just sat down to write to King William, determined now to end the conflict, and still perhaps hopeful that by his personal surrender, he might in some way obtain better terms for his troops.

To Bronsart he explained briefly the position, telling him that Wimpffen was now in command in MacMahon's place and that it would be he who had power to negotiate. For himself, he would be sending General Reille with his personal letter to the King. Bronsart withdrew, and with the sounds of battle dying down all along the front rode back through the Torcy gate and then trotted on up the hill above Frénois. As he neared the royal party, his emotions got the better of him; spurring his horse into a gallop and pointing back to the fortress, he shouted 'Der Kaiser ist da!' – an outburst which brought cheers from the entourage around the King. It did not, however, please Moltke, who quickly made plain to Bronsart his severe disapproval of so considerable a lapse from propriety in the Royal presence.[18] It was now 6.15 p.m. The news that Bronsart delivered at once raised important and hitherto unconsidered questions. The Royal party had by now been joined by the Crown Prince and Blumenthal who, with the others, watched as, at 6.45, General Reille, accompanied by Winterfeldt and a guard of honour of Prussian cuirassiers, made his way up the slope to where the Royal party stood. Dismounting about ten yards from the King, he walked up to him, doffing his cap, and handed him a letter with a large red seal. Those around stepped back, and the King broke the seal and read it. The letter was brief. It has been graphically described as 'not the least of the title deeds of the Second German Reich'[19]; and in its brief, sad, formal dignity it marked a watershed in European history:

A contemporary drawing of the battlefield near Bazeilles, following the end of the Battle of Sedan (Scheibert)

Clearing the Meuse of corpses following Sedan, by Pallandre (Rousset/*Combattants*)

> Monsieur mon frére,
>
> N'ayant pas pu mourir au milieu de mes troupes, il ne me reste qu'à remettre mon épée entre les mains de Votre Majesté. Je suis de Votre Majesté le bon frére. Napoleon.[20]

To William, its enormous significance was at once apparent. As he turned to show it to the Crown Prince and to discuss its implications with Bismarck and Moltke, the sad figure of Reille stood alone and apart. Sympathetically, the Crown Prince, who knew Reille well, went over to him and talked to him to ease his obvious discomfort. Meanwhile, Bismarck beckoned Count Hatzfeldt forward and instructed him in the drafting of a reply. 'Two chairs were placed one on the top of the other, and I was given pen and paper. The King and Bismarck dictated, and we drew up a draft of the answer. Afterwards the King sat down on one of the chairs; Alten held the other as a desk; and I held the ink-bottle, and dictated to the King the answer that Reille took with him.'[21] It was businesslike and to the point.

> While deeply regretting the circumstances under which we meet, I accept your Majesty's sword and beg that you will be good enough to depute an officer with full powers to treat upon the capitulation of the army, which has fought so bravely under your orders. On my part I have appointed General von Moltke to this duty.[22]

The King gave the letter to Reille; accompanied by his Prussian escort, Reille rode off back down to Sedan, and the King and his son briefly shared a moment of emotion as they embraced. The other members of the Royal entourage also permitted themselves the luxury of congratulations, at the end of a day that had decisively wrenched the course of European history into a new direction. The practical business of the Royal Headquarters went on as well, however. At 7.15, Moltke issued an order recording the position:

> Negotiations have been opened; accordingly attacks may not be made on our side during the night. But any attempt of the enemy to break through our line must be repelled by force. If the negotiations do not lead to a conclusion hostilities will begin again, but only after communication from here. As such the opening of artillery fire from the height east of Frénois may be taken.[23]

It was the first written order Moltke had issued all day. And the headquarters of the Third Army and the Army of the Meuse themselves now issued instructions for the night bivouacs, the troops being concentrated just behind the most advanced positions which had been reached but ready, nevertheless, to recommence hostilities should that be necessary.

On the battlefield, however, peace now reigned after the day's violence. Forbes, who had been above Floing when the guns finally fell silent, looked out over the scene as night fell.

> A strange uncanny silence and stillness succeeded to the thunderous noise and turmoil of the day. The smoke of the long cannonade still hung low on the uplands of Floing and Illy, and around the sombre fortifications of Sedan. The whole horizon was lurid with the reflection of fires. All along the valley of the Meuse were the bivouacs of the German hosts. 150,000 Teuton soldiers lay in a wide circle around their beaten and shattered foe .... The chant that filled with

solemn harmony the wide valley was Luther's hymn, the glorious *Nun danket alle Gott* ... to listen to this vast martial choir singing this noble hymn on the field of hard won victory was to understand, in some measure, under what inspiration that victory had been gained.[24]

20

Sedan: The Capitulation

As the German staffs dispersed to their various quarters for the night, the sombre awareness of the magnitude of their victory gave way to a considerable celebration. At Donchéry, where the hungry victors had soon eaten up all there was to be found in the hotel in the square, a good many toasts had been drunk by the time Bismarck appeared later that night in the diningroom. Not surprisingly for a man who commonly enjoyed an enormous appetite, he too was extremely hungry, and after reading to those present the text of Napoleon's letter, and proposing the health of the King and the Fatherland, he looked about for his supper. None appeared. An officer was sent to enquire. Forbes, who had enjoyed much popularity earlier when producing some sardines was among those present.

> Alas, the unhappy hostess protested, with many "mon Dieus!" that the Germans might eat her if they chose and welcome, but that the only food in the place was half a dozen dubious eggs. From a ham among our stores we contributed sundry slices and they with the dubious eggs, were prepared for the Chancellor's supper. But even so great a man as he was not exempt from the practical realisation of the adage that there is many a slip between the cup and the lip. Between kitchen and diningroom the dish was cut out and carried off by a privateering Uhlan officer; and it was not until after perquisition throughout the depleted little town that a beefsteak was found

The surrender at Sedan, painting by von Werner (Scheibert)

on which Bismarck at last supped, washing it down with a bottle of Donchéry champagne.[1]

His supper concluded, Bismarck went off to a house that had been designated as a meeting place with Wimpffen and his staff. That unhappy general had endured a most painful time before setting off to the negotiations. When Napoleon had again caused the white flag to be displayed, Wimpffen was, of course, not at the Sous-Préfecture, and in his absence it was Faure, his Chief of Staff, who signed the order for the cease-fire. When he learned of it, Wimpffen's response was to resign. Telling Ducrot of this, Napoleon asked him to take command, an invitation which Ducrot refused. When Wimpffen finally burst into the Sous-Préfecture at 8 p.m. Ducrot was sitting quietly in a corner of the room. Waving his arms, Wimpffen exclaimed to the Emperor: 'If I have lost the battle, if I have been beaten, it was because my orders were not carried out, because your generals refused to obey me.' This was too much for Ducrot, who jumped up to face Wimpffen. Demanding to know to whom he was referring, he shouted that his orders had been only too well obeyed and that the disaster was due to Wimpffen's presumption, and that he alone was responsible. Wimpffen, startled, retorted that in that case, it was no longer right for him to remain command. This provoked Ducrot still further. 'You took the command this morning, when you thought there was honour and profit in exercising it; I didn't dispute it then, when it was perhaps arguable. But now, you can't refuse. You alone must bear the shame of the capitulation.' Ducrot admitted that, in his own words, he was 'très exalté', and that the Emperor and his staff were obliged to intervene to calm him down. In the end Wimpffen grudgingly accepted the responsibility of conducting the negotiations and obeyed Napoleon's instructions to proceed to the meeting with Moltke.[2]

This was to be held at Donchéry. Accompanying Wimpffen there went a number of other officers including Faure, the Chief of Staff, Castelnau, who represented the Emperor, and Captain d'Orcet, a Cuirassier officer who was there to take notes, and whose vivid record of the negotiations was included in Ducrot's account of the battle. His description of the meeting is largely in accord with that of Verdy, who had returned to Royal Headquarters after dark with Nostitz from his extended visit to the front of the V and XI Corps. When he arrived, it was to learn of the message from Napoleon to the King; when he finally rejoined the rest of the staff, he found them still overwhelmed by the scale of the victory.[3] They were quartered in a house on the outskirts of Donchéry and it was to this house, at about 11 o'clock, that Wimpffen came.

He and his brother officers were shown to a room on the first floor lit by a couple of candelabra and an oil lamp. On the wall over a table a picture of Napoleon I looked down. After ten minutes, Moltke and Bismarck, with Podbielski, Verdy and a number of general staff officers including Count Nostitz, who was also there to take a note, came into the room. After brief introductions, they sat down. Moltke was flanked on his right by Podbielski and on his left by Bismarck, facing Wimpffen who sat alone, his colleagues in shadow behind him.

There was a moment's silence. Moltke waited impassively before Wimpffen, after pondering on how to begin the discussions, asked what would be the terms of surrender. 'They are very simple,' replied Moltke. 'The whole army is taken prisoner with all its arms and equipment; the officers will be left with their own arms as an acknowledgement of their courage, but they will be prisoners of war with the troops.' Hard as he tried, Wimpffen was quite unable to shift Moltke from an insistence on these terms, which he protested were much too hard. After some prolonged discussion, Wimpffen, rather unconvincingly, said he would go back to Sedan and the army would fight it out. Moltke interrupted him, pointing out to Wimpffen that his situation was quite impossible.

> Certainly you have some really excellent troops; your elite infantry are remarkable, your cavalry are audacious and brave, your artillery is admirable and has caused us a lot of injury, unfortunately; but a large part of your infantry is demoralised and we have taken 20,000 unwounded prisoners today ... you only have 80,000 men left. They are in no condition to break through our lines; I already surround you with 240,000 men and 500 guns, of which 300 are in position to fire on Sedan and the rest will be there at daybreak. If you want to satisfy yourself, I can have one of your officers shown round the various positions held by my troops and he will be able to point out precisely that it is as I say.

He went on to add that Wimpffen had neither supplies nor munitions. Wimpffen tried a different tack, suggesting that it was in the German interest to accord him more generous terms which, he said, would diminish the effect on the French of the defeat, and would enable an amicable relationship to develop between the two nations; whereas if the Germans insisted on the terms proposed, 'you will risk setting light an unending war between France and Prussia.'

Bismarck was quick to reply to this. Wimpffen's argument might appear convincing at first sight but, in fact, reliance could not be placed on a people's gratitude.

> If the French people were as others, if they had solid institutions like ours, if they had a sovereign securely established on the throne, we could believe in the gratitude of the Emperor and his son and put value on it; but in France for 80 years governments have been so unstable and so many, and have changed so quickly and unexpectedly that one can count on nothing from your country. To base hopes of friendship on a French sovereign would be for a neighbour an act of madness – it would be building castles in the air.

Bismarck warmed to his theme. It would be foolish to imagine that France could forgive the Germans their victory. The French had, in two centuries, invaded Germany thirty times. This time, moved by envy as before, the French had acted because they could not forgive Sadowa – as if they alone were entitled to victory and military glory. 'Today we have had enough; France must give up her pride, her aggressive and ambitious character; we wish now to be able to assure our children's future and for this we need a glacis; it means territory, fortresses and frontiers which will protect us for ever from an attack.' Wimpffen replied that Bismarck misjudged the French people – he was looking as things had been in 1815, not as they now were. 'Today the French are quite different; thanks to the prosperity of the Empire, men's instincts turned to investment, to business, to the arts ... not to dreams of glory.' Wimpffen claimed that the long-standing feud between France and England had been replaced by friendship. 'It will be the same for Germany if you act generously.' Bismarck displayed incredulity at Wimpffen's reference to Anglo-French friendship.

> I must stop you there, General; it isn't that France hasn't changed, but it was she who wanted the war, and it was to satisfy the popular desire for glory in the interests of the dynasty that Napoleon provoked it; we well know that there is a rational and sane part of France that doesn't push for war – but in spite of that she welcomed the idea voluntarily ... who knows what will happen? Perhaps you will form a government that respects nothing, that makes its laws in this way that will not recognise the capitulation you will have signed for the army, that will force the officers to break promises they will have given us?

The Germans wanted peace, he said – lasting peace, but on the terms already indicated, which could not be changed.

'Well', replied Wimpffen, 'it's equally impossible for me to sign such a surrender – we will begin the battle again.' Before Bismarck or Moltke could reply, Castelnau diffidently intervened. 'I think this is the moment that I should convey a message from the Emperor.' 'We're listening, General,' said Bismarck. 'The Emperor instructed me to say to the King of Prussia that he had surrendered his sword unconditionally and gave himself up entirely in the hope that the King would be moved by this to accord to the French army an honourable capitulation.' 'Is that all?' 'Yes.' 'But is it the sword of Napoleon III that has been surrendered? Is it that of France or his own? If it is that of France, the terms could be significantly altered and your message would have a most important character.' 'It is solely the sword of the Emperor.' 'In that case', said Moltke curtly, with a relief that was evident both to Bismarck and to d'Orcet, 'there can be no change in the conditions. For himself, the Emperor will obtain whatever he requires.' It seemed to Captain d'Orcet at this point that there was some difference of view between Bismarck and Moltke – between one who wanted to bring the war to an end and one who wanted it to continue.

Wimpffen repeated that the battle would have to recommence. Moltke said that the truce would expire at 4 a.m. 'At 4 o'clock precisely I will open fire.' At this they all stood up and the French made to leave. No one spoke.

The icy silence was broken by Bismarck who pointed out to Wimpffen the folly of further fighting. Moltke repeated his analysis of the hopeless position of the French army. Wimpffen bravely but unconvincingly disputed it. 'You don't even know the topography of Sedan,' said Moltke, pointing out cuttingly that the French army had been equipped at the outset of the war with maps of Germany but not of its own country. 'Well, I've told you – our positions are not only strong, they are impregnable.'

Wimpffen, who had no answer to this, again unavailingly tried to play for time, saying that he must consult with his colleagues but Moltke was implacable. It was only after a whispered discussion with Bismarck that he could finally be prevailed upon to extend the truce until 9 o'clock. With this, the French left and returned to Sedan; from this moment on, Wimpffen had effectively accepted the principle that capitulation was unavoidable.[4]

Bismarck went back to the hotel in Donchéry to snatch some sleep and Moltke sat down with Verdy to dictate to him the text of the capitulation. Around them, exhausted staff officers slept where they sat; it was 3 a.m. before Verdy got to bed.

It was to be a short night's rest for Bismarck; at 6 a.m. he was woken by his servant Engel calling to him that there was a French general outside: 'I don't understand what he wants.' Bismarck, jumping out of bed, looked out of his window to see Reille in the square below, and from him learned that Napoleon was on his way out of Sedan. Bismarck wasted no time; he dressed and went straight out, riding off as fast as he could towards Sedan to meet the Emperor.[5] Watching from a nearby window, Forbes had seen Reille arrive and then ride away, followed by Bismarck who

> in flat cap and undress uniform, his long cuirassier boots stained and dusty, as if he had slept in them, came outside, swung himself onto his big bay horse and rode away in Reille's track. I was close by him as he forced his masterful way through the chaos that all but blocked the Donchéry street. There was no redness about the deep-set eyes or weariness in the strong-lined face; it had been midnight when he drank his last glass of champagne in the Hôtel de Commerce, and he and Moltke had been wrestling with Wimpffen about the terms of capitulation for some three hours longer; yet here he was before the clock had chimed the hour of six, fresh, hearty, steady of hand and clear of throat, as the ringing voice proved in which he bade the throng of soldiery give him space to pass.[6]

Forbes followed on foot as Bismarck walked his horse through Donchéry's crowded streets and then over the Meuse bridge, before he cantered away down the road towards Sedan. Bismarck was also followed by Busch who had been woken by Engel's call and, seeing Bismarck's departure, also dressed quickly to go after him (finding time on his way out to note the books Bismarck had been reading that night – 'Daily Watchwords and Texts of the Moravian Brethren for 1870' and 'Daily Refreshment for Believing Christians').

Back in Sedan, Napoleon had been pondering overnight the situation, and had resolved to go himself to make a personal approach to King William. Perhaps because of his impotence during the futility of the previous day, he saw it as the only positive step now open to him; and maybe in direct discussion with his fellow sovereign, he could bypass the negotiators. This was certainly something that Bismarck intended to prevent at all costs and in any case, whatever Napoleon's arrival portended, it was obviously necessary that Bismarck be on hand. Napoleon, wearing his general's uniform with a blue cloak with scarlet lining, and accompanied by a number of his senior staff, left Sedan at 5 a.m. At the Torcy gate, a group of Zouaves shouted 'Vive 1'Empereur!' At the German picket line, Sheridan and Forsyth, who were looking for their carriage, stood talking to a German officer. As the landau emerged from Sedan, they were amazed to recognise in the senior officer seated in it and smoking a cigarette the Emperor Napoleon III and they, at once, followed it down the road towards Donchéry, 'inferring that there was something here more important at hand just then than the recovery of our trap.'[7]

Sheridan was able to witness the meeting between Emperor and Chancellor as the latter came cantering down the road towards Napoleon's carriage. Bismarck dismounted and saluted (noting as he did so what seemed to him the Emperor's involuntary start as he glanced at his revolver). The Emperor took off his cap as did his staff. Bismarck did the same but Napoleon said 'couvrez-vous donc.' Bismarck asked Napoleon his commands, and he replied that he wished to know if he could speak to the King. Bismarck replied quickly that this was not possible, as the King's quarters were some miles away; Napoleon asked if he could wait, so Bismarck suggested he should accompany him back to Donchéry. On the way, the time being now just after 7 o'clock, Napoleon noticed a cottage just by the road and suggested that he wait there. Bismarck's cousin, Count von Bismarck-Bohlen went over to it, reporting that it was a very humble dwelling. 'No matter,' said Napoleon and dismounting from his carriage, he went over to the back of the cottage, while Bismarck and Reille briefly went inside. On the Emperor's return, he and Bismarck went upstairs. For how long they were together there is a matter of dispute, since Bismarck recalled it as being three quarters of an hour, while Forbes, who had caught up with events as the party was returning towards Donchéry, reckoned it to be only ten minutes. At all events, when they emerged, Bismarck and Napoleon then sat outside the cottage on a pair of cane chairs, observed at a discreet distance by Napoleon's staff, by a group of German officers and by Sheridan, Forsyth and Forbes. Busch, too, had by now caught up with events, and had arrived at the cottage outside which he found half a dozen senior French officers waiting while a carriage stood on the road.

> Soon afterwards, a little thickset man came forward behind the house who wore a red cap with a gold border, a black paletot lined with red, with a hood and red trousers. He spoke first to the Frenchmen, some of whom were sitting on the bank near the potatoes. He wore white kid gloves and was smoking a cigarette. It was the Emperor. From the short distance at which I stood I could see his face perfectly. The look in his light grey eyes was somewhat soft and dreamy, like that of people who have lived hard. He wore his cap a little on the right, to which side his head also inclined … his whole appearance was a little unsoldier-like.[8]

For the discussions between them, we are left to rely on Bismarck's account alone. Napoleon, he said, complained that he had been forced into the war by public opinion. Bismarck replied, somewhat disingenuously, that in Germany the Spanish question had been regarded as concerning Spain alone. Napoleon then discussed the terms of capitulation. Bismarck replied that this, being a military question, was one for Moltke to deal with. On the other hand, he went on, it was open to them to talk about eventual peace terms, but Napoleon was not to be drawn on this, saying that he was a prisoner and referring Bismarck to the government in Paris. At this, Bismarck, understandably, began to lose interest. Outside the house, after a brief exchange of civilities about the previous day's fighting, Napoleon made a further attempt to reopen the terms of capitulation, suggesting that the army should be allowed to cross into Belgium to be interned. To this, Bismarck again said that it was a matter for the military, and the discussion turned to the question of a suitable lodgment for the Emperor.[9] Staff officers had, in the meantime, located suitable quarters in the Chateau de Bellevue just down the road that looked across the Iges peninsula towards Sedan and was felt to be suitable. Napoleon having agreed to the suggestion that he should go there to meet the King, Bismarck accordingly went off to change into full dress. At some time during this encounter, Moltke, who had been told of Napoleon's appearance while having a hasty coffee with his staff, appeared on the scene. Forbes did not observe his arrival during the meeting between Bismarck and the Emperor, but Bismarck records his having briefly joined the discussion before going off to Vendresse to see the King and this is confirmed by Verdy. When Moltke arrived, he went inside to see the Emperor.

> When I entered, he rose and asked me to take a seat, which was opposite him. To his proposals I could only answer, that nothing less than the capitulation of the whole army was demanded, and that I should have to give the signal for the renewal of the firing, if the army had not surrendered before 10 o'clock. "C'est bien dur," he sighed. But he was quiet and resigned to his fate.[10]

Then Napoleon was left at the cottage moodily walking up and down the potato field smoking, his hands behind his back or sitting reflectively outside the front of the cottage. At 9.45 a.m., Bismarck, now in full dress, reappeared, accompanied by Moltke who had seen the King to obtain his approval to the terms of capitulation and his confirmation that the proposed meeting with Napoleon would not take place until after the treaty was signed. Forbes watched Bismarck arrive,

> his burnished helmet flashing in the sun rays ... Wiping his hot face, Bismarck strode up to the Emperor and spoke with him for a few moments. Then he ordered up the carriage which Napoleon entered and the cortège, escorted by the cuirassier guard of honour, moved off at a walk towards the Chateau Bellevue.[11]

Meanwhile, Wimpffen had been discussing with his corps and divisional commanders the terms of the proposed capitulation. Some protested; Bellemare said that the conditions were unacceptable and that the town would have to be defended. Faure, the Chief of Staff, pointed out that there were victuals for no

Emperor Napoleon is escorted by Bismarck to King William on the morning following the Battle of Sedan, painting by Camphausen (Pflugk-Harttung)

more than 24 hours; Pellé suggested that in that case there should be a sortie.[12] After further discussion, however, the dissentients gave in and, accompanied again by Faure, Wimpffen set off once more, this time to the Chateau Bellevue. He had been preceded there by Winterfeld, who had been sent by Moltke to the French headquarters to make absolutely clear to Wimpffen that if the terms were not accepted, the bombardment would begin.

At the Chateau Bellevue, the Germans were waiting for them, and they quickly got down to business. Verdy and Faure sat down and wrote out two copies of the text of the capitulation. At 11 a.m., Moltke and Wimpffen signed it. Podbielski, whose pens were used, later gave one to Verdy as a souvenir.[13] The business done, Moltke went off to Frénois to see the King and the Crown Prince while Wimpffen, after a short conversation with Bismarck, who sympathetically appreciated his profound sadness, went upstairs for a word with Napoleon. 'The Emperor," he wrote, 'with tears in his eyes approached me, pressed my hand and embraced me.'[14] This painful duty accomplished, Wimpffen rode sadly back to Sedan 'la mort dans l'ame'. Forbes, who had managed on this day at any rate to be in the right place most of the time, watched the meeting that followed between the two sovereigns as Napoleon came down the steps of the Chateau to greet William.

> The German, tall, upright, bluff, square shouldered, with the flash of victory from the keen blue eyes under the helmet, and the glow of good fortune on the fresh old face; the Frenchman, bent with weary stoop of the shoulders, leaden face, his eye drooping, his lip quivering, bare headed and dishevelled. As the two clasped hands silently, Napoleon's handkerchief was at his eyes, and the King's face was working with emotion.[15]

Then, the two monarchs turned and went inside, withdrawing to a private room. The Crown Prince closed the door and for a quarter of an hour, King and Emperor had a painful and emotional conversation. William wrote later to Augusta:

> We were both very much affected. He asked what I was deciding with regard to him, whereupon I proposed Wilhelmshöhe to him which he accepted; he asked about going there, whether it was to be through Belgium or Paris, which latter had been arranged, but could still be altered (this was done). He asked to be allowed to take his suite with him, Generals Reille, Moskowa, Prince Murat II etc. and also to be allowed to retain his household, all of which I naturally accorded. Then he praised my army, particularly the artillery which was unrivalled, and found fault with the want of discipline in his own army ... the whole conversation seemed to do him good; I venture to believe I made the position very much easier for him, and we parted both deeply affected.[16]

When they came out, Napoleon, still very much moved, spoke briefly to the Crown Prince, saying that the King had treated him with much kindness. He came to the steps with William to see him off. Beside the Chateau, Verdy stood with the rest of the staff.

> With youthful alertness the tall figure of our sovereign sprang into the saddle; going off at a gallop, accompanied by his numerous and many-coloured followers who had not been able to find room in the small house and had stood about

> among the shrubs, on the narrow pathways far down into the park. They formed a brilliant and wild-looking cavalcade, which the Emperor thoughtfully followed with his eyes before he disappeared into the room. Outside the drums of the Bavarians struck up; their bands played *Heil dir im Siegerkranz* and the hurrah of the bivouacking troops followed the King along his ride; he was eager to express his thanks to his victorious troops on the battlefield. General von Moltke invited me into his carriage; silently we drove back to Donchéry where more work awaited us.[17]

Napoleon, too, sat down to write to his wife, to whom he had first sent a brief telegram following his meeting with William.

> I cannot tell you what I have suffered and am suffering. We made a march contrary to all the rules and to commonsense; it was bound to lead to a catastrophe and that is complete. I would rather have died than witness such a disastrous capitulation; and yet things being what they are it was the only way of avoiding the slaughter of 60,000 men.
>
> Then again, if only all my torments were concentrated here! I think of you, of our son, of our unfortunate country. May God protect you! What is going to happen in Paris?
>
> I have just seen the King. There were tears in his eyes when he spoke of the sorrow I must be feeling. He has put at my disposal one of his chateaux near Hesse-Cassel but what does it matter where I go? I am in despair. Adieu: I embrace you tenderly.[18]

The surrender terms themselves were brief; apart from officers who chose to be paroled, the whole French army was made prisoner of war. The problem of dealing with such a large mass of prisoners was enormous. A geographical accident had, however, provided the Germans with an ideal prison camp; the Iges peninsula, surrounded on three sides by the river Meuse and on the fourth by the line of the canal, was designated as the point to which, by detachments, the French troops were to be moved. 21,000 had been taken prisoner during the battle itself and these were already en route to prison camps; into the Iges peninsula now marched a further 83,000 men. In addition, the French had lost some 3,000 killed and 14,000 wounded while a further 3,000 men had got across the frontier and been interned in Belgium. The Germans had also captured over 1,000 wagons, 6,000 horses and 419 guns. The total German loss in the battle was 8,932 men, of which 3,022 were killed or missing and the remaining 5,910 wounded. The bulk of the casualties had fallen on the Third Army, with 6,707 in all. The heaviest losses had been sustained by the Bavarians; von der Tann's I Bavarian Corps had total casualties of 2,109, while Hartmann's II Bavarian Corps suffered 1,981. In the Army of the Meuse, most of the losses were borne by the Saxon XII Corps. which suffered a total of 1,427 casualties.[19]

The losses sustained by the German armies show clearly the extent of the skill and courage displayed by the French Army on September 1. Notwithstanding the unfavourable position in which they had fought the battle, and the almost total dominance of the German artillery, the French had put up a fierce struggle before their ultimate acceptance of a defeat that Moltke had days earlier rendered inevitable. Though totally defeated, the men who fought for the Second Empire that day and lived to recall it could feel pride in their hopeless endeavours.

Napoleon spent his last night in France at the Chateau Bellevue, reading that night from Bulwer Lytton's 'The Last of the Barons', which he found in a bookcase in the bedroom. Next morning early, in driving rain, he came out to the carriages of the Imperial headquarters that had assembled in the courtyard; and the cavalcade, with coachmen and outriders in gold and scarlet, and over 100 horses, escorted by a detachment of Death's Head Hussars clattered off down the road to Donchéry and to captivity at Wilhelmshöhe. On the way, the cavalcade passed the cottage of Monsieur Fournaise, to whose wife Napoleon had given, on the morning before, four 20 franc gold pieces, saying: 'This perhaps is the last hospitality which I shall receive in France.' Further on at Donchéry, the Emperor passed the houses at either side of the street at whose windows stood Bismarck and Moltke respectively, they each saluted; gravely the Emperor responded.

'He is now saluting his gravediggers', remarked Moltke to his staff. And across the street, as he watched the Imperial cavalcade receded into the distance, 'There', said Bismarck, 'is a dynasty on its way out.'

21

The End of the Empire

Bismarck's prophecy soon proved correct. The political consequences of Sedan were, in Paris, immediate and predictable. For two days after the battle, there continued to circulate the usual rumours of great victories. The first intimation of the capitulation of the Army of Châlons came on the morning of September 3 in the form of a telegram from Brussels; but it was not until 4.30 pm on that day, with the receipt of Napoleon's own telegram to Eugénie announcing the surrender of the army and that he too was made prisoner, that the government were in possession of hard news of the situation which they were obliged to accept. They now had to face the fearful implications of the defeat.

Eugénie's reaction to the news, immediately on hearing it from the Minister of the Interior, was briefly explosive. To her secretary Augustine Filon, and to Eugene Conti, one of the Emperor's secretaries, she exclaimed angrily her disbelief that Napoleon could have surrendered; then, in a furious tirade, her eyes blazing, she broke out into a denunciation of the Emperor for his betrayal. For a moment madness gripped her; then, as the two men went to her, she fainted.[1] But Eugénie was made of sterner stuff than that, and when she came to, she at once began to tackle her almost impossible situation. Her first move was to send for Trochu but, still resenting what he perceived a recent affront, he refused the invitation with the

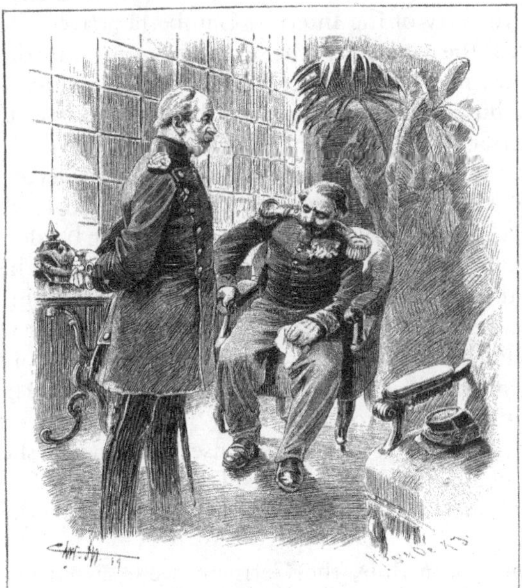

A meeting of two emperors, William and Napoleon, by Speyer (Bork)

implausible excuse that he had not dined. It was clear to the Empress that little support was to be had from him. Palikao, on hearing the grim news, also realised at once that Trochu was not to be relied upon in an insurrectionary situation, and sought to involve Trochu's subordinate officers direct – an insult to which, when he learned of it, Trochu reacted with predictable indignation. Meanwhile that night, at a session of the Corps Législatif, Jules Faure had moved a resolution proposing dethronement.

During the following morning the Council of Ministers held prolonged and anxious discussions, and had a meeting with a group of deputies. Following this they advised Eugénie that the only alternative to revolution was abdication; at first resolutely opposed to this course, Eugénie nevertheless reluctantly accepted the advice in the face of mounting disorder in the city. At the Palais Bourbon, the situation was fast deteriorating. When the next session of the Corps Legislatif began, Gambetta vainly appealed for order. Soon, however, the mob poured into the building. Favre seized his chance and called for an adjournment to the Hôtel de Ville to proclaim the Republic. Shouting approval, the Republican deputies, the cheering crowds, and a large number of Gardes Nationales followed him from the building. En route, they encountered Trochu, who willingly accepted Favre's suggestion that he should go to his headquarters to await the establishment of the new government.

At the Hôtel de Ville, with the mounting threat that the extreme Left might seize power, it was agreed that the government should be comprised of Republican deputies for Paris, and Gambetta thereupon proclaimed the Third Republic. The composition of the new ministry was hasty and chaotic. It was intended that Trochu should become President while Jules Favre assumed office as Foreign Minister. At the Ministry of the Interior, Gambetta arrived simultaneously with Picard; he secured the office by the expedient of immediately despatching telegrams in his own name as Minister. In this way he assumed the position that was soon to make him, for the next six months, the effective ruler of France and Moltke's real adversary for the remainder of the war.

While all this was going on, Eugénie had at 3.30pm ordered Filon to telegraph instructions to the aides accompanying the Prince Imperial, who was by now at Maubeuge, that they should make at once for the Belgian border, and by midnight Louis was in Namur.[2] Next day, watched by a large crowd, he left for Ostend. Meanwhile his father, learning of the fall of the Empire from the newsboys on Verviers Station as he travelled by rail through Belgium, was well on his way to captivity at Wilhelmshöhe, which he reached on the evening of September 5.

In Paris, Eugénie had been obliged to find sanctuary at the house of Dr Evans, her American dentist. At dawn on September 5, displaying her usual courage and resourcefulness, as well as a remarkable sense of humour, she left Paris. After experiencing various adventures she reached Deauville, where Sir John Burgoyne, a visiting English baronet, was finally prevailed upon to take her in his yacht to England.

Outside Sedan, meanwhile, the Germans were savouring their victory. At Donchéry Busch observed the King with Bismarck and a 'great retinue' passing through the town, intent on riding around the entire battlefield. The Crown

Prince was in the party and found on closer inspection that the nature of the battlefield was not at all what he had supposed.

> In the course of the ride I was able to get a really clear conception of what yesterday's battle meant; in particular I now realise the astonishing depth of the dips in the ground and the ravines that had impeded the advance of our infantry, but, on the other hand, had proved of extraordinary advantage to the enemy. At Floing I also examined the garden walls which had first of all to be demolished by our persistent artillery fire; these had been loopholed and constituted a regular fortification, while the heaps of dead artillery horses lying about testified to the obstinacy of the struggle.

He also encountered large numbers of French prisoners, and was shocked to find that many of them called out 'Vive la paix!' and appeared to be delighted to be on their way to captivity in Germany.[3]

Busch had stayed at Donchéry, and at about 1.30pm saw the beginning of the process of handling the huge numbers of prisoners.

> Some thousands of prisoners marched through the town on their way to Germany; partly on foot, partly on waggons – a general on horseback and sixty or seventy officers of different grades. There were cuirassiers with white helmets, blue hussars with white lace, and infantry of the 22nd and 52nd and 58th Regiments. The escort consisted of Württemburg infantry. About two o'clock there came two thousand more prisoners, amongst them negroes in Arab garb – broad shouldered figures with savage faces.[4]

It was with the prisoners that Moltke and his staff were immediately concerned. While they were being assembled in the Iges Peninsula, Moltke issued orders at noon on September 2 to the Third Army and the Army of the Meuse assigning the responsibility for dealing with them to the XI Corps and the I Bavarian Corps under the overall command of von der Tann.[5] The first problem was to feed them; Wimpffen had promised to send up supplies by rail from the fortress to a point just short of Donchéry. Considerable difficulties were however experienced in getting sufficient food to them.[6] It was Moltke's intention to evacuate them as soon as possible by using two railway lines, one through Remilly and the other through Pont à Mousson. He instructed the Third Army to appoint a Commandant of Sedan, and Blumenthal chose Major General von Bernhardi for this task. Moltke issued instructions to the latter on September 4 for the phased transportation of the prisoners to Germany. At this time the total number of prisoners was still unknown, but Moltke's intention was that they should be moved at the rate of 10,000 per day, in batches of 2,000 at a time.[7]

Although their captors did their best to provide adequately for them, for the French prisoners concentrated in the Iges Peninsula conditions were extremely unpleasant. There were only three small villages there, Villette, Glaire and Iges. There was little shelter and the weather was dreadful. When he joined his men in the camp, Commandant Vidal was appalled by what he found.

> There had been thrown there more than 70,000 men and 20,000 horses, all mixed together, infantry, cavalry, artillery, engineers, soldiers, officers, generals, all disarmed (with the exception of the officers), without shelter and without

> food; all resembled a collection of wild beasts given over, in the absence of all discipline, to the most brutal passions.[8]

As Vidal observed, the situation was even worse for the unfortunate inhabitants, who struggled in vain to prevent the looting of their villages. The peninsula quickly became known as the 'Camp de la Misère.'

Although Moltke's instructions were perfectly clear, the tension of the last few days found Blumenthal in a very short temper, and disposed to find fault with the orders he received. In the privacy of his diary he was sharply critical of Moltke and his staff:

> After everything had been carried out with such precision up to date, suddenly there set in the wildest confusion in the communication of orders, which nearly drove me mad with annoyance. The written orders of Moltke and Podbielski did not tally with the orders communicated verbally; in short, it looked as though they had intended to bring chaos and confusion into our counsels, then to withdraw and let the thing work out its own salvation ....There was nobody told off to take charge of all the arrangements in chief, and I have no idea who has brought the prisoners out of the fortress, or even whether they have been brought out at all.[9]

Blumenthal dashed off a testy note to Moltke about it that evening.

On the morning of September 3 Bismarck, who had received a present of five hundred cigars, gave them to Busch to distribute among the German wounded; when Busch got to the makeshift hospital he was prevailed on by the German soldiers to share them out among the French soldiers as well. Bismarck, meanwhile, set off in an open carriage from Donchéry to go over to Vendresse to dine with the King, getting thoroughly soaked in a heavy thunderstorm on the way.[10] After dinner he sat down to write a short account of recent events to his wife. Following a brief description of the battle, he hoped that Metz would soon surrender: 'then the lies of the Paris newspapers about everlasting victories will be at an end.' Bismarck had been suffering considerably from the weather, but his appetite was unaffected as he explained to Johanna:

> I mounted my horse yesterday morning at six and did not dismount until midnight, having ridden ten to eleven miles, was twice drenched and dried again, and have eaten nothing warm for the last three days. When, on the aforesaid midnight, I chanced upon a dish of stewed meat, I ate it like a wolf and then slept quite fast for six hours. Then I felt like a fish in the water, and what is more wonderful still, so does Röschen, who had no food or water for eighteen hours, and who did those eleven miles under me on a bad road and in darkness and rain: she took her food at once with a good appetite.[11]

Next day Bismarck moved on to Rethel. He was already turning over in his mind the basis of a possible peace settlement. After dinner that night he reflected out loud on what might be achieved: 'It is the fortresses of Metz and Strasbourg which we want and which we will take. Elsass is an idea of the professors.'[12] Whatever Bismarck might have thought of larger annexations, however, Moltke was of a different view. Writing to Stiehle on September 5 with his account of the closing stages of the Sedan campaign, and the capitulation of the Army of Châlons,

Moltke added one piece of information, which made his position entirely plain. 'I propose to return to their homes in Alsace and Lorraine all the German speaking troops. This will make clear at the same time our settled intention of not abandoning these two provinces.' At that time he had no news from Paris, but he recognised that 'a revolution is inevitable since the Emperor has left French soil. Bazaine is one of his creatures and has perhaps more particular regards to consider than the interests of France.' He ended his letter with a brief description of the Emperor's departure: 'At 3.am in pouring rain, Napoleon then drove with a numerous retinue and much baggage to the border, escorted by the body-squadron of the 1st Hussars, which looked splendid, to Bouillon. Can he have sacrificed 80,000 men to secure this retreat?'[13]

Moltke's views about Alsace and Lorraine were shared by all the military, and as the days passed and the public fervour at home for much more substantial annexations increased, Bismarck's own views began to harden. He may at first have been inclined to regard the retention of the two provinces as a 'professorial idea', but he certainly regarded it as a possible outcome of the war, as he had told the Crown Prince as early as September 3. During this conversation the Crown Prince was particularly interested to listen to the Chancellor's views on the establishment of a German Empire, but to his disappointment Bismarck hardly referred to it.

> Indeed I noticed that Count Bismarck is only in favour of the plan under certain conditions, and guarded myself accordingly more than ever now against even appearing, at this moment and in the enemy's country, to be desirous of hastening such a consummation, though I am convinced that it must come and will come.[14]

Bismarck had from the outset been anxious about the extent to which the Germans might be allowed a free hand. On September 6, however, he was sufficiently encouraged after reading a despatch from Paris announcing the formation of the new ministry to tell Blumenthal that 'we no longer need dread any interference on the part of the diplomatics. There should be no question of negotiations.'[15] But although Blumenthal saw things in such simple terms, Bismarck's anxiety about the policy of the other Great Powers never left him until the war was finally won, and it shaped his own attitude to all the critical decisions that remained to be made.

On Moltke's staff there was a strong feeling at first that the war was as good as over. Certainly no surprise was felt at the news of the dynasty's fall, and there was no expectation that whatever followed – Moltke predicted to his brother Fritz that this would be a military republic – French resistance would be very prolonged.

> 'By rights,' he wrote on September 11, 'the war ought to be ended now as France has no longer an army; one has capitulated and the other will certainly have to do so. At Metz this is the twenty-fourth day that 200,000 mouths have had to be fed. We hear from the prisoners that they have begun to eat horseflesh. Bazaine may make another desperate attempt to cut through the lines, but all necessary precautions to prevent it have been taken. In Paris there are no other soldiers left but the incomplete Corps Vinoy, and a very large number of gardes nationales, men who defend themselves behind ramparts and ditches, but who can never dare come out and fight our men in the open field. The difficulty is

> that there is no authority with whom peace can be concluded. The present Government was established in this manner: at the last ridiculous meeting a workman jumped upon the president's chair, rang the bell and proclaimed the republic.'[16]

The King, however, was not so sure. In a short speech, which he made to a group of princes forming part of his entourage, he concluded with the words: 'Gentlemen, believe me, the war is not yet over. We have achieved great and unlooked-for victories, but France will not yet give in. We may have much and bloody work still before us.'[17]

William's point was well made. The virtual destruction of the armies of the Second Empire in a few weeks was wholly unexpected, and should not be allowed to obscure the fact that the French nation was still a very formidable opponent. In spite of the well documented history of muddle and disorganisation that had characterised the French mobilisation and deployment, the French armies had fought bravely and well; and behind them, as Moltke was soon to discover, lay the vast resources of a large and powerful industrial nation. The superior organisation, training and management of the German armies had given Moltke the opportunity to win a series of stunning victories, and would stand them in good stead in the months ahead; but the speed and the extent of the French military recovery was so great that the task of bringing the war to a successful conclusion would tax Moltke and his armies to the utmost.

The Crown Prince was of the same opinion as his father. 'I am convinced the war will be continued all the same, and, thanks to the French system of misrepresentations, the struggle will be protracted in Paris to the bitter end. Then we shall advance before Paris, blockade the city, and when it is eventually taken there still remains the question whether a Government can be found that will be ready to satisfy our demand for the surrender of Alsace, and at the same time be strong enough to do it. How much then yet remains problematical for the future!'[18]

William was, though, entitled to moments of euphoria. At dinner on September 3 he proposed a toast to the army:

> 'You, General von Roon, have sharpened the sword; you, General von Moltke, have wielded it; you, Count Bismarck, have conducted my policy in such a able manner that, in thanking my army I think of you three in particular. Long live the army!'[19]

Moltke and his staff were not long distracted by these modest celebrations; whether or not the war would end quickly it must for the moment be got on with, and this, at once and with complete and characteristic efficiency, the German armies turned to do. At noon on September 3 Royal Headquarters issued general orders for the advance on Paris. A second, and bitterly prolonged phase of the war was under way.

Notes

Introduction

1. A Bucholz, *Moltke and the German Wars*, (New York 2001), p 10
2. ibid.
3. A J P Taylor, *From Napoleon to the Second International*, (London 1993), p 320
4. G A Craig, *The Politics of the Prussian Army*, (Oxford 1964), pp 215–16
5. D J Hughes, *Moltke on the Art of War*, (Novato California 1993), p 171
6. ibid, p 174
7. ibid, pp 174–5
8. Lieut. General von Caemmerer, *The Development of Strategical Science*, (London 1905), p 179
9. Bucholz, p 9
10. M Howard, *The Franco-Prussian War*, (London 1962), p 24
11. Bucholz, p 11

Chapter 1: From Nikolsburg to Ems

1. Field Marshal H von Moltke, *Letters to his Wife*, (London 1896), II, pp 197–8
2. quoted F E Whitton, *Moltke*, (London 1921), p 169
3. Ollivier, E. *The Franco-Prussian War and its Hidden Causes*, (London 1913), p 5
4. E A Pottinger, *Napoleon III and the German Crisis*, (Cambridge, Mass. 1968), pp 193–4
5. Sir V Wellesley and R Sencourt, *Conversations with Napoleon III*, (London 1934), p 295
6. Pottinger, p 183
7. Wellesley, pp 303–4
8. ibid, pp 304–5
9. ibid, p 306
10. ibid, p 314
11. J Ridley, *Napoleon III and Eugénie*, (London 1979), p 540
12. Wellesley, p 327
13 E Stoffel, *Military Reports addressed to the French War Minister*, (London 1872), p 302
14. V Benedetti, *Ma Mission en Prusse*, (Paris 1871), p 262
15. Field Marshal H von Moltke, *Letters to his Mother and his Brothers*, (London 1891), p 183
16. ibid, p 184
17. quoted Whitton, p 86
18. Prince O von Bismarck, *The Correspondence of William I & Bismarck*, (New York 1903), II, p 135
19. Bismarck, Prince O von *Reflections and Reminiscences*, (London 1898), II, p 57
20. quoted L Gall, *Bismarck The White Revolutionary*, (London 1986), I, p 343
21. Moltke, *Military Correspondence 1870–71*, (trans. H Bell) (Fort Leavenworth, Kansas), p 93

22. ibid, p 125
23. Moltke, *Letters to his Wife*, II, pp 200–2
24. Moltke, *Letters to his Mother and Brothers*, p 185
25. Moltke, *Letters to his Wife*, II, pp 215–16
26. Herms, M (trans), *Moltke, his Life and Character*, (London 1892), p 143
27. Bismarck, *Reflections and Reminiscences*, II, p 89
28. ibid, II, p 89
29. R H Lord, *The Origins of the War of 1870*, (Harvard 1924), p 21
30. quoted Gall, I, p 352
31. ibid, p 34
32. ibid, p 42
33. ibid, p 46
34. quoted R Millman, *British Foreign Policy and the Coming of the Franco-Prussian War*, (Oxford 1965) p 184
35. Ollivier, p 147
36. Benedetti, p 331
37. Ollivier, p 152
38. Benedetti, pp 349–57
39. Bismarck, *Reflections and Reminiscences*, II, p 92
40. Helms, M, *Moltke's Life*, p 214
41. Bismarck, *Reflections and Reminiscences*, II, p 93
42. Lord, p 192
43. Ollivier, p 181
44. Millman, p 189
45. Lord, p 87
46. ibid, pp 276–8
47. Bismarck, *Reflections and Reminiscences*, II, pp 95–101
48. Ollivier, p 309

Chapter 2: Strategic Planning

1. Bismarck, *Reflections and Reminiscences*, II, p 37
2. Moltke, *Military Correspondence*, pp 88–9
3. A Bucholz, *Moltke, Schlieffen and Prussian War Planning*, (New York 1991), pp 49–51
4. Moltke *Military Correspondence*, pp 93–6
5. ibid, pp 97–9
6. ibid, pp 100–2
7. Bucholz, *War Planning*, p 51
8. Moltke, *Military Correspondence*, pp 108–10
9. ibid, pp 111–13
10. ibid, pp 114–16
11. ibid, pp 117–18
12. ibid, p 121
13. ibid, p 124
14. ibid, p 126
15. ibid, p 130
16. ibid, p 136

17. ibid, pp 145–7
18. ibid, pp 138–9
19. ibid, p 150
20. ibid, p 152
21. ibid, p 157
22. ibid, p 159
23. ibid, pp 162–3
24. quoted Hughes, *Moltke on the Art of War*, (Novato, California 1994), pp 125–6
25. R Stadelmann, *Moltke und der Staat*, (Krefeld 1950), p 32

Chapter 3: The German Army after Königgrätz

1. Stoffel, p 44
2. ibid, p 149
3. ibid, p 86
4. quoted G A Craig, *The Battle of Königgrätz*, (London 1965), Stoffel, p 4
5. Stoffel, p 5
6. Stoffel, p 149
7. Prince Krafft zu Hohenlohe Ingelfingen, *Letters on Infantry*, (trans NL Walford) (London 1892), p 83
8. Stoffel, p 149
9. quoted Craig, *Königgrätz*, p 186
10. Hohenlohe, *Letters on Artillery*, (trans NL Walford) (London 1890), p 6
11. Stoffel, p 47
12. Hohenlohe, *Artillery*, p 30
13. Hughes, p 211
14. ibid, p 213
15. Stoffel, p 6
16. Hughes, p 209
17. ibid, p 223
18. D Ascoli, *A Day of Battle: Mars-la-Tour 16 August 1870*, (London 1987), p 67
19. General J von Verdy du Vernois, *With the Royal Headquarters in 1870–71*, (London 1897), p 22
20. Field Marshal Count A von Waldersee, *A Field Marshal's Memoirs*, (trans F Whyte) (London 1924), p 60
21. Verdy, p 22
22. Field Marshal Count K von Blumenthal, *Journals for 1866 and 1870–71*, (London 1903), pp 26–7
23. Crown Prince Frederick William, *The War Diary of the Emperor Frederick III 1870–71*, (London 1927), p 7
24. Waldersee, p 83
25. ibid, p 60
26. Blumenthal, p 13
27. ibid, p 57
28. Lieut Col Chesney and H Reeve, *The Military Resources of Prussia and France*, (London 1870), p 167

Chapter 4: The French Army and its Leaders

1. quoted Pottinger, p 196
2. Chesney and Reeve, pp 126 and 168
3. Ollivier, p 84
4. T J Adriance, *The Last Gaiter Button*, (Westpoint Conn 1987), p 24
5. Chesney and Reeve, p 141
6. Adriance, pp 33–4
7. R Holmes, *The Road to Sedan*, (London 1984), p 222
8. Holmes, p 202, GFR Henderson: *The Battle of Wörth*, (Yorktown, Surrey 1899), pp 3–4
9. quoted Holmes, p 204
10. Holmes, p 207
11. quoted Howard, p 36
12. Holmes, p 42
13. ibid, p 49
14. German Official Account: *The Franco-German War 1870–71*, (London 1874), I, p 16
15. Holmes, p 177
16. Holmes, p 49, quoting General Bonnal
17. AJ Barker, *The Vainglorious War*, (London 1970), p 266
18. P Turnbull, *Solferino: The Birth of a Nation*, (London 1985), p 108
19. ibid, p 113
20. Holmes, p 12
21. ibid, pp 60–1
22. S Eardley Wilmot, *Life of Vice Admiral Lord Lyons*, (London 1898), p 294
23. Holmes, p 12
24. ibid, pp 60–1
25. GP Cox, *The Halt in the Mud*, (Oxford 1994), p 181
26. Holmes, p 168
27. ibid, p 169
28. Howard, p 45
29. ibid, pp 46–8

Chapter 5: Mobilisation and Deployment

1. quoted Howard, p 48
2. Millman, p 188
3. R Fulford (ed), *Your Dear Letter, Private Correspondence of Queen Victoria and the Crown Princess of Prussia 1865–71*, (London 1981), p 284
4. ibid, p 287
5. Millman, p 192
6. Daily News: *Correspondence of the War between Germany and France 1870–71*, (London 1871), p 5
7. General P Sheridan, *Personal Memoirs*, (London 1888), II, p 359
8. F von Holstein, *Memoirs*, (Cambridge 1955), p 4
9. Adriance, p 49
10. ibid.
11. Holmes, p 177

12. ibid.
13. ibid, p 175
14. Moltke, *Military Correspondence 1870–71*, (ed S Wilkinson) (Oxford 1923), p 37
15. Official Account, I, p 60
16. Moltke, *Military Correspondence*, (ed S Wilkinson) pp 40–1
17. ibid, p 45
18. ibid, p 53
19. Official Account, I, p 25
20. ibid, appendix II
21. ibid, p 27
22. ibid, p 75
23. Moltke, *Military Correspondence*, (ed S Wilkinson), p 57
24. ibid, p 55
25. Crown Prince, p 19
26. Moltke, *Military Correspondence*, (ed S Wilkinson), p 58
27. A Forbes, *My Experiences of the War between France and Germany*, (London 1871), I, p 28
28. Moltke, *Military Correspondence*, (ed S Wilkinson), p 59
29. Verdy, pp 46–7
30. ibid, pp 43–4
31. K John, *The Prince Imperial*, (London 1939), p 189
32. Forbes, I, p 65

Chapter 6: The Opening Battles: Weissenburg and Wörth

1. Blumenthal, p 85
2. Moltke, *Military Correspondence*, (ed S Wilkinson), pp 66–7
3. Official Account, I, p 136
4. Crown Prince, pp 27–8
5. Hohenlohe, *Artillery*, p 31
6. Official Account, I, p 140
7. Henderson, *Wörth*, p 71
8. Blumenthal, p 87
9. ibid, p 88
10. Moltke, *Military Correspondence*, (ed S Wilkinson), p 74
11. Official Account, I, p 151
12. ibid, p 155
13. ibid, p 163
14. Henderson, p 48
15. Official Account, I, p 184
16. Hohenlohe, *Artillery*, p 34
17. Crown Prince, pp 38–9
18. Moltke, *Military Correspondence*, (ed S Wilkinson), p 75
19. ibid.
20. Blumenthal, pp 88–9
21. ibid, p 91

Chapter 7: The Opening Battles: Spicheren

1. Official Account, I, p 142
2. ibid, p 214
3. Moltke, *Military Correspondence,* (ed S Wilkinson), p 69
4. ibid, pp 69–70
5. ibid, p 70
6. ibid.
7. Official Account, I, p 103
8. Moltke, *Military Correspondence,* (ed S Wilkinson), p 71
9. Field Marshal H von Moltke, *The Franco-German War of 1870–71,* (London 1907), pp 19–20
10. Official Account, I, p 106
11. Field Marshal H von Moltke, *Correspondance Militaire de Maréchal de Moltke 1870–71,* (Paris n.d), V, p 285
12. Official Account, I, p 203
13. General von Pelet-Narbonne, *Cavalry On Service,* (London 1906), p 3
14. Official Account, I, p 234
15. ibid, p 243
16. Moltke, *Franco-German War,* p 25
17. Official Account, I, p 252
18. Hohenlohe, *Artillery,* pp 52–3
19. Official Account, I, p 254

Chapter 8: Borny-Colombey

1. quoted Howard, p 117
2. *Daily News,* p 23
3. Moltke, *Military Correspondence,* (ed S Wilkinson), p 77
4. ibid p 78
5. quoted T Aronson, *The Fall of the Third Napoleon,* (London, 1970), p 117
6. Official Account, I, p 288
7. Verdy, p 60
8. Moltke, *Military Correspondence,* (ed S Wilkinson), p 79
9. ibid, p 81
10. ibid, p 82
11. ibid, p 83
12. ibid, p 84
13. ibid, p 85
14. ibid, p 86
15. Verdy, p 62
16. Blumenthal, p 93
17. Official Account, I, p 299
18. Pelet-Narbonne, p 271
19. A von Schell, *The Operations of the First Army under General von Steinmetz,* (London 1873), p 86
20. Verdy, pp 64–5
21. ibid, p 67
22. Moltke, *Franco-German War,* p 33

23. Verdy, p 68
24. Schell, p 93
25. Marshal A Bazaine, *Episodes de la Guerre de 1870*, (Madrid 1883), p 71

Chapter 9: Mars La Tour

1. Moltke, *Military Correspondence*, (ed S Wilkinson), p 94
2. Pelet-Narbonne, p 30
3. Holmes, p 62
4. Verdy, p 70
5. Pelet-Narbonne, pp 319–20
6. Moltke, Military Correspondence, (ed S Wilkinson), p 95
7. Lieut Col. Bonie, 'The French Cavalry in 1870', in *Cavalry Studies for Two Great Wars*, (Kansas City, 1896), p 44
8. Official Account, I, p 373
9. ibid, Appendix XIX, p 125
10. quoted Major Kaehler, 'The German Cavalry in the Battle of Vionville-Mars La Tour', in *Cavalry Studies for Two Great Wars*, p 170
11. quoted Field Marshal Sir E Wood, *Achievements of Cavalry*, (London 1897) p 232
12. Hohenlohe, *Letters on Cavalry*, (London 1889), p 26
13. Official Account, I, p 412
14. ibid, p 412
15. F Hönig, *Twenty Four Hours of Moltke's Strategy*, (Woolwich 1895), p 22
16. quoted P Guedalla, *The Two Marshals*, (London 1943), p 186
17. quoted W McElwee, *The Art of War from Waterloo to Mons*, (London 1974), p 67
18. Official Account, I, p 418
19. Moltke, *Franco-German War*, p 45
20. Verdy, p 71
21. Moltke, *Military Correspondence*, (ed S Wilkinson), p 96
22. Verdy, p 72
23. Ascoli, p 339
24. ibid, p 213

Chapter 10: Gravelotte

1. Moltke, *Military Correspondence*, (ed S Wilkinson), p 97
2. Verdy, p 73
3. Hönig, p 29
4. Moltke, *Military Correspondence*, (ed S Wilkinson), p 98
5. Moltke, *Franco-German War*, p 47
6. Hönig, p 39
7. Moltke, *Military Correspondence*, (ed S Wilkinson), pp 98–9
8. Official Account, II, p 10
9. Verdy, p 79
10. ibid, p 86
11. Hönig, p 12
12. quoted Hönig, p 13
13. Hönig, p 24

14. Verdy, p 80
15. Moltke, *Military Correspondence*, (ed S Wilkinson), p 99
16. Official Account, II, p 16
17. Moltke, *Military Correspondence*, (ed S Wilkinson), p 99
18. Official Account, II, p 25
19. G Hooper, *The Campaign of Sedan*, (London 1908), p 213
20. Hönig, p 101
21. ibid, p 109
22. Waldersee, p 65
23. Howard, p 172
24. Hönig, p 131
25. ibid, p 133
26. Dick de Lonlay, *Francais et Allemands*, (Paris 1890), III, p 735
27. Moltke, *Franco-German War*, p 58
28. Hönig, p 149
29. Hohenlohe, *Artillery*, p 44
30. Hooper, p 220
31. Official Account, II, p 131
32. ibid, p 141
33. Verdy, p 92

Chapter 11: The Army of Châlons

1. Official Account, II, p 166
2. Moltke, *Military Correspondence*, (ed S Wilkinson), p 100
3. Hohenlohe, *Letters on Strategy*, (London 1898), II, p 8
4. Verdy, p 101
5. Crown Prince, p 63
6. Blumenthal, p 97
7. ibid, p 98
8. Crown Prince, p 64
9. Blumenthal, p 99
10. Crown Prince, p 65
11. ibid.
12. Blumenthal, p 99
13. H Helvig, *Operations of the I Bavarian Army Corps under General von der Tann*, (London 1874), I, 39
14. quoted Howard, p 185
15. Bazaine, p 91
16. Official Account, II, p 186
17. *Papiers et Correspondance de la Famille Imperiale*, (Paris 1870), p 44
18. *Official Account*, II, p 187
19. *Papiers et Correspondance*, p 62
20. ibid, p 46
21. Bazaine, p 163
22. Howard, p 190
23. *Papiers et Correspondance*, p 47
24. ibid, p 48

Chapter 12: MacMahon's Flank March

1. Helvig, I, p 48
2. Blumenthal, p 101
3. Sheridan, II, p 386
4. ibid, p 388
5. M Busch, *Bismarck in the Franco-German War 1870–71*, (London 1879), I, p 45
6. Crown Prince, p 69
7. Moltke, *Military Correspondence*, (ed S Wilkinson), p 106
8. Hohenlohe, *Strategy*, II, p 65
9. Official Account, II, pp 195–7
10. ibid, p 198
11. ibid, p 199
12. Blumenthal, p 102
13. Moltke, *Military Correspondence*, (ed S Wilkinson), p 108
14. Hohenlohe, *Strategy*, II, p 87
15. Official Account, II, pp 195–7
16. Forbes, I, p 219
17. Sheridan, II, p 389
18. Verdy, p 108
19. Busch, I, p 55
20. Moltke, *Franco-German War*, p 70
21. Official Account, II, p 200
22. ibid, p 201
23. ibid, p 204
24. Forbes, I, p 221
25. Verdy, p 111
26. Helvig, p 42
27. Blumenthal, p 103
28. Verdy, p 113
29. John, p 217
30. Bazaine, pp 164–7
31. Moltke, *Franco-German War*, p 70
32. Crown Prince, p 72
33. W H Russell, *My Diary during the Last Great War*, (London 1874), p 148
34. Hohenlohe, *Cavalry*, p 43
35. Official Account, II, p 215
36. E S May, *Guns and Cavalry*, (London 1896) pp 102–5
37. Hohenlohe, *Cavalry*, p 42
38. Blumenthal, p 105
39. Verdy, p 115
40. Moltke, *Franco-German War*, pp 72–3
41. Moltke, *Military Correspondence*, (ed S Wilkinson), p 116
42. Hooper, p 252
43. Official Account, II, p 220
44. Hooper, p 253
45. Official Account, II, p 220

46. Hooper, p 253
47. Helvig, I, pp 49–50
48. Blumenthal, pp 105–6
49. Sheridan, II, pp 393–4
50. Moltke, *Franco-German War*, p 75
51. Hohenlohe, *Cavalry*, pp 52–3
52. Moltke, *Military Correspondence*, (ed S Wilkinson), p 119

Chapter 13: Beaumont

1. Blumenthal, p 106
2. Moltke, *Military Correspondence*, (ed S Wilkinson), p 120
3. Official Account, II, pp 228–9
4. ibid, p 234
5. Helvig, I, p 53
6. Blumenthal, p 107
7. Crown Prince, p 76
8. Verdy, p 116
9. Moltke, *Military Correspondence*, (ed S Wilkinson), pp 121–2
10. Sheridan, II, p 396
11. Busch, I, p 75
12. Official Account, II, pp 238–9
13. Verdy, p 116
14. Russell, pp 155–6
15. Hooper, p 266
16. Verdy, p 116
17. Blumenthal, p 108
18. Russell, pp 157–8
19. Busch, I, p 76
20. Official Account, II, p 246
21. Hohenlohe, *Artillery*, p 45
22. Verdy, p 121
23. Sheridan, II, p 397
24. Official Account, II, p 264
25. ibid, p 276
26. Moltke, *Franco-German War*, p 81
27. Official Account, II, p 276
28. Moltke, *Franco-German War*, p 83
29. Verdy, p 125
30. Moltke, *Franco-German War*, p 82
31. Moltke, *Military Correspondence*, (ed S Wilkinson), p 122

Chapter 14: August 31

1. A Borbstaedt and F Dwyer, *The Franco-German War to the Catastrophe of Sedan*, (London 1873), p 231
2. Howard, p 203
3. Hooper, p 288
4. Official Account, II, p 288

5. General A Ducrot, *La Journée de Sedan*,(Paris 1872), p 7
6. ibid, p 10
7. ibid, p 11
8. ibid, p 14
9. Hooper, p 286
10. General E F de Wimpffen, *Sedan*, (Paris 1871), p 142
11. Hooper, p 290
12. Official Account, II, p 294
13. ibid, p 296
14. ibid, p 298
15. Helvig, I, p 71
16. Official Account, II, p 304

Chapter 15: Sedan: The Battlefield

1. Official Account, II, p 309
2. ibid.
3. ibid, p 309–10
4. ibid, p 490
5. ibid.
6. ibid, p 494
7. Moltke, *Military Correspondence*, (ed S Wilkinson), p 125
8. Official Account, II, Appendix XLIII
9. Blumenthal, p 110
10. ibid.
11. Official Account, II, p 306
12. ibid, p 307
13. Sheridan, II, p 398
14. Moltke, *Military Correspondence*, (ed S Wilkinson), p 125
15. Moltke, *Franco-German War*, p 86
16. Official Account, II, p 308
17. P Vidal, *Campagne de Sedan*, (Paris, 1910), p 141
18. Dr Sarazin, *Récits de la Dernière Guerre Franco-Allemand*, (1887), p 115, quoted Maj.Gen J F C Fuller, *Decisive Battles of the Western World*, (London 1956), III, p 122

Chapter 16: Sedan: The First Stages

1. Verdy, p 126
2. Crown Prince, p 82
3. Busch, I, p 94
4. ibid, p 95
5. ibid, p 97
6. Forbes, I, p 224
7. Russell, p 187
8. ibid, p 190
9. Helvig, I, p 77
10. Official Account, II, p 313
11. Helvig, I, p 82

12. Official Account, II, p 315
13. ibid, p 316
14. ibid, p 318
15. ibid, p 320
16. Ducrot, p 20
17. ibid, p 27
18. Official Account, II, p 311
19. Wimpffen, pp 158–9
20. Official Account, II, p 324
21. Howard, p 210
22. Ducrot, p 31
23. ibid, p 145
24. ibid, p 32
25. Hohenlohe, *Artillery*, p 90
26. Official Account, II, p 333
27. ibid, p 335
28. Hohenlohe, *Artillery*, pp 47–8
29. ibid, p 339

Chapter 17: The Advance of the Crown Prince

1. Blumenthal, p 111
2. Official Account, II, p 353
3. ibid, p 354
4. Moltke, *Franco-German War*, p 91
5. Official Account, II, p 355
6. Hohenlohe, *Artillery*, p 49
7. Blumenthal, p 111
8. Forbes, I, p 231
9. Official Account, II, pp 356–7
10. Hooper, pp 308–9
11. Official Account, II, p 360
12. Ducrot, p 33
13. Verdy, p 130
14. Official Account, II, p 345

Chapter 18: Sedan: Floing and Hill 812

1. Russell, p 191
2. Busch, I, p 98
3. H Abeken, *Bismarck's Pen*, (London 1911), p 275
4. Official Account, II, p 366
5. ibid, pp 362–3
6. ibid, p 363
7. ibid, p 367
8. ibid, p 368
9. ibid, p 371
10. Dick de Lonlay, I, p 714
11. quoted Captain Fitzgeorge, *The Battle of Sedan*, (London 1871), p 50

12. quoted ibid, p 48
13. Ducrot, p 37
14. Official Account, II, p 378
15. Verdy, p 133

Chapter 19: Sedan: The End of the Battle

1. Wimpffen, p 170
2. Ducrot, p 41
3. Dick de Lonlay, I, p 716
4. Aronson, p 170
5. Wimpffen, p 171
6. Official Account, II, p 384
7. Hohenlohe, *Artillery*, p 94
8. Official Account, II, p 387
9. ibid, p 388
10. ibid, p 395
11. Ducrot, p 47
12. Official Account, II, p 396
13. Wimpffen, p 173
14. Official Account, II, p 388
15. Ducrot, p 49
16. Sheridan, II, p 402
17. Official Account, II, p 401
18. A Forbes, *Memories and Studies of War and Peace*, (London 1895), p 77
19. Howard, p 218
20. Official Account, II, p 402
21. Count P Hatzfeldt, *Letters to his Wife 1870–71*, (London 1905), p 63
22. Official Account, II, Appendix XLVIII
23. Moltke, *Military Correspondence*, (ed S Wilkinson), p 126
24. Forbes, *Memories* p 80

Chapter 20: Sedan: The Capitulation

1. Forbes, *Memories*, p 81
2. Ducrot, pp 52–3
3. Verdy, p 135
4. Ducrot, pp 54–68; Verdy, pp 135–7; Forbes, *Memories*, pp 81–3; Howard, p 220–2; Wimpffen, pp 239–48
5. Busch, I, p 103
6. Forbes, *Memories*, p 84
7. Sheridan, II, p 406
8. Busch, I, p 104; also Sheridan II, pp 406–7 and Forbes, *Memories*, pp 84-5
9. Busch, I, pp 108–10
10. Moltke, *Moltke as a Correspondent*, (ed M Herms) London 1893, p 133
11. Forbes, *Memories*, p 89
12. Ducrot, pp 68–9
13. Verdy, p 140
14. Wimpffen, p 248

15. Forbes, *Memories*, p 91; quoted P Wiegler, *William the First, His Life and Times*, (London 1929), p 308
16. Verdy, p 141
17. Aronson, pp 180–1
18. Official Account, II, p 408 and Appendix L

Chapter 21: The End of the Empire

1. A Filon, *Recollections of the Empress Eugénie*, (London 1920), p 134
2. ibid, p 151
3. Crown Prince, pp 100–1
4. Busch, I, p 111
5. Moltke, *Correspondance Militaire*, I, pp 343–4
6. Blumenthal, p 115
7. Moltke, *Correspondance Militaire*, I, p 346
8. Vidal, pp 216–17
9. Blumenthal, p 115
10. Busch, I, p 118
11. Bismarck, *Letters to his Wife from the Seat of War 1870–71*, (London 1915), pp 46–7
12. Busch, I, p 122
13. Moltke, *Correspondence Militaire*, I, p 346
14. Crown Prince, p 102
15. Blumenthal, p 118
16. Moltke, *Moltke as a Correspondent*, p 135
17. Waldersee, p 68
18. Crown Prince, p 104
19. Verdy, p 147

APPENDIX I

German Forces (August 1st 1870)

Commander in Chief:	King William I of Prussia
Chief of Staff:	General of Infantry Baron von Moltke
Quartermaster General:	Lieutenant-General von Podbielski
Inspector General of Artillery:	General von Hindersin
Inspector General of Engineers:	Lieutenant-General von Kleist
Intendant General:	Lieutenant-General von Stosch

FIRST ARMY

Commander:	General of Infantry von Steinmetz
Chief of Staff:	Major-General von Sperling

I CORPS

Commander:	General of Cavalry Baron von Manteuffel
Chief of Staff:	Lieutenant-Colonel von der Burg

1st Infantry Division

Commander:	Major-General von Bentheim

1st Infantry Brigade (Major-General von Gayl)

1st East Prussian Grenadier Regiment Nr. 1 (Colonel von Massow)
3 battalions
5th East Prussian Infantry regiment Nr. 41 (Colonel Meerscheidt-Hüllessem)
3 battalions

2nd Infantry Brigade (Major-General von Falkenstein)

2nd East Prussian Grenadier Regiment Nr. 3 (Colonel von Legat)
3 battalions
6th East Prussian Infantry Regiment Nr. 43 (Colonel von Busse)
3 battalions

Divisional Troops

East Prussian Jäger Battalion Nr. 1 (Major von Plœtz)
1 battalion
'Lithuanian' Dragoon Regiment Nr. 1 (Lieutenant-Colonel von Massow)
4 squadrons
2 4 pounder batteries, 1st Artillery Regiment
2 6 pounder batteries, 1st Artillery Regiment
2 companies, 1st Pioneer Battalion

2nd Infantry Division

Commander:	Major-General von Pritzelwitz

3rd Infantry Brigade (Major-General von Memerty)

3rd East Prussian Grenadier Regiment Nr. 4 (Colonel von Tiezen and Hennig)
3 battalions
7th East Prussian Infantry Regiment Nr. 44 (Colonel von Böcking)
3 battalions

4th Infantry Brigade (Major-General von Zglitzky)

4th East Prussian Grenadier Regiment Nr. 5 (Colonel von Einem)
3 battalions
8th East Prussian Infantry Regiment Nr. 45 (Colonel von Mützschefal)
3 battalions

Divisional Troops

East Prussian Dragoon Regiment Nr. 10 (Colonel Baron von der Goltz)
2 4 pounder batteries, 1st Artillery Regiment
2 6 pounder batteries, 1st Artillery Regiment
1 company, 1st Pioneer Battalion

Corps Artillery (Colonel Junge)

2 4 pounder batteries, 1st Artillery Regiment
2 6 pounder batteries, 1st Artillery Regiment
2 4 pounder horse artillery batteries, 1st Artillery Regiment

1st Train Battalion

CORPS Total:
25 battalions, 8 squadrons, 3 companies, 14 batteries, train
28,800 men, 84 guns

VII CORPS

Commander: General of Infantry von Zastrow

13th Infantry Division

Commander: Lieutenant-General von Glümer

25th Infantry Brigade (Major-General Baron von der Osten-Sacken)

1st Westphalian Infantry-Regiment Nr.13 (Colonel von Frankenberg-Ludwigsdorff)
3 battalions
Hanoverian Fusilier Regiment Nr.73 (Colonel von Loebell)
3 battalions

26th Infantry Brigade (Major-General von der Goltz)

2nd Westphalian Infantry Regiment Nr. 15 (Colonel von Delitz)
3 battalions
6th Westphalian Infantry Regiment Nr. 55 (Colonel von Barby)
3 battalions

Divisional Troops

Westphalian Jäger Battalion Nr. 7 (Lieutenant-Colonel Reinike)
1 battalion
1st Westphalian Hussar Regiment Nr. 8 (Lieutenant-Colonel von Arendt)
4 squadrons
2 pioneer companies, 7th Pioneer Battalion

Divisional Artillery
2 4 pounder batteries, 7th Artillery Regiment
2 6 pounder batteries, 7th Artillery Regiment

14th Infantry Division

Commander: Lieutenant-General von Kameke

27th Infantry Brigade (Major-General von François)

Rhineland Fusilier Regiment Nr. 39 (Colonel von Eskens)
3 battalions
1st Hanoverian Infantry Regiment Nr. 74 (Colonel von Pannwitz)
3 battalions

28th Infantry Brigade (: Major-General von Woyna II)

5th Westphalian Infantry Regiment Nr. 53 (Colonel von Gerstein-Hohenstein)
3 battalions
2nd Hanoverian Infantry Regiment Nr. 77 (Colonel von Conrady)
3 battalions

Divisional Troops

Hanoverian Hussar Regiment Nr. 15 (Colonel von Cosel)
4 squadrons
1 pioneer company, 7th Pioneer Battalion

Divisional Artillery
2 4 pounder batteries, 7th Artillery Regiment
2 6 pounder batteries, 7th Artillery Regiment

Corps Artillery (Colonel Helden-Sarnowski)

2 4 pounder batteries, 7th Artillery Regiment
2 6 pounder batteries, 7th Artillery Regiment
2 4 pounder horse artillery batteries, 7th Artillery Regiment

7th Train Battalion

CORPS Total:
25 battalions, 8 squadrons, 3 companies, 14 batteries, train
28,800 men, 84 guns

VIII CORPS

Commander: General of Infantry von Goeben
Chief of Staff: Colonel von Witzendorff

15th Infantry Division

Commander: Lieutenant-General von Weltzien

29th Infantry Brigade (Major-General von Wedell)

East Prussian Fusilier Regiment Nr. 33 (Lieutenant-Colonel von Henning)
3 battalions
7th Brandenburg Infantry Regiment Nr. 60 (Colonel von Dannenberg)
3 battalions

30th Infantry Brigade (Major-General von Strubberg)

2nd Rhineland Infantry Regiment Nr. 28 (Colonel von Rosenzweig)
3 battalions
6th Rhineland Infantry Regiment Nr. 68 (Colonel von Sommerfeld)
3 battalions

Divisional Troops

Rhineland Jäger Battalion Nr. 8
1 battalion
1st Rhineland Hussar Regiment Nr. 7 (Colonel Baron Loë)
4 squadrons
1 pioneer company, 8th Pioneer Battalion

Divisional Artillery
2 4 pounder batteries, 8th Artillery Regiment
2 6 pounder batteries, 8th Artillery Regiment

16th Infantry Division

Commander: Lieutenant-General von Barnekow

31st Infantry Brigade (Major-General Count Neidhardt von Gneisenau)

3rd Rhineland Infantry Regiment Nr. 29 (Colonel von Blumröder)
3 battalions
7th Rhineland Infantry Regiment Nr. 69 (Colonel Beyer von Karger)
3 battalions

32nd Infantry Brigade (Colonel von Rex)

Fusilier Regiment Nr. 40 (Colonel von Eberstein)
3 battalions
4th Thuringian Infantry Regiment Nr. 72 (Colonel Mettler)
3 battalions

Divisional Troops

2nd Rhineland Hussar Regiment Nr. 9 (Colonel Wittich)
4 squadrons
2 pioneer companies, 8th Pioneer Battalion

Divisional Artillery
2 4 pounder batteries, 8th Artillery Regiment
2 6 pounder batteries, 8th Artillery Regiment

Corps Artillery

2 4 pounder batteries, 8th Artillery Regiment
2 6 pounder batteries, 8th Artillery Regiment
2 4 pounder horse artillery batteries, 8th Artillery Regiment

8th Train Battalion

CORPS Total:
25 battalions, 8 squadrons, 3 companies, 14 batteries, train
28,800 men, 84 guns

1st Cavalry Division

Commander: Lieutenant-General von Hartmann

1st Cavalry Brigade (Major-General von Lüderitz)

Pomeranian Cuirassier Regiment Nr. 2 (Colonel von Pfuhl)
4 squadrons
1st Pomeranian Uhlan regiment Nr. 4 (Lieutenant-Colonel von Radecke)
4 squadrons
2nd Pomeranian Uhlan Regiment Nr. 9 (Lieutenant-Colonel von Kleist)
4 squadrons

2nd Cavalry Brigade (Major-General Baumgarth)

East Prussian Cuirassier Regiment Nr. 3 (Colonel von Winterfeld)
4 squadrons
East Prussian Uhlan Regiment Nr. 8 (Colonel Winterfeld)
4 squadrons
'Lithuanian' Uhlan Regiment Nr. 12 (Colonel von Rosenberg)
4 squadrons

Divisional Artillery
1 4 pounder horse artillery battery, 1st Artillery Regiment

Division Total:
20 squadrons, one battery
3,600 men, 6 guns

3rd Cavalry Division

Commander: Lieutenant-General von der Groeben

6th Cavalry Brigade (Major-General von Mirus)

Rhineland Cuirassier Regiment Nr. 8 (Colonel Count von Rödern)
4 squadrons
Rhineland Uhlan Regiment Nr. 7 (Lieutenant-Colonel von Pestel)
4 squadrons

7th Cavalry Brigade (Major-General Count Dohna)

Westphalian Uhlan Regiment Nr. 5 (Colonel Baron von Reitzenstein)
4 squadrons
Hanoverian Uhlan Regiment Nr. 14 (Colonel von Lüderitz)
4 squadrons

Divisional Artillery
1 4 pounder horse artillery battery, 7th Artillery Regiment

Division Total:
16 squadrons, one battery
2,400 men, 6 guns

SECOND ARMY

Commander:	His Royal Highness, General of Cavalry Prince Frederick Charles of Prussia
Chief of Staff:	Major General von Stiehle

GUARD CORPS

Commander:	Prince Augustus of Württemberg
Chief of Staff:	Major-General von Dannenberg

1st Guard Infantry Division

Commander:	Major-General von Pape

1st Infantry Brigade (Major-General von Kessel)

1st Foot Guard Regiment (Colonel von Röder)
3 battalions
3rd Foot Guard Regiment (Colonel von Linsingen)
3 battalions

2nd Infantry Brigade (Major-General von Medem)

2nd Foot Guard Regiment (Colonel von Kanitz)
3 battalions
4th Foot Guard Regiment (Colonel von Neumann)
3 battalions
Guard Fusilier Regiment (Lieutenant-Colonel von Erkert)
3 battalions

Divisional Troops

Guard Jäger Battalion (Major von Arnim)

1 battalion
Guard Hussar Regiment (Lieutenant-Colonel von Hymmen)
4 squadons
1 company, Guard Pioneer Battalion

Divisional Artillery
2 4 pounder batteries, Guard Artillery Regiment
2 6 pounder batteries, Guard Artillery Regiment

2nd Guard Infantry Division

Commander: Lieutenant-General von Budritzki

3rd Infantry Brigade (Colonel Knappe von Knappstaedt)

1st Guard Grenadier Regiment (Colonel von Zeuner)
3 battalions
3rd Guard Grenadier Regiment (Colonel Zaluskowski)
3 battalions

4th Infantry Brigade (Major-General von Berger)

2nd Guard Grenadier Regiment (Colonel von Böhn)
3 battalions
4th Guard Grenadier Regiment (Colonel Baron von Waldersee)
3 battalions

Divisional Troops

Guard Schützen Battalion (Major von Fabeck)
1 battalion
2nd Guard Uhlan Regiment (Colonel Prince Henry von Hesse)
4 squadrons
2 pioneer companies, Guard Pioneer Battalion

Divisional Artillery
2 4 pounder batteries, Guard Artillery Regiment
2 6 pounder batteries, Guard Artillery Regiment

Guard Cavalry Division

Commander: Lieutenant-General Count von der Goltz

1st Cavalry Brigade (Major-General Count von Brandenburg I)

Guard du Corps Regiment (Colonel von Krosigk)
4 squadrons
Guard Cuirassier Regiment (Colonel Baron von Brandenstein)
4 squadrons

2nd Cavalry Brigade (Major-General Prince Albrecht of Prussia)

1st Guard Uhlan Regiment (Lieutenant-Colonel von Rochow)
4 squadrons

3rd Guard Uhlan Regiment (Colonel Prince Frederick William von Hohenlohe)
4 squadrons

3rd Cavalry Brigade (Major-General Count von Brandenburg II)

1st Guard Dragoon Regiment (Colonel von Auerswald)
4 squadrons
2nd Guard Dragoon Regiment (Colonel Fink zu Finkenstein)
4 squadrons

Divisional Artillery
3 4 pounder horse artillery batteries, Guard Artillery Regiment

Guard Corps Artillery

2 4 pounder batteries, Guard Artillery Regiment
2 6 pounder batteries, Guard Artillery Regiment
2 4 pounder horse artillery batteries, Guard Artillery Regiment

Guard Train Battalion

CORPS Total:
29 battalions, 32 squadrons, 3 companies, 17 batteries, train
37,000 men, 102 guns

II CORPS

Commander:	General of Infantry von Fransecky
Chief of staff:	Colonel von Wichmann

3rd Infantry Division

Commander:	Major-General von Hartmann

5th Infantry Brigade (Major-General von Koblinski)

1st Pomeranian Grenadier Regiment Nr. 2 (Colonel von Ziemietzky)
3 battalions
5th Pomeranian Infantry Regiment Nr. 42 (Colonel von Knesebeck)
3 battalions

6th Infantry Brigade (Colonel von der Decken)

3rd Pomeranian Infantry Regiment Nr. 14 (Colonel von Vosz)
3 battalions
7th Pomeranian Infantry regiment Nr. 54 (Colonel von Busse)
3 battalions

Divisional Troops

Pomeranian Jäger Battalion Nr. 2 (Major von Netzer)
1 battalion
Neumark Dragoon Regiment Nr. 3 (Colonel Baron von Willisen)
4 squadrons
1 pioneer company, 2nd Pioneer Batallion

Divisional Artillery
2 4 pounder batteries, 2nd Artillery Regiment
2 6 pounder batteries, 2nd Artillery Regiment

4th Infantry Division

Commander: Lieutenant-General Hann von Weyhern

7th Infantry Brigade (Major-General du Trossel)

2nd Pomeranian Infantry Grenadier Nr. 9 (Colonel Ferentheil von Gruppenberg)
3 battalions
6th Pomeranian Infantry Regiment Nr. 49 (lieutenant-Colonel Laurin)
3 battalions

8th Brigade (Major-General von Kettler)

4th Pomeranian Infantry Regiment Nr. 21 (Lieutenant-Colonel von Lobenthal)
3 battalions
8th Pomeranian Infantry Regiment Nr. 61 (Colonel von Wedell)
3 battalions

Divisional Troops

Pomeranian Dragoon Regiment Nr. 11 (Lieutenant-Colonel von Guretzky-Cornitz)
4 squadrons
2 pioneer Companies, 2nd Pioneer Battalion

Divisional Artillery
2 4 pounder batteries, 2nd Artillery Regiment
2 6 pounder batteries, 2nd Artillery Regiment

Corps Artillery

2 4 pounder batteries, 2nd Artillery Regiment
2 6 pounder batteries, 2nd Artillery Regiment
2 4 pounder horse artillery batteries, 2nd Artillery Regiment

2nd Train Battalion

CORPS Total
25 battalions, 8 squadrons, 3 companies, 14 batteries, train
28,800 men, 84 guns

III CORPS

Commander: Lieutenant-General von Alvensleben II
Chief of Staff: Colonel von Voigts-Rhetz

5th Infantry Division

Commander: Lieutenant-General von Stülpnagel

9th Brigade (Major-General von Döring)

Leib Grenadier Regiment Nr. 8 (Lieutenant-Colonel L'Estocq)
3 battalions
5th Brandenburg Infantry Regiment Nr. 48 (Colonel von Garrelts)
3 battalions

10th Brigade (Major-General von Schwerin)

2nd Brandenburg Grenadier Regiment Nr. 12 (Colonel von Reuter)
3 battalions
6th Brandenburg Infantry Regiment Nr. 52 (Colonel von Wulffen)
3 battalions

Divisional Troops

Brandenburg Jäger Battalion Nr. 3 (Major von Jena)
1 battalion
2nd Brandenburg Dragoon Regiment Nr. 12 (Major Pfieffer von Salomon)
4 squadrons
1 pioneer company, 3rd Pioneer Battalion

Divisional Artillery
2 4 pounder batteries, 3rd Artillery Regiment
2 6 pounder batteries, 3rd Artillery Regiment

6th Infantry Division

Commander: Lieutenant-General von Buddenbrock

11th Infantry Brigade (Major-General von Rothmaler)

3rd Brandenburg Infantry Regiment Nr. 20 (Colonel von Flotow)
3 battalions
Brandenburg Fusilier Regiment Nr. 35 (Colonel von Plessis)
3 battalions

12th Infantry Brigade (Colonel von Bismarck)

4th Brandenburg Infantry Regiment Nr. 24 (Colonel Count Dohna)
3 battalions
8th Brandenburg Infantry Regiment Nr. 64 (Colonel Buttlar-Brandenfels)
3 battalions

Divisional Troops

1st Brandenburg Dragoon Regiment Nr. 2 (Colonel von Drigalski)
4 squadrons
1 pioneer company, 3rd Pioneer Battalion

Divisional Artillery
2 4 pounder batteries, 3rd Artillery Regiment
2 6 pounder batteries, 3rd Artillery Regiment

Corps Artillery

2 4 pounder batteries, 3rd Artillery Regiment
2 6 pounder batteries, 3rd Artillery Regiment
2 4 pounder horse artillery batteries, 3rd Artillery Regiment
1 pioneer company, 3rd Pioneer Battalion

3rd Train Battalion

CORPS Total:
25 battalions, 8 squadrons, 3 companies, 14 batteries, train
28,800 men, 84 guns

IV CORPS

Commander:	General of Infantry von Alvensleben I
Chief of Staff:	Colonel von Thile

7th Infantry Division

Commander: Lieutenant-General von Schwarzhoff

13th Infantry Brigade (Major-General von Borries)

1st Magdeburg Infantry Regiment Nr. 26 (Colonel von Schmeling)
3 battalions
3rd Magdeburg Infantry Regiment Nr. 66 (Lieutenant-Colonel Finck von Finckenstein)
3 battalions

14th Infantry Brigade (Major-General von Zychlinski)

2nd Magdeburg Infantry Regiment Nr. 27 (Colonel Pressentin)
3 battalions
Anhalt Infantry Regiment Nr. 93 (Colonel von Krosigk)
3 battalions

Divisional Troops

Magdeburg Jäger Battalion Nr. 4 (Major von Lettow-Vorbeck)
1 battalion
Westphalian Dragoon Regiment Nr. 7 (Lieutenant-Colonel von Schleinitz)
4 squadrons
2 pioneer companies, 4th Pioneer Battalion

Divisional Artillery
2 4 pounder batteries, 4th Artillery Regiment
2 6 pounder batteries, 4th Artillery Regiment

8th Infantry Division

Commander: Lieutenant-General von Schöller

15th Infantry Brigade (Major-General von Kessler)

1st Thuringian Infantry Regiment Nr. 31 (Colonel von Bonin)
3 battalions
3rd Thuringian Infantry Regiment Nr. 71 (Colonel Klöden)
3 battalions

16th Infantry Brigade (Colonel von Scheffler)

Schleswig-Holstein Fusilier Regiment Nr. 86 (Colonel von Horn)
3 battalions
7th Thuringian Infantry Regiment Nr. 96 (Lieutenant-Colonel von Redern)
3 battalions

Divisional Troops

Thuringian Hussar Regiment Nr. 12 (Lieutenant-Colonel von Suckow)
4 squadrons
1 pioneer company, 4th Pioneer Battalion

Divisional Artillery
2 4 pounder batteries, 4th Artillery Regiment
2 6 pounder batteries, 4th Artillery Regiment

Corps Artillery

2 4 pounder batteries, 4th Artillery Regiment
2 6 pounder batteries, 4th Artillery Regiment
2 4 pounder horse artillery batteries, 4th Artillery Regiment

CORPS Total:
25 battalions, 8 squadrons, 3 companies, 14 batteries, train
28,800 men, 84 guns

IX CORPS

Commander:	General of Infantry von Manstein
Chief of Staff:	Major Bronsart von Schellendorff

18th Infantry Division

Commander:	Lieutenant General Baron von Wrangel

35th Infantry Brigade (Major-General von Blumenthal)

Magdeburg Fusilier Regiment Nr. 36 (Colonel von Brandenstein)
3 battalions
Schleswig Infantry Regiment Nr. 84 (Colonel Winckler)
3 battalions

36th Infantry Brigade (Major-General von Below)

2nd Silesian Grenadier Regiment Nr. 11 (Colonel von Schöning)
3 battalions

Holstein Infantry Regiment Nr. 85 (Colonel von Falkenhausen)
3 battalions

Divisional Troops

Lauenburg Jäger Battalion Nr. 9 (Major von Minckwitz)
1 battalion
Magdeburg Dragoon Regiment Nr. 6 (Colonel von Houwald)
4 squadrons
2 pioneer companies, 9th Pioneer Battalion

Divisional Artillery
2 4 pounder batteries, 9th Artillery Regiment
2 6 pounder batteries, 9th Artillery Regiment

25th (Grand Duchy of Hesse) Infantry Division

Commander: Lieutenant-General Prince Ludwig of Hesse

49th Infantry Brigade (Major-General von Wittich)

1st Hessian Leib-Guard Regiment (Lieutenant-Colonel Coulmann)
2 battalions
2nd Hessian Infantry Regiment (Colonel Krauss)
2 battalions
1st Hessian Guard Jäger Battalion (Major Anschütz)
1 battalion

50th Infantry Brigade (Major-General von Lyncker)

3rd Hessian Infantry Regiment (Lieutenant-Colonel von Stamm)
2 battalions
4th Hessian infantry Regiment (Colonel Zwenger)
2 battalions
2nd Hessian Jäger Batallion (Major Winter)
1 battalion

25th Hessian Cavalry Brigade (Major General von Schlotheim)

1st Hessian Chevauxlegers Regiment (Colonel Riedsel von Eisenach)
4 squadrons
2nd Hessian Chevauxlegers Regiment (Colonel von Bouchenröder)
4 squadrons

Divisional Artillery
5 Hessian 4 pounder batteries
1 Hessian 4 pounder horse artillery battery

Corps Artillery

2 4 pounder batteries, 9th Artillery Regiment
2 6 pounder batteries, 9th Artillery Regiment
1 4 pounder horse artillery battery, 9th Artillery Regiment
1 pioneer company, 9th Pioneer Batallion

1 Hessian pioneer company

9th Train Battalion
Hessian Train Battalion

CORPS Total:
23 battalions, 12 squadrons, 4 companies, 15 batteries, train
27,400 men, 90 guns

X CORPS

Commander: General of Infantry von Voigts-Rhetz
Chief of Staff: Colonel von Caprivi

19th Infantry Division

Commander: Lieutenant-General von Schwartzkoppen

37th Infantry-Brigade (Colonel Lehmann)

Friesian Infantry Regiment Nr. 78 (Colonel von Lyncker)
3 battalions
Oldenburg Infantry Regiment Nr. 91 (Colonel von Kamecke)
3 battalions

38th Infantry Brigade (Major-General von Wedell)

3rd Westphalian Infantry Regiment Nr. 16 (Colonel von Brixen)
3 battalions
8th Westphalian Infantry Regiment Nr. 57 (Colonel von Cranach)
3 battalions

Divisional Troops

Hanoverian Jäger Battalion Nr. 10 (Major Dunin von Przychowski)
1 battalion
1st Hanoverian Dragoon Regiment Nr. 9 (Lieutenant-Colonel von Hardenberg)
4 squadrons
2 pioneer companies, 10th Pioneer Battalion

Divisional Artillery
2 4 pounder batteries, 10th Artillery Regiment
2 6 pounder batteries, 10th Artillery Regiment

20th Infantry Division

Commander: Major-General von Kraatz-Koschlau

39th Infantry Brigade (Major-General von Woyna I)

7th Westphalian Infantry Regiment Nr. 56 (Colonel von Block)
3 battalions
3rd Hanoverian Infantry Regiment Nr. 79 (Colonel von Valentini)
3 battalions

40th Infantry Brigade (Major-General von Diringshofen)

4th Westphalian Infantry Regiment Nr. 17 (Colonel von Ehrenberg)
3 battalions
Brunswick Infantry Regiment Nr. 92 (Colonel von Haberlandt)
3 battalions

Divisional Troops

2nd Hanoverian Dragoon Regiment Nr. 16 (Lieutenant-Colonel von Waldow)
4 squadrons
1 pioneer company, 10th Pioneer Battalion

Divisional Artillery
2 4 pounder batteries, 10th Artillery Regiment
2 6 pounder batteries, 10th Artillery Regiment

Corps Artillery

2 4 pounder batteries, 10th Artillery Regiment
2 6 pounder batteries, 10th Artillery Regiment
2 4 pounder horse artillery batteries, 10th Artillery Regiment

10th Train Battalion

CORPS Total:
25 battalions, 8 squadrons, 3 companies, 14 batteries, train
28,800 men, 84 guns

XII ROYAL SAXON CORPS

Commander:	General of Infantry Crown Prince Albert of Saxony
Chief of Staff:	Lieutenant-Colonel von Zeschwitz

23rd Infantry Division/1st Infantry Division

Commander: Lieutenant-General Prince George of Saxony

45th Infantry Brigade/1st Infantry Brigade (Major-General Craushaar)

1st Leib Infantry Regiment Nr. 100 (Colonel Garten)
3 battalions
2nd Grenadier Regiment, Nr. 101 (Colonel von Seydlitz-Gerstenberg)
3 battalions
Fusilier Regiment Nr. 108 (Colonel Baron von Hausen)
3 battalions

46th Infantry Brigade/2nd Brigade (Colonel von Montbé)

3rd Infantry Regiment Nr. 102 (Colonel Rudorff)
3 battalions
4th Infantry Regiment Nr. 103 (Lieutenant-Colonel Dietrich)
3 battalions

Divisional Troops

1st Horse Regiment (Lieutenant-Colonel von Sahr)
4 squadrons
2 pioneer companies, 12th Pioneer Battalion

Divisional Artillery
2 4 pounder batteries, 12th Artillery Regiment
2 6 pounder batteries, 12th Artillery Regiment

24th Infantry Division/2nd Infantry Division

Commander: Major-General Nehrhoff von Holderberg

47th Infantry Brigade/3rd Brigade (Major-General Tauscher)

5th Infantry Regiment, Nr. 104 (Colonel von Elterlein)
3 battalions
6th Infantry Regiment Nr. 105 (Colonel von Tetau)
3 battalions
1st Saxon Jäger Battalion Nr. 12 (Major von Holtzendorff)
1 battalion

48th Infantry Brigade/4th Infantry Brigade (Colonel von Schulz)

7th Infantry Regiment Nr. 106 (Colonel von Abendroth)
3 battalions
8th Infantry Regiment Nr. 107 (Lieutenant Colonel von Schweinitz)
3 battalions
2nd Saxon Jäger Battalion Nr. 13 (Major von Götz)
1 battalion

Divisional Troops

2nd Horse Regiment (Major Genthe)
4 squadrons

Divisional Artillery
2 4 pounder batteries, 12th Artillery Regiment
2 6 pounder batteries, 12th Artillery Regiment
1 pioneer company, 12th Pioneer Battalion

Cavalry Division

Commander: Major-General Count zu Lippe

23rd Cavalry Brigade/1st Cavalry Brigade (Major-General Krug von Nidda)

Guard Horse regiment (Colonel von Carlowitz)
4 squadrons
1st Saxon Uhlan Regiment Nr. 17 (Colonel von Miltitz)
4 squadrons

24th Cavalry Brigade/2nd Cavalry Brigade (Colonel Senfft von Pilsach)

3rd Horse Regiment (Colonel von Standfest)
4 squadrons
2nd Saxon Uhlan Regiment Nr. 18 (Lieutenant-Colonel Trosky)
4 squadrons

12th Train Battalion

Corps Artillery

2 4 pounder batteries, 12th Artillery Regiment
2 6 pounder batteries, 12th Artillery Regiment
1 4 pounder horse artillery battery, 12th Artillery Regiment

CORPS Total:
29 battalions, 24 squadrons, 3 companies, 14 batteries, train
32,000 men, 84 guns

5th Cavalry Division

Commander: Lieutenant-General Baron von Rheinbaben

11th Cavalry Brigade (Major-General von Barby)

Westphalian Cuirassier Regiment Nr. 4 (Colonel von Arnim)
4 squadrons
1st Hanoverian Uhlan regiment Nr. 13 (Colonel von Schack)
4 squadrons
Oldenburg Dragoon Regiment Nr. 19 (Colonel Colonel von Trotha)
4 squadrons

12th Cavalry Brigade (Major-General von Bredow)

Magdeburg Cuirassier regiment Nr. 7 (Lieutenant-Colonel von Arisch)
4 squadrons
Altmark Uhlan Regiment Nr. 16 (Major von der Dollen)
4 squadrons
Schleswig-Holstein Dragoon Regiment Nr. 13 (Colonel von Brauchitsch)
4 squadrons

13th Cavalry Brigade (Major-General von Redern)

Magdeburg Hussar Regiment Nr. 10 (Colonel von Weise)
4 squadrons
2nd Westphalian Hussar Regiment Nr. 11 (Colonel Baron von Eller-Eberstein)
4 squadrons
Brunswick Hussar Regiment Nr. 17 (Lieutenant-Colonel von Rauch)
4 squadrons

Divisional Artillery
2 horse artillery batteries

Division Total:
36 squadrons, 2 batteries
5,400 men, 12 guns

6th Cavalry Division

Commander: Lieutenant-General Duke Wilhelm of Mecklenburg-Schwerin

14th Cavalry Brigade (Colonel Baron von Diepenbroick-Grüter)

Brandenburg Cuirassier Regiment Nr. 6 (Colonel Count Lynar)
4 squadrons
1st Brandenburg Uhlan Regiment Nr. 3 (Colonel von der Gröben)
4 squadrons
Schleswig-Holstein Uhlan Regiment Nr. 15 (Colonel von Alvensleben)
4 squadrons

15th Cavalry Brigade (Major-General von Rauch)

Brandenburg Hussar Regiment Nr. 3 (Colonel von Zieten)
4 squadrons
Schleswig-Holstein Hussar Regiment Nr. 16 (Colonel von Schmidt)
4 squadrons

Divisional Artillery
1 4 pounder horse artillery battery

Division Total:
20, squadrons, 1 battery
3,000 men, 6 guns

THIRD ARMY

Commander: General of Infantry Crown Prince Friedrich Wilhelm of Prussia
Chief of Staff: Lieutenant-General von Blumenthal

V CORPS

Commander: Lieutenant-General von Kirchbach
Chief of Staff: Colonel von der Esch

9th Infantry Division

Commander: Major-General von Sandrart

17th Infantry Brigade (Colonel von Bothmer)

3rd Posen Infantry regiment Nr. 58 (Colonel von Rex)
3 battalions
4th Posen Infantry Regiment Nr. 59 (Colonel von Eyl)
3 battalions

18th Infantry Brigade (Major-General Voigts-Rhetz)

3rd West Prussian Grenadier Regiment Nr. 7 (Colonel von Köthen)
3 battalions
2nd Lower Silesian Infantry Regiment Nr. 47 (Colonel von Burghoff)
3 battalions

Divisional Troops

1st Silesian Jäger Battalion Nr. 5 (Major von Boedicher)
1 battalion
1st Silesian Dragoon Regiment Nr. 4 (Lieutenant-Colonel von Schenck)
4 squadrons
1 pioneer company, 5th Pioneer Battalion

Divisional Artillery
2 4 pounder batteries, 5th Artillery Regiment
2 6 pounder batteries, 5th Artillery Regiment

10th Infantry Division

Commander: Major-General von Schmidt

19th Infantry Brigade (Colonel Henning u. Schönhoff)

1st West Prussian Grenadier Regiment Nr. 6 (Colonel Flöckher)
3 battalions
1st Lower Silesian Infantry Regiment Nr. 46 (Colonel von Stosch)
3 battalions

20th Infantry Brigade (Colonel Walther von Montbary)

Westphalian Fusilier Regiment Nr. 37 (Colonel von Heinemann)
3 battalions
3rd Lower Silesian Infantry Regiment Nr. 50 (Colonel Michelmann)
3 battalions

Divisional Troops

Kurmark Dragoon Regiment Nr. 14 (Colonel von Schon)
4 squadrons
2 pioneer companies, 5th Pioneer Battalion

Divisional Artillery
2 4 pounder batteries, 5th Artillery Regiment
2 6 pounder batteries, 5th Artillery Regiment

Corps Artillery

2 4 pounder batteries, 5th Artillery Regiment
2 6 pounder batteries, 5th Artillery Regiment
2 4 pounder horse artillery batteries, 5th Artillery Regiment

5th Train Battalion

CORPS Total:
25 battalions, 8 squadrons, 3 companies, 14 batteries, train
28,800 men, 84 guns

VI CORPS

Commander:	General of Cavalry von Tümpling
Chief of Staff:	Colonel von Salviati

11th Infantry Division

Commander:	Lieutenant General von Gordon

21st Infantry Brigade (Major-General von Malachowski)

1st Silesian Grenadier Regiment Nr. 10 (Colonel von Weller)
3 battalions
1st Posen Infantry Regiment Nr. 18 (Colonel von Bock)
3 battalions

22nd Infantry Brigade (Major-General von Eckartsberg)

Silesian Fusilier Regiment Nr. 38 (Colonel von Schmeling)
3 battalions
4th Lower Silesian Infantry Regiment Nr. 51 (Colonel Knipping)
3 battalions

Divisional Troops

2nd Silesian Jäger Battalion Nr. 6 (Major von Walther)
1 battalion
2nd Silesian Dragoon Regiment Nr. 8 (Lieutenant-Colonel von Winterfeld)
4 squadrons
1 pioneer company, 6th Pioneer Battalion

Divisional Artillery
2 4 pounder batteries, 6th Artillery Regiment
2 6 pounder batteries, 6th Artillery Regiment

12th Infantry Division

Commander:	Major-General von Hoffmann

23rd Infantry-Brigade (Major-General Gündell)

1st Upper Silesian Infantry Regiment Nr. 22 (Colonel von Quistorp)
3 battalions
3rd Upper Silesian Infantry Regiment Nr. 62 (Colonel von Bessell)
3 battalions

24th Infantry Brigade (Major-General von Fabeck)

2nd Upper Silesian Infantry Regiment Nr. 23 (Colonel von Briesen)
3 battalions
4th Upper Silesian Infantry Regiment Nr. 63 (Colonel von Thielau)
3 battalions

Divisional Troops

3rd Silesian Dragoon Regiment Nr. 15 (Colonel von Busse)
4 squadrons
2 pioneer companies, 6th Pioneer Battalion

Divisional Artillery
2 4 pounder batteries, 6th Artillery Regiment
2 6 pounder batteries, 6th Artillery Regiment

6th Train Battalion

Corps Artillery

2 4 pounder batteries, 6th Artillery Regiment
2 6 pounder batteries, 6th Artillery Regiment
2 4 pounder horse artillery batteries, 6th Artillery Regiment

CORPS Total:
25 battalions, 8 squadrons, 3 companies, 14 batteries, train
28,800 men, 84 guns

XI CORPS

Commander:	Lieutenant-General von Bose
Chief of Staff:	Major-General von Kaminski

21st Infantry Division

Commander:	Lieutenant-General von Schachtmeyer

41st Infantry Brigade (Colonel von Koblinski)

Hessian Fusilier Regiment Nr. 80 (Colonel von Colomb)
3 battalions
1st Nassau Infantry Regiment Nr. 87 (Colonel von Grolman)
3 battalions

42nd Infantry Brigade (Major-General von Thiele)

2nd Hessian Infantry Regiment Nr. 82 (Colonel von Grawert)
3 battalions
2nd Nassau Infantry Regiment Nr. 88 (Colonel Köhn von Jaski)
3 battalions

Divisional Troops

Hessian Jäger Battalion Nr. 11 (Major von Johnston)
1 battalion
2nd Hessian Hussar Regiment Nr. 14
4 squadrons
1 pioneer company, 11th Pioneer Battalion

Divisional Artillery
2 4 pounder batteries, 11th Artillery Regiment

2 6 pounder batteries, 11th Artillery Regiment

22nd Infantry Division

Commander: Lieutenant-General von Gersdorff

43rd Infantry Brigade (Colonel von Kontzki)

2nd Thuringian Infantry Regiment Nr. 32 (Colonel Förster)
3 battalions
6th Thuringian Infantry Regiment Nr. 95 (Colonel Beckedorff)
3 battalions

44th Infantry Brigade (Major-General von Schkopp)

3rd Hessian Infantry Regiment Nr. 83 (Colonel Marschall von Bieberstein)
3 battalions
5th Thuringian Infantry-Regiment Nr. 94 (Colonel Bessel)
3 battalions

Divisional Troops

1st Hessian Hussar Regiment Nr. 13 (Lieutenant-Colonel von Heuduck)
4 squadrons
2 pioneer companies, 11th Pioneer Battalion

Divisional Artillery
2 4 pounder batteries, 11th Artillery Regiment
2 6 pounder batteries, 11th Artillery Regiment

11th Train Battalion

Corps Artillery

2 4 pounder batteries, 11th Artillery Regiment
2 6 pounder batteries, 11th Artillery Regiment
2 4 pounder horse artillery batteries, 11th Artillery Regiment

CORPS Total:
25 battalions, 8 squadrons, 3 companies, 14 batteries, train
28,800 men, 84 guns

I BAVARIAN CORPS

Commander: General of Infantry Baron von der Tann-Rathsamhausen
Chief of Staff: Lieutenant-Colonel Heinleth

1st Infantry Division

Commander: Lieutenant-General von Stephan

1st Brigade (Major-General Dietl)

Leib Regiment (Colonel von Täuffenbach)

3 battalions
1st Infantry Regiment (Colonel Heckel)
2 battalions
2nd Jäger Battalion (Major Vallade)
1 battalion

2nd Brigade (Major-General von Orff)

2nd Infantry Regiment (Colonel von der Tann)
3 battalions
11th Infantry Regiment (Colonel von Schmidt)
2 battalions
4th Jäger Battalion (Major Reschreiter)
1 battalion

Divisional Troops

9th Jäger Battalion (Lieutenant-Colonel von Massenbach)
1 battalion
3rd Chevauxleger Regiment (Colonel A. von Leonrod)
4 squadrons

Divisional Artillery
2 4 pounder batteries, 1st Artillery Regiment
2 6 pounder batteries, 1st Artillery Regiment

2nd Infantry Division

Commander: Lieutenant-General Count zu Pappenheim

3rd Brigade (Major-General Schumacher)

3rd Infantry Regiment (Colonel Schuch)
3 battalions
12th Infantry Regiment (Colonel Narciss)
2 battalions
1st Jäger Battalion (Lieutenant-Colonel von Schmidt)
1 battalion

4th Brigade (Major-General Baron von der Tann)

10th Infantry Regiment (Colonel Baron von Guttenberg)
3 battalions
13th Infantry Regiment (Colonel von Ysenburg)
2 battalions
7th Jäger Battalion (Lieutenant-Colonel Schultheiss)
1 battalion

Divisional Troops

4th Chevauxleger Regiment (Colonel K. von Leonrod)
4 squadrons

Divisional Artillery

2 4 pounder batteries, 1st Artillery Regiment
2 6 pounder batteries, 1st Artillery Regiment

Cuirassier Brigade (Major-General von Tauch)

1st Cuirassier Regiment (Colonel Feichtmayr)
4 squadrons
2nd Cuirassier Regiment (Colonel Baumüller)
4 squadrons
6th Chevauxleger Regiment (Colonel Baron Krauss)
4 squadrons
(Attached) 1 horse artillery battery, 3rd Artillery Regiment
2 companies, engineers

Corps Artillery

6 6 pounder batteries, 3rd Artillery Regiment
1 4 pounder horse artillery battery, 3rd Artillery Regiment

Train battalion

Corps Total:
25 battalions, 20 squadrons, 3 companies, 16 batteries, train
33,750 men, 96 guns

II BAVARIAN CORPS

Commander:	General of Infantry von Hartmann
Chief of Staff:	Colonel Baron von Horn

3rd Infantry Division

Commander:	Lieutenant-General von Walther

5th Infantry Brigade (Major-General von Schleich)

6th Infantry Regiment (Colonel Bosmüller)
3 battalions
7th Infantry Regiment (Colonel Höfler)
2 battalions
8th Jäger Battalion (Lieutenant-Colonel Kohlermann)
1 battalion

6th Infantry Brigade (Colonel von Wissell)

14th Infantry Regiment (Colonel Diehl)
2 battalions
15th Infantry Regiment (Colonel Count Treuberg)
3 battalions
3rd Jäger Battalion (Lieutenant-Colonel von Horn)
1 battalion

Divisional Troops

1st Chevauxleger Regiment (Colonel von Grundherr)
4 squadrons

Divisional Artillery
2 4 pounder batteries, 2nd Artillery Regiment
2 6 pounder batteries, 2nd Artillery Regiment

4th Infantry Division

Commander: Lieutenant-General von Bothmer

7th Infantry Brigade (Major-General Thiereck)

5th Infantry Regiment (Colonel Mühlbauer)
2 battalions
9th Infantry Regiment (Colonel Heeg)
3 battalions
6th Jäger Battalion (Major Caries)
1 battalion

8th Infantry Brigade (Major-General Maillinger)

5 battalions (1 each from 1st, 5th, 7th, 11th, 14th Infantry Regiments)
5th Jäger Battalion (Lieutenant-Colonel v. Gumppenberg)
1 battalion

Divisional Troops

10th Jäger Battalion (Lieutenant-Colonel von Heckel)
1 battalion
2nd Chevauxleger Regiment (Colonel Horadam)
4 squadrons

Divisional Artillery
2 4 pounder batteries, 2nd Artillery Regiment
2 6 pounder batteries, 2nd Artillery Regiment

Uhlan Brigade (Major-General Baron von Mulzer)

1st Uhlan Regiment (Colonel Count M. Ysenburg)
4 squadrons
2nd Uhlan Regiment (Colonel Count Pflummers)
4 squadrons
5th Chevauxleger Regiment (Colonel Weinrich)
4 squadrons
(Attached) 1 4 pounder horse artillery battery, 2nd Artillery Regiment
2 companies, engineers

Corps Artillery

6 6 pounder batteries, 4th Artillery Regiment
1 4 pounder horse artillery battery, 4th Artillery Regiment

Train Battalion

CORPS Total:
25 battalions, 20 squadrons, 3 companies, 16 batteries, train
33,750 men, 96 guns

APPENDIX II

Imperial French Army (August 1st 1870)

Army of the Rhine

Commander in Chief:	Emperor Napoleon III
Major-General:	Marshal Edmond Le Boeuf
Aides to the Major-General:	General of Division Lebrun
	General of Division Jarras
Artillery Commander:	General of Division Soleille
Engineer Commander:	General of Division Coffinières de Nordeck
Intendant General:	Intendant General Wolff
Chief of Medical Services:	Baron Larrey

IMPERIAL GUARD

Commander:	General of Division Bourbaki
Chief of Staff:	General of Brigade d'Auvergne
Artillery Commander:	General of Brigade Pé de Arros

1st Guard Division

Commander:	General of Division Deligny

1st Brigade (General of Brigade Brincourt)

Guard Chasseur Battalion (Commandant Dufaure du Bessol)
1 battalion
1st Guard Voltigeur Regiment (Colonel Dumont)
3 battalions
2nd Guard Voltigeur Regiment (Colonel Peychaud)
3 battalions

2nd Brigade (General of Brigade Garnier)

3rd Guard Voltigeur Regiment (Colonel Lian)
3 battalions
4th Guard Voltigeur Regiment (Colonel Ponsard)
3 battalions

Divisional Artillery
2 4 pounder batteries
1 mitrailleuse battery
1 engineer company

2nd Guard Division

Commander: General of Division Picard

1st Brigade (General of Brigade Jeanningros)

Guard Zouave Regiment (Colonel Giraud)
2 battalions
1st Grenadier Regiment (Colonel Théologue)
3 battalions

2nd Brigade (General of Brigade le Poitevin de la Croix Vaubois)

3rd Grenadier Regiment (Colonel Lecointe)
3 battalions
4th Grenadier Regiment (Colonel Cousin)
3 battalions

Divisional Artillery
2 4 pounder batteries
1 mitrailleuse battery
1 engineer company

Guard Cavalry Division

Commander: General of Division Desvaux

1st Brigade (General of Brigade Halna du Fretay)

Guard Chasseur Regiment (Colonel de Montarby)
5 squadrons
Guides Regiment (Colonel de Percin-Northumberland)
5 squadrons

2nd Brigade (General of Brigade de France)

Guard Lancer Regiment (Colonel Latheulade)
5 squadrons
Guard Dragoon Regiment (Colonel Sautereau Dupart)
5 squadrons

3rd Brigade (General of Brigade du Preuil)

Guard Cuirassier Regiment (Colonel Dupressoir)
5 squadrons
Guard Carabinier Regiment (Colonel Petit)
5 squadrons

Divisional Artillery
2 4 pounder horse artillery batteries

Guard Reserve Artillery
4 4 pounder horse artillery batteries

1 engineer company

Guard Total:
24 battalions, 30 squadrons, 3 companies, 1 train squadron, 10 artillery batteries, 2 mitrailleuse batteries
1,047 officers, 21,028 men, 60 guns, 12 mitrailleuse

2nd CORPS

Commander: General of Division Frossard
Chief of Staff: General of Brigade Saget
Artillery Commander: General of Brigade Gagneur

1st Division

Commander: General of Division Vergé

1st Brigade (General of Brigade Letellier-Valazé)

3rd Chasseur Battalion (Commandant Thoina)
1 battalion
32nd Line Infantry Regiment (Colonel Merle)
3 battalions
55th Line Infantry Regiment (Colonel de Waldner de Freudenstein)
3 battalions

2nd Brigade (General of Brigade Jolivet)

76th Line Infantry Regiment (Colonel Brice)
3 battalions
77th Line Infantry Regiment (Colonel Fèvrier)
3 battalions

Divisional Artillery
2 4 pounder batteries
1 mitrailleuse battery

1 engineer company

2nd Division

Commander: General of Division Bataille

1st Brigade (General of Brigade Pouget)

12th Chasseur Battalion (Commandant Jeanne-Beaulieu)
1 battalion
8th Line Infantry Regiment (Colonel Haca)
3 battalions
23rd Line Infantry Regiment (Colonel Roland)
3 battalions

2nd Brigade (General of Division Fauvart-Bastoul)

66th Line Infantry Regiment (Colonel Ameller)
3 battalions
67th Line Infantry Regiment (Colonel Mangin)

3 battalions

Divisional Artillery
2 4 pounder batteries
1 mitrailleuse battery

1 engineer company

3rd Division

Commander: General of Division Merle de Labrugière de Laveaucoupet

1st Brigade (General of Brigade Doens)

10th Chasseur Battalion (Commandant Schenk)
1 battalion
2nd Line Infantry Regiment (Colonel de Saint-Hillier)
3 battalions
63rd Line Infantry Regiment (Colonel Zentz)
3 battalions

2nd Brigade (General of Brigade Micheler)

24th Line Infantry Regiment (Colonel d'Arguesse)
3 battalions
40th Line Infantry Regiment (Colonel Vittot)
3 battalions

Divisional Artillery
2 4 pounder batteries
1 mitrailleuse battery

1 engineer company

Cavalry Division

Commander: General of Division Marmier

1st Brigade (General of Brigade de Valabrègue

4th Chasseur Regiment (Colonel du Ferron)
5 squadrons
5th Chasseur Regiment (Colonel de Séréville)
5 squadrons

2nd Brigade (General of Brigade Bachelier)

7th Dragoon Regiment (Colonel de Gressot)
4 squadrons
12th Dragoon Regiment (Colonel D'Avocourt)
4 squadrons

Corps Reserve Artillery

2 12 pounder batteries

2 4 pounder batteries
2 4 pounder horse artillery batteries

1 engineer company
1 bridging train

2nd CORPS Total:
39 battalions, 18 squadrons, 4 companies, 12 batteries, 3 mitrailleuse batteries
1,172 officers, 27,956 men, 72 guns, 18 mitrailleuse

3rd CORPS

Commander:	Marshal Bazaine
Chief of Staff:	General of Brigade Manèque
Artillery Commander:	General of Division Grimaudet de Rochebouet

1st Division

Commander:	General of Division Montaudon

1st Brigade (General of Brigade Aymard)

18th Chasseur Battalion (Commandant Rigault)
1 battalion
51st Line Infantry Regiment (Colonel Delebecque)
3 battalions
62nd Line Infantry Regiment (Colonel Dauphin)
3 battalions

2nd Brigade (General of Brigade Clinchant)

81st Line Infantry Regiment (Colonel d'Albici)
3 battalions
95th Line infantry Regiment (Colonel Davout d'Auerstædt)
3 battalions

Divisional Artillery
2 4 pounder batteries
1 mitrailleuse battery

1 engineer company

2nd Division

Commander:	General of Division de Castagny

1st Brigade (General of Brigade Nayral)

15th Chasseur Battalion (Commandant Lafouge)
1 battalion
19th Line infantry Regiment (Colonel de Launay)
3 battalions
41st Line Infantry Regiment (Colonel Saussier)
3 battalions

2nd Brigade (General of Brigade Duplessis)

69th Line Infantry Regiment (Colonel le Tourneur)
3 battalions
90th Line Infantry Regiment (Colonel de Courcy)
3 battalions

Divisional Artillery
2 4 pounder batteries
1 mitrailleuse battery

1 engineer company

3rd Division

Commander: General of Division Metman

1st Brigade (General of Brigade de Potier)

7th Chasseur Battalion (Commandant Rigaud)
1 battalion
7th Line Infantry Regiment (Colonel Cotteret)
3 battalions
29th Line Infantry Regiment (Colonel Lalanne)
3 battalions

2nd Brigade (General of Brigade Arnaudeau)

59th Line Infantry Regiment (Colonel Duez)
3 battalions
71st Line Infantry Regiment (Colonel de Ferussac)
3 battalions

Divisional Artillery
2 4 pounder batteries
1 mitrailleuse battery

1 engineer company

4th Division

Commander: General of Division Decaen

1st Brigade (General of Brigade de Brauer)

11th Chasseur Battalion (Commandant de Paillot)
1 battalion
44th Line Infantry Regiment (Colonel Fournier)
3 battalions
60th Line Infantry Regiment (Colonel Boissie)
3 battalions

2nd Brigade (General of Brigade Sanglé-Ferrière)

80th Line Infantry Regiment (Colonel Janin)

3 battalions
85th Line Infantry Regiment (Colonel Planchut)
3 battalions

Divisional Artillery
2 4 pounder batteries
1 mitrailleuse battery

1 engineer company

Cavalry Division

Commander: General of Division Clérembault

1st Brigade (General of Brigade Bruchard)

2nd Chasseur Regiment (Colonel Pelletier)
5 squadrons
3rd Chasseur Regiment (Colonel Sanson de Sansal)
5 squadrons
10th Chasseur Regiment (Colonel Nérin)
5 squadrons

2nd Brigade (General de Brigade Gayrault de Maubranches)

2nd Dragoon Regiment (Colonel du Paty de Clam)
4 squadrons
4th Dragoon Regiment (Colonel Cornat)
4 squadrons

3rd Brigade (General of Brigade Bégougne de Juiniac)

5th Dragoon Regiment (Colonel Lachène)
4 squadrons
8th Dragoon Regiment (Colonel Boyer de Fonscolombe)
4 squadrons

Corps Reserve Artillery

2 12 pounder batteries
2 4 pounder batteries
4 4 pounder horse artillery batteries

½ engineer company
1 pontonnier company

3rd CORPS Total
52 battalions, 31 squadrons, 5½ companies, 16 batteries, 4 mitrailleuse batteries
1,704 officers, 41,574 men, 96 guns, 24 mitrailleuse

4th CORPS

Commander: General of Division Ladmirault
Chief of Staff: General of Brigade Osmont
Artillery Commander: General of Brigade Lafaille

1st Division

Commander: General of Division Courtot de Cissey

1st Brigade (General of Brigade Brayer)

20th Chasseur Battalion (Commandant de Labarrière)
1 battalion
1st Line Infantry Regiment (Colonel Frémont)
3 battalions
6th Line infantry Regiment (Colonel Labarthe)
3 battalions

2nd Brigade (General of Brigade de Goldberg)

57th Line Infantry Regiment (Colonel Giraud)
3 battalions
73rd Line Infantry Regiment (Colonel Supervielle)
3 battalions

Divisional Artillery
2 4 pounder batteries
1 mitrailleuse battery

1 engineer company

2nd Division

Commander: General of Division Rose

1st Brigade (General of Brigade Véron-Bellecourt)

5th Chasseur Battalion (Commandant Carré)
1 battalion
13th Line Infantry Regiment (Colonel Lion)
3 battalions
43rd Line Infantry Regiment (Colonel de Viville)
3 battalions

2nd Brigade (General of Brigade Pradier)

64th Line Infantry Regiment (Colonel Léger)
3 battalions
98th Line Infantry Regiment (Colonel Lechesne)
3 battalions

Divisional Artillery
2 4 pounder batteries
1 mitrailleuse battery

1 engineer company

3rd Division

Commander: General of Division Latrille, Count de Lorencez

1st Brigade (General of Brigade Pajol)

2nd Chasseur Battalion (Commandant le Tanneur)
1 battalion
15th Line Infantry Regiment (Colonel Fraboulet de Kerléadec)
3 battalions
33rd Line infantry Regiment (Colonel Bounetou)
3 battalions

2nd Brigade (General of Brigade Berger)

54th Line Infantry Regiment (Colonel Caillot)
3 Battalions
65th Line Infantry Regiment (Colonel Sée)
3 battalions

Divisional Artillery
2 4 pounder batteries
1 mitrailleuse battery

1 engineer company

Cavalry Division

Commander: General of Division Legrand

1st Brigade (General of Brigade Montaigu)

2nd Hussar Regiment (Colonel Carrelet)
5 squadrons
7th Hussar Regiment (Colonel Chaussée)
5 squadrons

2nd Brigade (General of Brigade Baron Gondrecourt)

3rd Dragoon Regiment (Colonel Bilhau)
4 squadrons
11th Dragoon Regiment (Colonel Huyn de Vernéville)
4 squadrons

Corps Reserve Artillery

2 12 pounder batteries
2 4 pounder batteries
2 4 pounder horse artillery batteries

1 engineer company
1 bridging train

4th CORPS Total:
39 battalions, 18 squadrons, 4 companies, 12 batteries, 3 mitrailleuse batteries
1,208 officers, 27,702 men, 72 guns, 18 mitrailleuse

6th CORPS

Commander: Marshal Canrobert
Chief of staff: General of Brigade Henry
Artillery Commander: General of Brigade Bertrand

1st Division

Commander: General of Division Tixier

1st Brigade (General of Brigade Péchot)

9th Chasseur Battalion (Commandant Mathelin)
1 battalion
4th Line Infantry Regiment (Colonel Vincendon)
3 battalions
10th Line Infantry Regiment (Colonel Ardant du Picq)
3 battalions

2nd Brigade (General of Brigade Leroy de Dais)

12th Line Infantry Regiment (Colonel Lebrun)
3 battalions
100th Line infantry Regiment (Colonel Grémion)
3 battalions

Divisional Artillery
2 4 pounder batteries
1 mitrailleuse battery

1 engineer company

2nd Division

Commander: General of division Bisson

1st Brigade (General of Brigade Noel)

9th Line Infantry Regiment (Colonel Roux)
3 battalions
14th Line Infantry Regiment (Colonel Louvent)
3 battalions

2nd Brigade (General of Brigade Maurice)

20th Line Infantry Regiment (de la Guigneraye)
3 battalions
31st Line Infantry Regiment (Colonel Sautereau)
3 battalions

Divisional Artillery
2 4 pounder batteries
1 mitrailleuse battery

1 engineer company

3rd Division

Commander: General of Division Lafont de Villiers

1st Brigade (General of Brigade Becquet de Sonnay)

75th Line infantry Regiment (Colonel Amadieu)
3 battalions
91st Line infantry Regiment (Colonel Daguerre)
3 battalions

2nd Brigade (General of Brigade Colin)

93rd Line infantry Regiment (Colonel Guazin)
3 battalions
94th Line infantry Regiment (Colonel de Geslin)
3 battalions

Divisional Artillery
3 4 pounder batteries

1 engineer company

4th Division

Commander: General of Division Levassor-Sorval

1st Brigade (General of Brigade de Marguenat)

25th Line Infantry Regiment (Colonel Gibon)
3 battalions
26th Line Infantry Regiment (Colonel Hanrion)
3 battalions

2nd Brigade (General of Brigade Count De Chanaleilles)

28th Line infantry regiment (Colonel Lamothe)
3 battalions
70th Line Infantry Regiment (Colonel Bertier)
3 battalions

Divisional Artillery
3 4 pounder batteries

1 engineer company

Cavalry Division

Commander: General of Division de Salignac Fénelon

1st Brigade (General of Brigade Tilliard)

6th Hussar Regiment (Colonel de Bauffremont)
5 squadrons
1st Chasseur Regiment (Colonel Bonvoust)
5 squadrons

2nd Brigade (General of Brigade Savaresse)

1st Lancer Regiment (Colonel Oudinot de Reggio)
5 squadrons
7th Lancer Regiment (Colonel Périer)
5 squadrons

3rd Brigade (General of Brigade Yvelin de Béville)

5th Cuirassier Regiment (Colonel Dubessey de Contensen)
4 squadrons
6th Cuirassier Regiment (Colonel Martin)
4 squadrons

Corps Reserve Artillery

2 12 pounder batteries
2 4 pounder batteries
2 4 pounder horse artillery batteries

6th CORPS Total (as intended)
52 battalions, 28 squadrons, 4 companies, 16 batteries, 2 mitrailleuse batteries
1,043 officers, 23,142 men, 96 guns, 12 mitrailleuse

CAVALRY RESERVE

1st Cavalry Division (as intended)

Commander: General of Division du Barail

1st Brigade (General of Brigade Margueritte)

1st Regiment, Chasseurs d'Afrique (Colonel Cliquot)
5 squadrons
3rd Regiment, Chasseurs d'Afrique (Colonel de Gallifet)
5 squadrons

2nd Brigade (General of Brigade de Lajaille)

2nd Regiment, Chasseurs d'Afrique (Colonel de la Martinière)
5 squadrons
4th Regiment, Chasseurs d'Afrique (Colonel de Quèlen)
5 squadrons

Divisional Artillery
2 4 pounder horse artillery batteries

3rd Cavalry Division

Commander: General of Division de Forton

1st Brigade (General of brigade Prince Murat)

1st Dragoon Regiment (Colonel de Forceville)
4 squadrons
9th Dragoon Regiment (Colonel Reboul)

4 squadrons

2nd Brigade (General of Brigade de Gramont, Duke of Esparre)

7th Cuirassier Regiment (Colonel Nitot)
4 squadrons
10th Cuirassier Regiment (Colonel Yuncker)
4 squadrons

Divisional Artillery
2 4 pounder horse artillery batteries

RESERVE CAVALRY Total:
52 squadrons, 6 batteries
464 officers, 6369 men, 36 guns

RESERVE ARTILLERY

Commander: General of Division Canu

1st division (Colonel Salvador)

8 12 pounder batteries

2nd division (Colonel Toussaint)

8 4 pounder horse artillery batteries

RESERVE ARTILLERY Total
16 batteries
96 guns

Army of Alsace

Commander: Marshal MacMahon, Duke of Magenta

1st CORPS

Commander: Marshal MacMahon
Chief of Staff: General of Brigade Colson
Artillery Commander: General of Division Forgeot

1st Division

Commander: General of Division Ducrot

1st Brigade (General of Brigade Morèno)

13th Chasseur Battalion (Commandant de Bonneville)
1 battalion
18th Line Infantry Regiment (Colonel Bréger)
3 battalions
96th Line Infantry Regiment (Colonel de Franchessin
3 battalions

2nd Brigade (General of Brigade Postis de Houlbec)

45th Line Infantry Regiment (Colonel Bertrand)
3 battalions
1st Zouave Regiment (Colonel Carteret-Trecourt)
3 battalions

Divisional Artillery
2 4 pounder batteries
1 mitrailleuse battery

1 engineer company

2nd Division

Commander: General of Division Abel Douay

1st Brigade (General of Brigade Pelletier de Montmarie)

16th Chasseur Battalion (Commandant d'Hugues)
1 battalion
50th Line Infantry Regiment (Colonel Ardouin)
3 battalions
74th Line Infantry Regiment (Colonel Theuvez)
3 battalions

2nd Brigade (General of Brigade Pellé)

78th Line Infantry Regiment (Colonel Carrey de Bellemare)
3 battalions
1st Algerian Tirailleur Regiment (Colonel de Morandy)
3 battalions

Divisional Artillery
2 4 pounder batteries
1 mitrailleuse battery

1 engineer company

3rd Division

Commander: General of Division Raoult

1st Brigade (General of Brigade L'Herillier)

8th Chasseur Battalion (Commandant Poyet)
1 battalion
36th Line Infantry Regiment (Colonel Krien)
3 battalions
2nd Zouave Regiment (Colonel Détrie)
3 battalions

2nd Brigade (General of Brigade Lefebvre)

48th Line Infantry regiment (Colonel Rogier)

3 battalions
2nd Algerian Tirailleur Regiment (Colonel Suzzoni)
3 battalions

Divisional Artillery
2 4 pounder batteries
1 mitrailleuse battery

1 engineer company

4th Division

Commander: General of Division Lartigue

1st Brigade (Colonel Fraboulet de Kerléadec)

1st Chasseur Battalion (Commandant Bureau)
1 battalion
56th Line Infantry Regiment (Colonel Ména)
3 battalions
3rd Zouave Regiment (Colonel Bocher)
3 battalions

2nd Brigade (General of Brigade Lacretelle)

87th Line Infantry Regiment (Colonel Blot)
3 battalions
3rd Algerian Tirailleur Regiment (Colonel Gandil)
3 battalions

Divisional Artillery
2 4 pounder batteries
1 mitrailleuse battery

1 engineer company

Cavalry Division

Commander: General of Division Duhesme

1st Brigade (General of Brigade Septeuil)

3rd Hussar Regiment (Colonel D'Espeuilles)
4 squadrons
11th Chasseur Regiment (Colonel Dastugue)
4 squadrons

2nd Brigade (General of Division Nansouty)

2nd Lancer Regiment (Colonel Poissonniers)
4 squadrons
6th Lancer Regiment (Colonel Tripart)
4 squadrons

3rd Brigade (General of Brigade Michel)

8th Cuirassier Regiment (Colonel) Guiot de la Rochère
4 squadrons
9th Cuirassier Regiment (Colonel Waternau)
4 squadrons

Corps Reserve Artillery

2 12 pounder batteries
2 4 pounder batteries
4 4 pounder horse artillery batteries

½ engineer company
1 train squadron

1st CORPS Total:
52 battalions, 26 squadrons, 4½ companies, 1 train squadron, 16 batteries, 4 mitrailleuse batteries
1,651 officers, 40,165 men, 96 guns, 24 mitrailleuse

5th CORPS

Commander:	General of Division de Failly
Chief of Staff:	General of Brigade Besson
Artillery Commander:	General of brigade Liedot

1st Division

Commander:	General of Division Goze

1st Brigade (General of Brigade Grenier)

4th Chasseur Battalion (Commandant Foncegrives)
1 battalion
11th Line Infantry Regiment (Colonel de Behagle)
3 battalions
46th Line Infantry Regiment (Colonel Pichon)
3 battalions

2nd Brigade (General of Brigade Baron Nicolas-Nicolas)

61st Line Infantry Regiment (Colonel du Moulin)
3 battalions
86th Line Infantry Regiment (Colonel Berthe)
3 battalions

Divisional Artillery
2 4 pounder batteries
1 mitrailleuse battery

1 engineer company

2nd Division

Commander: General of Division de L'Abadie D'Aydren

1st Brigade (General of Brigade Lapasset)

14th Chasseur Battalion (Commandant Planck)
1 battalion
84th Line Infantry Regiment (Colonel Benoit)
3 battalions
97th Line Infantry Regiment (Colonel Copmartin)
3 battalions

2nd Brigade (General of Brigade de Maussion)

49th Line Infantry Regiment (Colonel Kampf)
3 battalions
88th Line Infantry Regiment (Colonel Courty)
3 battalions

Divisional Artillery
2 4 pounder batteries
1 mitrailleuse battery

1 engineer company

3rd Division

Commander: General of Division Guyot de Lespart

1st Brigade (General of Brigade Abbatucci)

19th Chasseur Battalion (Commandant de Marqué)
17th Line Infantry Regiment (Colonel Weissemburger)
3 battalions
27th Line Infantry Regiment (Colonel de Barolet)
3 battalions

2nd Brigade (General of Brigade de Fontagnes de Couzan)

30th Line Infantry Regiment (Colonel Wirbel)
3 battalions
68th Line Infantry Regiment (Colonel Paturel)
3 battalions

Divisional Artillery
2 4 pounder batteries
1 mitrailleuse battery

1 engineer company

Cavalry Division

Commander: General of Division Brahaut

1st Brigade (General of Brigade Tilliard)

5th Hussar Regiment (Colonel Flogny)
5 squadrons
2nd Chasseur Regiment (Colonel de Tucé)
5 squadrons

2nd Brigade (General of Brigade de la Mortière)

3rd Lancer regiment (Colonel Thorel)
4 squadrons
5th Lancer Regiment (Colonel de Boerio)
4 squadrons

Corps Reserve Artillery

2 12 pounder batteries
2 4 pounder batteries
4 4 pounder horse artillery batteries

5th CORPS Total:
39 battalions, 18 squadrons, 4 companies, 12 batteries, 3 mitrailleuse batteries
1,174 officers, 20,243 men, 72 guns, 18 mitrailleuse

7th CORPS

Commander:	General of Division Félix Douay
Chief of Staff:	General of Brigade Renson
Artillery Commander:	General of Brigade Liegard

1st Division

Commander:	General of Division Conseil-Dumesnil

1st Brigade (General of Brigade Nicolai)

17th Chasseur Battalion (Commandant Merchier)
1 battalion
3rd Line Infantry Regiment (Colonel Champion)
3 battalions
21st Line Infantry Regiment (Colonel Morand)
3 battalions

2nd Brigade (General of Brigade Maire)

47th Line Infantry Regiment (Colonel de Gramont)
3 battalions
99th Line Infantry Regiment (Colonel Chagrin de Saint-Hilaire)
3 battalions

Divisional Artillery
2 4 pounder batteries
1 mitailleuse battery

1 engineer company

2nd Division

Commander: General of Division Liébert

1st Brigade (General of Brigade Guiomar)

6th Chasseur Battalion (Commandant Beaufort)
1 battalion
5th Line Infantry regiment (Colonel Boyer)
3 battalions
37th Line Infantry Regiment (Colonel de la Formy de la Blanchetée)
3 battalions

2nd Brigade (General of Brigade de la Bastide)

53rd Line Infantry Regiment (Colonel Japy)
3 battalions
89th Line infantry Regiment (Colonel Munier)
3 battalions

Divisional Artillery
2 4 pounder batteries
1 mitrailleuse battery

1 engineer company

3rd Division

Commander: General of Division Dumont

1st Brigade (General of Brigade Bordas)

52nd Line Infantry Regiment (Colonel Aveline)
3 battalions
79th Line Infantry Regiment (Colonel Bressolles)
3 battalions

2nd Brigade (General of Brigade Bittard des Portes)

82nd Line Infantry Regiment (Colonel Guys)
3 battalions
83rd Line Infantry Regiment (Colonel Séatelli)
3 battalions

Divisional Artillery
2 4 pounder batteries
1 mitrailleuse battery

1 engineer company

Cavalry Division

Commander: General of Division Baron Ameil

1st Brigade (General of Brigade Cambriels)

4th Hussar Regiment (Colonel de Lavigerie)
5 squadrons
4th Lancer Regiment (Colonel Féline)
4 squadrons
8th Lancer Regiment (Colonel de Dampierre)
4 squadrons

2nd Brigade (General of Brigade Jolif du Coulombier)

6th Hussar Regiment (Colonel Guillon)
5 squadrons
6th Dragoon Regiment (Colonel Tillion)
4 squadrons

Corps Artillery Reserve

2 12 pounder batteries
2 4 pounder batteries
2 4 pounder horse artillery batteries

7th CORPS Total:
38 battalions, 22 squadrons, 3 companies, 12 batteries, 3 mitrailleuse batteries
1,043 officers, 23,142 men, 72 guns, 18 mitrailleuse

CAVALRY RESERVE

2nd Division

Commander: General of Division Viscount Bonnemains

1st Brigade (General of Brigade Girard)

1st Cuirassier Regiment (Colonel de Vandœvre)
4 squadrons
4th Cuirassier Regiment (Colonel Billet)
4 squadrons

2nd Brigade (General of Brigade de Brauer)

2nd Cuirassier Regiment (Colonel Rossetti)
4 squadrons
3rd Cuirassier Regiment (Colonel Lafutsun de Lacarre)
4 squadrons

Divisional Artillery
2 4 pounder horse artillery batteries
16 squadrons, 12 guns

APPENDIX III

German Forces, Gravelotte-St.Privat (August 18th 1870)

FIRST ARMY

Commander: General of Infantry von Steinmetz

VII CORPS

Commander: General of Infantry von Zastrow

13th Infantry Division

Commander: Lieutenant-General von Glümer

25th Infantry Brigade (Major-General Baron von der Osten-Sacken)

1st Westphalian Infantry-Regiment Nr.13
Hanoverian Fusilier Regiment Nr.73
Westphalian Jäger Battalion Nr. 7

26th Infantry Brigade (Major-General von der Goltz)

2nd Westphalian Infantry Regiment Nr. 15
6th Westphalian Infantry Regiment Nr. 55

14th Infantry Division

Commander: Lieutenant-General von Kameke

27th Infantry Brigade (Major-General von François)

Rhineland Fusilier Regiment Nr. 39
1st Hanoverian Infantry Regiment Nr. 74 (-)
Hanoverian Hussar Regiment Nr. 15

28th Infantry Brigade (: Major-General von Woyna II)

5th Westphalian Infantry Regiment Nr. 53 (-)
2nd Hanoverian Infantry Regiment Nr. 77 (-)

Corps Artillery

13 batteries

VIII CORPS

Commander: General of Infantry von Goeben

15th Infantry Division

Commander: Lieutenant-General von Kummer

29th Infantry Brigade (Colonel Bock)

East Prussian Fusilier Regiment Nr. 33
7th Brandenburg Infantry Regiment Nr. 60

30th Infantry Brigade (Major-General von Strubberg)

2nd Rhineland Infantry Regiment Nr. 28
6th Rhineland Infantry Regiment Nr. 68

Divisional Troops

Rhineland Jäger Battalion Nr. 8
1st Rhineland Hussar Regiment Nr. 7

2 4 pounder batteries
2 6 pounder batteries

16th Infantry Division

Commander: Lieutenant-General von Barnekow

31st Infantry Brigade (Major-General Count Neidhardt von Gneisenau)

3rd Rhineland Infantry Regiment Nr. 29
7th Rhineland Infantry Regiment Nr. 69

32nd Infantry Brigade (Colonel von Rex)

Fusilier Regiment Nr. 40 (-)
4th Thuringian Infantry Regiment Nr. 72

Divisional Troops

2nd Rhineland Hussar Regiment Nr. 9

2 4 pounder batteries
2 6 pounder batteries

Corps Artillery

2 4 pounder batteries
2 6 pounder batteries
2 4 pounder horse artillery batteries

1st Cavalry Division

Commander: Lieutenant-General von Hartmann

1st Cavalry Brigade (Major-General von Lüderitz)

Pomeranian Cuirassier Regiment Nr. 2
1st Pomeranian Uhlan regiment Nr. 4
2nd Pomeranian Uhlan Regiment Nr. 9

2nd Cavalry Brigade (Major-General Baumgarth)

East Prussian Cuirassier Regiment Nr. 3

East Prussian Uhlan Regiment Nr. 8
'Lithuanian' Uhlan Regiment Nr. 12

1 4 pounder horse artillery battery

SECOND ARMY

Commander: His Royal Highness, General of Cavalry Prince Frederick Charles of Prussia

GUARD CORPS

Commander: Prince Augustus of Württemberg

1st Guard Infantry Division

Commander: Major-General von Pape

1st Infantry Brigade (Major-General von Kessel)

1st Foot Guard Regiment
3rd Foot Guard Regiment

2nd Infantry Brigade (Major-General von Medem)

2nd Foot Guard Regiment
4th Foot Guard Regiment
Guard Fusilier Regiment

Divisional Troops

Guard Jäger Battalion
Guard Hussar Regiment

2 4 pounder batteries
2 6 pounder batteries

2nd Guard Infantry Division

Commander: Lieutenant-General von Budritzki

3rd Infantry Brigade (Colonel Knappe von Knappstaedt)

1st Guard Grenadier Regiment
3rd Guard Grenadier Regiment

4th Infantry Brigade (Major-General von Berger)

2nd Guard Grenadier Regiment
4th Guard Grenadier Regiment

Divisional Troops

Guard Schützen Battalion
2nd Guard Uhlan Regiment

2 4 pounder batteries
2 6 pounder batteries

Guard Cavalry Division

Commander: Lieutenant-General Count von der Goltz

1st Cavalry Brigade (Major-General Count von Brandenburg I)

Guard du Corps Regiment
Guard Cuirassier Regiment

3rd Cavalry Brigade (Major-General Count von Brandenburg II)

1st Guard Dragoon Regiment
2nd Guard Dragoon Regiment

2 4 pounder horse artillery batteries

Guard Corps Artillery

2 4 pounder batteries
2 6 pounder batteries
2 4 pounder horse artillery batteries

II CORPS

Commander: General of Infantry von Fransecky

3rd Infantry Division

Commander: Major-General von Hartmann

5th Infantry Brigade (Major-General von Koblinski)

1st Pomeranian Grenadier Regiment Nr. 2
5th Pomeranian Infantry Regiment Nr. 42

6th Infantry Brigade (Colonel von der Decken)

3rd Pomeranian Infantry Regiment Nr. 14
7th Pomeranian Infantry Regiment Nr. 54

Divisional Troops

Pomeranian Jäger Battalion Nr. 2
Neumark Dragoon Regiment Nr. 3

2 4 pounder batteries
2 6 pounder batteries

4th Infantry Division

Commander: Lieutenant-General Hann von Weyhern

7th Infantry Brigade (Major-General du Trossel)

2nd Pomeranian Infantry Grenadier Nr. 9
6th Pomeranian Infantry Regiment Nr. 49

8th Brigade (Major-General von Kettler)

4th Pomeranian Infantry Regiment Nr. 21
8th Pomeranian Infantry Regiment Nr. 61

Divisional Troops

Pomeranian Dragoon Regiment Nr. 11

2 4 pounder batteries
2 6 pounder batteries

Corps Artillery

2 4 pounder batteries
2 6 pounder batteries
2 4 pounder horse artillery batteries

III CORPS

Corps Artillery

2 4 pounder batteries
2 6 pounder batteries
2 4 pounder horse artillery batteries

IX CORPS

Commander: General of Infantry von Manstein

18th Infantry Division

Commander: Lieutenant General Baron von Wrangel

35th Infantry Brigade (Major-General von Blumenthal)

Magdeburg Fusilier Regiment Nr. 36
Schleswig Infantry Regiment Nr. 84 (-)

36th Infantry Brigade (Major-General von Below)

2nd Silesian Grenadier Regiment Nr. 11
Holstein Infantry Regiment Nr. 85

Divisional Troops

Lauenburg Jäger Battalion Nr. 9
Magdeburg Dragoon Regiment Nr. 6

2 4 pounder batteries
2 6 pounder batteries

25th (Grand Duchy of Hesse) Infantry Division

Commander: Lieutenant-General Prince Ludwig of Hesse

49th Infantry Brigade (Major-General von Wittich)

1st Hessian Leib-Guard Regiment

2nd Hessian Infantry Regiment
1st Hessian Guard Jäger Battalion

50th Infantry Brigade (Major-General von Lyncker)

3rd Hessian Infantry Regiment
4th Hessian infantry Regiment
2nd Hessian Jäger Batallion

25th Hessian Cavalry Brigade (Major General von Schlotheim)

1st Hessian Chevauxlegers Regiment
2nd Hessian Chevauxlegers Regiment

5 Hessian 4 pounder batteries
1 Hessian 4 pounder horse artillery battery

Corps Artillery

2 4 pounder batteries
2 6 pounder batteries
1 4 pounder horse artillery battery

X CORPS

20th Infantry Division

Commander: Major-General von Kraatz-Koschlau

39th Infantry Brigade (Major-General von Woyna I)

7th Westphalian Infantry Regiment Nr. 56
3rd Hanoverian Infantry Regiment Nr. 79

40th Infantry Brigade (Major-General von Diringshofen)

4th Westphalian Infantry Regiment Nr. 17
Brunswick Infantry Regiment Nr. 92

Divisional Troops

2nd Hanoverian Dragoon Regiment Nr. 16
Hanoverian Jäger Battalion Nr. 10 (19th Division)

2 4 pounder batteries,
2 6 pounder batteries

Corps Artillery

2 4 pounder batteries
2 6 pounder batteries
2 4 pounder horse artillery batteries

XII ROYAL SAXON CORPS

Commander: General of Infantry Crown Prince Albert of Saxony

23rd Infantry Division/1st Infantry Division

Commander: Lieutenant-General Prince George of Saxony

45th Infantry Brigade/1st Infantry Brigade (Major-General Craushaar)

1st Leib Infantry Regiment Nr. 100
2nd Grenadier Regiment, Nr. 101
Fusilier Regiment Nr. 108

46th Infantry Brigade/2nd Brigade (Colonel von Montbé)

3rd Infantry Regiment Nr. 102
4th Infantry Regiment Nr. 103

Divisional Troops

1st Horse Regiment

Divisional Artillery
2 4 pounder batteries
2 6 pounder batteries

24th Infantry Division/2nd Infantry Division

Commander: Major-General Nehrhoff von Holderberg

47th Infantry Brigade/3rd Brigade (Colonel Leonhardi)

5th Infantry Regiment, Nr. 104
6th Infantry Regiment Nr. 105
1st Saxon Jäger Battalion Nr. 12

48th Infantry Brigade/4th Infantry Brigade (Colonel Schulz)

7th Infantry Regiment Nr. 106
8th Infantry Regiment Nr. 107
2nd Saxon Jäger Battalion Nr. 13

Divisional Troops

2nd Horse Regiment

2 4 pounder batteries
2 6 pounder batteries

Cavalry Division

Guard Horse Regiment
3rd Horse Regiment

Corps Artillery

2 4 pounder batteries
2 6 pounder batteries
1 4 pounder horse artillery battery

5th Cavalry Division

Commander: Lieutenant-General Baron von Rheinbaben

11th Cavalry Brigade (Major-General von Barby)

Westphalian Cuirassier Regiment Nr. 4
1st Hanoverian Uhlan Regiment Nr. 13
Oldenburg Dragoon Regiment Nr. 19

12th Cavalry Brigade (Major-General von Bredow)

Magdeburg Cuirassier Regiment Nr. 7 (2 sqdns.)
Altmark Uhlan Regiment Nr. 16 (2 sqdns.)
Schleswig-Holstein Dragoon Regiment Nr. 13

13th Cavalry Brigade (Major-General von Redern)

Magdeburg Hussar Regiment Nr. 10
2nd Westphalian Hussar Regiment Nr. 11
Brunswick Hussar Regiment Nr. 17

4 horse artillery batteries

6th Cavalry Division

Commander: Lieutenant-General Duke Wilhelm of Mecklenburg-Schwerin

14th Cavalry Brigade (Colonel Baron von Diepenbroick-Grüter)

Brandenburg Cuirassier Regiment Nr. 6
1st Brandenburg Uhlan Regiment Nr. 3
Schleswig-Holstein Uhlan Regiment Nr. 15

15th Cavalry Brigade (Major-General von Rauch)

Brandenburg Hussar Regiment Nr. 3
Schleswig-Holstein Hussar Regiment Nr. 16

1 4 pounder horse artillery battery

Forces engaged: 188, 332 men, 732 guns

Note: Units marked thus (-) were reduced in strength due to previous losses

APPENDIX IV

French Forces, Gravelotte-St.Privat (August 18th 1870)

Army of the Rhine

Commander: Marshal Bazaine

IMPERIAL GUARD

Commander: General of Division Bourbaki

1st Guard Division

Commander: General of Division Deligny

1st Brigade (General of Brigade Brincourt)

Guard Chasseur Battalion
1st Guard Voltigeur Regiment
2nd Guard Voltigeur Regiment

2nd Brigade (General of Brigade Garnier)

3rd Guard Voltigeur Regiment
4th Guard Voltigeur Regiment

2 4 pounder batteries
1 mitrailleuse battery

2nd Guard Division

Commander: General of Division Picard

1st Brigade (General of Brigade Jeanningros)

Guard Zouave Regiment
1st Grenadier Regiment

2nd Brigade (General of Brigade le Poitevin de la Croix Vaubois)

3rd Grenadier Regiment (2 bttns.)
4th Grenadier Regiment

2 4 pounder batteries
1 mitrailleuse battery

Guard Cavalry Division

Commander: General of Division Desvaux

1st Brigade (General of Brigade Halna du Fretay)

Guard Chasseur Regiment
Guides Regiment (4 sdns.)

2nd Brigade (General of Brigade de France)

Guard Lancer Regiment
Guard Dragoon Regiment

3rd Brigade (General of Brigade Du Preuil)

Guard Cuirassier Regiment
Guard Carabinier Regiment

2 4 pounder horse artillery batteries

Guard Reserve Artillery
4 4 pounder horse artillery batteries

2nd CORPS

Commander: General of Division Frossard

1st Division

Commander: General of Division Vergé

1st Brigade (General of Brigade Letellier-Valazé)

3rd Chasseur Battalion
32nd Line Infantry Regiment
55th Line Infantry Regiment (-)

2nd Brigade (General of Brigade Jolivet)

76th Line Infantry Regiment
77th Line Infantry Regiment (-)

3 4 pounder batteries

2nd Division

Commander: General of Division Bastoul

1st Brigade (General of Brigade Pouget)

12th Chasseur Battalion
8th Line Infantry Regiment
23rd Line Infantry Regiment

2nd Brigade (General of Division-Bastoul)

66th Line Infantry Regiment (-)
67th Line Infantry Regiment (-)

2 4 pounder batteries
1 mitrailleuse battery

Cavalry Division

Commander: General of Division Marmier

1st Brigade (General of Brigade de Valabrègue)

4th Chasseur Regiment
5th Chasseur Regiment

2nd Brigade (General of Brigade Bachelier)

7th Dragoon Regiment (2 sqdns.)
12th Dragoon Regiment

Corps Artillery

2 12 pounder batteries
2 4 pounder batteries
2 4 pounder horse artillery batteries

3rd CORPS

Commander: Marshal Bazaine

1st Division

Commander: General of Division Montaudon

1st Brigade (General of Brigade Plombin)

18th Chasseur Battalion
51st Line Infantry Regiment
62nd Line Infantry Regiment

2nd Brigade (General of Brigade Clinchant)

81st Line Infantry Regiment
95th Line infantry Regiment

1 4 pounder batteries

2nd Division

Commander: General of Brigade Nayral

1st Brigade (General of Brigade Nayral)

19th Line infantry Regiment (-)
41st Line Infantry Regiment

2nd Brigade (General of Brigade Duplessis)

69th Line Infantry Regiment
90th Line Infantry Regiment (-)

2 4 pounder batteries

3rd Division

Commander: General of Division Metman

1st Brigade (General of Brigade de Potier)

7th Chasseur Battalion
7th Line Infantry Regiment
29th Line Infantry Regiment

2nd Brigade (General of Brigade Arnaudeau)

59th Line Infantry Regiment
71st Line Infantry Regiment

2 4 pounder batteries
1 mitrailleuse battery

4th Division

Commander: General of Division Aymard

1st Brigade (General of Brigade de Brauer)

11th Chasseur Battalion
44th Line Infantry Regiment (-)
60th Line Infantry Regiment

2nd Brigade (General of Brigade Sanglé-Ferrière)

80th Line Infantry Regiment
85th Line Infantry Regiment (-)

2 4 pounder batteries

Cavalry Division

Commander: General of Division Clérembault

1st Brigade (General of Brigade Bruchard)

2nd Chasseur Regiment
3rd Chasseur Regiment
10th Chasseur Regiment

2nd Brigade (General de Brigade Gayrault de Maubranches)

2nd Dragoon Regiment
4th Dragoon Regiment

3rd Brigade (General of Brigade Bégougne de Juiniac)

5th Dragoon Regiment

Corps Reserve Artillery

2 12 pounder batteries
2 4 pounder batteries
2 4 pounder horse artillery batteries

4th CORPS

Commander: General of Division Ladmirault

1st Division

Commander: General of Division Courtot de Cissey

1st Brigade (General of Brigade Brayer)

20th Chasseur Battalion
1st Line Infantry Regiment
6th Line infantry Regiment

2nd Brigade (General of Brigade de Goldberg)

57th Line Infantry Regiment
73rd Line Infantry Regiment

2 4 pounder batteries
1 mitrailleuse battery

2nd Division

Commander: General of Brigade Grenier

1st Brigade (General of Brigade Véron-Bellecourt)

5th Chasseur Battalion
13th Line Infantry Regiment
43rd Line Infantry Regiment (-)

2nd Brigade (General of Brigade Pradier)

64th Line Infantry Regiment
98th Line Infantry Regiment

2 4 pounder batteries
1 mitrailleuse battery

3rd Division

Commander: General of Division Latrille, Count de Lorencez

1st Brigade (General of Brigade Pajol)

2nd Chasseur Battalion
15th Line Infantry Regiment
33rd Line infantry Regiment

2nd Brigade (General of Brigade Berger)

54th Line Infantry Regiment
65th Line Infantry Regiment

2 4 pounder batteries
1 mitrailleuse battery

Cavalry Division

Commander: General of Division Legrand

1st Brigade (General of Brigade Montaigu)

2nd Hussar Regiment
7th Hussar Regiment

2nd Brigade: (General of Brigade Baron Gondrecourt)

3rd Dragoon Regiment
11th Dragoon Regiment

Corps Reserve Artillery

2 12 pounder batteries
2 4 pounder batteries
2 4 pounder horse artillery batteries

5th CORPS

2nd Division

1st Brigade (General of Brigade Lapasset)

14th Chasseur Battalion
84th Line Infantry Regiment
97th Line Infantry Regiment (-)

1 4 pounder battery

Cavalry Division

3rd Lancer Regiment

6th CORPS

Commander: Marshal Canrobert

1st Division

Commander: General of Division Tixier

1st Brigade (General of Brigade Péchot)

9th Chasseur Battalion
4th Line Infantry Regiment
10th Line Infantry Regiment (-)

2nd Brigade (General of Brigade Leroy de Dais)

12th line Infantry Regiment (-)
100th Line infantry Regiment

2 4 pounder batteries
1 mitrailleuse battery

2nd Division

Commander: General of Division Bisson

1st Brigade (General of Brigade Noel)

9th Line Infantry Regiment

2 12 pounder batteries

3rd Division

Commander: General of Division Lafont de Villiers

1st Brigade (General of Brigade Becquet de Sonnay)

75th Line infantry Regiment (-)
91st Line infantry Regiment

2nd Brigade (General of Brigade Colin)

93rd Line infantry Regiment (-)
94th Line infantry Regiment

3 4 pounder batteries
1 engineer company

4th Division

Commander: General of Division Levassor-Sorval

1st Brigade (General of Brigade de Marguenat)

25th Line Infantry Regiment
26th Line Infantry Regiment (-)

2nd Brigade (General of Brigade Count De Chanaleilles)
28th Line infantry regiment
70th Line Infantry Regiment

2 4 pounder horse artillery batteries

1st Reserve Cavalry Division

Commander: General of Division du Barail

2nd Regiment, Chasseurs d'Afrique
2nd Chasseur Regiment
3rd Chasseur Regiment

3rd Cavalry Division

Commander: General of Division de Forton

1st Brigade (General of Brigade Prince Murat)

1st Dragoon Regiment
9th Dragoon Regiment

2nd Brigade (General of Brigade de Gramont, Duke of Esparre)

7th Cuirassier Regiment
10th Cuirassier Regiment

2 4 pounder horse artillery batteries

ARMY RESERVE ARTILLERY
2 12 pounder batteries
6 4 pounder horse artillery batteries

Forces engaged: 112,800, 520 guns (of some 140,000 present)

Note: Units marked thus (-) were reduced in strength due to previous losses

APPENDIX V

Terms of the Capitulation at Sedan

The following treaty has been concluded between the undersigned, the Chief of the General Staff of H.M. the King of Prussia, Commander in Chief of the German Army, and the Commander in Chief of the French Army, both acting with full powers from King William and the Emperor Napoleon.

Art. 1. The French Army, under the command of General de Wimpffen, at the present time invested by superior forces in Sedan, are prisoners of war.

Art. 2. In consequence of the brave defence of this army, exceptions are made in favour of such general and other officers, including the higher officials with officers' rank, as bind themselves by their written word of honour not to take up arms against Germany, nor to act in any way prejudicial to her interests until the close of the present war. The officers and officials, who accept these conditions, will retain their arms and private property.

Art. 3. All other arms, inclusive of the entire war material, such as colours, eagles, standards, guns, horses, treasurer chests, military carriages, ammunition, &c., will be delivered up to some military authority in Sedan appointed for this purpose by the French Commander in Chief, with a view to their being handed over without delay to the German agents.

Art. 4. The fortress of Sedan will then be surrendered in its present state to H.M. the King of Prussia, by the evening of 2nd September at the latest.

Art. 5. Those officers who do not accept the obligation mentioned in Art. 2, and the men disarmed, are to be marched off by regiments in parade order. This measure is to take effect from the 2nd September, and be completed by the 3rd. The detachments are to be brought to the ground encircled by the Meuse near Iges, with a view to their being handed over to the German agents by their officers, who will then resign the command to the non-commissioned officers.

Art. 6. The army surgeons will remain behind without exception for the purpose of tending the wounded.

Frénois 2nd September 1870.

(Signed) v. Moltke
(Signed) de Wimpffen

Bibliography

ABBOTT, JSC, *Prussia and the Franco-Prussian War,* (London 1871)
ABEKEN, H, *Bismarck's Pen,* (London 1911)
ADDINGTON, LH, *The Blitzkrieg Era and the German General Staff 1865–1941,*
(New Brunswick, NJ 1971)
ADRIANCE, TJ, *The Last Gaiter Button,* (Westpoint, Connecticut 1987)
ALLNUTT, H, *Historical Diary of the War Between France and Germany 1870–71,*
(London 1871)
(ANON), *Papiers et Correspondance de la Famille Imperiale,* (Paris 1870)
(ANON), *Le Général Chanzy,* (Paris 1896)
ARONSON, T, *The Fall of the Third Napoleon,* (London 1970)
ASCOLI, D, *A Day of Battle: Mars la Tour 16 August 1870,* (London 1987)
AURELLE de PALADINES, General C d', *La Première Armée de la Loire,* (Paris 1871)
BALDICK, R, *The Siege of Paris,* (London 1964)
BARKER, AJ, *The Vainglorious War,* (London 1970)
BAUNARD, Monsignor, *Le Général de Sonis,* (Paris 1903)
BAZAINE, Marshal A, *Episodes de la Guerre de 1870,* (Madrid 1883)
BENEDETTI, V, *Ma Mission en Prusse,* (Paris 1871)
BIBESCO, Prince G, *Campagne de 1870: Belfort, Reims, Sedan,* (Paris 1872)
BIRD, Brevet-Major WD, *Lectures on the Strategy of the Franco-German War 1870,* (London 1909)
BISMARCK, Prince O von, *The Correspondence of William I and Bismarck,* (New York 1903)
BISMARCK, Prince O von, *Letters to his Wife from the Seat of War 1870–1871,* (London 1915)
BISMARCK, Prince O von, *Reflections and Reminiscences,* (London 1898)
BLUME, W, *The Operations of the German Armies in France,* (London 1872)
BLUMENTHAL, Field Marshal Count K von, *Journals for 1866 and 1870–71,* (London 1903)
BOGUSLAWSKI, A von, *Tactical Deductions from the War of 1870–71* (trans Colonel L Graham), (London 1872)
BONIE, Lieutenant Colonel, 'The French Cavalry in 1870' in: *Cavalry Studies from Two Great Wars,* (Kansas City 1896)
BONNAL, General H, *La Manoeuvre de Saint Privat,* (Paris 1904)
BONNIN, G (ed), *Bismarck and the Hohenzollern Candidature for the Spanish Throne,* (London 1957)
BORBSTAEDT, A and DWYER, F, *The Franco- German War to the Catastrophe of Sedan,* (London 1911)
BOWLES,TG, *The Defence of Paris,* (London 1871)
BRESLER, F, *Napoleon III: A Life,* (London 1999)
BROCKETT, LP, *The Franco-German War of 1870–71,* (New York 1871)

BRONSART von SCHELLENDORFF, General P, *The Duties of the General Staff,* (London 1905)
BUCHOLZ, A, *Moltke and the German Wars,* (New York 2001)
BUCHOLZ, A, *Moltke, Schlieffen and Prussian War Planning,* (New York 1991)
BURY, JPT, *Gambetta and the National Defence: A Republican Dictatorship in France,* (London 1964)
BURY, JPT and TOMBS, RP, *Thiers 1797–1877: A Political Life,* (London 1871)
BUSCH, M, *Bismarck in the Franco-German War 1870–71,* (London 1879)
BUSCH, M, *Bismarck: Some Secret Pages of his History,* (London 1898)
CAEMMERER, Lieutenant General von, *The Development of Strategical Science,* (London 1905)
CANE, Brigadier General JP du, *The Campaign in Alsace August 1870,* (London 1912)
CARR, W, *The Origins of the Wars of German Unification,* (London 1991)
CARTIER, V, *Le General Trochu,* (Paris 1914)
CHABOT, Colonel Jules de, *La Cavalerie Allemande pendant la Guerre de 1870–71,* (Paris 1899)
CHANZY, General A, *La Deuxième Armée de la Loire,* (Paris 1871)
CHAPELLE, Count de la, *The War of 1870,* (London 1870)
CHESNEY, Lieutenant Colonel C and REEVE, H, *The Military Resources of Prussia and France,* (London 1870)
COX, GP, *The Halt in the Mud,* (Oxford 1894)
CRAIG, GA, *The Battle of Königgrätz,* (London 1965)
CRAIG, GA, *The Politics of the Prussian Army,* (Oxford 1964)
CREVELD, M van, *Supplying War,* (Cambridge 1977)
'DAILY NEWS', *Correspondence of the War between Germany and France, 1870–71, (London 1871)*
DEMETER. K, *The German Officer Corps in Society and State 1650–1945,* (London 1965)
DUCROT, General A, *La Journée de Sedan,* (Paris 1872)
ELLIOT-WRIGHT P, *Gravelotte-St Privat 1870,* (Westport, Connecticut 2005)
FAIDHERBE, General L, *Campagne de l'Armée du Nord,* (Paris 1871)
FILON, A, *Recollections of the Empress Eugénie,* (London 1920)
FITZGEORGE, Captain, *The Battle of Sedan,* (London 1871)
FOERSTER, W, *Prinz Friedrich Karl von Preussen,* (Stuttgart 1910)
FORBES, A, *Memories and Studies of War and Peace,* (London 1895)
FORBES, A, *My Experiences of the War between France and Germany,* (London 1871)
FRANKLYN, HB, *The Great Battles of 1870 and Blockade of Metz,* (London 1887)
FREDERICK WILLIAM, Crown Prince *The War Diary of the Emperor Frederick III* (trans AR Allinson), (London 1927)
FRENCH GENERAL STAFF, *La Guerre de 1870–71,* (Paris 1901)
FREYCINET, C de, *La Guerre en Province,* (Paris 1872)
FRIEDRICH, O, *Blood and Iron,* (New York 1995)

FROSSARD, General, *Rapport sur les Opérations de Deuxième Corps,* (Paris 1872)
FULFORD, R (ed) *Your Dear Letter: Private Correspondence Of Queen Victoria and the Crown Princess Of Prussia 1865–71,* (London 1981)
FULLER, Major General JFC, *Decisive Battles of the Western World,* (London 1956)
FURSE, Colonel GA, *The Organisation and Administration of Lines of Communication in War,* (London 1894)
GALL, L, *Bismarck: The White Revolutionary,* (London 1896)
GERMAN GENERAL STAFF, *Official Account of the Franco-German War 1870–1871* (trans Capt FCH Clarke), London 1874)
GHEUSI, PB, *Gambetta: Life and Letters,* (London 1910)
GHIO, A (ed), *Procés de Maréchal Bazaine,* (Paris 1874)
GIESBERG, RI, *The Treaty of Frankfort,* (Philadelphia 1966)
GOLTZ, C von der, *Leon Gambetta und Seine Armeen,* (Berlin 1877)
GÖRLITZ, W, *The German General Staff,* (London 1953)
GUEDALLA, P, *The Two Marshals,* (London 1943)
HALE, Colonel LONSDALE, *The 'People's War' in France 1870–71,* (London 1904)
HATZFELDT, Count P, *Letters to his Wife 1870–71,* (London 1905)
HELMS, M, *Moltke, his Life and Character,* (London 1892)
HELVIG, H, *Operations of the I Bavarian Corps under General von der Tann,* (trans G Schwabe), (London 1874)
HENDERSON, Colonel GFR, *The Battle of Spicheren,* (London n.d)
HENDERSON, Colonel GFR, *The Battle of Wörth, (Yorktown Surrey 1899)*
HERISSON, Count d', *Journal of a Staff Officer in Paris during The Events of 1870 and 1871,* (London 1885)
HEYDE, E and FROESE, A, *Geschichte der Belagerung von Paris im Jahre 1870/71,* (Berlin 1874)
HIBBERT, C, *Garibaldi and his Enemies,* (London 1965)
HOFFBAUER, Captain E, *The German Artillery in the Battles Near Metz,* (London 1874)
HOHENLOHE-INGELFINGEN, Prince Kraft zu, *Letters on Artillery,* (trans NL Walford), (London 1890)
HOHENLOHE-INGELFINGEN, Prince Kraft zu, *Letters on Cavalry,* (trans NL Walford), (London 1889)
HOHENLOHE-INGELFINGEN, Prince Kraft zu, *Letters on Infantry,* (trans NL Walford), (London 1892)
HOHENLOHE-INGELFINGEN, Prince Kraft zu, *Letters on Strategy,* (London 1898)
HOLLYDAY, FBM, *Bismarck's Rival,* (Durham, N Carolina 1960)
HOLMES, R, *The Road to Sedan,* (London 1984)
HOLSTEIN, F von, *Memoirs,* Cambridge 1955)
HÖNIG, F, *Inquiries concerning the Tactics of the Future,* (trans Captain HM Bowes), (London 1899)
HÖNIG, F, *Twenty Four Hours of Moltke's Strategy,* (trans NL Walford), (Woolwich 1895)

HOOPER, G, *The Campaign of Sedan,* (London 1908)
HORNE, A, *The Fall of Paris,* (London 1965)
HOWARD, M, *The Franco-Prussian War,* (London 1962)
HOWES, Colonel P, *The Catalytic Wars,* (London 1998)
HOZIER, Captain HM (ed), *The Franco-Prussian War: Its Causes Incidents and Consequences,* (London n.d)
HUGHES, DJ, *Moltke on the Art of War,* (Novato, California 1993)
JOHN, K, *The Prince Imperial,* (London 1939)
JOUBERT, L, *La Bataille de Sedan,* (Paris 1873)
KAEHLER, Major, 'The German Cavalry in the Battle of Vionville-Mars-la-Tour' in: *Cavalry Studies from two Great Wars,* (Kansas City 1896)
KRETSCHMANN H von, *Kriegsbriefe aus dem Jahren 1870–71,* (Stuttgart 1904)
LABOUCHÈRE, H, *Diary of the Besieged Resident in Paris,* (London 1871)
LÖHLEIN, L, *The Operations of the Corps of General von Werder,* (Chatham n.d)
LONLAY, Dick de, *Francais et Allemands, (Paris 1890)*
LORD, RH, *The Origins of the War of 1870,* (Harvard 1924)
MAGUIRE, TM, *The Franco-German War July 15-August 18, 1870,* (London 1909)
MAUNI, R de, *Eight Months on Duty,* (London 1872)
MAURICE, Major General (ed), *The Franco-German War 1870–71,* (London 1900)
MAY, Major ES, *Field Artillery with the Other Arms,* (London 1898)
MAY, Major ES, *Guns and Cavalry,* (London 1896)
McCABE, JD, *History of the War between Germany and France, (New York 1871)*
McELWEE, W, *The Art of War from Waterloo to Mons,* (London 1974)
MILLMAN, R, *British Foreign Policy and the Coming of the Franco-Prussian War,* (Oxford 1965)
MOLTKE, Field Marshal H von, *Correspondance Militaire de Maréchal de Moltke,* (Paris n.d)
MOLTKE, Field Marshal H von, *Letters to his Mother and his Brothers,* (trans C Bell & H Fischer) (London 1891)
MOLTKE, Field Marshal H von, *Letters to his Wife,* (London 1896)
MOLTKE, Field Marshal H von, *Military Correspondence 1870–71,* (ed. S Wilkinson) (Oxford 1923)
MOLTKE, Field Marshal H von, *Military Correspondence 1870–71,* (trans. H Bell), (Fort Leavenworth, Kansas n.d)
MOLTKE, Field Marshal H von, *Moltke as a Correspondent,* (ed. M Herms), (London 1893)
MOLTKE, Field Marshal H von, *The Franco- German War of 1870–71,* (London 1907)
MOLTKE, Field Marshal H von, *Strategy: Its Theory and Application,*(Westport, Connecticut 1971)
MORRIS, W O'Connor, *Moltke,* (London 1893)
NASO, E von, *Moltke,* (Hamburg 1937)

NEWDIGATE, Colonel E (trans), *The Army of the North German Confederation,* (London 1872)
OLLIER, E, *Cassell's Illustrated History of the War between France and Germany,* (London n.d)
OLLIVIER, E, *The Franco-Prussian War and its Hidden Causes,* (London 1913)
ORTHOLAN, Henri, *L'Armée de la Loire,* (Paris 2005)
PARET, P (ed), *Makers of Modern Strategy,* (Oxford 1994)
PATRY, L, *The Reality of War* (trans D Fermer), (London 2001)
PELET-NARBONNE, General von, *Cavalry on Service,* (London 1906)
PFLANZE, O, *Bismarck and the Development of Germany,*(Princeton, New Jersey 1990)
POTTINGER, EA, *Napoleon III and the German Crisis,* (Cambridge, Massachusetts 1968)
PRATT, Lieutenant Colonel SC, *Saarbrück to Paris 1870,* (London 1914)
RICH, E, *A History of the Franco-German War,* (London 1884)
RIDLEY, J, *Napoleon III and Eugènie,* (London 1979)
RIEZ, MG Martiny de, *La Guerre de 1870–71,* (Laon 1871)
RODD, R, *Frederick: Crown Prince and Emperor,* (London 1888)
ROBINSON, GT, *The Fall of Metz,* (London 1871)
ROSINSKI, H, *The German Army,* (London 1939)
SARAZIN, Doctor, *Récits de la Dernière Guerre, Franco-Allemand,*(Paris 1887)
RUSSELL, WH, *My Diary during the Last Great War,* (London 1874)
RÜSTOW, W, *The War for the Rhine Frontier 1870,* (London 1871–2)
SCHEIBERT, J, *Franco-German War 1870–71,* (trans JA Ferrier), (Chatham 1891)
SCHELL, Major A von, *The Operations of the First Army under General von Goeben,* (London 1873)
SCHELL, Major A von, *The Operations of the First Army under General von Steinmetz,* (London 1873)
SENCOURT, R, *Napoleon III: The Modern Emperor,* (London 1933)
SHERIDAN, General P, *Personal Memoirs,* (London 1888)
SHOWALTER, D, *Railroads and Rifles: Soldiers, Technology and the Unification of Germany,* (Hamden, Connecticut 1975)
SHOWALTER, D, *The Wars of German Unification,* (London 2004)
STADELMANN, R, *Moltke und der Staat,* (Krefeld 1950)
STANNARD, H, *Gambetta,* (London 1921)
STOFFEL, E, *Military Reports addressed to the French War Minister,* (London 1872)
STONE, D, *First Reich,* (London 2002)
STONE, Captain FG, *Tactical Studies from the Franco-German War of 1870–71,* (London 1886)
STOSCH, General A von, *Denkwurdigkeiten,* (Berlin 1904)
STRAUSS. GLM, *Men who have made the New German Empire,* (London 1875)
TAYLOR, AJP, *Bismarck,* (London 1955)
TAYLOR, AJP, *From Napoleon to the Second International,* (London 1993)
'THE TIMES', *The Campaign of 1870–71,* (London 1871)
THOMPSON, JM, *Louis Napoleon and the Second Empire,* (Oxford 1954)

TIEDEMANN, Colonel B von, *The Siege Operations in the Campaign against France1870–71,* (trans. Major Tyler) (London 1877)
TOVEY, Lieutenant Colonel, *The Elements of Strategy,* (London 1904)
TURNBULL, P, *The Birth of a Nation,* (London 1985)
VERDY du VERNOIS, General J von, *With the Royal Headquarters in 1870–71,* (London 1924)
VIDAL, Commandant P, *Campagne de Sedan,* (Paris 1910)
VIZETELLY, EA, *My Days of Adventure: The Fall of France 1870–1871,* (London 1914)
WALDERSEE, Field Marshal, Count A von, *A Field Marshal's Memoirs* (trans F Whyte), (London 1924)
WARTENSLEBEN, Colonel H von, *Operations of the First Army under General von Manteuffel,* (London 1873)
WARTENSLEBEN, Colonel H von, *Operations of the South Army,* (London 1872)
WASHBURNE, EB, *Correspondence relating to the Franco-German War and Insurrection of the Commune,* (Washington DC 1878)
WAWRO, G, *The Franco- Prussian War,* (Cambridge 2003)
WELLESLEY, Sir V and SENCOURT, R, *Conversations with Napoleon III,* (London 1934)
WETZEL, D, *A Duel of Giants,* (Madison, Wisconsin 2001)
WHITTON, Lieutenant Colonel FE, *Moltke,* (London 1921)
WIEGLER, P, *William the First: his Life and Times,* (London 1929)
WILKINSON, Spencer, *The Brain of An Army,* (London 1895)
WILMOT, S Eardley, *Life of Vice Admiral Lord Lyons,* (London 1898)
WILSON, R, *The Franco- German War,* (Edinburgh 1881)
WIMPFFEN, General EF de, *Sedan,* (Paris 1871)
WITTICH, General L von, *Journal de Guerre,* (Paris 1902)
WOOD, Field Marshal Sir E, *Achievements of Cavalry,* (London 1897)

Index

BOOKS IN THIS SERIES:

1. *The Battle of Majuba Hill The Transvaal Campaign 1880–1881* John Laband (ISBN 978-1-911512-38-7)
2. *For Queen and Company Vignettes of the Irish Soldier in the Indian Mutiny* David Truesdale (ISBN 978-1-911512-79-0)
3. *The Furthest Garrison Imperial Regiments in New Zealand 1840–1870* Adam Davis (ISBN 978-1-911628-29-3)
4. *Victory Over Disease Resolving the Medical Crisis in the Crimean War, 1854–1856* Michael Hinton (ISBN 978-1-911628-31-6)
5. *Journey Through the Wilderness Garnet Wolseley's Canadian Red River Expedition of 1870* Paul McNicholls (ISBN 978-1-911628-30-9)
6. *Kitchener The Man Not The Myth* Anne Samson (ISBN 978-1-912866-45-8)
7. *The British and the Sikhs Discovery, Warfare and Friendship c1700–1900* Gurinder Singh Mann (ISBN 978-1-911628-24-8)
8. *Bazaine 1870 Scapegoat for a Nation* Quintin Barry (ISBN 978-1-913336-08-0)
9. *Redcoats in the Classroom The British Army's Schools For Soldiers and Their Children During the 19th Century* Howard R. Clarke (ISBN 978-1-912866-47-2)
10. *The Rescue They Called a Raid The Jameson Raid 1895–96* David Snape (ISBN 978-1-913118-77-8)
11. *Hungary 1848 The Winter Campaign* Christopher Pringle (ISBN 978-1-913118-78-5)
12. *The War of the Two Brothers The Portuguese Civil War 1828-1834* Sérgio Veludo Coelho (ISBN 978-1-914059-26-1)
14. *Forgotten Victorian Generals Studies in the Exercise of Command and Control in the British Army 1837–1901* Christopher Brice (editor) (ISBN 978-1-910777-20-6)
15. *The German War of 1866 The Bohemian and Moravian Campaign* Theodore Fontane (ISBN 978-1-914059-29-2)
16. *Dust of Glory The First Anglo-Afghan War 1839–1842, its Causes and Course* Bill Whitburn (ISBN 978-1-914059-33-9)
17. *Saarbruck to Sedan The Franco-German War 1870–1871 Volume 1* Ralph Weaver (ISBN 978-1-914059-88-9)
18. *The Battle of Lissa 1866 How the Industrial Revolution Changed the Face of Naval Warfare* Quintin Barry (ISBN 978-1-914059-92-6)
19. *The Zulu Kingdom and the Boer Invasion of 1837–1840* John Laband (ISBN 978-1-914059-89-6)
20. *The Fire of Venture Was in His Veins* Major Allan Wilson and the Shangani Patrol 1893 David Snape (ISBN 978-1-914059-90-2)
21. *From the Atacama to the Andes Battles of the War of the Pacific 1879–1883* Alan Curtis (ISBN 978-1-914059-90-2)
22. *The Rise of the Sikh Soldier The Sikh Warrior Through the Ages, c1700–1900* Gurinder Singh Mann (ISBN 978-1-915070-52-4)
23. *Victorian Crusaders British and Irish Volunteers in the Papal Army 1860–70* Nicholas Schofield (ISBN 978-1-915070-53-1)
24. *The Battle for the Swiepwald Austria's Fatal Blunder at Königgrätz, the climactic battle of the Austro-Prussian War, 3 July 1866* Ernst Heidrich (ISBN 978-1-915070-49-4)
25. *British Military Panoramas Battle in The Round, 1800–1914* Ian F.W. Beckett (ISBN 978-1-915113-84-9)
26. *Onwards to Omdurman The Anglo-Egyptian Campaign to Reconquer the Sudan, 1896–1898* Keith Surridge (ISBN 978-1-915070-51-7)
27. *Hungary 1849 The Summer Campaign* Wilhelm Ramming, Christopher Pringle (editor) (ISBN 978-1-915113-80-1)
28. *Line in the Sand French Foreign Legion Forts and Fortifications in Morocco 1900–1926* Richard Jeynes (ISBN 978-1-915113-83-2)
29. *The Republic Fights Back The Franco-German War 1870-1871 Volume 2* Ralph Weaver (ISBN 978-1-915070-50-0)
30. *Controlling the Frontier Southern Africa 1806–1828, The Cape Frontier Wars and The Fetcani Alarm* Hugh Driver (ISBN 978-1-915113-78-8)
31. *The Battle of Magersfontein Victory and defeat on the South African veld, 10–12 December 1899* Garth Benneyworth (ISBN 978-1-915113-79-5)
32. *Too Little Too Late The Campaign in West and South Germany June–July 1866* Michael Embree (ISBN 978-1-804513-77-4)
33. *The Destruction of the Imperial Army* Volume 1: The Opening Engagements of the Franco-German War 1870–71 Grenville Bird (ISBN 978-1-915113-81-8)
34. *Kitchener* The Man Not the Myth Anne Samson (ISBN 978-1-804513-84-2)
35. *From Ironclads to Dreadnoughts* The Development of the German Battleship, 1864–1918 Dirk Nottelmann & David M. Sullivan (ISBN 978-1-804511-84-8)
36. *The Destruction of the Imperial Army* Volume 2: The Battles around Metz Grenville Bird (ISBN 978-1-804511-85-5)
37. *More Work Than Glory* Buffalo Soldiers in the United States Army, 1866–1916 John P Langellier (ISBN 978-1-804513-34-7)
38. *The Spioenkop Campaign* The Battles to Relieve Ladysmith 17–27 January 1900 Robert Davidson (ISBN 978-1-804513-31-6)
39. *The Destruction of the Imperial Army* Volume 3: *The Sedan Campaign 1870* Grenville Bird (ISBN 978-1-804513-32-3)
40. *The Destruction of the Imperial Army* Volume 4: *Sedan, Strasbourg and Metz* 1870 Grenville Bird (ISBN 978-1-804514-59-7)
41. *Memorandum on the Prussian Army in Relation to the Campaign of 1866* Lieutenant Colonel W.E.M Reilly (ISBN 978-1-804516-27-0)
42. *Black Week: The British Army and Defeat in Anglo-Boer War 1899-1900* Quintin Barry (ISBN 978-1-804511-86-2)
43. *War in the East. A Military History of the Russo-Turkish War 1877-78* Quintin Barry (ISBN 978-1-804517-30-7)
44. *The First Schleswig-Holstein War 1848-50* Nick Svendsen (ISBN 978-1-804517-36-9)
45. *The Hundred Thousand Sons of St Louis* Ralph Weaver (ISBN 978-1-804517-37-6)
46. *Bismarck's First War: The Campaign in Schleswig and Jutland 1864* Michael Embree (ISBN 978-1-804517-38-3)
47. *The Honvéd War. Armies of the Hungarian War of Independence 1848-49* Nigel James Smith (ISBN 978-1-804514-60-3)
48. *Radestzky's Marches. The Campaigns of 1848 and 1849 in Upper Italy* Michael Embree (ISBN 978-1-804517-42-0)
49. *The Campaign on the Loire 1870-71: Orléans and Le Mans* Quintin Barry (ISBN 978-1-804517-82-6)
50. *The British Empire's Regulars 1880-1914: Soldiers of Britain, India and Africa* Wendell Scholander (ISBN 978-1-804515-62-4)
51. *The Last Throw of the Dice: Bourbaki and Werder in Eastern France 1870-71* Quintin Barry (ISBN 978-1-804517-78-9)
52. *Three Weeks in November. A Military History of the Swiss Civil War of 1847* Ralph Weaver (ISBN 978-1-804518-49-6)
53. *The Battle of Wörth August 6th 1870* Lieut.-Col. G.F.R. Henderson (ISBN 978-1-804517-90-1)
54. *The Battle of Spicheren August 6th 1870* Lieut.-Col. G.F.R. Henderson (ISBN 978-1-804518-50-2)
55. *The Serbian Army in the Wars for Independence against Turkey 1876-1878* Dusan M. Babac (ISBN 978-1-804518-69-4)
56. *The Campaign in Alsace August 1870* Brigadier-General J.P. Du Cane, C.B. (ISBN 978-1-804518-82-3)
57. *The Franco-Prussian War 1870-71 Volume 1* Quintin Barry (ISBN 978-1-806721-04-7)
58. *The Franco-Prussian War 1870-71 Volume 2* Quintin Barry (ISBN 978-1-806721-05-4)